FIREFIGHTERS

FIREFIGHTERS

JoEllen L. Kelly, Ph.D., Editor-in-Chief

Robert A. Yatsuk, Fire Captain/Paramedic (Ret)
Managing Editor

J. Gordon Routley, Contributing Editor

NATIONAL FALLEN FIREFIGHTERS FOUNDATION
BEAUX ARTS EDITIONS

National Fallen Firefighters Foundation

In 1992, the U.S. Congress created the National Fallen Firefighters Foundation to lead a nationwide effort to honor America's firefighters who die in the line of duty and to provide necessary resources to assist their survivors in the rebuilding of their lives. Since then, the Foundation has developed and expanded many programs to honor and remember our nation's fallen fire heroes and to provide resources to assist their families and coworkers.

The Foundation provides a variety of resources to survivors of fallen firefighters and fire service personnel. During the National Memorial Weekend, family members and coworkers of fallen firefighters participate in Family Day support programs.

Foundation scholarships are available to eligible children and spouses of fallen firefighters. In addition to financial support, families get emotional assistance through the Fire Service Survivor Support Network. This especially benefits families in small communities who may not have access to needed resources.

Senior fire officers receive specialized training from the Foundation in how to handle line-of-duty deaths and support survivors. The training program, "Taking Care of Our Own," is offered at sites across the country. A Chief-to-Chief Network gives senior officials a place to turn for professional and personal support. The Foundation serves as a clearinghouse for departments in locating information on survivor benefits and support.

The Foundation is a 501(c) 3 nonprofit organization located at the National Emergency Training Center in Emmitsburg, Maryland. It is registered as a corporation in the State of Maryland and receives funding through private donations from individuals, organizations, corporations, and foundations.

The Congressional Fire Services Institute recognized the National Fallen Firefighters Foundation as the Fire Service Organization of the Year in 2003. The award cited the Foundation for its passion, leadership, and hard work in providing comfort to the survivors of our firefighting heroes.

Information about the Foundation and its programs is available at: www.firehero.org.

National Fallen Firefighters Foundation
Post Office Drawer 498
Emmitsburg, Maryland 21727
www.firehero.org
e-mail: firehero@firehero.org
(301) 447-1365; fax: (301) 447-1645

Beaux Arts Editions
Published by Universe Publishing
A Division of Rizzoli International Publications, Inc.
300 Park Avenue South
New York, NY 10010
www.rizzoliusa.com

© 2003 National Fallen Firefighters Foundation

2009 2010 2011 2012 / 10 9 8 7 6 5 4 3 2

Design: Lori S. Malkin
Project Editor: James O. Muschett

ISBN-13: 978-0-88363-619-0

Printed in China

Contents

Prologue: Heroes for All Time

This volume bears eloquent witness to the achievements of our fire-fighters, over a history as long and inspiring as the history of our nation. It appears at an especially appropriate time. While approximately 100 firefighters lose their lives in the line of duty each year, in 2001, 442 perished. The devastating attacks of September 11th focused the nation's attention, in a manner we will forever remember, on all the dangers and challenges that firefighters face as they carry out their unwavering mission of service to the common good, wherever they are called, and whatever the sacrifice that they and their families are called upon to make. If, in the past, the role firefighters play in our lives was so fundamental that too often it went unnoticed, that will never again be the case.

In these pages you will find a moving portrait of the great firefighting family. It is in the finest tradition of the large, loving, and supportive family. At its center are the nearly 1.1 million men and women currently on active duty in over 26,000 firehouses across the nation. But it reaches out, to every locality in the nation, across many generations and through many branches. Spouses and children, parents and siblings are all members of this extraordinary family; so, too, are those who have retired from service and the newest recruits just beginning their service.

While the setting may change, our firefighters' commitment never wavers. Perhaps they are called upon to work in the tunnel fire in Baltimore, the forest fire in Oregon, the warehouse fire in Worcester, or the cataclysm of the World Trade Center. Or they may be working in our neighborhoods, fighting fires caused by gas explosions and short circuits and, too often and too irresponsibly, sheer carelessness or even deliberate malice. They go about their work knowing they have the support of every colleague, and indeed of every member of the great extended family.

In every case they face the same daunting challenges. And think what is expected of them. To combat a fire effectively, firefighters must understand its chemical properties. To gauge the condition of a structure, they must understand structural engineering. To treat the injured, they must know medicine. To deal with the panic that gets in the way of rescue, they must be psychologists and sociologists. Every fire has the potential to be fatal, and they respond to all with equal determination.

Today more than ever, Americans have reason to reflect on the role that our firefighters play in the lives of our families and our communities. Perhaps you have a child who pauses at the sight of every fire engine, or whose very favorite outing is a trip to the neighborhood firehouse. Or perhaps you grew up, as I did, in a small town or city with a firehouse close by. I loved that firehouse. It was an anchor in my community of Salisbury, on Maryland's Eastern Shore. Indeed, my profound respect for our firefighters and my commitment to seeing they receive the national recognition they so rightly deserve began with the inspiration of my early years.

Page 6–7: The legion of heroes that protect America come from all walks of life. ("Protecting Our Nation," Chas Fagan, courtesy of Congressional Fire Services Institute and State Farm Insurance)

With the upper floors of both towers of the World Trade Center engulfed in smoke, the tragic nightmare of September 11, 2001, was beginning to unfold. (© Chris Collins/Corbis)

Three firefighters attack the flames head-on. Protected behind a wide fog stream, they are able to advance to the seat of the fire and make an effort to either hold it in check or proceed with extinguishment. (© Bill Stormont/Corbis)

I therefore feel honored and privileged to have some small part in this excellent book. Of the many responsibilities and challenges I have faced in more than thirty years in the United States Congress, first in the House of Representatives and since 1977 in the Senate, unquestionably one of the most rewarding has been the opportunity to serve as both a co-chair and as chairman of the Congressional Fire Services Caucus. The caucus, the largest bipartisan and bicameral coalition in the Congress, works on behalf of our nation's firefighters and to promote fire safety. Over the years, we have championed a number of bills critical to the fire service, including legislation, now public law, establishing and funding the Assistance to Firefighters Grant Program. Thus far, the program has competitively awarded more than $450 million to ensure that firefighters across the nation are best equipped to serve their communities.

I am also pleased to have played a role in the establishment of the National Fallen Firefighters Memorial and the National Fallen Firefighters Foundation. The Foundation's mandate is great. It assures the necessary financial support for the Memorial and for our annual service of remembrance. It offers support to the families of those we have lost, and provides assistance to communities across the nation seeking to build memorials to their own firefighters.

Our National Memorial, located in Emmitsburg, Maryland, like this book, commands us to contemplate the mission that our firefighters undertake, year after year, decade after decade, with every succeeding generation. It is a mission of steadfastness, of service to the common good, of sacrifice. It is a mission that our firefighters' families embrace. I salute them for it, and, on behalf of our nation, I thank them for it.

Senator Paul S. Sarbanes
Maryland

National Fallen Firefighters Foundation

The entire world learned about heroism and what it means to be a firefighter on September 11, 2001. At the World Trade Center in New York, at the Pentagon in Arlington, Virginia, and in a field near Shanksville, Pennsylvania, career and volunteer firefighters responded to the alarms. Almost 3,000 innocent lives were lost, but many more thousands were saved by firefighters who risked their own lives to protect others—as they do, every hour of every day.

The casualties included 347 firefighters who died in the line of duty that day, and their sacrifice brought back the words expressed long ago by Chief Edward Croker, a legendary leader of the Fire Department of New York, who said; "The risks are plain . . . when a man becomes a fireman; his act of bravery has been accomplished."

A century later, those words are still true and apply to every man and woman in the fire-rescue service. Each year, approximately 100 firefighters die in the line of duty, and thousands are injured as they carry out their mission of saving lives and property. And Chief Croker's words also apply to their families, who must perform their own act of bravery by rebuilding their lives without the loved ones they have lost. It is the mission of the

National Fallen Firefighters Foundation to honor our fallen comrades and to help their families on that long and difficult journey.

But even as we honor the dead by caring for the living, there must be an investigation to determine how and why a firefighter died in the line-of-duty. Every effort must be made to discover what went wrong—what new lessons were learned, what old lessons were ignored, and what steps must be taken to prevent it from happening again. We can never accept a line-of-duty death as inevitable, even though a firefighter's work is inherently dangerous, and we know that each year more names will be added to the monument at the National Fallen Firefighters Memorial in Emmitsburg, Maryland.

In response to requests from the fire service, the Foundation has created a unique program to train senior fire officers on how to cope with a line-of-duty death when it strikes their department. Known as *Taking Care of Our Own*, the course is taught on a regional basis throughout the country and at the National Fire Academy. The demand for this training has been overwhelming, and well-received by the fire service. It has led to the establishment of a network of fire chiefs who have had a line-of-duty death in their own department, and who can offer guidance to another chief when tragedy occurs.

The Foundation's staff attempts to reach out to every fire department and every family by offering support from professional counselors, chaplains, and fire officers who are trained to do this type of work. An important resource is the Fire Service Survivors Network, a peer group made up of people who care and understand because they have experienced a line-of-duty death in their own family. Each year, the new survivors tell us that this relationship with others who have been through the same ordeal is a major step on their road to recovery. It is especially gratifying when a survivor from a previous year feels ready to start helping others and joins the network.

To assist families in planning for the future, we have established the Sarbanes Scholarship Fund, named in honor of Maryland Senator Paul Sarbanes, who introduced the Act of Congress that created the Foundation. In partnership with the National Association of State Fire Marshals, State Farm Insurance, ICMA Retirement Corporation, and MasterGuard Corporation, this program provides college scholarships for the children of fallen firefighters, and funds for spouses who need special training to join or rejoin the workforce. Like most of the Foundation's activities, this program is funded primarily by donations from the private sector. Applications for these grants are increasing every year, and the Foundation is committed to raising the money that is required for every qualified applicant to receive the scholarship aid they need and deserve.

The annual National Fallen Firefighters Memorial Weekend is held in early October in Emmitsburg, on the campus of the National Fire Academy. Thousands of firefighters from across the nation participate, with many serving as family escorts or honor guards. They come from the smallest volunteer fire companies and the largest career departments, bonded together to honor their fallen comrades, and to bring comfort to their families. The theme of the weekend is "going forward to the future" and it begins with

Constructed in 1981, this seven-foot stone monument features a sculpted Maltese Cross, the traditional symbol of the fire service. At the base of the monument, an eternal flame symbolizes the spirit of all firefighters—past, present, and future. Plaques encircling the monument list the names of the men and women of the fire service who have died in service to their communities since 1981. Whenever a firefighter dies in the line of duty, fire officials post a notice of the death at the monument and lower flags at the site to half-staff. (Bill Green)

The Candlelight Service for fallen firefighters in 2002 required a much larger space for the many families and departments represented. Many Bagpipers and Honor Guards participated to honor their fallen comrades. They assemble here in front of The Basilica of the National Shrine of the Immaculate Conception in Washington, D.C., as the participants enter. (Bill Green)

Opposite, bottom: *The National Fallen Firefighters Foundation National Memorial Service on October 11, 2001, was a particularly somber one due to the recent events of September 11. Shown here (left to right): Hal Bruno, Chairman of the Board; President George W. Bush; First Lady Laura Bush; and Chief Ron Siarnicki, Executive Director. (Bill Green)*

In tribute to all fallen firefighters, the Honor Guard from New Haven, Connecticut, forms up in front of The Basilica of the National Shrine of the Immaculate Conception. They stand quiet and still in solemn recognition of the ultimate sacrifice made by so many in 2001. (Bill Green)

As the Candlelight Service begins, two representatives of the many Honor Guards in attendance proceed up the aisle of The Basilica of the National Shrine of the Immaculate Conception. As they approach each row, they pass the flame of their candles to the candles of all in the assembly, uniting everyone with the purpose of honoring the fallen. (Bill Green)

Right: *The National Memorial Service for 2002 was held in the MCI Center in Washington, D.C. Leading the procession of Honor Guards, at the beginning of the tribute, were three special representatives of the fire service. (Bill Green)*

Opposite: *The Basilica of the National Shrine of the Immaculate Conception is the largest Catholic Church in the Americas and among the largest in the world. The Great Upper Church (seen here) accommodates more than six thousand people. The 2002 Candlelight Service was all the more meaningful having been observed in this inspirational place. (Bill Green)*

Saturday's Family Day, which includes group sessions and special activities for the spouses, children, and parents of the fallen firefighters. Saturday night's dinner is followed by an inspiring candlelight ceremony and musical program. Sunday's program opens with a nondenominational prayer service in the historic Fallen Firefighters Chapel. The honor guards then lead a stirring and colorful "Sea of Blue" to the site of the Fallen Firefighters Monument for a ceremony that is rich in the traditions of the American fire-rescue service. As the roll of honor is called, each family comes forward to receive a red rose and an American flag, a flag that has been flown over the U.S. Capitol building. The keynote speaker and honor guard unveil the new plaque that lists the names of all firefighters who died in the line of duty the previous year. President George W. Bush is among the many national leaders who have delivered the keynote address.

In 2002, the Memorial Weekend was temporarily moved to Washington, D.C., to accommodate the huge crowd that honored 442 firefighters who died in the line-of-duty, including the 347 lost at the World Trade Center. (The Foundation has been fully involved in assisting the FDNY Counseling Unit since the September 11 attack.) The ceremony will continue to be held in Emmitsburg, where plans are underway to create a memorial park and visitor's center at the Fallen Firefighters Monument.

Over the years, the Foundation has relied heavily on input from family members to determine which aspects of the weekend activities and programs are most helpful to them. Many report that their spirits were lifted and that they gained emotional strength by being part of a national observance that honored their fallen firefighter. For some, it provides an additional support system that is available even after they leave Emmitsburg. Typical is the response of a young widow with three children, who told us, "I have never been so proud in all of my life and I know that my husband would feel the same."

To the National Fallen Firefighters Foundation, that means "mission accomplished."

Hal Bruno
Chairman, National Fallen Firefighters Foundation
Board of Directors

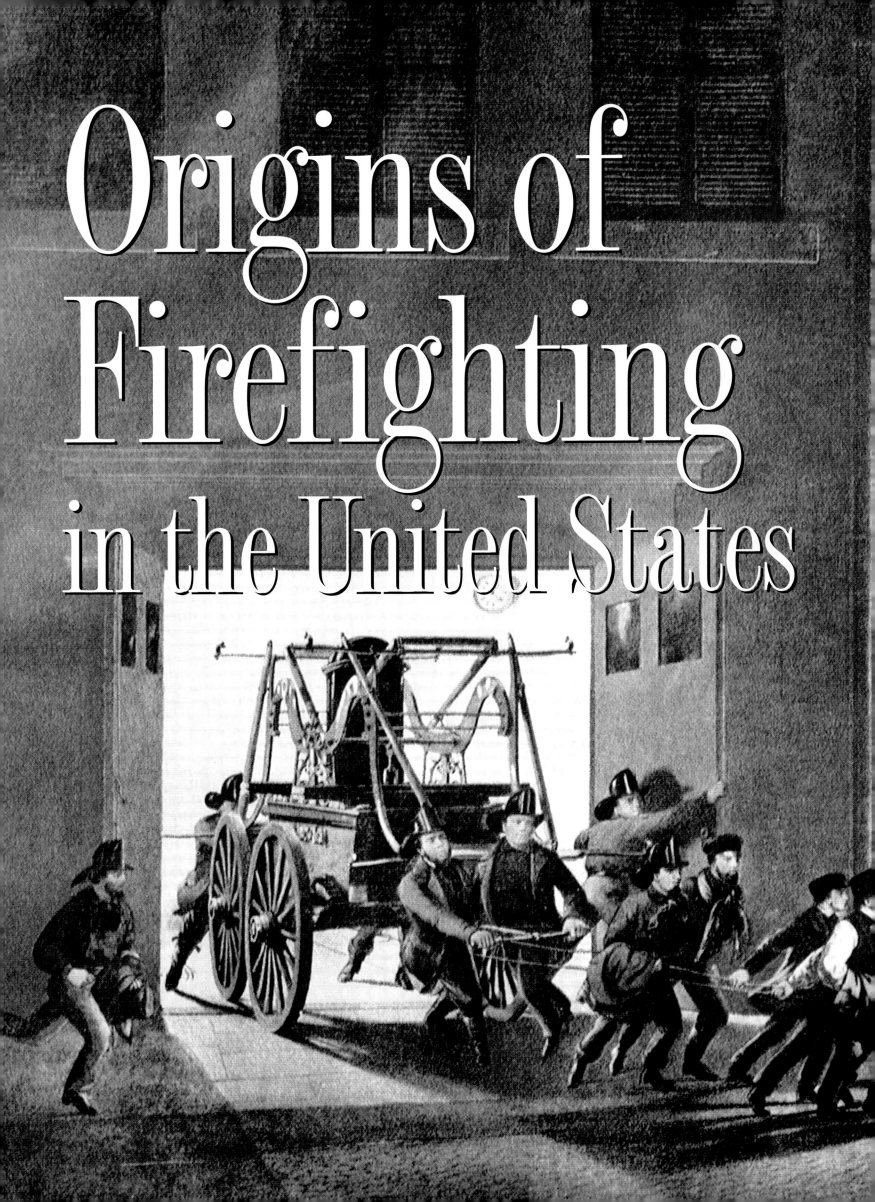

Origins of Firefighting
in the United States

Origins of Firefighting in the United States

John A. Granito, Ed.D.

In 2001, there was a fire alarm every eighteen seconds someplace in the United States, including a residential fire call every eighty seconds. When all other types of alarms to fire departments are added to these—including emergency medical requests—a call for help sounds somewhere in the nation approximately every one and a half seconds. We know that fire departments are crucial to the well-being of our people, our communities, and our environment—but fire stations and fire trucks do not mitigate fires by themselves. The work, of course, is done by firefighters, whose story is exciting, fascinating, and important to understand, especially at this time in our nation's history.

From our founding to this day, destructive fires in the United States have amassed a shocking toll of injury, death, and destruction. The

National Fire Protection Association (NFPA), which compiles such statistics, and from which most of the data in this chapter are drawn, reports that in 2001 our nation's fire departments responded to about 1.75 million fires, with more than 500,000 of them occurring in structures, and almost 400,000 of those in residences. In fact, residential fires alone in 2001 killed 3,140 civilians and injured about 16,000 more. The total number of United States civilian fire deaths in 2001, including those killed in the September 11th terrorist attacks, was almost 6,200. The national property fire loss in

2001, without the 9/11 incidents, is estimated at about $10.5 billion, with an additional $44 billion related to 9/11. At least twenty fires in 2001 exceeded $10 million each in property loss and, dismayingly, an estimated 45,500 structure fires in 2001 were intentionally set. Each year fires kill more Americans than all other natural disasters combined.

From the very beginnings of our country, destructive fires have impacted significantly, and often fearfully, on the development of communities and the lives of their people. Indeed, very early journals describe the devastating 1608 fire in Virginia's Jamestown settlement, and one in 1623 which destroyed a portion of the Plymouth Plantation. But the early settlers and Pilgrims could hardly have been surprised, since destructive fires had been commonplace in England, foreshadowing the 1666 Great Fire of London, which consumed five-sixths of inner London and left 100,000 people homeless. That destruction in London, coupled with such colonial experiences as the 1653 Boston Waterfront Fire (which burned about a third of the city's homes and several warehouses), and the 1655 burning of large areas of New Amsterdam (New York) focused colonial attention on the necessity to create both fire prevention ordinances and organized firefighting measures.

Both of these needs were addressed early on, in 1692, by the Massachusetts Bay Assembly with "An Act for Building with Stone or Brick in the Town of Boston, and Preventing Fire." This lengthy and detailed act called for stone and brick construction (slate or tile for roofs), the enlargement of streets and lanes, and the presence of ladders, a cistern, a night watchman, and other fire protection devices. Additional colonial populated areas, including New York, Philadelphia, and Charleston, created similar safeguards. Philadelphia obtained a hand-pumped "fire engine" in 1719, years after Boston's 1654 model appeared there, but before New York's two engines arrived from London toward the end of 1731. The New York engines arrived just in time; four days after their arrival they were used successfully to stop a spreading fire.

While historians occasionally argue over just which city created the first fire department, undoubtedly the appearance of hand-pumping devices (with men pulling them) necessitated plans for organizing people who could fight fires. In smaller communities, everyone, including women and older children, helped with the bucket brigade (which brought water to the pumper from a water source), but operating the pumping handles or "brakes" on the pumpers required strong, practiced, and dedicated men. Many times, these men would get used to the routine of working together and would form into town and city fire companies. Typically, these companies also functioned as social organizations, and often developed a good deal of local political clout.

A term which today's firefighters use, "making a run," comes directly from those long-ago days when pulling the hand-pumped engine on ropes, at a run, was the only way to get it to a fire. And when our modern hydrants are sometimes called "fireplugs," we're remembering that water mains were once made of hollowed logs, with access holes stopped with wooden plugs. The term "plug-ugly," meaning a city ruffian, stems from the tough men who at the sounding of a fire alarm would

A Currier & Ives fireman's certificate, ca. 1877, depicts several heroic firefighting scenes. (Library of Congress)

Benjamin Franklin is often said to have been the father of the American fire service. Here we see him and other volunteers as they work with a hand pumper at the Union Fire Company in Philadelphia. (J. Riegel, Jr., Heritage of Flames, The Illustrated History of Early American Firefighting, *Artisan Books, Pound Ridge, New York, 1977)*

Opposite: *A factory fire in Fall River, Massachusetts, in 1874, illustrates the increasingly complex task of firemen as the nation became more industrialized. Such large buildings, along with lax or nonexistent fire codes, created buildings that had a great deal of flammable material within them, lack of sufficient exits, and no internal fire protection systems. When fires such as this occurred, the local departments were soon overwhelmed. As shown here, panic often ensued and many fell to their death rather than face the smoke and flame and an uncertain rescue. This led to the necessity to have full-time crews to combat the increased fire danger. Volunteers began to form into official fire departments. (© Corbis)*

guard the nearest fireplug until their own company arrived. The goal of the fire company at the fireplug was to pump water, in relay, to the tub of another company's hand pumper, nearer the fire, faster than the men at those pumping handles could force the water from their tub out through the nozzle. This overflowing was called "washing the tub," and was viewed by the men supplying the water with great pride and joy. A hand pumper and its company that went for many years without being washed would become famous.

These early hand pumpers were the source of tremendous pride for well-established and fledgling companies alike. Such was case for New York City's Company No. 5, housed in downtown Manhattan. Company 5 boasted many well-known members who spared little expense in adorning their famous engine. In many other cases, also, the members' pride was expressed in lavishly and artistically painted and gilded pumpers, such as that of Philadelphia's early-nineteenth-century pumper from the Weccacoe Fire Company. That pride is still expressed today in the gold striping and beautiful painted logos that can be seen on contemporary fire trucks.

Perhaps the greatest humiliation to settle on a fire company, however, was arriving at the fire after a more distant company had made a faster run, or being passed on the street by a faster running company. If a fireplug were available, the first arriving company would access it, thus blocking the late arrivals from its use. Fighting between the companies would sometimes occur as frustration and embarrassment overcame public duty. Even today, firefighters use the term "taking a hydrant," and can become quite vocal when another department crosses the boundary line, unbidden, to attack "their" fire before they even arrive at the scene.

But the characteristics of firefighters that strike home to citizens are not these. Rather, they are overwhelmingly positive and described by such words as dedicated, courageous, and unselfish. Of all municipal departments, most residents rate their fire department as providing the best local service, and their firefighters as people who will do whatever is necessary to rescue and protect them, even at the risk of death—a risk which is realized about 100 times a year in the United States. And this community sense of the worth of fire departments and their members

A New York City firefighter opens a fire hydrant to engage the high-pressure hoses, ca. 1908. Photographed by George Grantham Bain. (Corbis)

is applied to both career firefighters who staff the stations around the clock as full-time employees, and the volunteer or "call" firefighters who respond to alarms from home or work.

Imagine, if you will, that we're standing in the truck bay area of a modern fire station. Firefighters refer to the trucks as "apparatus," and in stations that have on-duty crews, the firefighters are assigned to a specific apparatus and to a specific riding position—the company officer next to the driver, and crewmembers in the jump seats at the rear of the cab. At one time firefighters "rode the back step," or even the side running boards, but safety now dictates that all be seated and belted, and in a fully enclosed cab. In most instances the firefighters don protective gear before the truck rolls, to save valuable seconds at the incident where search and rescue work are often needed immediately.

With firefighters already on-duty in the station, the "let's roll" command can come less than a minute after the dispatch alarm is sounded, and just a few minutes after a citizen calls 911. Modern stations, while not equipped with a famous ankle-breaking brass slide pole, are designed for the fastest and safest possible turnout of the crews. In the most modern stations, the sounding of the alarm will automatically turn on lights and even shut off the kitchen stove to save time. A computer printer or fast fax machine will rattle off the address and other information on what company officers refer to as a "rip and go" sheet. Increasingly, apparatus are being equipped with interactive onboard computers to provide vital information about the location, the structure, special preplanned tactics, and even any special evacuation needs of those who live or work there.

If we could tour the station, we would find an area or a glassed-in office called the watch desk, with communication equipment, a district map, and other aids to a quick and safe response, such as a switch to activate a red traffic light in front of the station. Hopefully, we'd find an administrative office and a classroom area in even the smallest station, along with a bunk area, a kitchen-eating area, and a ready room, plus an exercise area. Near the apparatus bays we should find equipment storage and repair areas, plus racks along the bay walls where each firefighter hangs their protective gear when not on duty. On-duty crews usually arrange their gear next to their riding position during the day. The self-contained breathing masks and their compressed air tanks are kept on the apparatus, usually mounted on a special seat back to facilitate quick donning.

At night, some firefighters arrange their protective clothing on the floor next to their bunk, so that when an alarm sounds they can step into their bunker pants—each leg of which they had fitted over a boot—pull up the suspenders, and thus have half their required gear on in one quick step. A common term for the protective clothing is a throwback to the old days of horse-drawn apparatus, when the trained horses, upon hearing the alarm bell, would back into their assigned spaces next to the tongues of the pumper. One pull on a rope and their harnesses would drop into place from the ceiling hangars, making a "quick hitch" of the team, and the company was ready to "turn out" of the station. Thus, today, protective clothing arranged alongside a bunk at night is sometimes called a "quick hitch," and the clothing itself is still referred to by many as "turnouts." Good

In this January 1943 photo of a Washington, D.C., firehouse, a fireman slides down a brass pole from the upper levels of the firehouse. Originally used to allow a rapid response to the engine room, these poles were responsible for many in-station injuries to firefighters. (© Corbis)

Firefighters often arrange their boots and pants next to their bunks to facilitate a rapid response when the alarm sounds. Here one such fireman sleeps soundly but is prepared to spring into action at a moment's notice. (© Bettmann/Corbis)

This classic firehouse scene shows firemen pulling a hand-drawn fire engine as other firemen scramble to readiness to answer an alarm, ca. 1857. (Marian S. Carson Collection, Library of Congress)

The first fire engine made in the United States was constructed in 1654 by Joseph Jencks of Lynn, Massachusetts, who offered it to the Selectmen of Boston at the time of the first Great Fire. (Library of Congress)

advice to a new probationary firefighter—a "probie"—is to arrange your turnouts in a quick hitch for a fast response! Now, as always in emergency response, time is of the essence, both for on-duty firefighters and the volunteers who have to hurry to their stations when an alarm sounds.

There are today 1,078,300 career and volunteer firefighters in the United States; of these, 784,700 are volunteers. Our nation's earliest fire-fighting groups were, through necessity, composed of volunteers, and that tradition has lasted for almost four centuries. In fact, of NFPA's estimated 26,350 fire departments in the United States, about 87 percent are totally or mostly volunteer. Because career departments, composed entirely or mostly of full-time firefighters, tend to be located in population centers, NFPA statistics indicate that the 13 percent of career departments protect about 62 percent of the population. But in most states, and especially in the smaller cities, towns, villages, and counties, volunteer firefighters provide service.

However, greatly increased training requirements, heavier emergency response workloads, increased family responsibilities, home town and job mobility, and time-consuming department administrative work are making it difficult for many to give the long hours necessary to be volunteer firefighters. The recruitment and retention of volunteer firefighters have become major challenges throughout the nation.

One way to sense the difficulty many volunteer departments have in maintaining adequate numbers of active members is to consider the downward spiral of the rate of volunteers per 1,000 people. In 1983, the United States had about 3.8 volunteer firefighters for every 1,000 inhabitants.

In 2000, we had about 2.8 volunteers for every 1,000. Some volunteer departments have broken tradition by employing a number of full-time career firefighters to maintain operational viability, and it's estimated that about 20 percent of the nation's fire departments use this combination of career and volunteer members.

Actually, what we are experiencing today in this shifting of firefighters is somewhat similar to our nation's earlier history, when cities grew in size and population, departments were organized, and full-time duty crews finally became necessary. An old adage tells us that the three principal causes of fires are men, women, and children, and so as more densely populated cities emerged, the number of fire alarms increased, as did the magnitude of structure fires.

Just as London had experienced conflagrations, so did many cities here, and some several times. Despite fire prevention efforts, including inspections by the fire wardens appointed in many colonial communities, cities such as Boston, New York, Philadelphia, Charleston, and smaller towns as well suffered from large-scale fires in the period prior to the Revolutionary War. Obviously, a structured organization of firefighting resources was called for, and the volunteers, typically augmented by hand pumpers, formed official fire departments.

In December 1737, for example, the New York Volunteer Department was established by the general assembly of the colony. As described in *Fire Department City of New York*, the thirty appointed "Firemen of the City of New York" were to be "strong, able, discreet, honest and sober men . . . ready at a call by night and by day." A station was built in front of City Hall, and the now official volunteer department assumed protection of New York's 1,200 houses and 9,000 people.

Boston's organized volunteer fire companies grew in number, and by 1758 there were nine of them. Four years earlier, Charlestown, across the river from Boston, boasted five pumpers, and it is said that Benjamin Franklin himself founded Philadelphia's Union Volunteer Fire

As this eighteenth-century illustration depicts, hand pumpers required "many hands." The village pump provided water for the bucket brigade. The bucket brigade moved the water from the village pump to the hand pumper and then through the hose to the fire. Other volunteers were involved in "laddering the building" for rescue and access; and still others removed contents from the building to a safer location. (New York Public Library, Print Collection)

In colonial times, firefighting was accomplished by bucket brigades. As firefighting techniques evolved, the flow of water from such brigades was used to fill hand-operated fire pumps that sent water through hoses to those directly fighting the blaze (©Bettmann/Corbis)

The ladder truck of the Columbus, Ohio, fire department, ca. 1912, photographed in action. (Library of Congress)

Opposite, top: *The massive New York World building fire in 1882 drew crowds of fire-fighters and onlookers. (© Museum of the City of New York/Corbis)*

Bottom, left: *A horse drawn hose reel was used in Cincinnati around 1853. This piece of equipment was configured to enhance the operation of the city's first steam pumper. Also, that year the volunteer companies were disbanded in favor of a paid, career depart-ment. (Cincinnati Museum)*

Bottom, right: *Many famous Americans were volunteer firefighters. Among them were Thomas Jefferson, Benjamin Franklin, Samuel Adams, Paul Revere, Alexander Hamilton, John Hancock, John Jay, John Barry, Aaron Burr, and Benedict Arnold. George Washington is seen here commanding the crews at a fire. (Brown Brothers)*

Company—perhaps America's first—in 1736, with thirty prominent citizens as members.

Very likely firefighting is the only absolutely essential community service performed in many communities solely by volunteers. That is true today, and it certainly was true prior to the American Revolution. It's understandable, then, that men prominent in business, politics, and government would join the very important volunteer fire companies. These associations benefited both the community and the individual members. John Hancock was appointed a Boston firewarden in 1766, and six years later he bought Boston its tenth pumper. Samuel Adams served as a Boston firewarden for nine years, and Paul Revere became a chief firewarden and helped found the Massachusetts Charitable Fire Society. George Washington was an honorary member of the Friendship Fire Company of Alexandria and donated a pumper to his department.

Many accounts recall that retired President Washington, manning a hand pumper at an Alexandria marketplace fire, shamed two fashionably dressed spectators into joining him in pumping the handles. There is evidence as well that such notables as Alexander Hamilton, John Jay, and even Aaron Burr and Benedict Arnold also were volunteers.

While volunteer firefighters are still very much present and serve with great loyalty, distinction, and professionalism in well over 20,000 fire departments, around the middle of the 1800s many cities began to realize that a full-time force of firefighters was necessary. In some communities the threat of conflagration was very great, and more and more volunteers were necessary to man the hand pumpers. As well, volunteer company rivalry and outright battles cost public support. A large-scale volunteer battle, said to involve more than a dozen companies, that took place at a Cincinnati fire in 1851 lead to the disbanding of that city's volunteer companies two years later.

During the Civil War, "The First Fire Zouaves" (firemen from New York City) formed an elite regiment within the Union Army under the command of Colonel Elmer E. Ellsworth. These soldiers performed admirably throughout the War, but nowhere more so than when they were temporarily stationed in Washington, D.C., in 1861, and fought the Willard Hotel Fire. Noted by the press for their great skill and precision, the Fire Zouaves of New York may have encouraged some cities to transi-

tion from volunteer to "career" departments once they witnessed the efficiency of reliable on-duty forces. As a further point of interest, Ellsworth was the first Union officer killed in the Civil War, when he tore down a Confederate flag in Alexandria, Virginia. Abraham Lincoln was so moved by this event that he ordered Ellsworth's body to lie in state in the East Room of the White House. He quickly became a Union martyr and "Avenge Ellsworth" became a battle cry for Union troops. (A photograph of Colonel Ellsworth appears later in this book.)

The greatest facilitator of this trend, however, was the invention of the steam-powered fire pumpers. One pumper, tended by a few men, could easily out-pump several hand pumpers. Cincinnati's paid department, formed on April 1, 1853, was likely America's first. Providence, Rhode Island, followed in 1854. After several delaying actions and injunctions, New York City followed in August 1865, following the total destruction of P. T. Barnum's Museum and Zoo despite the work of the volunteers, one of whom is said to have killed an escaping tiger with an ax!

Albany, New York's, paid department began on June 1, 1867, and the city of Philadelphia created its fire department in 1871, the year of the infamous Chicago Fire, and a year before the1872 Great Fire of Boston. The Boston fire destroyed nearly 800 buildings and killed thirteen people, nine of whom were firefighters. More than thirty insurance companies were severely impacted or forced to close. At the time, Boston had 106 career firefighters, forty-two fire vehicles, and 363

When King David Kalakaua died in 1891, firefighters draped black bunting on their stations to show their respect for the king. Kalakaua was a member of Engine Company No. 4, originally an all-Hawaiian company. (Honolulu Fire Department)

The P.T. Barnum Museum and Zoo falls to the ravages of fire in August 1865. Following its total loss, New York City established its career fire department. (© Bettman/Corbis)

on-call firefighters, but area communities still had to send firefighters and pumpers by rail to assist.

Many other cities suffered large fire losses during the last half of the nineteenth century and into the twentieth as well, and more and more paid full-time firefighters were employed. At the time of the 1906 San Francisco earthquake and fire, that city employed 600 firefighters who, augmented by mutual aid departments, fought that fire for three days.

What happened in our country is that these large-loss fires—sometimes devastating conflagrations—focused public attention on the need for improved fire protection, and this involved forcing change on the proud,

Right: *A composite photo of the officers of the Albany, New York, Fire Department in 1900. Note that the background for the photo is a Maltese Cross, the traditional symbol of firefighters. (Reprinted from* The History of the Albany Fire Department 1867-1967, *ed. Warren W. Abriel (1967))*

Far right: *This Milwaukee banner commemorates the heroic services rendered to Kinosha, Wisconsin. The Milwaukee Fire Department provided assistance to Kinosha during a major fire in 1892. (Collection of Virginia Kloiber)*

Opposite, bottom: *The change to motorized apparatus may have been inevitable, but many firemen resisted the change and clung to what they knew best. In this 1914 photograph of the Middletown, Ohio, fire department, horses and motorized apparatus work side by side. (Library of Congress)*

typically conservative, steeped-in-precedent and bound-by-tradition volunteer fire companies. To this day, firefighters joke about the description "three hundred years of history unimpeded by progress!" This unkind observation, of course, is hardly accurate, but tradition causes change to be wrenching. And the fire service was wrenched by several monumental changes during the period from 1850 to about 1920.

These changes involved, first, the urban shift from volunteers and their hand pumpers to paid, full-time firefighters and horse-drawn steam pumpers—especially in the growing cities. Then, beginning a few years after the start of the twentieth century, came the shift from horse-drawn apparatus to motorized vehicles, although the move to completely motorized fire trucks was a slow one. For example, Engine Companies 2

Top, left: An American steam pumper manufactured in 1901 was given to the city of Albany, New York, in 1926. (Reprinted from Albany Fire Department, 1867–1967, One Hundred Years of Service, *by Warren Abriel and Joseph Winchell.)*

Above: Battalion Chief Barend Geel of Albany in his horse-drawn rig, a common form of transportation for chief officers. (Reprinted from Albany Fire Department, 1867–1967, One Hundred Years of Service, *by Warren Abriel and Joseph Winchell.)*

Below: In the early 1900s, with the advent of motorized apparatus, the chiefs also began using the automobile instead of horse-drawn transportation. (Reprinted from Albany Fire Department, 1867–1967, One Hundred Years of Service, *by Warren Abriel and Joseph Winchell.)*

Left: The firemen of Steamer 6 outside of quarters, about 1886. (Reprinted from Albany Fire Department, 1867–1967, One Hundred Years of Service, *by Warren Abriel and Joseph Winchell.)*

Above: *A team of horses pulls a steam pumper through the streets of New York City as the department dashes to an alarm in the early twentieth century. (New York Public Library, Picture Collection)*

Top, right: *This steamer, from New Haven, Connecticut, was caught on film by a newspaper photographer. All of the excitement comes to life—three horses are ably handled by their driver, a fireman rides on the rear of the steamer, and smoke billows from the chimney of the steam engine. (Brown Brothers)*

and 9 and Ladder Company 1 of the Albany (NY) Fire Department became motorized as late as December 1921, although some other Albany companies became motorized as early as 1913. Actually, a few departments had obtained early self-propelled steam engines, with Hartford having one in 1901, and New York City and Boston as early as 1872. Incidentally, these early models were chain driven, and their tendency to skid around corners led to the invention of today's automotive differential gear.

The first pumper to be self-propelled by a gasoline engine was delivered to Wayne, Pennsylvania, in 1906. The San Francisco Fire Chief is reported to have had an electric auto in 1901, and a steam-driven "Locomobile" was used by the New York City chief that same year. New York City obtained its first motorized fire truck in 1909.

Since many volunteer companies were very much (and still are) providing active service, the volunteers had to deal with what they saw as the incursion of paid firefighters, the phasing out of hand pumpers in

The rainy day did not dampen the mood during the review ceremony of the inaugural trip of Engine 91, in New York City, on March 20, 1913. (Bain Collection, Library of Congress)

favor of heavy steamers and horses, and finally, the takeover by gasoline-powered pumps and motorized vehicles. In many cases, two or more of these profound organizational and technological changes took place during a firefighter's career. There were repercussions, and dire predictions that history was witnessing the sun setting on the volunteer service.

Today there are movements on the part of some career firefighter labor groups to prohibit their members from belonging to a volunteer department in neighborhoods where they may live. During the last part of the 1800s, the new paid firefighters sometimes had to fear repercussions from resentful and replaced community volunteers. Histories of the United States fire service are replete with tales and photos of the contests—always intense and sometimes bitter—which pitted, first, hand pumpers operated by volunteers against steam engines and, later, horse-drawn apparatus against motorized trucks.

Early paid firefighters most often worked shifts which today would be unheard of: twenty-four hours on duty, continuously, for a month, with only one twenty-four hour period off duty. In some departments, families were allowed to have Sunday dinner in the station with their firefighter husbands and fathers. Today's firefighting labor unions fight hard for the voice of their members, which includes input regarding scheduling and staffing.

Once there was very little focus on firefighter safety, and today's protective clothing, self-contained breathing apparatus (SCBA), and insistence on approved operating procedures would have been seen by many an old "smoke eater" as the stuff of weaklings. The focus for much of the history of

Top, left: *Early gasoline-powered pumpers provided their own means of propulsion as well as power for the pump. This Alameda, California, pumper was placed in service in 1907 with a 600 gallon per minute pumping capacity. (Waterous Company)*

Above: *A 900-gallon-per-minute Waterous pumper was New York City's first gasoline pumper. (Waterous Company)*

This ca. 1902 photograph captures Chicago firemen with two fire engines in the foreground while others fight a fire in the background. (Library of Congress)

In some departments, families were allowed to have Sunday dinner in the station with their firemen husbands and fathers. Here, members of the Milwaukee Fire Department Company 18 celebrate "St. Sylvester's Eve" (New Year's Eve) in 1914 with off-duty members and family. (Collection of Virginia Kloiber)

"Sussex" the rescue dog locates a training victim in this 1942 rescue exercise. Once located, Sussex leaves the victim to summon help, before returning to the injured to stand watch until assistance arrives. (© Bettmann/ Corbis)

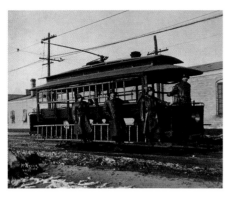

The Duluth, Minnesota, fire trolley ran from 1907 to 1930. In this photo from the 1920s, the ever-vigilant firemen pose in their turnout gear. Ladders hang on the sides, and fire equipment, including an electric pump and hoses, is stored inside the car. (St. Louis County Historical Society, Hugh McKenzie photographer)

On December 20, 1922, Engine Company 205 in Brooklyn Heights, New York City, made its final run utilizing horse power. This was a special run that ended with a ceremony at Borough Hall. The age of the horse-drawn steamer had officially ended in New York. (New York City Fire Museum)

the fire service was on "taking the punishment" and ignoring the likely consequences. Today's firefighters are encouraged to "work smarter" and to make their safety and survivability a high priority. Firefighting is dangerous, an occupation that kills scores of firefighters in their best years—about 100 annually. In 2001, 442 firefighters died in the line of duty (347 of them at the World Trade Center), men and women from thirty-four states across the country. Additionally, reported injuries to firefighters have ranged annually between 85,000 and 100,000. Burn injuries are considered the worst, but firefighters often are injured from falls and in vehicle accidents. According to the United States Fire Administration, heart attacks are the leading cause of firefighter deaths, accounting for almost one-third of the total in 2002.

Until well after World War II, very few fire departments became noted for providing services other than response to fires and related emergencies, plus fire inspections. Almost all departments viewed their public safety role as quite limited. It wasn't until the early 1970s that basic emergency medical life support and advanced life support services conducted by specially trained firefighters began to appear in such city departments as Seattle, Miami, Los Angeles, and Columbus (OH). In the following twenty years, many fire departments moved to provide some level and type of emergency medical services (EMS), and today medical calls typically exceed fire alarms in those departments. Almost 60 percent of the departments in the United States, both career and volunteer, provide either basic or advanced EMS.

From the 1920s well into the 1960s, most firefighters and their departments experienced little significant change in their mission, in their daily tasks, in their operating procedures, and in the technologies that provided them with the apparatus and tools of their trade. Some improvements appeared in pumps and apparatus, in protective clothing and, certainly in breathing equipment. Some firefighters would observe often that some advancements in technology typically generated new dangers in firefighting, but seldom improvements in effectiveness and safety. Fortunately, that has been reversed.

Almost a half block of buildings on the Bowery and Twelfth Street at Coney Island, New York, were destroyed by flames that were whipped up by heavy winds on February 6, 1933. Pictured are the ruins after the firemen extinguished the blaze. (© Bettmann/Corbis)

Firemen carry hose up an aerial ladder as they battle a three-alarm fire in the Gowanus section of Brooklyn, New York, in January 1962. The fire started in the basement of a four-story apartment building and quickly spread to an adjacent building. There were no injuries. (© Bettmann/Corbis)

31

Consider, however, that only ten years after the end of the World War I, our nation fell into a devastating economic depression that made the secure position of a city firefighter one to be treasured and envied. Those men were hardly eager to jeopardize their jobs by forming aggressive labor groups seeking provisions for greater safety, insisting on shorter work hours, or displaying unrest because of an officer's disregard for their well-being and long-term health. That type of environment is not conducive to organizational change, and relatively little did occur, even during the 1940 war years and well into the decade following, when shifts often were eighty-five hours a week.

Indeed, many returning military veterans were happy to join a familiar para-military organization, to take orders without complaint, and to perform with dedication and often heroically. Awards, medals, points toward promotion, plus the recognition of fellow firefighters and the public provided strong motivation for many to live up to the popular image of firefighters. Individual firefighters, and in some areas entire departments, strove to match and enhance the popular image of strong, brave, and dedicated protectors.

Imagine, then, the dismay, confusion, and anger felt by many firefighters when during the 1960s they and policemen in many cities became prime targets in incidents of civil unrest, riots, and arson. By the early 1970s, there was an increased focus on the challenges facing fire departments and their firefighters. This attention led in 1973 to the publication of a seminal report, *America Burning*, issued by the National Commission on Fire Prevention and Control. This report generated widespread agreement and discomfort throughout the U.S. fire service, and in the federal government. It pointed out that the United States surpassed all other industrialized nations in annual fire death rates and property loss, and that the fire service itself, the federal government, designers of buildings, and the American public itself must share the blame.

While several newer reports have been issued by various committees and fire service organizations since *America Burning* (which itself has been revisited and updated twice), few have had such impact. The report pointed out that the nation's firefighters are among those paying most heavily for the poor national fire record, as evidenced by death and injury rates and by debilitating, long-lasting, and often fatal illnesses.

Following the publication of *America Burning*, several federal agencies began to work to improve the national record relative to fire protection. Encouraged by fire service organizations, with strong efforts by the International Association of Fire Fighters (IAFF) and the National Fire Protection Association (NFPA), the NFPA *1500 Standard on Fire Department Occupational Safety and Health Program* was issued in 1987. This controversial standard and its updates, augmented by regulations issued by the federal Occupational Safety and Health Administration (OSHA), have done a great deal to reduce firefighter death, injury, and illness rates.

By almost any measure, the impact of *America Burning* and other efforts did result in greatly improving the fire situation in the U.S. Beginning in the 1980s, fire departments began to extend the list of services they would provide, both as a result of new community needs and a desire to

A stunning action photo of a firefighter operating a deck pipe from a pumper, ca. 1920s. Photographed by George Rinhart. (© Underwood & Underwood/Corbis)

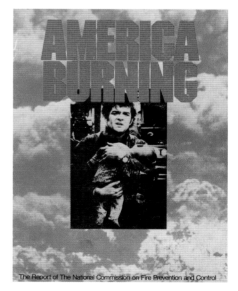

In 1973, a report was issued by the National Commission on Fire Prevention and Control. This report was a turning point in the fire service in the United States. Its impact was felt throughout the country and is still referred to today as the pivotal beginning of efforts to reduce fire deaths and property loss. (United States Fire Administration)

As homes are built on land that was for ages forested wildland, the incidents of wildland fires in urban settings increases. What was once a fire that affected mostly flora and fauna in remote areas of the country, now is a threat to whole communities that did not exist a hundred years ago. Here, fire devastates the area around Los Alamos, New Mexico, in May 2000. (B. Gutierrez/Denver Rocky Mountain News/Corbis Sygma)

maintain productivity in the face of declining fire incidents. These additional services, which place vastly increased training, knowledge, and skill requirements on firefighters, include advanced emergency medical services, hazardous materials incident mitigation, various technical rescue specialties such as rope rescue, trench collapse, and confined space rescue, plus natural disaster response and "weapons of mass destruction" incident readiness. In addition, public safety education and health screening programs are commonplace services for many departments.

In most communities, firefighters have seen that the demand for this wider variety of services has grown, and many firefighters have needed to become specialists in one of the newer demand areas. Teams of experienced specialists have been formed into urban search and rescue teams, which are now dispatched regularly to large-scale national, and even international disasters. As a result of vastly broader missions, many fire departments are called fire-rescue departments. It's commonplace today to see uniform shoulder patches on what were once called "firemen," denoting emergency medical, technical rescue, or hazardous materials expertise. And, of course, the term "fireman" holds no validity today, since there currently are about 6,100 women nationally in career departments and many thousands more in volunteer departments.

Another technical specialty that has a long and venerated history in the fire service is wildland firefighting. Our great national treasure, the American West, has experienced some of history's most intense wildfires, and we continue to read and see accounts of such fires each fire season. As former wildland has been built upon, we now have what are termed *wildland-urban interface* fires. These call for specialists and special equipment for both forest fires and structural fires. Once viewed as a "California problem" (such as the 1991 Oakland fire, which destroyed 2,900 structures and killed twenty-five people), recent years have seen devastating wildland and urban interface fires in many states, and the tragic deaths of wildland firefighters.

One such fire drew international attention, with Russia even offering to send two huge slurry bombers to aid. During May 2000, the Cerro Grande wildland-urban interface fire in New Mexico burned almost 18,000 acres, left 350 families homeless, and destroyed 112 small

buildings at the Los Alamos National Laboratory. Los Alamos County fire-fighters, aided by men and women from sixty-six other departments—career and volunteer—plus U.S. Forest Service Hotshot Crews, fought this fire for over a week. At one point, the famous and vital federal laboratory at Los Alamos was threatened. Large wildland fires in 2001 and 2002 further emphasized this type of danger to the nation, and to the men and women who fight them.

The chapters in this book describe in detail these and many other aspects of the work of firefighters which remain basic to the safety of our communities. And while much has changed over the more than 300 years of firefighting history, the dedication of firefighters remains as key to the profession today as it has in the past.

There are many stories to tell about the firefighters of this country, and many are told in this book. But I like the story of a man from New Jersey, a local person who started young and stayed with firefighting his entire life. Fireman Frank Walsh joined the Hackensack Volunteer Fire Department and rose to become volunteer captain of Hook and Ladder #2. The paid department was organized in 1911, and he was one of six men appointed to it in February 1912. He was promoted to lieutenant three years later, captain in 1924, and assistant chief in 1929. In 1937 he became acting chief. When the city shifted to a council-manager form of government in 1938, a director of public safety was appointed and the police chief and fire chief positions were abolished. Chief Walsh then became Captain Walsh until 1940, when the chiefs' positions were reestablished and he was named fire chief. He retired at age 65 in 1946, with an annual pension of $1,750, which was 50 percent of his annual salary.

One of the best-known early fire chiefs in New Jersey, Chief Walsh issued a statement in 1942 that echoed then, and still does now, what most firefighters—men and women—believe: "The greatest uniform that a man can wear is that of a fireman. It is greater than even the army or the navy. Theirs reminds us of the loss of human life, whereas that of the fireman is dedicated to its saving. But on one account only is it the greatest uniform that a man can wear—if he wears it rightly and if he honors God."

Damage to a Los Alamos lab caused by wildland fires May 21. 2000. This emphasizes the threat that wildland fire pose not only to the land and urban environments, but to national security. (© Gilbert Liz/Corbis Sygma)

Fireman Frank Walsh, who is standing in the middle of the row of firemen in front of the pumper, joined the Hackensack Volunteer Fire Department and was Captain of Hook and Ladder #2. (Collection of Joan McCaffrey, granddaughter of Chief Walsh)

Becoming a Firefighter

Becoming a Firefighter
Fire Service Training and Education

Steven T. Edwards

Training is the foundation upon which the every fire service is built. Fire departments that care about their members strongly support training throughout all phases of a firefighter's career. Firefighters are expected to be well-trained in order to provide a high level of service to the public, and in order to insure their own safety, as well. The survivability of a firefighter during an emergency incident in many cases depends on his or her level of training. Unfortunately, the history of the fire and rescue service is laden with the sacrifices made by firefighters in the line of duty. Proper training is one way to increase safety to prevent firefighter tragedies in the future.

There are few other public service professions that spend as much on-duty time in training as the fire service. From the recruit's first day on the job, firefighters are consistently involved in training to help them develop the skills to meet whatever challenge lies ahead. Firefighters never know what the next incident may demand. It could be a house fire, a truck accident with hazardous materials, a choking baby, or something as simple as a person locked out of their house. As a firefighter, one has to be ready for anything at anytime. This means that firefighter training must cover a wide variety of subjects and circumstances.

There is no question that specialization and the technology available to today's firefighter or emergency medical technician requires a higher level

Above: An *Aerial Ladder Short Course conducted at the University of Maryland in the early 1960s. (University of Maryland Fire and Rescue Institute)*

Pages 36–37: *Fire instructors ignite a training fire for a group of new firefighters. (Massachusetts Firefighting Academy)*

Opposite: *A graduating class of firefighter trainees in Stillwater, Oklahoma, during the early 1930s. (Oklahoma State University Fire Service Training)*

of knowledge and ability than in the past. Fire service training is a cumulative process that continues throughout one's entire career. Firefighters achieve certain milestones in training and are certified to increasingly higher levels, but the need for on-going training and preparation never stops. There are many highly developed training academies, schools, and institutions devoted to the continuing education and professionalism of fire service personnel.

Becoming a Firefighter

Before one is allowed into a fire training program, he or she has to be selected for the position. This is a very competitive process in most fire departments, one where many thousands may apply for the few available vacancies. A department may have only one recruit per fire school per year, and a typical class in a career fire department may consist of only thirty trainees—or fewer. Fire departments have a large number of applicants, not because the salaries are so high, but because the work is challenging and worthwhile.

The selection process involves judging firefighter candidates on a variety of dimensions, ranging from those which are observable and measurable (for example, years of experience and education), to the abstract and personal (predicted leadership potential).The fire service typically attracts people who enjoy risk and who love physical challenges. The vast majority of firefighter applicants are not selected for the position. Those who are appointed truly represent an elite group of applicants. Most fire departments utilize a multi-step process to select firefighter candidates. The process will consist of a number of selection tools sequenced to fit the needs of the particular fire department. Selection is usually based on a combination of written examination, a physical ability test, an oral interview, a background and reference check, and a thorough medical examination.

Firefighters must learn how to tie knots in order to hoist equipment and for many other purposes. (Louisiana State University Fire/Rescue Training)

Unquestionably, it's the physical ability test that knocks out many applicants, especially females. This is a controversial issue within the fire service, but it remains a fact that physical strength is absolutely essential for an active firefighter. The day a candidate receives *the letter* appointing him or her to the fire department is usually one of great satisfaction. Many have described this as the happiest day of their lives. Hopefully, it's the beginning of a long and rewarding career.

The fire service is unique in that you may serve for a fire department as a paid, career firefighter, or serve as a volunteer member. It is estimated that there are approximately 293,600 paid or career firefighters in the United States, and approximately 784,700 volunteer members. In most cases, volunteer applicants are not subject to all the same requirements as applicants for career positions. Over 26,000 communities in the United States depend wholly, or in part, on volunteer fire and EMS personnel. Almost all of them are struggling to recruit and retain qualified volunteer members. Applicants are welcome in the volunteer fire service, with the hope that training (both in the classroom and in drills) and hands-on experience will allow them to serve the community in a skilled and accomplished manner.

Recruit (Rookie) School

Regardless of whether it is a paid, volunteer or combination department, all fire departments have to train new firefighters. The public holds high expectations for fire service personnel, and this expectation begins with the trainees. The training that firefighters receive is designed to respond directly to the types of incidents they will encounter. Training, therefore, is not only physically demanding, it is often dangerous. It is an unfortunate fact that recruit firefighters have been killed or injured during training evolutions.

Recruit or "rookie" school is where it all begins. It is very critical that recruit school be taught by experienced members of the department—

A firefighter trainee listens to instruction during a firefighting training session at the Colorado Fire Fighters Academy in Durango, Colorado. (© Layne Kennedy/Corbis)

Fire training exercises are demanding and physically challenging. (University of Illinois Fire Service Training Institute)

Aerial ladders must be placed with pinpoint accuracy so that if firefighters must leave the roof, it can be rapidly accomplished. (Baltimore County Fire Department)

members who will teach not only techniques, but who will also indoctrinate the recruit in the discipline of the fire service. Recruit school is a probationary period where firefighters are first exposed to the mental, physical, and emotional aspects of becoming a firefighter. Even after the strenuous selection process, some candidates don't get past this hurdle,

Firefighters enter the burn building during a training evolution and successfully extinguish the fire. (University of Maryland Fire and Rescue Institute)

FROM THE VERY FIRST DAY, I'VE LOVED IT!— CHIEF DENNIS COMPTON

It was January 18, 1971. We reported to the Phoenix, Arizona, Fire Department Training Academy at 7:00 a.m. sharp. I was dressed in a new uniform, anxious about what the day might be like, and hopeful that I would be able to prove myself as a capable firefighter. As I entered the academy, I was one member of a class of thirteen recruits.

I had never considered becoming a firefighter until about nine months earlier. A friend had approached me about taking the test. Fresh out of the Army, it seemed like a good thing to do. Then I began meeting other firefighters, and it wasn't long before I was sure that I wanted to become one of them. Now, on that January day in 1971, I had accomplished that . . . or at least I had one foot in the door.

Almost all the class members became immediate friends (and still are to this day). It was obvious that a good sense of humor would be necessary to get along in the group and to deal with the stress associated with being constantly evaluated. We met our interim training officer, an old Battalion Chief named Jake Siken. He would be with us until Captain Jim Walker returned from sick leave.

I remember being challenged by all there was to learn, and much like boot camp in the military, there was little tolerance for error. I can honestly say that the day I graduated from the Phoenix Recruit Academy was one of the most satisfying experiences in my life.

From those first days, I knew that the fire service would be my lifetime career. It felt good to be able to perform difficult, and at times, risky tasks, and it felt good to be part of the fire service family. Wearing a firefighter's uniform and the thrill of helping others was a real high, and it still is. From the first day, I couldn't believe I could be lucky enough to be selected as a firefighter. It's now 2003, and I still can't believe I have been so lucky. I loved my first day, and I'll love being a firefighter until the day I die.

and are excused from the process. Recruit school is designed to train new firefighters to a level of proficiency that will allow them to function as part of a team that responds to emergencies.

The school can be very intimidating. When the recruit firefighters first step onto the grounds of the training academy, they see a bewildering series of obstacle courses and towers designed for ladder work and repelling. During classroom work, books are distributed that are reminiscent of college science textbooks. The recruit is exposed to equipment and apparatus, but has no idea what they are used for. The "burn building" (the firefighting structural burn building) ominously looms with its windows blackened from many live fire training exercises. A recruit may ask him or herself, "Am I up to this? Do I have what it takes to be a firefighter?" In all cases, they'll know soon enough.

Across the United States, recruit school usually lasts anywhere from sixteen to twenty-two weeks. Much like boot camp, its goals are not only to impart specific technical knowledge and skills, but to bring the trainee into the culture of firefighting. In terms of building a knowledge base, the recruits are expected to learn the basics of roughly seven general subject areas within firefighting:

Basics of Firefighting: Recruits are taught to handle hoses; the proper use of personal protective equipment (PPE), including self-contained breathing apparatus (SCBA); search procedures; forcible entry techniques; ventilation procedures; and the use of various firefighting tools, including extrication equipment.

Fire engines can pump over 1,500 gallons of water per minute. (Pennsylvania State Fire Academy)

Above: *An instructor is teaching new recruits the principles of hydraulic theory and how to operate fire department pumps. (Prince George's County Fire/EMS Department)*

Right: *Firefighters must learn how to operate the pumps on fire apparatus in order to get water to the fire. (Louisiana State University Fire/Rescue Training)*

Opposite, top: *Extricating people trapped in vehicle accidents is something that every firefighter must learn. (Baltimore County Fire Department)*

Rescue: Rescue techniques will include the principles and procedures of removing victims from vehicles accidents; confined-space entry and egress; the use of hydraulic rescue tools as well as the use of specialized rescue equipment.

Medical: Recruits are taught the mechanics of transporting patients safely to a hospital, and standard pre-hospital procedures, ranging from airway management to the use of automatic external defibrillators (AED). Rookies

are also taught CPR and are certified either as medical first responders or emergency medical technicians. Firefighters who eventually cross-train as paramedics are highly valued within their departments.

Hazardous Materials: Recruits are taught the techniques of donning chemical protective clothing; how to recognizing the hazards of specific chemicals; and how to control the spread of hazardous materials to protect life, property, and the environment.

Above, left: *Many firefighters are needed to handle the hoses necessary to extinguish large fires involving flammable liquids.* (North Carolina Fire Service Training)

Above: *Firefighters practicing the use of hydraulic rescue tools to pry and cut the metal that may trap someone in a car.* (Baltimore County Fire Department)

Driver Training: Recruits are taught to drive a variety of fire apparatus; they learn hydraulic theory and how to operate nozzles and other appliances. Complex mathematical formulas relating to water pressure and pump operations are expected to be memorized.

Ladders: The proper use of ladders is considered core knowledge in the fire service. Recruits are taught to successfully place ground ladders up to fifty feet in length; how to use aerial ladder equipment and elevated platforms to reach heights up to 150 feet.

Special Services: Increasingly, even new recruits are expected to respond to highly unusual situations. It is not unusual in urban areas, for example, for new firefighters to receive anti-terrorism training, including preparation for weapons of mass destruction events, including chemical, biological, and nuclear emergencies.

When the great day arrives, graduation, a career firefighter will usually have met the requirements for several National Fire Protection Association (NFPA) professional qualification standards. He or she will be a certified Level I or II Firefighter and as an Emergency Medical Technician (EMT). As well, the recruit will have completed Hazardous Materials Operations, Rescue Technician, and perhaps several other standards, some of which have been approved for equivalent college credit.

The National Fire Academy

Denis Onieal, Ed.D., *Superintendent National Fire Academy*

*T*he landmark 1973 report, AMERICA BURNING: The Report of the National Commission on Fire Prevention and Control, *called for the creation of a United States Fire Administration (originally the National Fire Prevention and Control Administration), and specifically "the establishment of a National Fire Academy (NFA) to provide specialized training in areas important to the fire services and to assist State and local jurisdictions in their training programs."*

Since its inception, the NFA's responsibility has been to promote the professional development of the fire and the emergency response community and its allied professionals. To supplement and support state and local fire service training programs, the NFA delivers educational and training courses having a national focus.

The NFA began operating in 1974 with a core curriculum and small cadre of instructors who traveled around the nation conducting courses in cooperation with local fire agencies. For those first six years, it was an academy without "bricks and mortar."

In March 1979, the federal government purchased the former St. Joseph's College in Emmitsburg, Maryland, as the site for the NFA. The first NFA classes on the Emmitsburg campus were held in January 1980, and the NFA has grown steadily since that time. From its humble beginnings in 1974, the academy's course offerings were revised, improved, and expanded each year. In 2001, the NFA trained over 50,000 fire and emergency services personnel.

The Emmitsburg NFA campus is located a few miles south of the Pennsylvania border, 75 miles north of Washington, D.C. Today, the 107-acre campus houses the United States Fire Administration and its training arm, the NFA, the Emergency Management Institute, the National Fire Data Center, the National Fire Programs offices, the Urban Search and Rescue program, the

offices of the National Fallen Firefighters Foundation, and the National Fallen Firefighters Memorial. The campus, known as the National Emergency Training Center (NETC), has modern, fully equipped classrooms, lodging for students, a learning resource center, and dining and recreational facilities.

Through its courses and programs, the NFA works to enhance the ability of fire and emergency services and allied professionals to deal more effectively with fire and related emergencies. The academy's delivery systems are diverse. Courses are delivered at the Emmitsburg resident facility, and throughout the nation, in cooperation with state and local fire-training organizations and local colleges and universities. The NFA continues to expand its technology-based training through the Internet and CD-ROM self-study. Most of the NFA's courses undergo a rigorous evaluation by the American Council on Education, and students receive college credit recommendations for successful completion of those courses.

For those interested in pursuing higher education, the Degrees At a Distance Program extends NFA's academic outreach through a network of seven colleges and universities. Fire service personnel who cannot attend college due to work hours and location are able to earn their degree in fire technology and management through independent study. The NFA also distributes baccalaureate-level materials to four-year colleges and universities for traditional classroom use.

Any person with substantial involvement in fire prevention and control, emergency medical services, fire-related emergency management activities, or allied professions is eligible to apply for NFA courses.

National, State and Local Fire Training Academies

After completion of recruit school, there are numerous types and levels of training and educational programs available to firefighters throughout the United States. Each has a specific role to play in the training process at the local, state, or national level. Fire training programs can range from six

Many state fire training programs use mobile training props in order to maximize training throughout the entire state. (Iowa Fire Service Training Bureau)

A special prop is used to simulate an aircraft fire for firefighters to train in this very specific environment. (South Carolina Fire Academy)

51

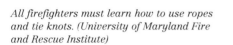

Much of what recruit firefighters must learn is accomplished in the classroom environment. (University of Maryland Fire and Rescue Institute)

All firefighters must learn how to use ropes and tie knots. (University of Maryland Fire and Rescue Institute)

Training to sharpen their skills, firefighters with advanced emergency medical training use a realistic scenario to ensure that their techniques and knowledge are current. Upon initial training, skills tests are given. Continuing education ensures that they remain up to high standards. (Paul Ramirez/Phoenix Fire Department)

hours, to several hundred hours depending upon the course content. Fire departments that provide emergency medical services (EMS) have additional training requirements depending upon the level of service provided. Local fire training academies operate at the city, county, or municipal level and generally provide the training services to one fire department or to a specific geographical region. Most large city fire departments will have their own fire training academy that is used to create the situations that the firefighters of that jurisdiction will encounter. The training academies are staffed by experienced and professional fire service instructors who guide and manage the training programs to best serve their community.

State fire training programs are operated in every state and provide training to a large geographical area and large numbers of firefighters. Many state fire training programs or state fire training academies are associated with universities or colleges. Several university-based state fire training programs began at land grant universities in the 1930s.

MY FIRST FIRE — *Steven T. Edwards*

We had been in training for several weeks and it was now time for our first live fire training exercise. Everyone was apprehensive, but no one wanted to show it. I remember this fire as though it was yesterday, even though it was more than thirty years ago.

As I stood outside the burn building ready to go, I could see the instructor light the fire. A large cloud of dark black smoke appeared, followed by the bright orange and red flames. I was surprised that I could feel the heat from the fire and I was still outside. My position was on the nozzle, so I was the first one to enter and extinguish the fire.

As my team crawled down the hallway on bended knees toward the burn room, the heat grew more intense. I was sweating from the combination of heavy gear, breathing apparatus, and anxiety. As I entered the room, flames were issuing out at the top of the doorway. I could feel my wrists and ears starting to burn from the intense heat that was 200–300 degrees at the floor and approximately 1,000 degrees at the ceiling. I reached up to open the nozzle, because I thought that would cool everything down. I didn't know at the time that water turns to steam, expands 1,600 times in volume, and is intensely hot. With the thermo balance in the burn room disrupted by the water from the hose line, it drove me to the floor.

The room was now totally dark and I couldn't see my hand in front of my face. I could hear the instructor yelling to stay down and to open the nozzle again. I did this and in a few seconds it got cooler and the smoke started to lift off of the floor so that I could see again. My neck, ears, and wrists hurt from the heat and the associated pain. I felt relieved that it

was over as we backed the hose line out the door. I then felt a wonderful sense of pride at what I had accomplished and that I was ready for a real fire.

As I exited the burn building the next group of firefighters was ready to take their turn. One of them nervously asked me how it was; of course I replied as if I was a veteran of many fires: "Nothing to it. A piece of cake." I didn't fully appreciate this training exercise until I encountered my first real fire a couple of weeks later—but that's another story.

Steve Edwards became the fourth Fire Chief of Prince George's County, Maryland, in 1990.

Universities such as Iowa State, University of Illinois, University of Maryland, Louisiana State University, University of Missouri, Texas A&M, Oklahoma State University, and others have their origins in this era. Several states use the community college delivery system to provide training for firefighters within their state. Other state fire training programs are a part of state government or are based under the auspices of a separate state level board or commission. Many state fire training academies have large training facilities and regional training systems so that they can train large numbers of students. Each year the state fire training programs in the United States cumulatively train over 750,000 firefighters.

The National Fire Academy (NFA) is located in Emmitsburg, Maryland, and is structured within the United States Fire Administration of the Federal Emergency Management Agency (FEMA). The National Fire Academy promotes the professional development of the fire and emergency response community and its allied professionals. To supplement and support state

The campus of FEMA's National Emergency Training Center (which includes the National Fire Academy), located in Emmitsburg, Maryland, offers a beautiful environment for first responders, emergency managers, and educators to learn state-of-the-art disaster management and response. (Jocelyn Augustino/FEMA News Photo)

and local fire service training programs, the NFA delivers educational and training courses having a national focus. Courses are delivered at the resident facility in Emmitsburg and throughout the United States in cooperation with state and local training programs as well as various colleges and universities. The National Fire Academy supports programs for firefighters pursuing degrees. The Degrees at a Distance Program extends NFA's academic outreach through a network of seven colleges and universities. Fire service personnel who cannot attend college due to shift work hours and locations are able to earn a degree in fire technology and management through independent study. Many fire officers have pursued this option as well as continued on to complete advanced degrees at various universities and colleges.

In order to conduct realistic fire training programs there must be training props and equipment that can replicate real fires and other emergencies. In essence, fire training agencies have to construct a building that can be set on fire and burned several times each day. This takes structures that have been specially designed and constructed for this purpose. Firefighting structural burn buildings are constructed with materials that have been tested and proven to withstand the constant heating and then rapid cooling that they are exposed to. Special fire brick, coatings, and high temperature tiles are used to protect the structural elements of the building. These buildings are very expensive to construct and locate due to environmental concerns and other issues. Many new fire training props use propane gas as the fuel to reduce the environmental concerns of burning petroleum based fuels and Class A combustibles such as wood products. Fire training centers must also have tall structures that firefighters can climb, rappel from, and use for many training functions. These building are generally from five to ten stories and are designed to facilitate a large number of

Just before a dangerous flashover, Colorado Firefighter Academy students kneel beneath 800 degree heat in a smoking fire. Training structures are built to be used over and over while withstanding constant high temperatures. (© Layne Kennedy/Corbis)

training scenarios. Firefighter trainees need a place to learn how to lift and place ground ladders, use the aerial ladder trucks that can reach up to 150 feet, rappel out of upper floors, simulate high-angle rescues, advance hose lines, and perform many other tasks. Buildings such as this are in constant use at any fire training academy.

Many fire training centers include elaborate props for training in the numerous specialized rescues that firefighters are called upon to perform. Confined space rescue props are used to simulate rescues from below ground or tight spaces, hazardous materials spills from tank trucks are simulated, building collapses are replicated, mass causality events are set up and then responded to, and a host of other activities are regularly created for training purposes. The innovativeness of these props and the realism of the training environment are critical to the success of the firefighter training program.

Fire training academies must have adequate classroom space to conduct didactic training sessions. Much of what firefighter trainees receive is hands-on training, but a lot of class work is required also. Firefighter students, for example, must learn hydraulic theory to operate pumps and move water, the different phases of combustion, medical training, and techniques for their survival. In general, before any training prop is used on the drill ground the recruits have already attended classroom sessions to learn the principles and how to safely encounter such dangers.

The future of fire service training is moving toward the use of higher levels of technology. Much of the coursework previously taught at the fire training academy is now available on-line in computer-assisted or distance-learning programs. Fire simulators that use computer graphics and programs to train command-level fire officers are used by many departments. Human patient simulators driven by computers and other devices are used in emergency medical training for firefighters and paramedics. Systems that will use virtual reality techniques to simulate fires in a realistic manner without ever having to burn anything are on the horizon. As technology advances, so will the world of fire service training.

Fire Service Certification Systems

There is a great deal of training and education occurring in the fire service on a daily basis throughout the United States. How firefighters measure, compare, and quantify this training is important to their profession. If the training is accomplished in accordance with national standards and the results are certified by an independent body or organization, then highly trained firefighters will be the result. The general public expects qualified, competent, and professional personnel, be they volunteer or career, to respond to emergencies. There must be a system to ensure this and provide standards that are recognized as being professional in terms of intellect, competence, and responsibility.

The first step in this process is the establishment of national standards against which one can be evaluated. In the firefighting profession the undisputed leader in this field is the National Fire Protection Association

Firefighters train in an evolution to remove a victim from a burning building. While the firefighter on the ladder secures the victim between himself and the bed of the ladder, another "heels" the ladder for safety, and a third monitors his progress and stands ready to assist at the bottom of the ladder. (© Richard T. Nowitz/Corbis)

Training is a constant in the fire service and realistic training is essential. The evolution above provides exposure to heat, smoke, and flame. Firefighters regularly attend these classes to help them prepare for actual emergency conditions. (© Bill Stormont/Corbis)

Firefighters receive extensive training as "Emergency Medical Technicians" in order to provide emergency medical care to citizens. (Prince George's County Fire/EMS Department)

Firefighter trainees maintain their physical ability and agility by performing regular exercise, not unlike the military. Regular physical training is necessary to be prepared for the unexpected. (© Layne Kennedy/Corbis)

(NFPA). The mission of the NFPA, which was organized in 1896, is to reduce the burden of fire on the quality of life by advocating scientifically based consensus codes and standards, and supporting research and education for fire and related safety issues. The NFPA consensus process is dependent upon personnel from a wide range of professional backgrounds who serve on more than 200 technical committees, each reflecting a balance of affected interests.

In the fire and rescue service the primary document that guides training and certification systems is the NFPA 1000 Standard on Fire Service Professional Qualifications Accreditation and Certification Systems. The minimum criteria for certification as well as the assessment and validation requirements of the certifying agencies are established in this standard. The professional standards that have been developed in this series of

standards are widely used and acknowledged within North America. Many fire service training programs have been designed to meet the minimum requirements of the professional qualification standards. The NFPA professional qualification system standards that are eligible for certification in most states are as follows:

- NFPA 1001 Standard for Fire Fighter Professional Qualifications
- NFPA 1002 Standard for Fire Apparatus Driver/Operator Professional Qualifications
- NFPA 1003 Standard for Airport Fire Fighter Professional Qualifications
- NFPA 1021 Standard for Fire Officer Professional Qualifications
- NFPA 1031 Standard for Professional Qualifications for Fire Inspector
- NFPA 1033 Standard for Professional Qualifications for Fire Investigator

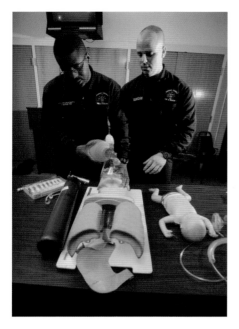

Firefighter trainees practice Cardiopulmonary Resuscitation (CPR) during recruit training school. These basic life support skills are critical to the performance of their duties once they begin responding to actual emergencies. (© Richard T. Nowitz/Corbis)

A firefighter places a ladder at the base of a training structure. The handling and placement of ground ladders is essential to many firefighting operations. Ladders are used for rescues and access to the location of the fire. Hoselines, tools, and other equipment can be taken up a ladder as dictated by the emergency incident. (© Richard T. Nowitz/Corbis)

■ NFPA 1035 Standard for Professional Qualifications for Public Educator

■ NFPA 1041 Standard for Professional Qualifications for Fire Service Instructor

The professional qualification system of the NFPA has established national standards to which individual training programs and performance can be evaluated. The NFPA standards are now in the job performance requirement (JPR) format that makes it easier to evaluate performance as it relates to the knowledge, skills, and abilities of a particular standard. In addition, the standards are revised every five years so that they remain current and reflect the true status of the fire and rescue services. Individuals within the fire service that have been certified as meeting the national standards may be recognized at the local, state, and national level for demonstrated proficiency within the standard to which they have been certified. Their credibility is enhanced on an individual and departmental level. Certification is a statement of accomplishment and it will improve one's worth and transferability to other departments, if that is desired. Being certified to national standards improves the professionalism of the fire and rescue service.

The National Board of Fire Service Professional Qualifications (NBFSPQ), commonly referred to as the "pro board," has established a national firefighter certification system. This board consists of representatives of the following organizations: International Association of Fire Chiefs, National Fire Protection Association, North American Fire Training Directors, North American Association of State Fire Marshals, and the International Association of Arson Investigators. This board establishes the criteria and the requirements for the certification of fire personnel to the national professional qualifications standards. The board also establishes the accreditation process for state and local certifications systems. Generally, the NBFSPQ only accredits one entity in each state as the certifying body of that state. The NBFSPQ has a well-defined process for accreditation that includes an extensive site visit by the accreditation team and then a recommendation is made to the board. Once a state is accredited, there are then requirements for re-accreditation at specific intervals. The International Fire Service Accreditation Congress (IFSAC) was established in 1991 as a national accrediting body for the certification of fire personnel and for the accreditation of college level fire service educational programs. IFSAC grew out of a national meeting hosted by the National Association of State Directors of Fire Training and Education in 1990 and is located at and supported by Oklahoma State University. The IFSAC system consists of an Accreditation Congress which is composed of one representative of each state or entity participating in the program and a Board of Governors consisting of seven members from the Accreditation Congress. The Accreditation Congress establishes the policy for the IFSAC system. In addition, there is a Degree Assembly which coordinates the accreditation of college-level fire service degree programs. The IFSAC system uses the NFPA professional qualifications standards for certification purposes.

Many fire departments have sought to obtain recognition for their training programs and to increase their value to firefighters by having

them evaluated for equivalent college credit. The American Council on Education (ACE) is an independent, nonprofit organization founded in 1918 and serves as an umbrella organization for colleges and universities. Upon request, the ACE College Credit Recommendation Service will conduct a site visit by education experts of the training facilities, curriculum, record-keeping, evaluation, and testing procedures of that jurisdiction. If approved, the training courses of the fire department will be listed in the National Guide to Educational Credit for Training Programs, which is available to academic advisors for reference while counseling students and awarding equivalent college credit.

The approval and listing of fire department training programs in the ACE guide provides a step toward "seamless education" wherein an individual may progress toward higher education without the restriction of system boundaries. The recognition of training programs will validate and emphasize the fire department's commitment to high-quality education and provide another positive incentive for firefighters to take the training programs. It enhances and brings recognition to a department's entire training effort and is highly recommended.

It should be noted that fire service training is not absolutely lockstep across the United States. As with most things having to do with government service delivery, the quality and type of training may vary somewhat from jurisdiction to jurisdiction. But, it remains remarkable, nonetheless, how well trained most firefighters are in the United States. The decision to pursue firefighting as a career or avocation means that the young person is embarking on a journey of lifelong learning. Whereas other professions may talk about continuing education, the fire service promotes and depends on it. There is no other choice.

A firefighter recruit class proudly poses for a class photo, having successfully completed their initial training to become a firefighter. The ropes around their waists are those that they carried throughout the training process and on which they practiced their rope tying techniques. Although they have completed the "basic training" for a firefighter, they know that their entire career will involve training and retraining to keep them prepared for whatever they may encounter in the future. (Montgomery County Fire and Rescue Service)

Firefighters training to become smokejumpers with the U.S. Forest Service undergo a routine of ground and low-level evolutions before they ever take off in an airplane. This tower is part of the Forest Service Smokejumping Training Center in Missoula, Montana. (© Kevin R. Morris/Corbis)

Tools of the Trade

Tools of the Trade

Kansas Firefighter's Museum

Above: *This 3/4-inch booster line is carried on the pumper on a hose reel. Because it is a rigid hose, it can be easily rolled up on a reel, charged with water without having to be fully unrolled, and does not need to be stored flat as with other fire hose. (Craig Hacker)*

Left: *Looking from the bottom of an aerial ladder to its tip enables a view of the two fly sections on top of the bed section. This particular aerial ladder extends to seventy-five feet. (Craig Hacker)*

Pages 60–61: *A firefighter in full protective clothing, self-contained breathing apparatus, and carrying a pick-head axe emerges from a training evolution. Constant training with the gear and equipment they will use on an actual fire is critical to maintain skill and confidence with the equipment. (Paul Ramirez/ Phoenix Fire Department)*

T he public image of the firefighter is closely associated with the distinctive appearance of a firefighter dressed and equipped for action. The unique protective clothing and special tools, which are essential for the functions that firefighters perform, have become trademarks of the profession. Virtually all of the tools and equipment used by firefighters have been specially developed or adapted for the tasks that must be performed and the extreme conditions of the firefighter's work environment.

A large part of the work of firefighters is a highly advanced form of manual labor, requiring the participants to perform strenuous physical tasks and face an array of challenges, while working under extremely hazardous conditions. Protective clothing and equipment provide the ability for firefighters to enter and work in areas where no one else could survive. The tools of the trade are the weapons used by firefighters to attack the fire, which requires a variety of different actions. Everything

Opposite: *Two firefighters cut through a metal wall to gain access to the fire. The saw has a gasoline-powered engine and a metal cutting saw blade. These saws are widely deployed throughout the fire service for, among other uses, cutting through walls, roofs, and to free victims trapped in crushed automobiles. (Paul Ramirez/Phoenix Fire Department)*

Top, left: This emergency fire escape kit from 1895 was designed to allow escape from upper floors by apartment occupants. A predecessor of the escape ladder, this item allowed an individual to sit in a sling and lower himself to the ground or to a point of safety away from the fire. (Craig Hacker)

Top, right: The mud pick was developed to clean clay from horse hooves. Horses, just like their modern-day equivalent, the pumper, required maintenance. Without clean hooves, the horses could develop injuries or slip and fall responding to an alarm. (Craig Hacker)

Above: Rather than just scooping up water and throwing it on the fire, these bucket pumps allowed the user to apply a stream of water to a more specific point for extinguishment. (Craig Hacker)

Below, left to right:
Hand pump extinguishers utilized water for extinguishment and came in sizes from two to five gallons. The extinguisher was pumped with one hand and the nozzle was held in the other and directed at the base of the fire. (Craig Hacker)

Soda and acid extinguishers are, except for water, the oldest, best known, and the most commonly used extinguisher. Utilizing sulfuric acid and bicarbonate of soda, these extinguishers are inverted to start the reaction of the acid and the soda. (Craig Hacker)

Dry powder tubes are sheet metal tubes with a mixture of bicarbonate of soda and other materials in powder form. Various methods of activation were used according to individual directions on the tubes. (Craig Hacker)

Carbon dioxide (CO2) extinguishers put out fires primarily by removing the oxygen that a fire needs to burn. The secondary effect is cooling the burning material with the cold CO2 that is expelled during operation. (Craig Hacker)

must be extra-strong, extra-powerful, extra-tough, and extra-durable to function effectively under these conditions, including the firefighter who must be able to perform strenuous work while wearing all of the protective clothing and equipment.

The history of firefighting in America involves an intricate combination of progress and tradition. The tools of the trade have seen continuous advancement over 200 years, while still maintaining many loyal attachments to the past. It has always been a challenge to introduce anything radically new to the fire service and almost impossible to abandon anything tried and true. The changes have often been incremental, developing adaptations of existing tools and equipment to gradually introduce new technology. Many of the items in use today can be traced back to fairly basic and primitive origins.

As the role of the firefighter has expanded far beyond fighting fires, the variety of different types of protective clothing and equipment has increased tremendously, and the selection of tools has become larger and much more specialized. Within the past fifty years the catalog of specialized tools and equipment used by firefighters has expanded tremendously. The inventory of tools and equipment carried on fire apparatus now includes a long list of sophisticated items for a wide range of situations.

Top, left: *The sprinkler head maintenance kit was designed for use at fires to shut down sprinkler flow and provide replacement heads. This kit contained replacement sprinklers, a wrench, and tools to stop the flow of water from an activated sprinkler head before the water could be turned off. (Craig Hacker)*

Top, right: *Emergency road flares, made by Toledo, shown as a boxed set and running board mounted set. The set includes three road flares and a container of fuel for refilling. These flares would be used on the scene of an emergency as a warning of danger in the area. (Craig Hacker)*

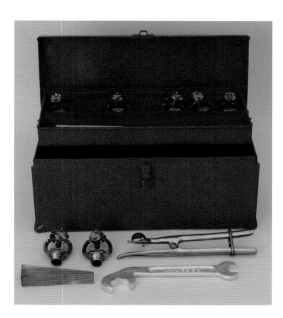

Center, clockwise from upper left:
The first fire watch alerting devices were the hand rattles, followed by the Muffin Bell, and finally the mouth siren. All were hand-operated fire-warning devices utilized in the 1800s. Before the use of alarm boxes and electronic fire detection devices, individuals would patrol buildings or city streets (particularly at night) looking for fires. Once a fire was detected, they would sound the alarm by activating one of the items shown and warn those in the vicinity to evacuate. (Craig Hacker)

In-station alarm bells "ring out" in fire companies from the late 1800s through today. Firefighters are often engaged in duties at various locations around the fire station. Alarm bells alert them of the necessity to assemble at the apparatus to respond to an alarm. (Craig Hacker)

This auto alarm call box set includes the bell and activators as used in the early 1920s. The activators would be pulled by employees or ordinary citizens and ring the alarm to warn those in the building of a fire. (Craig Hacker)

Electric fire alarm bells, from 1893, alerted the public to fire. These are another example of bells that could be used in a variety of locations. Businesses, warehouses, manufacturers, even homes could be outfitted with these warning devices. (Craig Hacker)

Below: *These carbon tetrachloride "hand grenades" were made of glass and thrown at the seat of the fire where they would break and release the extinguishing agent. (Craig Hacker)*

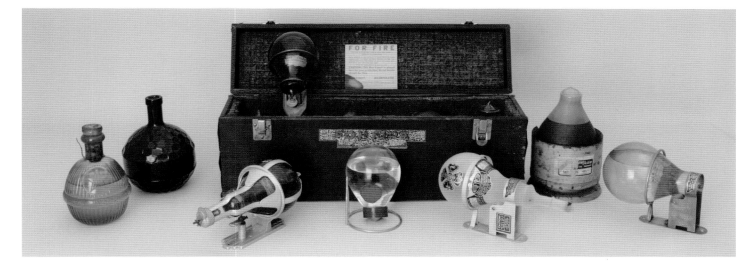

Protective Clothing

The clothing worn by firefighters must provide protection from the heat of the fire as well as a tremendous array of physical hazards that are likely to be encountered inside a burning building, or in any of the other environments where the firefighters fight fires. The skin that provides the exterior covering of the human body is easily burned, cut, scraped, bruised, battered, and attacked by a host of agents that are likely to be encountered by a firefighter. Today's ensembles for interior structural firefighting wrap every square inch of the firefighter's body with a combination of materials that provide an extremely tough outer layer, an impermeable barrier to prevent liquids from penetrating, and a thermal insulating layer to provide protection from the extreme heat produced by the fire.

The protective clothing must be tough enough to resist all of the hazards and still light and flexible enough to allow the user to move and work while wearing it. It must provide impact protection for areas that can be easily injured, particularly the head, and extra layers at the knees and elbows to allow a firefighter to crawl across a hot floor or over broken glass. The footwear must allow wading through hot or cold liquids, stop nails that are stepped upon from penetrating through the sole, and protect the toes from the impact of a misdirected sledgehammer. The gloves must allow a tool to be gripped and operated, while keeping the hands dry and preventing cuts or burns. The entire ensemble must be easily donned, allowing the firefighter to be fully dressed for combat in less than sixty seconds.

Prior to the development of modern protective ensembles, most firefighters had impressive collections of battle scars from past encounters with hostile situations. For more than a hundred years, the typical American firefighter wore a variation of a rubber or canvas raincoat to stay warm and dry, a leather helmet with a wide brim to protect the head against impacts and keep falling water and burning debris from going down the neck, and rubber boots to keep the feet dry. Gloves were optional. The generations of firefighters who wore that level of protective clothing could prove how tough they were just by taking off their shirts and showing off their old wounds.

The primary protection against being burned while wearing this type of clothing was distance. If the firefighters maintained a respectful distance from the flames, any burns they suffered would be relatively small and quick to heal. Even as newer and more protective ensembles became popular, many firefighters insisted on keeping their ears uncovered as a temperature gauge. The skin on the ears would provide a fast and painful warning when temperatures were approaching the threshold of serious injury.

One of the major problems with this type of protection was that it left very little margin for error. If the primitive warning system managed to keep the firefighter out of serious trouble, a minor ear burn was considered acceptable. When conditions changed very rapidly the results were often disastrous, because the clothing provided very little protection from a fully involved fire environment. Most of the materials that were used to construct protective clothing up until the 1960s would quickly char, melt, or burn if they came into direct contact with a fire, leaving no protection for the user.

The evolution of the modern "turnout" clothing is a result of new materials and manufacturing processes that were by-products of the space age. A series of scientific research projects measured and defined the conditions that are likely to be encountered in a firefighter's work environment, then supported the design and testing of new ensembles using newly developed materials and manufacturing methods. These ensembles included coats and pants, gloves, footwear, protective hoods, and helmets, all designed to work as a system to protect the entire body. This research allowed for the development of greatly advanced standards for protective clothing in the 1970s. Most of the protective ensembles worn today are the results of further advancements from the clothing that was introduced at that time.

The blending of progress with tradition is most clearly evident in the evolution of the firefighter's helmet. The traditional shape of the American firefighter's helmet dates back to the nineteenth century when durable leather was used to develop a very practical design that would provide impact protection to the head, while deflecting water and burning embers away from the face and neck. The basic shape was widely adopted and then gradually adapted by different fire departments and manufacturers until there were probably hundreds of variations reflecting different styles and preferences. While each design incorporated

The classic-style fire helmet has been used since the early 1900s. These helmets made of leather and metal protected the firefighter from falling debris while operating on the fireground. (Craig Hacker)

All modern helmets are made of material that is OSHA approved, but the design is based on the traditional leather fire helmet. Still in the classic shape, these helmets have undergone various improvements, particularly in the area of the headliner and suspension system on the interior of the helmet. (Craig Hacker)

The modern-style fire helmet replaced the classic style in the mid 1970s and are still in use today on a number of fire departments. The polycarbonate material provided a helmet with the ability to absorb forces from falling objects on the emergency scene, thus protecting the firefighter's head from injury. (Craig Hacker)

unique features and decorative details, the basic shape of a firefighter's helmet was easily recognized.

Through the twentieth century several different materials were adapted for use as firefighter's helmets, including aluminum, fiberglass, and several different plastics, with most retaining the same basic geometry. A few radically different designs were also introduced, but the traditional style continued to be much more popular than any of the new models. Many fire departments and tens of thousands of firefighters continued to wear traditional leather helmets and actively resisted any proposal to adopt more modern designs.

It was only after consensus standards were developed to define scientifically validated performance criteria for firefighters' helmets that many fire departments switched to more modern designs. Even after the standards were widely accepted, many firefighters resisted any change to the traditional design and maintained a firm grip on their traditional leather head coverings. Helmet manufacturers responded by incorporating new materials and technologies into new models that retained the traditional shape and decorative features, including leather outer coverings, while meeting the new performance standards.

At the beginning of the new millennium the traditional helmet is still preferred by many firefighters, even if the "leather look" is meticulously crafted from space age materials. Several fire departments that had adopted more modern-looking helmets in order to meet the performance standards have gone back to the traditional look, successfully maintaining the link between progress and tradition.

Below: The MSA canister mask provided early breathing capabilities for entering dangerous environments. These masks contained no fresh air or oxygen, but relied upon a filter system to remove harmful particulates from the surrounding air. After use the filter would be changed for a new one. (Craig Hacker)

Opposite, bottom left: The Scott Sling Pak contained twenty-two cubic feet of air and lasted for fifteen minutes under extreme exertion. In many departments these packs were used for short durations and for quick initial action on the fire scene . Most have been discontinued due to their small air capacity. (Craig Hacker)

Opposite, bottom right: The complete modern S.C.B.A. (Self Contained Breathing Apparatus) set includes a harness to hold the bottle and attach the unit to the firefighter's back (much like a backpack), an air bottle for containing the supply of air, and a mask to allow the firefighter to breathe fresh air while working in a hazardous or smoky place. (Craig Hacker)

Breathing Apparatus

The part of the human body that is most vulnerable to a fire environment is the respiratory system. Inhalation of the concentration of carbon monoxide produced by a typical interior structure fire would be fatal within seconds in many cases. In addition, a fire may release dozens of other products of combustion, some of which are even more toxic than carbon monoxide. Most civilian fire fatalities result from asphyxiation and, before self-contained breathing apparatus became available, hundreds of firefighters died from smoke inhalation and thousands were injured.

Early attempts to protect the lungs of firefighters relied on the filtering properties of a long moustache. For generations firefighters were affectionately nicknamed "smoke eaters" due to their apparent ability to work in conditions that were beyond comprehension to the spectators. Interior firefighting often involved a period of intense work and smoke

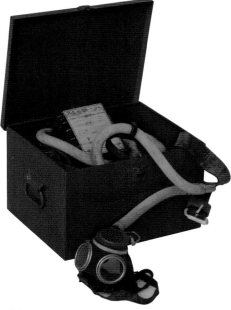

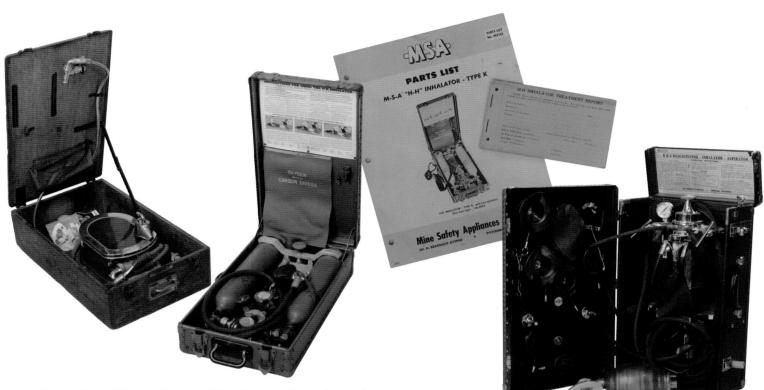

inhalation, followed by sticking the head out through a window to vomit and inhale some fresh air. This was repeated in cycles until the fire was extinguished, or the firefighter had to be dragged out of the building. Many of the hardy smoke eaters enjoyed an occasional cigarette break during long duration fires.

While the smoke eaters were great firefighters, far too many of them died from smoke inhalation or from respiratory diseases or cancers that resulted from repeated and extended exposures. This trend only began to change with the introduction of self-contained breathing apparatus in the 1950s, and it would take more than thirty years before this level of protection became mandatory for all interior firefighters.

The true first breathing apparatus used by firefighters dates back to the turn of the past century when some primitive designs that allowed outside air to be pumped in to a firefighter were developed. A few special rescue squads were trained and equipped to use this equipment, but it was much too cumbersome and complicated for general use.

The first generation of breathing apparatus to be widely used by firefighters was the canister mask that used a filter to trap particulate

Left to right: *Draeger Pulmotor Oxygen Apparatus; MSA Model H-H Inhalator–Type K; E&J Resuscitator; Bag Mask.*

The ability to provide artificial respiration to a nonbreathing patient has been a challenge to the medical community and firefighters for years. While medical facilities were able to use larger, more powerful units that could operate over long periods of time, firefighters required light-weight portable units that could be utilized in field situations. Above are examples of that evolution. The first three units represent the stages of development for the mechanical artificial respiration units used up until the advent of the bag mask. The bag mask replaced mechanical resuscitators and is the current tool of choice for fieldwork. (All photos Craig Hacker)

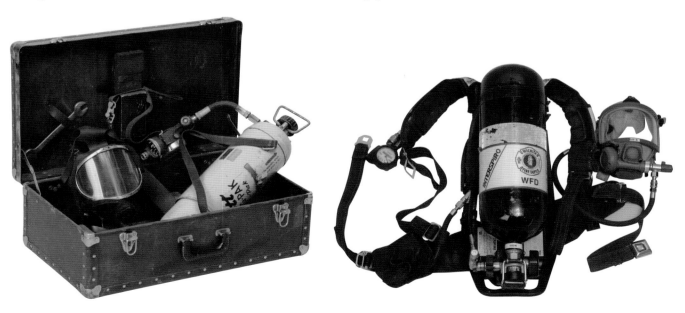

Opposite top, left: *Four different types of ground ladders in use by the fire service today. From left to right: A-frame ladder, folding ladder, roof ladder, and extension ladder. (Craig Hacker)*

Opposite top, center: *The roof ladder is a straight ladder consisting of one section. The unique feature of this ladder is the retractable hooks at the tip end that allow this ladder to be "hooked" over the ridge of a pitched roof. From there firefighters can work on a steep roof with some degree of security. (Craig Hacker)*

Opposite top, right: *An extension ladder is comprised of a bed section and one or more fly sections depending on the length of the ladder. The bed section remains stationary as the fly sections are raised to the appropriate height. (Craig Hacker)*

Opposite middle, left: *Ladders are stored on pumpers and ladder trucks when not in use. Here are several sizes of ladders stored in a compartment at the rear of a ladder truck. Also note a ladder hung on the outside of the right side of the truck. (Craig Hacker)*

Opposite middle, right: *The largest ladders in the fire service are those permanently attached to a ladder truck. These aerial ladders are moved by hydraulic systems operated by the truck's driver. Extending to lengths of seventy-five feet or more, they may be positioned to get firefighters to upper levels for fire suppression or rescue, and can facilitate the use of master stream devices to put massive amounts of water on a large fire. (Craig Hacker)*

Above: *A Thermal Imaging Camera uses heat generated by the human body to detect fire victims in heavy smoke situations. It also works well to locate the seat of the fire and hot spots in walls or roofs. Other applications include finding lost children at night by scanning a wooded area and detecting the heat from their body. This may be done from a helicopter above the search area. (Craig Hacker)*

Right: *A life belt is used in conjunction with ladders and ropes. Life belts are worn by members of rescue and ladder companies and allow firefighters to secure themselves to a ladder or rope for safety and rescue purposes. (Craig Hacker)*

70

matter and a chemical cartridge to absorb and neutralize the carbon monoxide. These masks worked well as long as the smoke contained only carbon particles and carbon monoxide, as long as the neutralizing chemicals were still effective, and as long as there was enough oxygen left in the filtered air to support life. They provided a tremendous improvement over a moustache or a wet towel, but they had very serious limitations.

The self-contained breathing apparatus (SCBA) that is in general use today dates back to just before World War II when the technology was developed to provide breathing air for the crews of high-altitude aircraft. In principle, it is very similar to the equipment that is used by SCUBA divers. This type of apparatus uses a tank of compressed air to provide a breathing air supply that is independent of the outside atmosphere. A regulator releases the air slowly as the user inhales and the exhaled air is released outside the mask.

Most SCBA units are nominally rated to provide a thirty-minute air supply, but firefighters working in fire conditions usually consume this volume of air within about twelve minutes. Longer duration systems with larger air tanks and higher storage pressures are also available, up to sixty-minute rated units. Other types of breathing apparatus that can provide even longer operating durations are available, but they are not widely used for firefighting.

Most fire departments began to introduce SCBA in the 1950s, but its use was resisted by many firefighters who were accustomed to working without the extra weight and encumbrance. At first the SCBA was reserved for special teams and special situations, then gradually all firefighters were trained to use them. During the 1970s and 1980s, SCBA became standard equipment on all fire apparatus, and occupational health and safety regulations began to mandate their use at every fire.

As the technology has improved, more advanced units have been introduced that are lighter in weight and more reliable. Today an SCBA is part of the standard ensemble of protective clothing and every firefighter is trained to work with an SCBA from the first day at the training academy. The result over the past thirty years has been the most significant advance in firefighter health and safety in our history.

Tools and Equipment

Firefighters use many different types of tools and equipment to perform specialized functions. These range from simple devices, such as hoses, ladders, and axes, to portable radios and thermal imaging cameras.

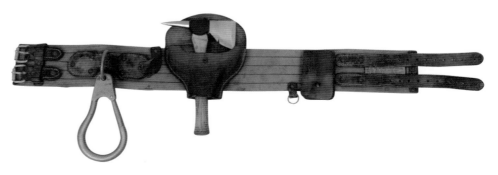

The art of applying water to extinguish burning materials may appear to be very simple, but it requires a complex array of equipment that can be adapted to all kinds of situations and circumstances. Fire departments use a tremendous assortment of equipment to move, deliver, and apply water, as well as other extinguishing agents.

Bottom, left: *Ropes have been used in the fire service for many purposes. In this rescue drill, different sizes of rope and several types of knots are used depending on the purpose. Ropes are also rated as to their strength and must be properly maintained to keep their integrity. (Craig Hacker)*

Below: *Various pieces of equipment are employed to assist in roping operations. Shown is equipment that act as connectors, junctions, and rope controllers. (Craig Hacker)*

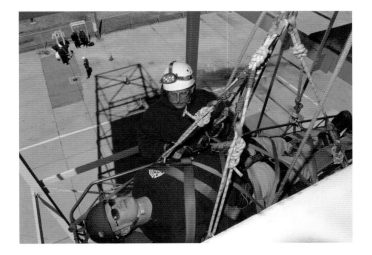

Top row, left to right:
This is an early model (ca. 1850) leather fire brigade bucket. The earliest models were riveted. (Craig Hacker)

With the advent of readily manufactured rubber came the heavy rubber bucket, which replaced leather to prevent rotting. (Craig Hacker)

The composition bucket was a further improvement on the heavy rubber bucket to increase serviceability. (Craig Hacker)

Not all bucket brigades were armed with water. Here is a metal dry chemical bucket that would use a powder instead of water to extinguish fires. (Craig Hacker)

Right: *Examples of metal fire brigade buckets include pointed and round bottoms along with a conical bucket. (Craig Hacker)*

Opposite, top: *This large-diameter hose is connected to the intake of a tanker. Tankers are utilized to carry large amounts of water to a fire scene in areas that are not serviced by hydrants. The tanker would fill its tank utilizing a distant hydrant connected by this type of hose. Once full, the tanker would respond to the scene and dump its water into a portable folding tank by means of the large red square "dump valve" next to the hose intake. (Craig Hacker)*

Right: *Wooden water mains, this one dated 1882, were built with wood strips and wrapped with a steel strap. Some of the older cities in the U.S. still have a few of these mains in operation today. As the wooden mains eventually rot or burst, they are replaced with modern materials. (Craig Hacker)*

Above: *A swinging hose rack is usually equipped with one-inch hose and utilized for an initial attack on fires by occupants. However, they were considered unreliable because of poor maintenance. (Craig Hacker)*

Right: *Extra hose is stored in the fire station on a hose rack. This allows hose to be rolled up and protected from damage and excessive dirt. It is particularly important to do this to protect the threads of the hose coupling. If they become damaged, sections of hose may not be properly coupled. (Craig Hacker)*

In colonial times individual homeowners were required to keep special leather buckets on hand, ready to form bucket brigades to deliver water from a well or lake to the scene of a fire. The organization of volunteer fire companies soon led to the development of the first fire hoses, made from riveted leather, as well as hand-operated pumps and a variety of brass nozzles and fittings to connect the hoses together.

The designs became more sophisticated as new materials and manufacturing methods became available. Leather hoses were replaced with rubber, then woven cotton jackets were developed to withstand

higher pressures and protect the rubber liner from wear and abrasion. Over the years, stronger, lighter weight, and more durable synthetic fibers were introduced to produce hose that is much lighter and more flexible and much more resistant to the rotting and mildew that used to attack hose that had not been thoroughly dried after use.

In order to move greater volumes of water, larger hoses were developed. For decades the standard fire hose was 2-1/2 inches in diameter and expected to flow 250 gallons of water per minute. Modern supply hoses are often 5 inches in diameter and easily deliver more than 1,500 gallons of water per minute. Lightweight hose materials and couplings made from high-strength alloys make this new hose comparable in weight to the old cotton double-jacketed hose that was used less than fifty years ago.

Above: *Efficiency is achieved on a pumper by the way hose is stored or "racked" in the hose beds. This particular method is in the "cross beds" and is used mainly for initial attack lines. The loops of hose or "ears" allow the firefighter to pull a specific amount of hose out of the bed, shoulder it and proceed to the fire. The next firefighter grabs the next load and follows. (Craig Hacker)*

Left: *Hose couplings are used to connect like sizes of hoses one after the other in order to lay hose over long distances. However, there are adapters available to connect hoses of different sizes together for a special purpose. (Craig Hacker)*

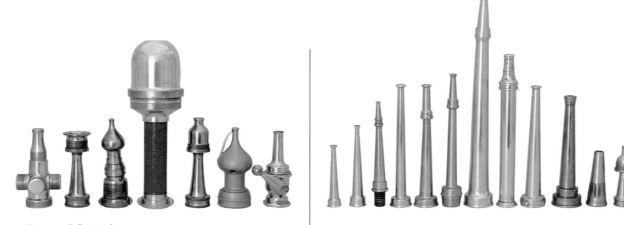

Top row, left to right:
These specialty nozzles are examples of the ingenuity within the fire service to develop the tools needed. Each of these unusual designs had a purpose based on a need that was discovered at previous fires. (Craig Hacker)

Brass nozzles of the late 1800s were made with various size tips. The tip size determined the amount of water that could be pumped through it. These nozzles did not have built-in shut-off valves. (Craig Hacker)

An 1896 Heart Phillips deck pipe was used for heavy stream applications. This nozzle utilizes different sizes of deck pipe tips to achieve the needed flow of water to the fire. (Craig Hacker)

Second row, left to right:
The Bresnan Distributor was a specific cellar nozzle with nine holes in the head that rotates when pressurized. As with other cellar nozzles, the Bresnan Distributor was used through a hole in the floor above when a cellar could not be entered. (Craig Hacker)

Hard suction hose strainers are made of chrome and brass and are usually five to six inches in diameter. The conical strainer is used at the engine intake. These strainers are designed for one particular purpose, to prevent rocks, sand, and other matter from entering the pump and causing damage. When a natural source of water is used such as a river or lake, this is especially helpful. Because hydrant water does not usually contain these contaminants, they are not necessary when using a hydrant. (Craig Hacker)

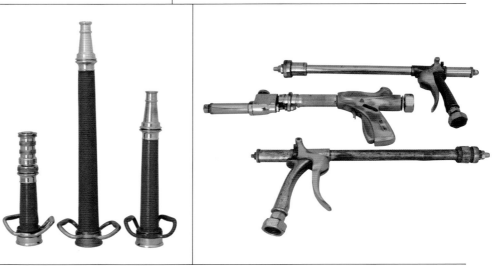

Third row, left to right:
The red cord wrapping allowed the firefighter to grip these early model "playpipes" without his fingers slipping off of the brass when it became wet. The term playpipe comes from the action of "playing the water on the fire" or to put the water on the fire. (Craig Hacker)

High pressure gun nozzles were able to create their high pressure by being used on a rigid hose booster line that was stored on a hose reel on a pumper. The small diameter, coupled with the ability of the rigid hose to withstand higher pressure than ordinary hose, allowed a much more forceful and concentrated water stream. (Craig Hacker)

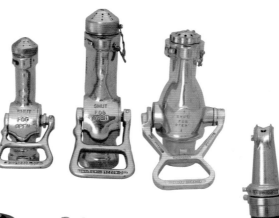

Bottom row, clockwise from top:
These three California fog nozzles are examples of a specialty nozzle developed as an innovation for the fire service. Equipment is constantly being altered and improved upon for higher efficiency. (Craig Hacker)

An early fog nozzle, dated 1932, was equipped with a rounded tip and designated the "Akron Rooker Lug 3A Fog Nozzle." This nozzle had several small holes at the tip to break up the water stream and create the "fog" effect. (Craig Hacker)

Introduced in the middle 1960s, fog nozzles represented a significant improvement. Each reinvention of an existing piece of equipment strives to improve on the predecessor hoping to allow the firefighters to do their jobs better. (Craig Hacker)

Top row, left to right:
This nozzle generated a chemical foam and was capable of extinguishing flammable liquid fires. Unlike some of the larger nozzles, this nozzle was easily carried by one person. (Craig Hacker)

The foam eductor is designed for mechanical foam applied through a one-inch hose line. It worked best on small fires. The small hose was placed into the container of foam and with the water flowing through the nozzle the foam was drawn into the nozzle and mixed with air. (Craig Hacker)

Second row, left to right:
Pictured are the one- and two-inch sizes of Cooper hose jackets. They are utilized for stopping leaks in hose lines or connecting hose of different sizes together. A quick alternative to replacing a section of damaged hose during a fire emergency, these jackets allow water to continue to flow to the fire while making a temporary repair. (Craig Hacker)

Hose rollers are utilized for hoisting or lowering equipment and to prevent cutting or chafing on sharp edges on roofs or windowsills. Ropes and hoses easily pass over the rollers on this tool to prevent damage. (Craig Hacker)

Third row, top to bottom:
A hose jack (top) is used to control backpressure on a charged hose line when the line is operated in a fixed position. A Hose Stick (middle) is used by two firefighters to back up a nozzle-man on a charged hose line. (Craig Hacker)

Cantilever hose crimpers are designed to crimp large-diameter hose under pressure for replacement of nozzles or extending hose length. These allow a quick and temporary way to stop water flow while making adjustments and repairs. (Craig Hacker)

Bottom, counter-clockwise from upper right:
This hand-made coupling thread dresser is used to clean damaged threads on two-inch hose lines at the fire scene. These tools come in various sizes to accommodate all sizes of hose. If the threads of a hose become damaged, they will not couple with another hose and could cause damage to that hose's thread. (Craig Hacker)

Screw type hose clamp (cantilever hose crimper behind) is designed to crimp all sizes of hose to control water flow. At times hose sections need to be replaced because they have burst or are leaking heavily. The hose clamp allows the water supply to be shut down quickly and temporarily to allow the repair to be made. (Craig Hacker)

Hand spanners are used to tighten assorted sizes of couplings on hoses. When connecting hoses together, it is important to have a good seal so as not to have water leaks. Hydrant wrenches are utilized to remove hydrant caps and to "turn the water on." (Craig Hacker)

A metal strap spanner is attached to a length of leather. The spanner end was used to tighten couplings and the strap end was used to secure the hose to a ladder or fire escape. (Craig Hacker)

75

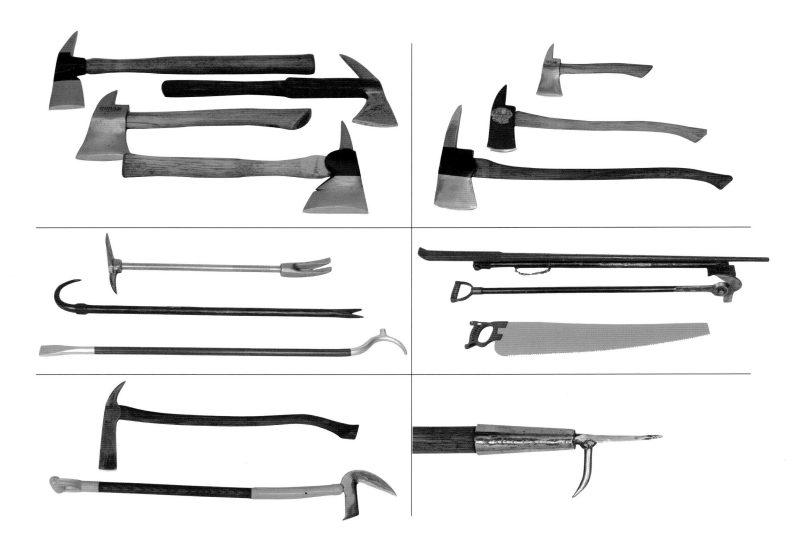

Implements of Destruction

One large category of firefighting tools is sometimes described as "implements of destruction." These devices are used to forcibly open doors and windows to get past locked doors and into burning buildings, to open up walls and ceilings to expose fire that may be burning in void spaces, to cut through roofs to create ventilation openings, to rip apart burning objects to reveal hidden fire, and for a myriad of similar purposes that all involve the application of mechanical force to some type of object or structure. This activity is often accomplished with very simple tools, such as an ax, pike pole, pry-bar, or sledgehammer. For tougher jobs the firefighter may use a battering ram, a gasoline-powered chain saw or circular saw, hydraudaulic cutters or spreaders, a jackhammer, or an acetylene torch.

The origins of many of the special tools go back to the early days of firefighting. Hook and ladder crews date back to the days when firefighters carried long poles with hooks to pull down burning roofing materials that had been ignited by hot coals from a chimney. Today there are dozens of different styles of pike poles that are used primarily to open holes in walls and ceilings, with different head designs, different types of handles, and a range of lengths for different situations. Some head styles are preferred for drywall, others for older lath and plaster construction, and still others for antique tin ceilings. The common factor is that all of the designs were developed and adapted by firefighters to meet their particular requirements and preferences. Most fire departments have

their favorite tools, often because they were first manufactured in the back room of a local firehouse.

Many ladder companies proudly claim that they can open any door, although the ability to close the door after they are finished with it may be questionable. A century ago the battering ram was a favorite tool for opening locked doors. The Halligan tool, a multipurpose pry-bar, is an example of a tool that was designed by a firefighter and refined over many years to allow the user to quickly open several types of locked doors. It incorporates several tools into one and is used by thousands of firefighters every day. For more delicate forcible entry jobs there is the K-tool, also designed by a firefighter, that allows a complete cylinder lock to be extracted from a door in a few seconds.

Where industrial tools have been adapted for firefighting, such as gasoline-powered chain saws and circular saws, the manufacturers have often developed special models to meet the demands of firefighters. In many cases firefighters have taken their suggestions for stronger, tougher, and more powerful equipment to the manufacturers, who have then produced special adaptations of their equipment for the fire service.

All photos in this chapter taken by Craig Hacker are of tools and equipment located at the Kansas Firefighter's Museum in Wichita.

Right: *A hand lantern is a primary hand-held source of light from the early 1900s to today. Firefighters always need a portable source of light in order to find their way around a dark and smoky environment. These battery-operated units are suited for that task. (Craig Hacker)*

Bottom, left: *The earliest known method of fire ground communication was the fire trumpet, which came in various sizes. Walkie-Talkies were designed during World War II and adapted to the fire service. Initial models were too heavy for fire ground use. Today, all line officers carry individual radios and they have become much more portable and durable. (Craig Hacker)*

Bottom, right: *Lanterns shown were manufactured by the Dietz Lantern Company and dated 1907. Utilized to light the operating area before the availability of portable generators or battery operated hand lights, these kerosene-fired lanterns were in wide used on the fireground. (Craig Hacker)*

Fire
Apparatus

Fire
Apparatus

John A. Calderone

The aerial ladder operator utilizes the remote control panel to position the ladder and master stream device. Due to heavy smoke conditions, and a hazardous materials situation, the operator has donned full protective clothing and self-contained breathing apparatus at this multi-alarm fire. (Paul Ramirez/Phoenix Fire Department)

Hand- and Horse-Drawn Era

Since man's first encounter with fire, we have been engaged in a continuing battle to suppress and contain its awesome and mighty power. The most effective means to do so, as we shall discover, have changed greatly over time. The development of fire-fighting apparatus reflects advances in technology, and has been influenced by war, experimentation and innovation, legislative requirements, and social change. Add to this the ever-expanding missions of fire departments, and it's easy to see how changes in apparatus design and delivery have both reinforced and challenged many proud fire department traditions.

Citizen bucket brigades were the earliest form of organized fire protection in North America. This was followed by hand pumpers, or hand tubs, which had long, parallel handles requiring many volunteers to pump up and down rapidly, pumping water from its tub. The effectiveness of hand pumpers was limited by the capability of the volunteers to pump before becoming exhausted. While primitive by today's standards, hand pumpers were a giant leap over the bucket brigades. The earliest hand pumpers were imported from England in the 1700s, and for the next hundred years, were copied and refined by American manufacturers.

The next firefighting advancement came, again from England, with the development of the steam pumper during the 1800s. A practical steam pumper was constructed in New York around 1840; however, volunteer firefighters perceived it as a threat to their existence. With a bare

This 1879 Silsby 600 gpm steamer was operated by Salisbury, Maryland. With a bare minimum of manpower, the horse-drawn steam pumper could supply continuous water, without wearing out the great number of volunteers that the hand pumpers did. (Joel Woods)

Pages 78–79: A ladder truck from the San Francisco Fire Department is a blur of lights and sirens as it answers a call in the dark of night. (George Hall)

The Hope Fire Company of Allentown, New Jersey, operated this hand-drawn hand pumper, built in 1818, which required many volunteers to pump up and down rapidly, pumping water from its tub. The effectiveness of hand pumpers was limited by the capability of the volunteers to pump before becoming exhausted. (John A. Calderone)

81

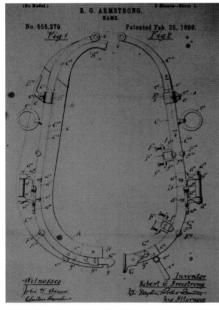

Top: *The Armstrong Hitch was an innovation that allowed firefighters to quickly attach the hitch for a horse-drawn wagon to the horse when preparing to respond to an alarm. Shown here, firefighters prepare to bring the horses into position under the hitch. Once the horses were ready, the hitch was quickly lowered and attached to the horse for a rapid response. (Kansas Firefighter's Museum)*

Above: *This original patent drawing of the "Armstrong Hitch" illustrates the details of an invention by R.G. Armstrong of Wichita, Kansas, in 1896. His invention allowed for rapid hitching of horses to horse-drawn fire apparatus. (Kansas Firefighter's Museum)*

minimum of manpower, the steam pumper could supply continuous water, without wearing out the great number of volunteers that the hand pumpers had done. Volunteers correctly predicted that their ranks would be greatly diminished.

The widespread introduction of steamers, and the beginning of the end of the volunteers in major American cities, was signaled by the establishment of the first paid firefighting force in the United States, in Cincinnati, during 1853. This also marked the start of what many consider the most colorful firefighting era, marked by the introduction of new concepts, inventions, technological advances, and the establishment of many traditions associated with the paid career service. Several of these innovations included the telegraph alarm system for dispatching, alarm box running assignment cards, sliding poles in fire stations, and the introduction of horses.

When cities established paid fire departments, they could no longer afford to pay the large number of men that were required to pull hand-drawn apparatus to the scene. Consequently, horses were introduced to pull equipment and apparatus. Simultaneously, steamers replaced the hand pumpers for the same reason: they required less manpower. While horses now hauled the apparatus to fires, firefighters were still running to the scene, and arriving there fatigued. Prior to the horses, there was never a need for anyone to ride on the apparatus. Everyone was needed to pull it to the fire. During the 1860s, fire departments started to install what became known as "running boards" on the sides of ladder trucks, so-called because they took the place of firefighters running to the scene. At the time, this was a major innovation in apparatus design, which probably added greatly to firefighter vitality when they arrived on the scene.

Engine companies in the early horse-drawn era usually responded with both a steamer and separate hose reel. Some departments utilized separate hose companies instead of two-piece engine companies. The hose reel was redesigned with seats topside and a rear step. Later, as hose capable of being packed flat was introduced in the late 1880s, hose wagons replaced the hose reels.

As horse-drawn ladder trucks grew longer to accommodate longer ladders, the tiller position to steer the rear wheels was developed. The ladder truck's capability was taken a step further with the development of the wood aerial ladder, up to 85-feet in height. The first successful wood aerial was patented by Daniel Hayes in 1868. The tillerman on these ladder trucks sat beneath the aerial, not on top as later became common. Many firefighters were required to raise, rotate, and extend these early aerials via a series of manually cranked gears and pulleys. During the early 1900s, several manufacturers developed spring raising mechanisms for their aerial ladders.

The horse-drawn chemical wagon was developed to provide for a quick knockdown while steamers were set up and hose lines were stretched. These chemical wagons carried tanks containing bicarbonate of soda, activated by mixing with sulfuric acid, then expelled by the resulting chemical reaction through a small-diameter hose line. Many early paid departments operated separate chemical companies. Eventually, this chemical equipment was installed on hose wagons, called combination wagons, which were operated by standard engine companies.

Many larger fire departments operated horse-drawn water towers. These were elevating masts equipped with a large monitor atop that was capable of applying a large-caliber stream to upper floors of burning

The first successful wood aerial was patented by Daniel Hayes in 1868. The tillerman on these Hayes ladder trucks, like this one that served Lynchburg, Virginia, sat beneath the aerial, not on top as later became common. (Joel Woods)

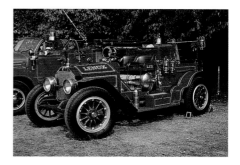

American LaFrance constructed their first of what was to become a long line of full-custom fire apparatus during 1910. The combination chemical hose wagon was delivered to Lenox, Massachusetts. (John A. Calderone)

83

Reno Steamer #1 and San Benadino Hose Cart #1 (California State Firefighter's Association Steamer Team)—The Steamer (in front and most visible), owned by Dave and Barbara Hubert, shows the horses Luke, Rocket, and Jimmy, driver Gene Hilty, "Blaze" the fire dog, and the firefighter (at rear) Dave Hubert. The wagon (behind the steamer) shows the horses Jay and Jiggs, Belgian draft horses owned by Sioux Munyon the driver, and firefighters Allen Bone and Steve Shaw. (Mitch Mendler; E.M.T. Fire Fighter/Paramedic San Diego Fire & Life Safety Services)

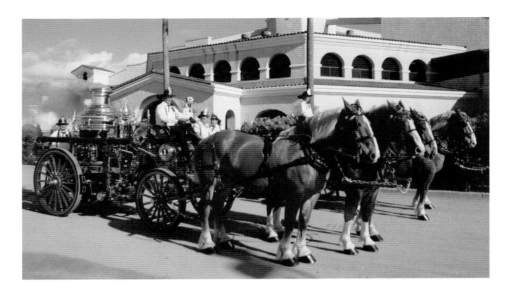

Above: *Steam driven apparatus needed to be lubricated on a regular basis—prior, during, and after an emergency response. This oiler (brass with nickel plating) would be used for that purpose. (Craig Hacker)*

Above: *A close-up of the fire bell on the steamer Reno #1 owned by Dave and Barbara Hubert (California State Firefighter's Association Steamer Team). (Mitch Mendler; E.M.T. Fire Fighter/Paramedic San Diego Fire & Life Safety Services)*

structures. Amoskeag, a manufacturer of steam pumpers, constructed a self-propelled steamer in 1867. Sprockets connected a shaft on the pump to the rear wheels. The driver steered and controlled the brakes while the engineer, on the rear step, controlled the speed using a locomotive-style throttle. Needless to say, this set-up led to much confusion in the vehicle's operation. While a good number of these innovative vehicles were produced, they proved to be heavier and slower than horse-drawn steamers, and many were eventually converted into horse-drawn units.

Early hand-drawn and horse-drawn apparatus were lavishly adorned with striping, paintings, and logos. This evolved into ornate gold leafing and stripes outlined to accent color schemes, unit numbers, and department names. Steamers were especially attractive, with all of their polished chrome and other brightwork, in addition to their paint schemes. Horse-drawn apparatus colors were as varied as today's apparatus, with dark green, brown, maroon, white, red, and combinations of these being popular.

Early Motorization

The earliest motorized vehicles to serve fire departments in any numbers were runabouts assigned to chief officers. These were basically standard production model automobiles that were placed into service with minor or no modifications. Just as steam power was perceived by volunteer firefighters as a threat, motorized vehicles were deemed by firefighters to be unreliable and prone to breakdowns—unlike their beloved horses. It would be several decades before this changeover took place nationwide, with horse-drawn vehicles continuing in production during the interim.

The size and weight of horse-drawn apparatus had grown to the point where most horse teams running at top speed began to become exhausted and slow down after about a half-mile. The average response distances were usually longer than this. A motorized fire company could be operated at approximately one-third the cost of a horse-drawn unit of the same type. This took into account such costs as gasoline, oil, and maintenance versus feed, horse shoeing, harnesses, stable equipment, and veterinary services. By 1915, these costs had risen to five times the cost of a motorized fire company. The time for motorization was at hand.

Above: *Prior to responding to an alarm with steam-driven apparatus "steamers," the engineer would have to "fire" the boilers. In order to do so, he would likely use a type of hand torch as seen here. These torches date to 1902. (Craig Hacker)*

Bottom, left: *Starting in 1912, the Christie Front Drive Auto Company began producing the first of approximately 600 two-wheel tractors like this one used to motorize an 1899 American steamer for Wayne, New Jersey. Throughout America, these practical units were used to motorize fleets of relatively new horse-drawn steamers, ladder trucks, and water towers. They provided a stopgap alternative to purchasing large numbers of motorized vehicles. (John A. Calderone)*

Bottom, right: *Constructed by American LaFrance on a 1921 Ford chassis, this double tank chemical wagon, which protected Commack, New York, was typical of early motorized chemical units. (John A. Calderone)*

Opposite, bottom, right: *A close-up of the "bright work" of Reno Steamer #1, a 1902 "American" Metropolitan Steam Fire Engine builders number 2823, owned by Dave and Barbara Hubert (California State Firefighter's Association Steamer Team). This adornment on steamers was typical of the era and a source of great pride to those firefighters who operated them. (Mitch Mendler; E.M.T. Fire Fighter/Paramedic San Diego Fire & Life Safety Services)*

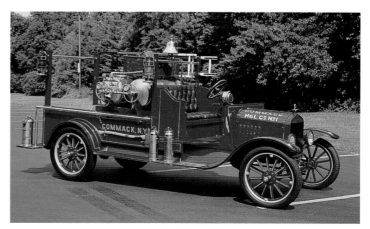

Top, left: *Loaded with chrome and gold leaf trim, this 1923 American LaFrance pumper was once assigned to Engine 7 in Toronto, Ontario. (John A. Calderone)*

Top, right: *Hamilton, Massachusetts, Engine 1 served with this 1924 Seagrave pumper equipped with a 350 gpm pump and 200-gallon tank. (John A. Calderone)*

Two examples of sirens (friction wheel drive and belt drive) and one apparatus mounted red light used in the mid 1920s. (Craig Hacker)

Before the advent of motorized or electronic sirens, fire apparatus was equipped with hand-operated sirens (these were further preceded by bells). Here are two examples of early models. Also shown is a brass search light utilized on fire apparatus. (Craig Hacker)

Above: *These examples of electronic sirens represent those used from the 1930s through the 1960s. While electronic sirens are still in wide use today, many fire departments have gone back to mechanical sirens because they better penetrate the modern sound-resistant automobile. (Craig Hacker)*

Generally, the year 1906 is accepted as the start of the motorized era of the fire service in America. During that year, Waterous delivered a unique motorized pumper, equipped with two gasoline-powered motors, one for propulsion and the other for pumping, to the Radnor Fire Company of Wayne, Pennsylvania. Springfield, Massachusetts, took delivery of a Combination Ladder Company squad body constructed on a Knox chassis during the same year. By the end of 1906, Knox and Combination Ladder Company, originally a manufacturer of horse-drawn fire apparatus, were advertising a wide range of motorized fire apparatus. The following year, both American LaFrance and Seagrave produced their first motorized fire apparatus. The American LaFrance was built on a Simplex chassis.

A good number of early-motorized fire apparatus were constructed on touring car and similar chassis. Most were chain-driven with wood-spoked, solid rubber tires. Very few had windshields. White was an extremely popular color for early motorized fire apparatus, as were the darker shades of red.

During 1909, a giant forward leap in apparatus development took place. Up until this time, most engine companies operated as two piece companies utilizing a steamer and separate hose wagon. A small manufacturer located in New Jersey known as the Tea Tray Company constructed the first triple combination pumper on an American Mors chassis. This apparatus was delivered to Middletown, New York, and incorporated a pump, hose bed, and chemical tanks. In effect it was a pumper, hose wagon, and chemical wagon all in one apparatus. Eventually booster equipment replaced the chemical tanks as pumpers evolved. This innovative apparatus slowly changed the manner in which most fire departments operated. It allowed for engine companies to operate with a single apparatus and permitted fire departments to eliminate separate hose and chemi-

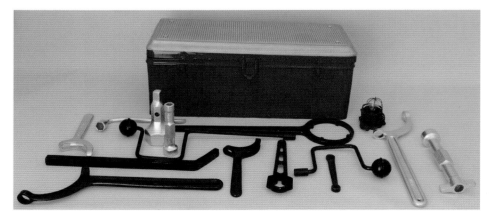

cal companies. Also in 1909, the International Motor Company (later to be known as Mack Trucks) delivered a motorized tractor to Allentown, Pennsylvania, which was used to power a former horse-drawn ladder truck. This is believed to be the first motorized ladder truck in the United States.

New concepts were being tried during the early-motorized era. Electric motors mounted inside each wheel hub, which were supplied by battery power, were introduced by the Couple Gear Freight Wheel Company in 1910. The limitations of storage batteries and the lack of recharging facilities handicapped these vehicles. The apparatus so powered were notoriously slow and often depleted the batteries before their assignments were completed. Nevertheless, many of these were sold, especially tractors that were used to power former horse-drawn units. This was a cheap, fast way for fire departments to replace their horse teams.

American LaFrance constructed their first of what was to become a long line of full-custom fire apparatus in 1910. It was a combination chemical hose wagon, which was delivered to Lenox, Massachusetts. The following year, Ahrens-Fox introduced a motorized pumper with the piston pump located at the front of the vehicle, ahead of the motor, instead of the conventional design with the pump either under or to the rear of the driver's seat. American LaFrance and Mack followed with the introduction of rotary gear pumpers while Seagrave introduced a centrifugal pumper.

Starting in 1912, the Christie Front Drive Auto Company began producing the first of approximately 600 two-wheel tractors. In cities throughout America, these practical units were used to motorize fleets of relatively new horse-drawn steamers, ladder trucks, and water towers, providing a stopgap alternative to purchasing large numbers of motorized vehicles. Other manufacturers introduced tractors of their own design. The market for these tractors lasted about ten years and allowed many fire departments to utilize their horse-drawn apparatus for its intended lifespan.

Most fire horses had disappeared from the firehouses by the early 1920s. By this time, the motor vehicle had developed to the point where it was relatively reliable and faster than the horses. An added benefit of motorization was a healthier environment in the fire station. The horses were generally housed on the apparatus floor near the apparatus for quick response. Basically a stable, along with somewhat unsanitary conditions that needed constant attention, this area was shared closely by firefighters in their daily firehouse routine. When the horses left, so did many health hazards associated with them. Firefighters no longer lived in barns.

Top, left: Tillered ladder trucks were common in most major cities. This 1927 Ahrens-Fox 75-foot aerial once served Kansas City, Missouri, as its Ladder 13. (John A. Calderone)

Top, right: Most engine companies operated with two pieces of apparatus, a pumper and separate hose wagon. Verplank, New York, operated this 1930 Sanford hose wagon. (John A. Calderone)

The fire engines and ladders of a team of firefighters can be seen as they fight a blaze at the U.S. Capitol on January 4, 1930. Many lengths of double-jacketed cotton hose lie on the grounds of the Capitol as three aerial ladders access the roof area below the dome. (© Corbis)

Opposite, bottom, right: This 1929 Ahrens-Fox Running Board Toolbox contained a complete set of tools for the assigned apparatus. This set of tools allowed the driver/operator to make basic repairs and adjustments to the fire engine, whether at the station or on the scene of an emergency. (Craig Hacker)

The quad allowed fire departments to provide limited ladder company functions while saving on manpower and the purchase of a separate ladder truck. This 1949 American LaFrance 750 gpm quad with a 750-gallon tank protected Carbondale, Pennsylvania. (John A. Calderone)

Also during the 1920s, a new type of fire apparatus, the quad, was introduced. This vehicle was a stretched triple combination pumper chassis with a fourth function added. It also carried a complement of ground ladders similar to a city service truck. Usually assigned to engine companies located in areas remote from ladder companies, where building height did not call for an aerial ladder, these apparatus allowed fire departments to provide limited ladder company functions while saving on manpower and the purchase of a separate ladder truck.

Most fire apparatus manufacturers built apparatus on their own custom-built chassis. During the 1920s, numerous commercial vehicle manufacturers marketed their chassis to fire apparatus manufacturers, allowing smaller manufacturers to specialize in body design and firefighting capabilities while using less expensive, commercially available chassis. This proved popular with smaller and less active fire departments. By the end of the 1920s, shaft-driven fire apparatus became standard, replacing chain-drive. Left-hand drive had also become standard by this time.

Monroe, Wisconsin, took delivery of the first custom-built enclosed cab fire apparatus, a pumper, from Pirsch in 1928. It was revolutionary and ahead of its time. Open-cab pumpers continued as standard well into the 1950s. In 1929, Mack Trucks introduced an aerial ladder that was raised and lowered through a power-take-off mechanism from the motor.

Bottom, left: Many fire departments operated separate floodlight trucks to provide fire-ground lighting. Mineola, New York, utilized this 1938 Diamond-T chassis with bodywork constructed by Ward LaFrance. (John A. Calderone)

Bottom, right: Shelton, Connecticut's, 1939 Ahrens-Fox pumper represented the epitome of the piston pumper's classic design style. (John A. Calderone)

The Depression Years

Like all industries, the fire apparatus manufacturers were hit hard by the stock market crash in 1929. Cash-short fire departments were unable to purchase new apparatus. This lasted into the mid-1930s, when orders for new fire apparatus bottomed-out and new orders started to trickle in. Most fire departments had entered the Depression with fleets of first generation motorized vehicles. By this time, these vehicles were beyond their useful life expectancy.

Once considered unnecessary, windshields began to be installed by the manufacturers during the 1930s. While providing a small degree of protection from the elements, windshields allowed drivers to see more safely, preventing constant squinting from the wind hitting the driver's face.

Pirsch introduced a hydraulic-mechanical aerial ladder mechanism, which allowed, for the first time, one firefighter to control all three ladder functions: raise, rotate, and extend. Before this mechanism, the muscle power of several firefighters was required to hand crank the aerial. Pirsch quickly followed this innovation with another, the first 100-foot metal aerial ladder. Prior aerial ladders were built of wood and were no longer than 85 feet in height.

Several different manufacturers produced designs for fully enclosed apparatus during the mid-1930s. All firefighters were provided with fully enclosed riding positions on these vehicles. Several sedan cab style pumpers, with completely enclosed rear bodies having bench seating, were constructed. From a safety standpoint, this was a significant design change for fire apparatus. However, this concept was way ahead of its time, and didn't really catch on until forced upon the fire service by the civil disturbances of the 1960s.

Top, left: *Metal aerial ladders were introduced during the 1930s. American LaFrance pioneered the fixed tiller seat position behind the aerial, as shown on Wildwood, New Jersey's, 1940 tiller. This design allowed for portable ladders to be removed without removing the tiller steering column. (John A. Calderone)*

Top, right: *American LaFrance introduced the first cab-forward fire apparatus in 1939, starting a revolution in fire apparatus design. This 1941 model served Avon, Connecticut, and was equipped with an 85-foot aerial. (John A. Calderone)*

A general view of the scene where an explosion blew out a wall of a four-story building occupied by a furniture company in Chicago in 1948. The blast caused one wall of the building to collapse and the unsupported floors of the building to tilt, causing the furniture they contained to shower into the street. The blast did not cause a fire. (©Bettmann/Corbis)

Pirsch aerials, with their unique truss construction, were popular in many fire departments. This 1952 Pirsch 100-foot tiller served as Ladder 7 in Milwaukee. (John A. Calderone)

Top, left: *The Mack L-Model chassis was introduced in 1940 and gained widespread use as the basis for almost every type of fire apparatus for the next thirteen years. This 1948 model, with a 750 gpm pump and 200-gallon tank, was operated by the Enterprise Fire Company of Hamilton Township, New Jersey. (John A. Calderone)*

Top, right: *This 1950 Ward LaFrance 750 gpm pumper from Archville, New York, typified 1950s fire apparatus design. (John A. Calderone)*

Right: *This 1949 Walter airport crash rig design was among the first of this type apparatus designed specifically to protect civilian airports. It was operated by Pan American World Airways, who provided contract operations for Teterboro Airport in New Jersey. (John A. Calderone)*

Firemen put out a blaze at a loft building used by the Grossman and Ozer mattress manufacturer in New York City in the late 1930s (© Underwood & Underwood/Corbis)

Some enclosure, albeit minor, of fire apparatus cabs did take place in the 1930s with the introduction of half-doors to open cab models. While still permitting the maximum visibility provided by an open cab, these doors provided a better degree of protection than no doors at all.

The fully enclosed apparatus design did not die in the 1930s. Several manufacturers adopted this design to rescue apparatus, bringing to life the heavy rescue. Up to this time, most rescue apparatus were similar to hose wagons in design, usually having bench seats in the rear body and with equipment carried either in the body or mounted on the running boards. Fully enclosed van style vehicles, carrying firefighters and equipment inside or in exterior compartments, were introduced to replace these. The most common rescue body style was the walk-through design where it was possible to enter via the cab doors and walk through the body, exiting at the rear doors.

American LaFrance introduced the first cab-forward fire apparatus in 1939, starting a revolution in fire apparatus design. Conventional apparatus had the engine located forward of the cab while this new design placed the cab in front of the engine, offering much better visibility for the driver, and a shorter turning radius. Eventually, the majority of custom-built fire apparatus would be constructed with cab-forward designs. The first diesel-powered fire apparatus also appeared in 1939. This was a pumper utilizing a Cummins Diesel engine, which was built by the New Stutz Fire Engine Company. While eventually almost every piece of fire apparatus constructed would be diesel powered, this innovation caught on very slowly and diesels in large numbers only started to appear in the 1960s.

Another new type fire apparatus started to emerge in the 1930s, the quint. While the quad had four distinct functions, pumper—hose wagon, booster equipment, and service ladder—the quint added the fifth function of being equipped with an aerial device on a quad-style chassis. Utilized like the quad, this apparatus was capable of providing both engine and ladder company functions to a limited degree. While not capable of performing all functions required by separate apparatus with their own staff, the quint continues to fill a void for some departments.

As the United States entered World War II, all of America's manufacturing capacity was directed to the war effort. Most fire apparatus produced were destined for military service. This 1941 Chevrolet airfield crash truck was typical of hundreds produced for the U.S. Army. (John A. Calderone)

World War II

With the Depression years behind them, most fire apparatus manufacturers had rebounded and were working at capacity to replace worn-out fleets of fire apparatus as the United States entered World War II. All of America's manufacturing capacity was directed to the war effort once the United States entered the war in 1941. Restrictions were placed on the use of many materials. Production of fire apparatus, deemed essential to the war effort, continued, but most apparatus produced were destined for military service. Civilian procurement of fire apparatus had to be justified to and approved by the government, and was extremely limited. A portion of the manufacturing capacity of fire apparatus manufacturers was also allocated to producing military vehicles, aircraft parts, and other items needed by the military. Fire apparatus produced during this time period was rather bland in appearance, having no chrome parts or brightwork due to restrictions on the use of certain materials.

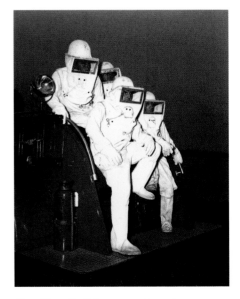

Four Navy firefighters wearing asbestos fire-protection suits sit on the back of a fire engine. The suits are white and have a square window for the face. The photo was taken at Naval Air Station, New York City, ca. 1939–1945. (© Corbis)

The two-way radio was, perhaps, the greatest innovation for the fire service coming out of World War II. It allowed firefighters to more easily communicate with their dispatchers and with others on the scene of an emergency. A great deal of versatility and flexibility was added to fireground operations. (© Corbis)

A firefighter climbs to the top of an aerial ladder. This piece of equipment has long allowed firefighters to quickly gain access to the upper reaches of tall buildings. This capability makes for quicker rescues and the application of large amounts of water through the large hose and nozzle devices (ladder pipes) attached to the tip of these pieces of apparatus. (© Bill Stormont/Corbis)

Several major developments and innovations came directly from new wartime technology. Because of the development of larger aircraft, the military developed larger aircraft crash rescue vehicles. When the war ended, many of these relatively new vehicles found their way to the numerous new civilian airports rapidly being established. The U.S. Navy pioneered the use of high-pressure fog for shipboard fire fighting. The John Bean Division of FMC adopted this concept to the structural fire-fighting vehicles it produced. Carbon dioxide was found to be an effective extinguishing agent for aircraft crash fires during the War. Aircraft crash apparatus equipped with large quantities of carbon dioxide, special applicator nozzles, and booms that could extend out over the burning aircraft, became popular following the War.

Perhaps the biggest innovation coming out of the war was the advance in two-way radio technology. Equipping fire apparatus with two-way radios revolutionized the fire service, providing far greater mobility and flexibility in operations. Prior to radios, when apparatus were dispatched to an alarm, they could not be called back while responding. All assigned units had to respond to the incident location, determine if their services were required, then usually respond back to their stations. Once they left the station, apparatus were out of touch with the dispatcher until they returned. During the time away from the station, apparatus could not be redeployed to another alarm. Radios gave the fire service a tool, taken for granted today, that allows in-service training and inspections and provides the tactical operations and dispatching in use today.

Fire apparatus chassis design continued despite the War with two of the most well-known models developed during these years. The Mack L-Model chassis was introduced in 1940,and gained widespread use as the basis for almost every type of fire apparatus for the next thirteen years. Full size mock-ups of one of the most esthetically pleasing and popular fire apparatus models, American LaFrance's 700 Series, were constructed during the War. Production was started as quickly as possible after the War and this model sold in great numbers in various configurations. It has become an icon for American fire apparatus.

Many of the fire apparatus in use by municipalities at the end of World War II were the same apparatus that were in service during the Depression. First the lack of funding, then wartime restrictions prevented their replacement. Fire apparatus manufacturers were now having a difficult time keeping up with new orders because there were so many apparatus in need of replacement.

The Growth Years

In the years following World War II, there was a general expansion and growth period in the United States. Fire departments and fire apparatus manufacturers worked hard to keep up with this record growth period. An overabundance of surplus military vehicles, released into the civilian sector, became a windfall for many fire departments, especially smaller and rural departments with limited funding. All types of military vehicles,

jeeps, cargo trucks, tankers, half-tracks, armored cars, and amphibious vehicles were the subjects of conversions. These vehicles were retrofitted with various fire-fighting capabilities and served well for many years. Although not as widespread as it was following World War II, this trend of converting former military vehicles into fire-fighting apparatus, particularly forestry units, continues to this day.

During 1947, Maxim introduced its own metal aerial ladder design. Maxim formed an alliance with Mack Trucks to market their aerial on a Mack chassis. Mack aggressively marketed these aerials resulting in many different models of Mack fire apparatus produced with Maxim aerials.

A west coast bus manufacturer, the Crown Coach Corporation, constructed an open-cab, cab-forward pumper in 1949. Called the Firecoach, this design became extremely popular with west coast fire departments.

While most fire departments were moving towards cab-forward designs, Seagrave, to celebrate its 70th anniversary, produced a redesigned larger conventional cab chassis characterized by a wide front grille and a siren recessed into the nose of the hood. While this model did sell well, it was Seagrave's last conventional design. Cab-forward apparatus would soon dominate the market.

With the ever-increasing size of military aircraft, the Air Force looked to acquire a larger capacity crash rescue vehicle. A contract was awarded to American LaFrance for the construction of over eleven-hundred O-10 and O-11 model crash trucks, the first mass-produced

Top, left: While most fire departments were moving toward cab-forward designs, Seagrave, to celebrate its seventieth anniversary, produced a redesigned larger conventional cab chassis. This 1951 model pumper served Boyertown, Pennsylvania. (John A. Calderone)

Top, right: Mack L-Model apparatus were popular in many fire departments. Engine 1 in Elizabeth, New Jersey, operated this 1952 model with an oversize deck gun. (John A. Calderone)

The U.S. Air Force, to acquire a larger capacity crash rescue vehicle, awarded a contract to American LaFrance for the construction of over 1,100 O-10 and O-11 model crash trucks, the first mass-produced airport crash apparatus. This one is a 1952 Type O-11A. (John A. Calderone)

airport crash apparatus. Designed to be air transportable, these vehicles incorporated such innovations as crew cabs, remote-controlled roof-mounted foam turrets, pump-and-roll capabilities, and swing-out hose reels.

A rear-mount aerial was introduced in 1952 by Maxim, built on a conventional cab pumper chassis utilizing a German-made Magirus aerial ladder. This short, maneuverable ladder truck design was still years ahead of its time and only a handful were sold.

Mack's popular L-model chassis was replaced in 1954 by a restyled cab with more streamlined, rounded lines. This new B-Model chassis proved just as popular as the L-Model it replaced.

A rounded, cab-forward design was introduced in 1956 by Ahrens-Fox, by this time merged with bus manufacturer C.D. Beck. This chassis was so popular that it was continued in production after Mack Trucks acquired C.D. Beck and was marketed as Mack's C-Model chassis. A handful of similar chassis were also produced by Approved Fire Apparatus, a small regional manufacturer.

Introduced in 1957 and probably used for more fire apparatus than any other commercial chassis, Ford's tilt-cab C Series chassis has been used by virtually every fire apparatus manufacturer. For over thirty years, all types of fire apparatus have been constructed on this chassis, with its cab built by the Budd Company.

The insight of Chicago's Fire Commissioner in 1958 led to the construction of the first fire service elevating platform. Chicago purchased a 50-foot Pitman boom, mounted it on a 1958 GMC chassis, outfitted the basket with a monitor nozzle supplied by a hose line attached to the side of the boom and coined the term Snorkel to describe the rather crude apparatus. (Jim Regan)

New Ideas

As with almost all heavy trucks in use up to this time, fire apparatus were equipped with manual shift transmissions. An automatic transmission for fire service use was introduced by Mack Trucks in 1957. Like most changes in the fire service, this concept took some time to catch on. It was almost ten years before widespread use of automatic transmissions in fire apparatus. Today, it is rare to encounter a newly constructed fire apparatus that does not have an automatic transmission.

The insight of Chicago's fire commissioner in 1958 led to a historic development in fire apparatus design, one which revolutionized firefighting tactics. While observing a utility crew at work in an elevated bucket truck, the commissioner saw immediate use for this equipment in the fire service. Chicago purchased a 50-foot Pitman boom, mounted it on a GMC chassis, outfitted the basket with a monitor nozzle supplied by a hose line attached to the side of the boom, and coined the term Snorkel to describe the apparatus. While crude in appearance, lessons learned from its fireground performance led to refinements in design and components. The elevating platform allowed for pinpoint accuracy in applying elevated streams, a stable platform to ventilate and perform other tasks from, and

Bottom, left: *Mack Trucks, in conjunction with the New York City Fire Department, designed and constructed the most powerful land-based pumper ever built. Delivered in 1965, the Super Pumper was rated at 8,800 gpm at 350 psi. (John A. Calderone)*

Bottom, right: *Tender 1 was the companion hose wagon to the Super Pumper. It carried large diameter hose, a large monitor, sections of hard suction, and various fittings. (John A. Calderone)*

Top, left: *The small, short wheelbase Jeep cab-forward chassis was a popular choice for fire departments protecting areas with narrow streets, tight congested areas, industrial facilities, and amusement areas. The Edgewater Park Volunteer Fire Department, New York, protects a tightly packed beach community with narrow pathways by utilizing this 1964 Jeep 500 gpm pumper constructed by Howe Fire Apparatus. (John A. Calderone)*

Top, right: *American LaFrance marketed its own elevating platform design, called the Aero-Chief. Tenafly, New Jersey, operated this 70-foot Aero-Chief constructed in 1966. (John A. Calderone)*

Above: *A firefighter climbs an aerial ladder with a length of hose in the early 1960s. Aerial ladders allow firefighters to get tools and equipment to the upper levels of buildings quickly. (© William Gottlieb/Corbis)*

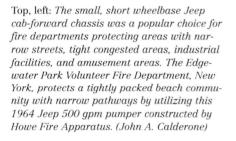

Right: *Hi-Ranger designed an aerial platform boom of open truss construction. This 85-foot Hi-Ranger boom was mounted on a 1967 Ward LaFrance chassis that served Mineola, New York. (John A. Calderone)*

a less stressful way to remove trapped occupants or injured victims. In the beginning, these apparatus responded as special units, but eventually, most departments assigned them as regular ladder company apparatus. Other manufacturers followed with their own various designs for articulated boom elevating platforms.

The rear-mount aerial design surfaced again in the late 1950s and early 1960s. Rear-mounts built on FWD, Mack, Maxim, and Seagrave chassis were part of a small trend that lasted several years. The fire service, still not ready to embrace these shorter, more compact ladder trucks, would wait almost another ten years before purchasing the rear-mount in quantity.

With pneumatic air brakes becoming popular on fire apparatus in the late 1950s, the air horn was introduced as a supplement to the siren and bell. It was a natural extension of the air brake system and added to the audible warning system of the apparatus. During the early 1960s, electronic sirens started to appear on fire apparatus. At first, these were installed in addition to the mechanical sirens, but eventually the electronic siren replaced the mechanical siren.

Mack Trucks began to aggressively market diesel-powered fire apparatus in the early 1960s. Marketing points included better mileage, less maintenance, and more cost effective than gasoline engines. In a few short years, diesel-powered apparatus were becoming more commonplace.

Fire apparatus manufacturers were racing against each other in a competition to develop what each thought would be the best elevating platform design. Sutphen introduced a telescopic boom of aluminum

truss construction in 1963. This was followed by Mack Trucks in 1964 with the introduction of the Aerialscope, a solid telescopic boom. Initially constructed by Truco, then Eaton, and followed by Baker, this boom evolved into that currently produced by Aerialscope, Inc.

Episodes of violent civil unrest categorized many major cities throughout the nation during the mid-1960s. The riots and resulting fires severely overtaxed fire departments. Apparatus and firefighters became targets for bricks, bottles, fire bombs, and even bullets. Rioters removed exposed tools and equipment from apparatus. The bulk of the apparatus then in service were open-cab units. Many fire departments experiencing these incidents began to construct makeshift cabs, roof enclosures over back steps, enclosed tiller seats, and even individual personnel enclosures resembling telephone booths on their existing apparatus. This resulted in some very strange-looking fire apparatus. As quickly as possible, enclosed cab apparatus were purchased. Firefighters were no longer permitted to ride the rear step of pumpers in some departments. More than any other single factor, these events led to the rapid design and introduction of apparatus equipped with crew cabs and designed to carry all tools and equipment in locked compartments.

The Young Crusader, an attention-getting futuristic cab design, was introduced in 1966. This was a low-profile, full-width cab that had a roomier interior and large, low-cut windows producing excellent visibility.

The introduction in 1966 of Mack's MB chassis, known as the Post Office truck because of that agency's wide spread use of this chassis, added to the rapidly occurring design changes in the apparatus industry.

Top, left: The New York City Fire Department added plywood cabs and tiller enclosures to protect its firefighters during periods of civil unrest. Assigned to Ladder 170, this 1953 American LaFrance 85-foot tiller has been so retrofitted. (John A. Calderone)

Top, right: During the civil disturbances of the 1960s, firefighters and their apparatus became targets and often encountered objects thrown at them while responding. Boston added a roof over the cab and enclosed the rear step of this 1962 Ward LaFrance 1,000 gpm pumper to protect its firefighters. (John A. Calderone)

Above: While police battled rioters, firemen were battling major fires throughout the night of August 13, 1965, in the Watts neighborhood of Los Angeles, California, where arsonists put the torch to more than half a dozen structures (© Bettmann/Corbis)

Left: The Young Crusader, a low-profile, full-width, futuristic cab design, was introduced in 1966. Elmont, New York, operated this 1968 model equipped with an 85-foot Snorkel boom. (John A. Calderone)

Top, left: *Introduced in 1966, Mack's flat-faced MB chassis, the Post Office truck, quickly became a popular chassis for fire apparatus production, especially to mount bodywork from other manufacturers. Chicago, Milwaukee, and New York operated quite a few of these vehicles. FDNY Ladder 39 had a 1969 Mack MB tractor retrofitted to its 1948 American LaFrance aerial. (John A. Calderone)*

Top, right: *The civil unrest of the 1960s forced fire departments to reexamine apparatus riding positions. The New York City Fire Department wanted all its personnel inside an enclosed cab. Working with Mack Trucks, the first attempt at a crew cab was the production of an R-Model chassis with a four-door cab. Five pumpers of this design were acquired in 1969. While a good start, they had many drawbacks. (John A. Calderone)*

This flat-faced model quickly became a popular chassis for fire apparatus production, especially to mount bodywork from other manufacturers on. Two additional newly designed chassis, both destined to become among the most popular fire apparatus chassis, were introduced by Mack Trucks the following year. A boxy, cab-forward design, the CF-Model, replaced the classic C-Model, while the short, conventional R-Model replaced the popular B-Model chassis.

The time had almost arrived for the rear-mount aerial. In 1967, Seagrave started marketing a rear-mount with rear steering, known as the Rear Admiral. The driver could control the rear-wheels from the cab, making this short ladder truck highly maneuverable. Although several Rear Admirals were built with this four-wheel steering, most were delivered with conventional two-wheel steering. American LaFrance introduced its rear-mount model, the Ladder Chief, the following year.

The top-mount pump panel was another design innovation introduced in 1967. Introduced by Howe, this design placed the pump operator
in an elevated position behind the cab and out of the street. This provided
a better overall view of operations and was significantly safer than a position in the street. However, many inner city fire departments felt that this
position needlessly exposed the operator and made him an easy target.

Another innovation was the Squrt boom, a 54-foot articulated
device that could be mounted on new pumpers and hose wagons or
retrofitted to older apparatus. This boom provided elevated stream
capabilities at a fraction of the cost of an elevating platform. A telescopic
model, the Tele-Squrt, would follow in a few years, available in various
lengths. The Command Tower, a 22-foot telescopic platform that could
be mounted on a pumper and equipped with a deck pipe, was introduced by Ward LaFrance in an attempt to compete.

Calavar, a firm that manufactured elevating platforms used to service aircraft introduced its Firebird in 1969. This was the largest elevating
platform produced for fire fighting up to this time and was a combination
telescopic and articulated boom. It was available in heights up to 150 feet.
The apparatus was quite large and required an even larger set-up area on
the fireground, resulting in only a small number of these units sold.

The wide-scale introduction of cross-lay hose beds with preconnected hose lines also took place in the mid- to late 1960s. Up to this
time, most hose was carried in the rear hose beds not connected to any
outlets. It had to be stretched in sufficient lengths, broken at the hose
bed, then manually connected to a supply outlet. The pumper would generally proceed to the front of the fire building, firefighters would start

Above: *A few years after the Squrt was
introduced, a telescopic model, called the
Tele-Squrt, was developed. The New York City
Fire Department had a 55-foot Tele-Squrt
retrofitted to this 1970 Mack pumper that
was originally equipped with an articulating
model. (John A. Calderone)*

Opposite, center left: *Mack introduced the
boxy, cab-forward CF-Model, to replace the
classic C-Model in 1967. It became one of
the most popular fire apparatus chassis ever
produced. Engine 9 in Sayerville, New Jersey,
operated this 1969 model with a 1,000 gpm
pump and 500-gallon tank. (John A. Calderone)*

Opposite, center right: *The short, conventional
R-Model was introduced by Mack Trucks to
replace the popular B-Model chassis. Carlstadt,
New Jersey, operated this 1971 R-Model 1250
gpm pumper as Engine 2. (John A. Calderone)*

Opposite, bottom left: *In 1967, Seagrave
started marketing a rear-mount with a rear-
steering option, known as the Rear Admiral.
Although several Rear Admirals were built
with this four-wheel steering, most were
delivered with conventional two-wheel steering. Chicago's Ladder 20 operated this 1969
100-foot Rear Admiral. (John A. Calderone)*

Opposite, bottom right: *The Squrt boom, a
54-foot articulated device that could be
mounted on new pumpers and hose wagons
or retrofitted to older apparatus, provided
elevated stream capabilities at a fraction of
the cost of an elevating platform. Columbus,
Ohio, had Squrts mounted on hose wagons
that were built by Allegheny on GMC chassis.
(John A. Calderone)*

The Providence Body Company built this heavy rescue vehicle on a 1969 Brockway chassis. Baltimore acquired it for use as a spare rescue. (John A. Calderone)

Above, left: *Calavar manufactured elevating platforms used to service aircraft. In 1969 it introduced its Firebird, the largest elevating platform produced for firefighting up to this time. This was a combination telescopic and articulated boom available in heights up to 150 feet. Manhasset-Lakeville, New York, operated this 125-foot model built on a 1974 Hendrickson chassis. (John A. Calderone)*

Above, right: *Military vehicles are constructed to have the maximum number of parts interchangeable. Military fire apparatus, especially those that could be deployed into battle areas, were no exception. American Air Filter constructed this 750 gpm structural-foam pumper, with a military designation of 530C, on a 1973 Kaiser standard military chassis. It was assigned to the Aberdeen Proving Grounds in Maryland. (John A. Calderone)*

stretching the hose line, and the pumper would then move forward to a hydrant. The primary reason that spurred development of pre-connected hand lines and related new attack tactics was a widespread lack of sufficient manpower. As the pumper arrived at the scene, it either dropped a supply line and firefighter at a hydrant as it approached the fire, or went directly to a position as close as possible to the fire and was supplied by the next pumper to arrive, working off its booster tank in the meantime. With the pumper in a position close to the fire, firefighters would stretch the smaller diameter preconnected lines to the fire. This was an efficient operation with less manpower and was adequate for most structural fires in smaller buildings such as dwellings.

Change and Turmoil

Probably the most emotional and controversial issue to ever confront the fire apparatus field was created by Ward LaFrance in the early 1970s. At that time, an aggressive marketing campaign, touting the color lime green as being more visible, and therefore a safer color for fire apparatus, drove a wedge through the fire service. While traditional-minded fire service people stood behind the color red, so-called progressive fire service personnel preached the advantages of the new color.

In the early 1970s, Ward LaFrance introduced the color lime green for fire apparatus, sparking the most emotional and controversial issue to ever confront the fire apparatus field. Newark, New Jersey, was among the first departments to embrace the new color as seen on this 1974 Ward LaFrance Tele-Squrt. (John A. Calderone)

Fire departments of all sizes were quick to switch to the new color, a surprise considering that most changes and innovations took at least ten years to gain a substantial hold in the fire service. At one point, more new apparatus were being delivered in the new color than in traditional red. However, after about ten years, a slow trend back to red was noticed. Departments that had jumped on the new color started changing back to red apparatus. Many lime-green apparatus were repainted red. Almost every major department that tried the new color gave it up over the years. Newark, New Jersey, one of the first departments to embrace lime green, and also one of the last holdouts, moved away from that color in the mid-1990s. The debate, to some degree, continues to this day; however, few new apparatus are delivered in lime green.

It is difficult to pinpoint a single reason for the return to red apparatus. The new color's lack of recognition as a fire truck was probably an important factor. We have all been conditioned since childhood to recognize red fire trucks. This lack of recognition has been documented as a contributing factor in accidents involving lime-green apparatus. Another problem with this color was the inability of firefighters to keep up the vehicle's shiny, like-new appearance. There was a perception that these vehicles did not instill the pride that traditionally colored red apparatus did in the fire service. While any of these reasons can be argued as being unjustified, nevertheless, they were all factors. One major city that was

Top, left: *The Ford C-Series chassis was used for many years as the basis for fire apparatus. This 1976 model served Avon, Connecticut, with a canopy cab, 1,250 gpm pump, and bodywork added by Middlesex. (John A. Calderone)*

Top, right: *A recession in the mid-1970s caused many fire departments to downsize, sometimes combining the functions of both an engine and ladder company into a single apparatus like this 1981 America LaFrance operated by Engine 3 in Clifton, New Jersey. It is equipped with a 1,500 gpm pump, 300-gallon tank, and 75-foot aerial. (John A. Calderone)*

A third alarm fire in Brooklyn, New York, on Box 1546 at Ocean Avenue and Parkside Avenue. The elevating platform provides a basket that carries firefighters and their equipment. The direction and elevation of the platform can be controlled from a remote pedestal in the basket. Here the firefighters direct a master stream into the fire. (Steve Spak)

Pages 104–105: *An aerial ladder deploys dual master stream devices at a working fire. (Paul Ramirez/Phoenix Fire Department)*

considering changing its fleet from red to lime green undertook a controlled pilot program over several years. A number of lime-green pumpers were placed in service and a control group of red pumpers responding to the same alarms was established. The final results of this study indicated that the lime-green apparatus were involved in more accidents than the red apparatus in the control group.

A new type of aerial device was introduced by Grove, a manufacturer of cranes and heavy-duty aerial ladders, in 1972. This design incorporated an elevating platform basket mounted to the tip of an aerial ladder, combining the best features of both. LTI acquired Grove two years later, and this design was subsequently copied by almost every apparatus manufacturer.

A new manufacturer with non-traditional ideas started constructing fire apparatus in 1974. Emergency-One would quickly become one of the largest fire apparatus builders, due largely to building all-aluminum modular bodies resulting in fast delivery times unheard of in the fire apparatus industry.

A recession in the mid-1970s had dire effects on many industries. Municipal governments were especially hard hit with severe financial restrictions imposed. Simultaneously, production costs for new apparatus skyrocketed. Many cities, especially the larger cities in the Northeast, were especially hard hit by this recession and funds to purchase new apparatus evaporated. Some major fire departments that routinely purchased groups of apparatus every year, went for several years without purchasing any new pieces. This, unfortunately, was the beginning of the end for many of the well-established, traditional fire apparatus manufacturers. Many manufacturers were forced to reorganize, or completely shut down. Sometimes, smaller, spin-off manufacturers came into being with the former company's employees. For such a small industry, acquisitions and mergers took place at an unprecedented rate.

Ward LaFrance and Maxim combined resources in 1976 in an effort to continue to construct fire apparatus. This kept Ward LaFrance alive for four more years. Maxim lasted until 1990. Van Pelt, Sanford, Crown, Beck, Grumman, Hahn, Pirsch, Mack Trucks, and American LaFrance all ceased production or stopped constructing fire apparatus. American LaFrance would reemerge several years later and become a major player again.

The apparatus refurbishing industry came of age during the early 1980s, mainly because many fire departments were still financially strapped and the cost of new apparatus continued to escalate. The life span of an existing apparatus could be substantially extended by a complete overhaul, and rebuilt at a fraction of the cost of a new replacement. Another factor that allowed this sub-industry to rapidly take hold was a decision by New York City, in 1980, to dispose of a large number of mechanically sound, but battle-scarred, ten- to twelve-year-old vehicles. These apparatus were purchased by many small departments at bargain prices and were then rebuilt. Firms dedicated to rebuilding fire apparatus sprang up as a result, and most major manufacturers followed, some establishing dedicated refurbishing centers.

A pumper chassis with a rear-mounted engine, called the Hush, was introduced by Emergency-One in 1985. This innovative design allowed for a quiet cab environment, better weight distribution, and more personnel to be carried in the cab. Another innovative design was the European Bronto Skylift's three-section articulating boom, available in greater heights than most platforms manufactured in the United States.

Top, left: The apparatus refurbishing industry came of age during the early 1980s. This Mack tractor pulling an American LaFrance tiller originally protected Dover, Delaware. It was eventually refurbished by Pierce and later purchased by Baltimore, Maryland. (John A. Calderone)

Top, right: Emergency-One introduced a pumper chassis with a rear-mounted engine, called the Hush because the design allowed for a quiet cab environment, better weight distribution, and more personnel to be carried in the cab. This 1992 model is lettered for a fictitious New York City Fire Department unit, Squad 55, as seen on the television series Third Watch. *(John A. Calderone)*

Below: Part of the reason that the apparatus refurbishing industry flourished was New York City Fire Department selling a large number of relatively young, but heavily used, apparatus at bargain prices. This 1974 Seagrave 100-foot tiller once served FDNY Ladder 6 in Chinatown. It then served in two small fire departments before being purchased by Baltimore, Maryland. (John A. Calderone)

Above: *This helicopter is one of the Honolulu Fire Department's most important pieces of emergency equipment. The present aircraft is a McDonnell Douglas 520N light turbine helicopter that was purchased in 1995 at a cost of $887,000. It is best known by its radio call signal, Air 1. (Honolulu Fire Department)*

Contemporary Apparatus

Current standards call for enclosed, seated positions equipped with seat belts for all firefighters riding apparatus. Two-tone color schemes with wide reflective stripes are standard. Roll-up compartment doors are becoming more common on fire apparatus. These have been used in Europe for quite some time and offer unobstructed access to the compartments, especially when the apparatus is positioned close to obstructions.

There is a current trend back to mechanical sirens on fire apparatus. Automobile soundproofing and entertainment systems often block or

Right: *Current standards call for enclosed, seated positions equipped with seat belts for all firefighters riding apparatus. Two-tone color schemes with wide reflective stripes are standard. Roll-up compartment doors are becoming more common on fire apparatus, like this 1998 Emergency-One 1,250 gpm pumper assigned to Engine 17 in Jersey City. (John A. Calderone)*

Opposite, bottom left: *Ocean rescue presents unique problems with breaking waves and dangerous currents. A jet-ski from the Honolulu Fire Department provides a specialized tool highly suited for these conditions. Because of their power and maneuverability, these pieces of equipment allow quick access to victims in rough surf. (Honolulu Fire Department)*

Left: *One of the best known of the Honolulu Fire Department's historic fireboats was the* Abner T. Longley. *She was named after Abner Townsend "Jack" Longley, a fifteen-year member of the territorial Board of Harbor Commissioners, and christened on May 22, 1951. On November 16, 1993, the* Abner T. Longley *was decommissioned after forty-two years of service. (Honolulu Fire Department)*

Above: *The Honolulu Fire Department's helicopter section is housed in a hangar on Kapalulu Place off of Lagoon Drive at the east end of the Honolulu International Airport. From this location, Air 1 responds to brush fires, where it makes water drops and serves as an observation platform for the Incident Commander. Air 1 is also an essential asset for search and rescue missions, especially in high surf (here seen during a rescue in a rocky tide pool) and in inaccessible mountain areas. The helicopter averages over 700 flying hours a year and responds to more than 300 alarms annually. Flight hours include fire operations, search, rescue, training, and administrative flights. (Honolulu Fire Department)*

Above: *A firefighter operates the pumps at the scene of a fire. Water is brought into the pump by way of hoses connected to a fire hydrant or from another pumper through hoses called "supply lines." Hoses called "attack lines" are connected to the pumper and provide water for the firefighters at the fire. (George Hall)*

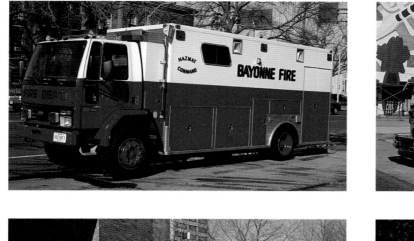

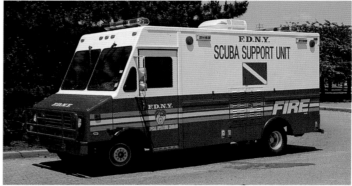

Top, left: *During the late 1980s and early 1990s, many departments formed haz-mat response teams and equipped specialized vehicles to deal with chemical releases. Bayonne, New Jersey, utilizes this 1994 Ford with body built by Marion. (John A. Calderone)*

Top, right: *Emergency-One built this heavy rescue truck in 1993 for Rescue 1 in Baltimore, Maryland. (John A. Calderone)*

Above, left: *Exposure to certain hazardous substances requires on-scene decontamination. The equipment to conduct a proper, safe decontamination procedure requires its own dedicated apparatus. Jersey City, New Jersey, operates this 1982 International that was retrofitted as a decontamination unit in 1997. (John A. Calderone)*

Above, right: *The New York City Fire Department's SCUBA Support Unit, a 1994 Ford/Utilimaster, is used to support SCUBA training drills and prolonged dive operations. (John A. Calderone)*

muffle the sound produced by electronic sirens. The louder mechanical sirens have returned as an essential safety factor.

Most contemporary fire apparatus are constructed with air-conditioned cabs, more as a safety factor than for firefighter comfort. The introduction of improved bunker gear over the last decade has made air-conditioned apparatus a requirement.

All-wheel, and rear-wheel steering options are becoming more popular. Apparatus have greatly increased in size and weight while at the same time traffic congestion and the street layout of new housing developments have made it more difficult to maneuver responding apparatus.

In recent years, there has been widespread use of highly specialized vehicles dedicated to a specific purpose. Haz-mat, heavy rescue, SCUBA, collapse, cave-in, confined space, cliff rescue, rehab, terrorism response, and other specific functions have become so highly developed, with such specialized equipment, that apparatus devoted exclusively to these functions have evolved.

Left: *Phoenix Ladder 11 in the smoke of a fire at 38th Street and Broadway. The aerial master stream was placed in service at this multiple alarm fire. (Paul Ramirez/Phoenix Fire Department)*

Above: *A member of a military fire department decontaminates a fellow firefighter's protective suit at the end of an exercise involving a simulated hazardous chemical spill. (U.S. Department of Defense)*

Opposite, bottom left: *Yonkers, New York, acquired this former military 1967 Kaiser and outfitted it as a Command Post vehicle. (John A. Calderone)*

Opposite, bottom right: *SuperVac constructed New York City Fire Department's Collapse Rescue trailer, which is pulled by a 1995 Ford tractor. (John A. Calderone)*

Below, left: *Rehab Units became common in many fire departments following the adoption of bunker gear to replace older style turnout gear. While bunker gear provides a greater degree of protection, its use, especially in hot weather, rapidly dehydrates firefighters. Originally a mobile medical unit, this 1983 American LaFrance with a Saulsbury body was one of two converted into rehab units by the New York City Fire Department during 1994. (John A. Calderone)*

Below, right: *During 1992, Uniondale, New York, converted this former military 1967 Kaiser into a forestry unit, equipped with a 60 gpm pump and 450-gallon tank. (John A. Calderone)*

Multi-functional apparatus have developed as a result of staffing shortages in both paid and volunteer departments. To maximize the use of available personnel, single vehicles have been designed to perform the functions of several individual apparatus. These are usually built on three-axle chassis and are larger and bulkier. Quints, foam-pumpers, rescue-pumpers, transport-pumpers, pumper-tankers, ladder tenders, and others are all used by various fire departments to meet individual needs.

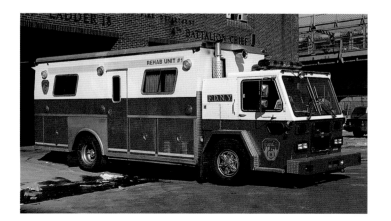

American fire apparatus are also taking on a more international appearance. While American fire apparatus manufacturers are now marketing their products worldwide, several European fire apparatus manufacturers have formed alliances with corporations in the United States to market their products as well. There are more American fire apparatus built on foreign chassis today than ever before. There is also a very subtle trend in fire apparatus body design that is leaning toward European-style fire apparatus.

Fire apparatus design will continue to constantly evolve to fulfill the needs of fire departments. Those needs also continually evolve and change to meet the needs and demands of a constantly changing society. The result is that there will always be something new and interesting in fire apparatus design.

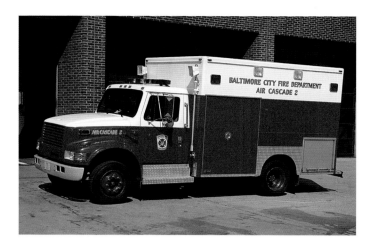

Firefighters in the Popular Imagination

Firefighters in the Popular Imagination

Chief Ronny J. Coleman (Ret)

"What do you want to be when you grow up?"

"A fireman."

"Why?"

"Ride in the red trucks. Zoom . . . Zoom . . . Zoom."

Many adults have had this conversation with a child, or have been the child wanting to be a firefighter when he grows up. Undoubtedly, the image of the firefighter, borrowed from the media and popular culture, remains one of the most powerful professional images for American children, one which was recently reinforced by the heroism of firefighters on September 11, 2001.

No one knows for sure the name of the very first pop culture firefighter, but we do know that the firefighter as an image has been a staple in contemporary popular media since mass-produced books, films, and television came on the scene. In modern society, we rely a great deal upon the media to create images of professional groups, public figures, and even our heroes. Some have even achieved fame, or celebrity, based solely on these images. As we shall see, the fire service in the popular imagination has been molded over time by a mixture of both real-world accomplishments and the larger-than-life escapades of our favorite film and television characters.

Since ancient times, both fire and firefighting have been popular themes for artisans and craftsmen. Turning back the pages of history, we find early representations in classical Rome, where images of firefighter-soldiers were popular. In A.D. 304, Florian von Lorch (who lived near the River Enns in present-day Austria) was martyred for his Christian beliefs. It was said that in his youth, Florian was able to put out a fire through prayer alone. Believers profess that he once saved an entire city being

Pages 112–113: *Children are fascinated by firefighters from a very early age. Maybe it is the red lights and siren on the fast fire engine, maybe the uniform, or the opportunity to spray water. Whatever the reason, children cannot seem to resist the opportunity to act out the tasks of their favorite heroes. (Collection of Ronald J. Siarnicki)*

Opposite: *A grouping of stamps from around the world commemorating firefighters. From the upper left and going clockwise: the 300th anniversary of volunteer firemen celebrated in 1948. Next an Australian stamp recognizes a 1929 Ahrens-Fox fire engine. A U.S. twenty-cent stamp commemorates an 1860 steam pumper. A Greek stamp praising firefighters in 1980. Germany issued this stamp with a fireboat in action. Finally, a British stamp illustrating a 1766 hand-drawn hand-operated pumper. (Collection of Delores Granito)*

This statue of St. Florian, the patron saint of firefighters, by the Viennese sculptor Josef Josephu (1889–1970) resides in the Vienna Fire Department Museum. St. Florian's feast day is the fourth of May, a day which is celebrated through Europe and Australia as International Firefighters' Day. (Courtesy of Marc Baron, grandson of the sculptor)

Opposite, top: On the morning of September 2, 1666, a fire that destroyed medieval London began. Within five days, the city was ravaged. An area one and a half miles by half a mile lay in ashes: 373 acres inside the city wall, 63 acres outside, 87 churches, and 13,200 houses. Amazingly, only six people were definitely known to have died, but probably many more did. Ironically, the Great Fire is often thought to have eliminated the sources of the Plague, which had taken the lives of some 68,000 Londoners during the previous two years. To control the fire, many buildings were pulled down or blown up to create a fire break. However Old St. Paul's Cathedral was spared destruction only to succumb to the fire later. (Courtesy of the London Fire Brigade)

Opposite, bottom: Benjamin Franklin truly was the messenger for fire prevention in the colonies. It was in regards to fire prevention that Franklin wrote his famous saying: "In the first place, an Ounce of Prevention is worth a Pound of Cure," in 1734. In a letter to the Pennsylvania Gazette, *he offered advice to families regarding the proper disposal of hot coals, and to bakers, coopers, and others, he proffered guidance regarding safe fire practices associated with their endeavors. ("Benjamin Franklin, The Fireman," Charles Washington Wright. Courtesy CIGNA Museum and Art Collection, Philadelphia)*

ravaged by fire with one bucket of water. At the time of his death, he was set on fire twice and survived both times before he was finally drowned. Eventually, Florian was sainted by the Roman Catholic Church; he is the patron saint of Poland. St. Florian is regarded as the patron of firefighters, and is said to intercede as a powerful protector in danger from fire and water. Throughout Europe and the United States, images of St. Florian adorn firehouses, public buildings, and the homes of firefighters.

During the ancient period, fires were considered a subject worthy of being depicted in public art, and seved as reminders to the public that fires were a dangerous threat to their communities. Throughout antiquity, and well into the Renaissance, art was used as a way to remind people of a fire's great destructive capabilities. Paintings of raging conflagrations in major Renaissance cities can be found in art galleries around the world. The Great Fire of London in 1666 virtually destroyed Britain's largest city. A commemorative pillar was constructed on the site where the fire started (in a bakery) to remind Londoners of just how serious fire can be. It can still be visited today.

In Europe, from the early 1500s through the 1700s, news about great fires was initially depicted in woodcuts that were then used to illustrate books. As printing became more popular, it was not uncommon for many of these woodcut images to work their way into both formal and popular histories. Although organized firefighting was just beginning, all people recognized the responsibility of fighting fires as a basic social obligation. The image of the firefighter/neighbor, as popularized in the woodcuts, was based on the belief that neighbors have a duty to each other. In other words, if a farm or a group of shops were lost, then community stability could suffer. Clearly during this period there is much popular emphasis on the fear of the destruction of fire, as well there should have been.

Major fires occurred in the capital cities of Europe almost continuously from the Dark Ages through the Renaissance. Fires were often characterized as uncontrollable enemies, and were described vividly with exciting illustrations. And almost always, "firemen" using the technology of the day (buckets), were unable to stop the advances of fire. Fire was seen as an equal opportunity danger—wiping out the great palaces of Europe, and humble country farms alike.

As time went on, and immigration to the New World progressed, communities in the British colonies needed to depict fire and firefighters. Quickly, popular media and culture created the image of the American firefighter in an extremely positive light. For example, it is common "knowledge" that the founder of what we can call organized firefighting in Philadelphia was Benjamin Franklin. In 1727, he and several friends formed the Junto, Philadelphia's famous discussion group, which proposed the idea that firefighting become an organized function of society through the formation of community fire brigades. In Spanish, Junto means "together."

Although we don't really know the extent of Franklin's contribution to the brigade concept in America, it probably wasn't an accident that this absolutely vital role in the colonies became associated with one of its most beloved figures. One of the most popular and enduring portraits of

Franklin, painted after his death, shows him wearing a fire helmet, albeit one which did not exist during his lifetime! Nonetheless, popular images of well-loved figures can be very helpful in getting the point across—in this case, firefighting is so critical that even Dr. Franklin does it.

This is not to say that Franklin's interest in fire and firefighting was anything less than sincere. Quite the opposite. Beginning in 1733, Franklin's widely read annual, *Poor Richard's Almanac*, advanced the concept of organizing fire protection. Franklin, writing in his persona of Poor Richard, described an incident when he was almost "roasted alive" by a fire that started in a bedpan of warming coals under his bed. On a more serious note, there is documentation that Franklin corresponded with a number of scientists in Europe, and contributed to articles having to do with fire-suppression techniques, including fire-resistant construction methods and theories about extinquishing agents.

What we know for sure is that Benjamin Franklin was influential at both the popular level (the image in the fire helmet, for example) and at the scientific and intellectual levels. His passion for controlling fires was genuine, and his actions to raise awareness in both ordinary citizens and the scientific community about fire controls are commendable. The Union Fire Company, Philadelphia's first firefighting organization, was founded by

Franklin in 1736, and was followed in swift succession by volunteer fire companies in all the other colonies. Today, one of the most prestigious awards any firefighter can receive is the Benjamin Franklin Fire Service Award for Valor, cosponsored by the International Association of Fire Chiefs and Motorola, Inc.

After the American Revolution, fires remained a constant threat to the new nation. With the rise of industrialization came cities and a history of industrial and commercial fires on the North American continent. Entire industries, which tended to cluster inside urban regions, could be wiped out in the course of a single large fire. In the War of 1812, the British used fire as a weapon to destroy our new capital city, Washington, D.C. During her escape, First Lady Dolly Madison is credited with saving Gilbert Stuart's priceless portrait of George Washington. Newspaper accounts of major fires that occurred between 1800 and about 1840 almost always characterized those who were fighting the fires as being brave, courageous, and heroic.

One of the earliest American examples of art creating the image of the firefighter was done by two artists who were interested in producing a series of lithographs of American life. Nathaniel Currier and James Merritt Ives, perhaps the greatest popularizers of early twentieth-century middle-class culture, are important figures in this story due to the enormous popularity and availability of their prints. Folklore regarding Currier recounts

From 1834 until 1907, the lithography shop of "Currier & Ives" produced in excess of one million prints, which included more than 7,500 different titles. James Meritt Ives once described their business as "Publishers of Cheap and Popular Pictures." These included disaster scenes, sentimental images, sports, humor, hunting scenes, politics, religion, city and rural scenes, trains, ships, firefighters, famous race horses, historical portraits, and just about any other topic that illustrated popular American life. ("The American Fireman: Always Ready [1858]." Courtesy of The Currier and Ives Foundation)

Above: The excitement of firefighting can capture one's imagination from an early age. Here, a child in full turnout gear pretends to answer a call. (Collection of Ronald J. Siarnicki/photo by Ronald J. Siarnicki)

his great love of firefighters, and how he often used himself as the firefighter model in his prints. In 1835, Nathaniel Currier produced a disaster print called *Ruins of the Planter's Hotel, New Orleans, which fell at two O'clock on the Morning of the 15th of May 1835, burying 50 persons, 40 of whom Escaped with their Lives.* Currier and Ives' first firemen print as a team was probably *Merchants Exchange Fire in New York City.*

Prior to the widespread use of photographic images in the late nineteenth century, the lithographs of Currier and Ives, and others, served as the primary means of documenting the role of firefighting in the United States. Currier and Ives prints created indelible images of the burgeoning fire service, most notably in their classic series, *Life of a Fireman.* One of the most famous of that series, *The American Fireman, Always Ready* (1858) illustrates the dedication of a single fireman readying the wagon for action.

Illustrations of catastrophic fires were a recurring image in the Currier and Ives repertoire, from the *Great Fire of 1835*, which destroyed 600 buildings below Wall Street, to the 1858 burning of New York's reportedly fireproof Crystal Palace, to the *Great Fire at Chicago, October*

Opposite, top: This wood engraving "celebrates" the actions of British General Robert Ross, who led his troops into the new capital city at about 8 p.m. on the evening of August 24, 1814. They encountered little resistance as most of the public officials, including President Madison and his wife, had already fled the city. Ross and his men torched the president's house, the Capitol (which then housed the Library of Congress), the Navy Yard, and several American warships. In 1815, Congress approved the purchase of Thomas Jefferson's library to replace the one lost in the fire. ("The Taking of the City of Washington in America," G. Thompson, Library of Congress)

Opposite, bottom: The Benjamin Franklin Fire Service Award for Valor honors the firefighter for his or her expert training, professional service, and dedication to duty displayed in the saving of a human life. Often, the nominees have been the recipients of medals within their own departments for heroism. The award also serves to raise public awareness of both individual heroism and issues facing the fire service.

119

Above: *Of course, Currier and Ives would have interpreted the most famous disaster of its day. They note that the "Fire commenced on Sunday evening, October 8th, and continued until Tuesday, October 10th, consuming the business portion of the City, public buildings, hotels, newspaper offices, railroad depots and extending over an area of five square miles. About 500 lives were lost and property valued at 200 million dollars was destroyed." ("The Great Fire at Chicago, October 8th 1871." Courtesy of The Currier and Ives Foundation)*

Below, left: *In 1853, New York's Crystal Palace for the Exhibition of the Industry of All Ages opened, modeled after the London Crystal Palace built in 1851. This iron and glass exhibition building was the first iron and glass structure in the U.S. The Crystal Palace burned and collapsed in 1858. ("Burning of the New York Crystal Palace [1858]," Currier and Ives, from the collection of Ronny J. Coleman)*

8th, 1871. A rare print of a saltpeter factory in New York shows the miraculous survival of a worker who was thrown from the roof of an exploding warehouse.

One of the most interesting characters in the emerging fire iconography of the nineteenth and early twentieth centuries was the fire chief, and often these images were borrowed from real life. It was not uncommon for fire chiefs of that era to have flamboyant reputations that were eventually reflected in their public images. Volunteer fire chiefs such as William Macy "Boss" Tweed of New York's Tammany Hall, Jim Decker, also from New York City, and others often found themselves represented in newspapers and magazines as leaders of courageous bands of firefighters. Reputedly, Boss Tweed signed up for Engine Company 6 on Gouvernor Street in 1848. By 1850, he was the foreman. It was not unusual for these chiefs to take on a cult status within their respective cities.

The rise of the fire chief as a popular figure was not only an American phenomenon. In England, Captain Sir Eyre Massey Shaw, founder and first chief officer of the Metropolitan (London) Fire Brigade, was the inspiration for the song "I Am the Captain of the Pinafore," by Gilbert and Sullivan in their famous operetta, *H.M.S. Pinafore* (1878).

John Decker was to be the last of the larger-than-life type of fire chief heading up the New York volunteers. At the height of the infamous draft riots during the Civil War, he climbed upon one of his apparatus and delivered an impassioned speech that stopped the rioters long enough to allow the firefighters to handle the fires being set by the crowds.

Chief Fire Marshal Robert Williams of the Chicago Fire Department was the top command officer during the Great Chicago Fire of October 1871, and is fondly recalled for his leadership during that most-remembered American fire. By the way, the fire probably did start on Mrs. O'Leary's property—but most likely not by the cow! It had been an extremely hot, dry summer, and it wouldn't have taken much to start a fire within the city.

As during the Revolution, in the Civil War fire was utilized as a major weapon of destruction. Union Army General William Tecumseh Sherman, for example, in his famous and controversial March to the Sea (1864), was popularly credited with "burning" a swath of destruction from Atlanta to the Atlantic coast. Enlistment rolls from both the Confederate and Union armies indicate that volunteer firefighters joined both sides to do their duty. It has been documented that the first Union officer to die in the Civil War, Colonel Elmer E. Ellsworth, was the head of a group of firemen (The First Fire Zouaves) who had volunteered from New York. Almost every Civil War battlefield museum will have on display examples of special uniforms worn exclusively by firefighters.

Decidedly, the Civil War helped cement the image of the firefighter as a soldier-hero in the great battle against fire. Viewed as neutrals, firefighters in images emanating from this period are characterized as being ready and able to respond to any battlefield emergency. The rise of *Harper's Weekly* journal, and others with widespread popularity

Above: *New York Fire Department Fire Chief John Decker. Draft rioters were filling New York City with terror during the summer of 1863. When the mobs set fire to the first government building, Chief Decker rushed to conduct the fire ground operations, but the rioters just moved to other sites. When they began their attack on the Colored Orphan Asylum, Decker was knocked unconscious as he tried to intervene. When he came around, he talked the rioters down and saved his own life. (Drawing courtesy of the New York City Fire Department)*

Opposite, bottom, right: *This colored lithograph is one in a series of "disaster prints" done by Currier and Ives. Although fairly common, a factory explosion represented an exciting event, and the public yearned for graphic interpretation. Lithography involves grinding a piece of limestone flat and smooth, then drawing in mirror image on the stone with a special grease pencil. After the application of a series of compounds, the stone is then placed in a press and used as a printing block to impart black on white images to paper. ("View of the Terrific Explosion at the Great Fire in New York, From Broad Street, July 19, 1845," Currier and Ives, Museum of the City of New York/J. Clarence Davies Collection)*

Left: Harper's Weekly *was published from 1857 to 1912, featuring its famous woodblock prints that depicted stories of the day. Before the rise of the "weeklies," newspapers typically did not have any pictorial images. Americans loved the weeklies and this new form of mass media quickly became popular. Here we see a fireman's parade in honor of the Prince of Wales, Prince Albert, consort to Queen Victoria. (*Harper's Weekly, *October 20, 1860, from the collection of Ronny J. Coleman)*

Above: *Mathew Brady documented the Civil War with his battleground photographs and portraits of Civil War leaders. Colonel Ellsworth, the first Union officer to be killed in the four-year-long struggle, commanded the 11th New York Fire Zouaves, which participated in the invasion of northern Virginia on May 24, 1861. Ellsworth was admired by President Lincoln. Ellsworth's funeral services were held in the White House, where thousands of mourners viewed his corpse. ("Colonel Elmer E. Ellsworth (1860)," Mathew Brady, Chicago Historical Society)*

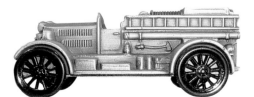

Toy fire trucks are the joy of many a child. They come in simple form, as with this stamped model, and more complicated versions with many moving parts and some that even squirt water. (Collection of Ronald J. Siarnicki/photo by Ronald J. Siarnicki)

among the middle classes, truly helped fix the image of the "can-do" firefighter in America's consciousness. Famous Civil War photographer Mathew Brady took many photos of battlefield scenes and soldiers, including Colonel Elmer Ellsworth.

The last half of the nineteenth century saw the rise of a popular form of literature known as the dime novel. Dime novels were cheaply produced weekly (or monthly) serialized paperbacks aimed primarily at working-class boys. Firemen and the world of firefighting were often depicted in the dime novels, with such titles as *Sam Spark, The Brave Young Fireman; Still Alarm Sam; The Daring Boy Fireman;* or, *Randy Rollins, The Boy Fireman.* Even Frank Merriwell, one of the most famous protagonists throughout the period of the dime novels, took his hand to firefighting in the Tip-Top Weekly Series, *The Fireman*.

Of course, the invention and acceptance of the photographic image throughout mass culture at the end of the nineteenth century propelled the image of the firefighter into all facets of American society. The firefighters in these early photographs were almost always posed (a custom borrowed from portrait painting) wearing formal uniforms, complete with high boots and the quintessential American fire helmet. They were almost always found holding a nozzle, a trumpet, or a fire ax, perhaps to indicate rank.

Whereas these early photo-portraits lacked the quality of action, in short order the amazing medium of photography demonstrated that its great gift was in capturing people in extraordinary environments. Many major urban factory and industrial fires occurred at the turn of the century, and photographers (most of whom worked for the daily tabloids) were on hand to capture the action. Firefighters began to appear regularly on the front of newspapers—heroes in the limelight.

Newspaper archives from this period are filled with photographs of firefighters battling huge urban blazes. What's interesting is that the bucket brigades, found in the Currier and Ives prints, are gone. This was the dawn of a new age of technology that had finally made its way into

FRANK LESLIE'S **ILLUSTRATED** NEWSPAPER

Entered according to Act of Congress, in the year 1887 by Mrs. Frank Leslie, in the Office of the Librarian of Congress at Washington.— Entered at the Post Office, New York, N. Y., as Second-class Matter.

1,667.—Vol. LXV.] NEW YORK—FOR THE WEEK ENDING AUGUST 27, 1887. [Price, 10 Cents.

. "OLD BLACK JOKE," THE OLDEST HAND-ENGINE IN THE UNITED STATES. 2. GRAND FIREMEN'S PARADE, AUGUST 17TH.— THE PROCESSION PASSING THE CITY HALL.

Top right and above: *The widespread availability of printed sheet music at the beginning of the nineteenth century allowed ordinary citizens the opportunity to expand their musical horizons. Waltzes, marches, and the like were played in the parlors of middle-class homes with increasing popularity. Firemen and their exciting fast-paced lives were a natural and popular theme for this new music awareness. Harry J. Lincoln's* Midnight March *is considered one of the best examples of the firehouse marches. (*The Midnight Fire Alarm *and* March Montello *sheet music from the collection of Ronny J. Coleman)*

Top, left: *Much like* Harper's Weekly, *Frank Leslie's newspapers were the antecedents of today's modern photojournalism. This representation of the fifteenth Annual Convention of the New York State Firemen's Association in 1887 shows an exciting and patriotic firemen's event—not much different from today's conventions. Many of the weeklies were successful because they relied on sensationalism to evoke curiosity and loyalty in the reader. (*Frank Leslie's Illustrated Newspaper, *August 27, 1887, from the collection of Ronny J. Coleman)*

the fire service. Hosecarts and steam engines were becoming ubiquitous elements in the developing firefighting partnership between man and machine. By the end of the nineteenth century, firefighters had also formed state firemen associations, groups that survive to this day as powerful political entities.

Firemen bands and ensembles were very popular around the turn of the twentieth century, and into the 1950s or so. Firehouse music must have been a welcome antidote to the many long hours the men were required to stay on duty. (It wasn't unusual for a firefighter to work six days straight without going home.) Marches were an especially popular musical genre, and firefighters were popular subjects. One of the most

In 1949, the "FIREHOUSE FIVE" was formed by a group of writers, animators, producers, and directors at the Walt Disney Studios. The group was originally made up of Ward Kimball on trombone, Clarke Mallory on clarinet, Frank Thomas on piano, Ed Penner on bass sax, Jim McDonald on drums, Johnny Lucas on trumpet, and Harper Goff on banjo. In the "Opera House" at Disneyland, they performed in red shirts, firemen's suspenders, and fire hats. In 1989, Ward Kimball was named a Disney Legend. ("Firehouse 5 Plus 2 Goes to a Fire!" Goodtime Jazz Records)

Firehouse bands must have helped pass the time and the long hours between the excitement of running to a call. Although concert bands are no longer as popular in the U.S. fire service, drum and bagpipe bands still flourish. Many fire service members are laid to rest with the sounds of a lone piper in the background. (©Bettman/Corbis)

Many toys have been created depicting firefighters and caricatures of firefighters. This endearing statue of a clown shows him only getting a drop of water from his fire hose—because he is standing on it, evidenced by the bulge in the hose behind his foot. (Collection of Ronald J. Siarnicki/photo by Ronald J. Siarnicki)

prolific march composers was Harry J. Lincoln, whose *The Midnight Fire Alarm* is a joyful and jaunty tribute to the fireman's life.

No image-maker in the history of mankind, however, can match the power of the moving motion picture and its stepchild, television. Shortly after the invention of the moving picture in the early 1890s, the firefighter became a focal point for early filmmakers. In 1898, a black-and-white silent film was made entitled *Alarm of Fire in a Soubrettes Boarding House*. One of the first portrayals of firefighters by the film industry was in *The Fire Chief's Daughter*, a melodrama in 1910, starring Francis Boggs and Kathleen Williams. In 1916, Charlie Chaplin directed and starred in a twenty-minute black-and-white silent film called *The Fireman*. The Keystone Cops had several films in which firefighting equipment, such as the tillered aerial ladder, played a major part in their outrageous chases.

Fatty Arbuckle, an extremely popular comic-actor in the early years of film, starred in a 1919 film called *The Garage*, where he was a part-time mechanic and part-time firefighter. The Our Gang ensemble made several comedies where the firefighter was seen as a jolly and well-liked fellow. Almost all of these early films were comedies, or spoofs, and it's interesting that the transition of the fireman image from print mediums (where he is depicted as having the best of American virtues) did not carry over to film. Often, in the early American cinema, firefighters are used as foils for practical jokes, and are shown to be lazy, overweight, and even dull-witted.

There is no record as to how actual firefighters reacted to these images. Firefighters, however, value humor as a tremendous remedy to combat the seriousness of their profession, and one can imagine firemen of the 1920s laughing right along with the audience, all the while knowing

how basically un-funny firefighting can be. The popular boys' book series based on the escapades of Tom Swift (an adventurer and inventor) took a turn at firefighting in a novel by Victor Appleton called *Tom Swift Among the Firefighters* (1921).

Through the first half of the twentieth century, this emphasis on humor continued to be the context for portrayals the fire service, in spite of the fact that this was one of the most dangerous periods for firefighters in American history. For example, The Three Stooges, in their inimitable style, made a film in which they portrayed firefighters as complete buffoons. In *False Alarms* (1936), Larry, Moe, and Curly are inept firemen who almost lose their jobs. Curly sneaks out of the station and is then encouraged by his girlfriend and her friends to call Moe and Larry to join them. Instead of calling them on the telephone, Curly pulls the fire alarm. To get to the fire on time, Moe and Larry take the captain's car and crash it.

But not all films of the 1930s were comedies. Cowboy star Johnny Mack Brown starred in a film called *Fire Alarm* (1932), one of the first films made with the firefighter as the true hero. In it, he plays a young firefighter named Charlie. After rescuing a cat from a burning building, Charlie and his pal Fishy try to impress the cat's pretty owners, Pat and Gertie, but soon their attention is diverted by the need to battle another blaze in the apartment next door.

While American cities experienced catastrophic industrial fires, movie-going America laughed at firemen. Research in metropolitan newspapers of that era reveals photo after photo of extremely complex fire ground operations, and firefighters in various stages of physical

False Alarms by the Three Stooges *(Curly, Larry, and Moe) was released on August 16, 1936. It was seventeen minutes long, took four days to make, and contained twelve slaps and three pokes. A zany and lighthearted look at the job of firemen. (Columbia Pictures, Inc.)*

On January 9, 1912, Engine Company 4 of the New York City Fire Department responded and went to work on the fire at the Equitable Building on Lower Broadway. The cold weather that day caused the spray from hose lines to blow back on the steamer and coat it and everything around with a thick layer of ice. The firemen likewise could not escape the freezing water as they attempted to extinguish the fire. Through all of this the steamer continued to puff smoke and fill the hoses. (Collection of Paul Hashagen)

125

The work of Stevan Dohanos is often compared with that of Norman Rockwell, as both painted during the 1940s and 1950s, concentrating on middle-class American life. His work also was regularly featured on covers of the Saturday Evening Post, the most powerful image-maker of its day. It is often commented, that while Rockwell embraced the American Dream, Dohanos looked with a more skeptical eye. In the 1960s, Dohanos also held the position of chairman of the National Stamp Advisory Committee, which selected art for postage stamps. ("Christmas at the Fire Station," Saturday Evening Post, December 16, 1950, Stevan Dohanos. Reprinted with permission of Curtis Publishing)

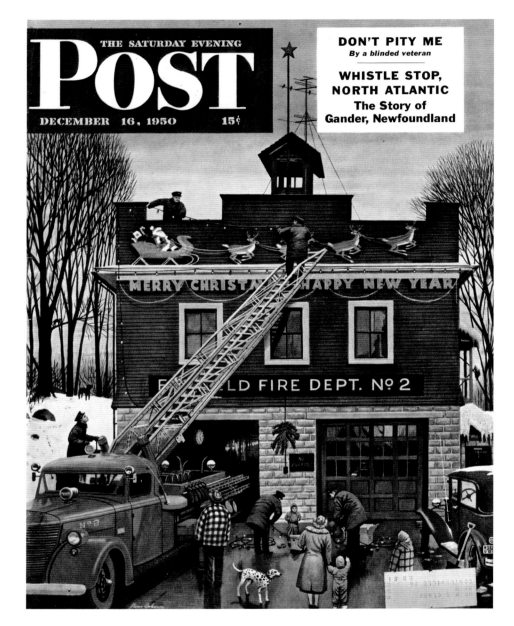

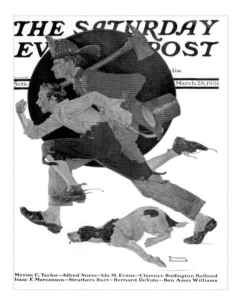

The exuberance of the fireman, with a lad and a hound in tow, virtually carries our eye off the magazine's cover. Rockwell's admiration for firefighters and the "tools of their trade" is obvious in this portrait. ("To The Rescue," Saturday Evening Post, March 28, 1931, Norman Rockwell. Printed by Permission of the Norman Rockwell Family Agency Copyright © 2003 the Norman Rockwell Family Entities)

As toys developed over the years, they have become more action oriented. This "Snorkel" has tires that roll and a boom that moves up and down. (Collection of Ronald J. Siarnicki/photo by Ronald J. Siarnicki)

exhaustion. Images offered to the public during these years were quite polarized—lazy and inept versus real-life working firefighters.

Television was introduced to American homes on a wide-scale basis during the early 1950s. In 1958, comedian-actor Ed Wynne was a feature character in the Texaco Comedy Hour, in which he portrayed a fire chief of some ineptitude. This was one of the earliest shows featuring a fireman, and it was sponsored by Texaco (maker of the "Fire Chief's" gasoline). Although never malicious, Wynne chose to perpetuate the general film image of firefighters as companionable family men with "relaxed" professional standards.

This image by Wynne and others was, of course, challenged by real-life events, and in other sets of images that were very popular during World War II and into the 1950s. The drawings and paintings of Norman Rockwell and Stevan Dohanos, among others, best illustrated on covers of the *Saturday Evening Post,* portray firefighters as representing the best of American life. Rockwell loved to portray firemen working and relaxing together. Among his collection are indelible images of firemen and firehouse life, such as his 1931 masterpiece, *To The Rescue.*

The good-natured approach to firefighters in the Rockwell and Dohanos paintings and illustrations portray them as dependable, stable, down to earth, and provide a balance to the comic image that was perpetuated in film and early television. These illustrations, with their sentimental qualities, portray an era of firefighting that, like much of Rockwell's work in particular, probably existed only as an idealized type. Rockwell loved painting the working man in action, and firefighters provided an excellent emotional landscape upon which he could portray the best of American life. And he kept at it, throughout the turbulent 1960s, when firefighters were often caught up in the "antiestablishment" backlash. His painting *The American LaFrance is Here!* (1971) is an especially sentimental and charming tribute to the American firefighter and the community.

The 1950s are also remembered as the heyday for comic books, and firefighters were not overlooked in this genre either. Perhaps one of the most interesting fireman of the era was DC Comics superhero, Fireman Fred Farrell. Farrell was the son of Fred "Smoky" Farrell, a fireman who had given his life in the line of duty. *The School for Smoke-Eaters* (1956) opens with young Fred about to take his final exam to earn his fireman's badge with the Center City Fire Department. Fred's struggle to establish a reputation in light of his father's achievements is a theme that would not be lost on any son of a firefighter, especially one who had died in the line of duty.

During the era of World War II and on into the 1960s, there were also several films that were made which began to offer a more realistic and gritty image of firefighting. One of these, *Red Skies of Montana* (1952), featured Richard Widmark as a USDA Forest Service firefighter, a brave man who is called a coward by a rookie fireman who holds Widmark responsible for his father's death. The turning point of the film comes in the course of a terrible wildfire, when Widmark and his team (including the rookie) are stranded. Much like Ed Pulaski (the real-life hero of the Big Blowup Fire in 1910), Widmark leads his men to safety, with minimal regard for his own survival. The true macho salute to firefighters however,

The excitement generated by the arrival of a new piece of equipment for the local volunteer fire department is still celebrated with great joy today. ("The American LaFrance is Here!" Norman Rockwell. Printed by Permission of the Norman Rockwell Family Agency Copyright © 2003 the Norman Rockwell Family Entities)

Above and left: *Richard Widmark and Jeffrey Hunter, among others, star in the 1952 film* Red Skies of Montana *about "Smoke Jumpers" in Montana. These firefighters are dropped into areas of forest inaccessible to wheeled vehicles and tasked with the job of cutting off and stopping wildfires. The photo above shows a fight between the two principals using "Pulaskis," a tool developed specifically for wildland firefighting by Edward Pulaski, a member of the U.S. Forest Service. The photo at left is the fire crew radioing for assistance after surviving a "crown fire" by digging holes in the ground and covering up with wet canvas tarps. (Warner Brothers Television)*

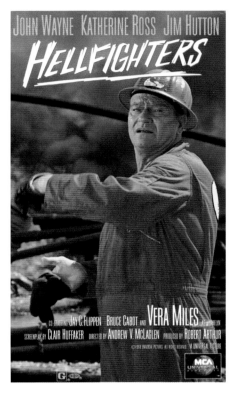

Above: *John Wayne stars in the 1968 film* Hellfighters, *highlighting the career of Red Adair and his crew of Texas oil well firefighters. Their process involved cooling hose streams around the burning wellhead and then carefully introducing a quantity of nitroglycerin into the flame. If all worked well, when the nitroglycerin exploded, it would generate enough pressure to effectively blow out the flame. (Universal Studios)*

Right: Fahrenheit 451, *the 1966 science fiction film based on the Ray Bradbury novel, shows a different type of firefighter. Fire prevention has reached its goal and all structures are now fireproof. There is no need for traditional firefighters. However, books have been banned and it is now the job of firefighters to go to the scene of any books found, seize them, and start a fire to destroy them. One firefighter, Montag, eventually becomes very curious about these books, hides some, and reads them. He eventually joins the resistance to preserve the knowledge of books. (Universal Studios)*

Opposite, top: *"Emergency!" originally aired between 1972 and 1977 on NBC. It consisted of 132 one-hour episodes with one two-hour pilot movie, and four two-hour sequel movies. The show centers around Station 51 and Rampart Emergency Hospital. Station 51 contains a squad and an engine with a normal crew of six, two of which are paramedics. It follows the characters of paramedics John Gage and Roy DeSoto to the point when they are promoted to captains. (From the collection of emergencyfans.com)*

did not come until 1968 when John Wayne portrayed a fictionalized version of the world's most famous industrial firefighter, Paul N. "Red" Adair, in a movie called *Hellfighters*. Wayne's character was called Chance Buckman, and this film brilliantly highlights Adair's development of tactics for handling oil well fires. Interestingly, the story of Red Adair would have been well served by a John Wayne-type sequel in 1991, when Adair and his team extinguished 117 of the burning oil well fires ignited by Iraqi troops retreating from Kuwait at the conclusion of the first Persian Gulf war.

Another interesting, albeit quirky film from the 1960s was *Fahrenheit 451* (1967), based on the novel by science fiction writer Ray Bradbury. Set in a futuristic American city where all printed material is banned (because it encourages free thinking and independence), the movie focuses on the plight of a young firefighter named Montag. In this city, it is the job of firefighters to "hunt down subversives and burn their caches of books." While on duty, Montag confiscates some of the banned material and begins to have doubts about his society. The title of the book comes from the fact that 451degrees is the temperature at which paper catches fire and starts to burn.

If we were to think about the representation of firefighting and fire-fighters throughout the 1960s, the image of firefighting and firefighters remained fairly stable, even if the industry itself was struggling with alarmingly high civilian fire death rates, significant firefighter mortality, and an ever-increasing menu of responsibilities. In film and on television, at least, firefighters remained fairly untormented characters—amiable, happy, dependable, and true to the cause.

But that was about to change. And it began with the creation of a television series called "Rescue 8", which dealt with two firefighters from the Los Angeles Fire Department. Debuted in 1958, this black-and-white show starred Jim Davis and Lang Jeffries. "Rescue 8" took a bold step in trying to capture the real-world life of urban firefighters, and it was loved by many firefighters for its reality base. However, the show that really gave a face to firefighting was "Emergency!", which premiered on NBC (in living color) in 1972.

Actually, "Emergency!" gave two faces to firefighting: Los Angeles County firefighter/paramedics Johnny Gage and Roy DeSoto. Gage and DeSoto (who responded to a seemingly endless array of emergencies in

For the rugged child, this piece of fire apparatus has an off-road look. This truck is complete with an open bed in the rear for hauling equipment and lug tires to make it through the toughest sandbox. (Collection of Ronald J. Siarnicki/photo by Ronald J. Siarnicki)

Dennis Smith's Report From Engine Co. 82 *(1972), was a best-seller and an eye-opener for the millions of nonfirefighters who were drawn in by its vivid descriptions of big city incidents and life in the firehouse. Smith later went on to become founding editor of* Firehouse Magazine, *one of the most influential and enduring fire periodicals. His* Report from Ground Zero: The Story of the Rescue Efforts at the World Trade Center *(2002) may well become the defining "insider" description of the World Trade Center Towers. (Pocket Books)*

Steve McQueen and Paul Newman star in The Towering Inferno, *the 1974 film about a fire chief and an architect who end up working together to deal with a massive fire and many lives in danger in the world's tallest building in San Francisco. Concerns over fire and life safety and the inherent hazards of fires in tall buildings come to light. (Warner Brothers/20th Century Fox)*

their unit, Squad 51) entered the lexicon of American pop culture. Their names and images became synonymous with American firefighting in the 1970s. Gage and DeSoto were hip, sometimes troubled characters, who gave the American public a good sense of the stress and workload associated with first responders. James O. Page, an early and enduring advocate of Fire-EMS in the United States, was an advisor to this show, and undoubtedly was responsible for much of its realism.

Surely, the phenomenon and realism of "Emergency!" can be debated, but no one can debate the impact that Gage, DeSoto, and Squad 51 had on American popular culture. For a time, Squad 51 became shorthand for all rescue units. So strong were the images of the firefighters that the actors who portrayed them initially had difficulty obtaining other roles after the show ended. "Emergency!" offered a relatively realistic set of images to the viewers. This was, for example, the first time the role of the firefighter/paramedic was explored. The migration into the paramedic world did a great deal to boost the image of the firefighter as possessing ever-increasing competence and professionalism. Anecdotally, many of today's firefighters recall the impact "Emergency!" had on their own career choices.

During the same time period, CBS produced a show called "Code Red" (1981–1982) a family saga starring Lorne Greene of "Bonanza" fame as Chief Joe Rorcheck. Although it did not achieve the popularity of "Emergency!", the concept of intergenerational fire service did ring true for many American firefighter families.

In the field of popular nonfiction, Dennis Smith broke the mold in 1972 with his best-seller, *Report From Engine Co. 82*. This book, which tells the story of "The Big House," one of the South Bronx's busiest fire stations, remains a classic in the field of firefighter memoir. It is an excellent book and one which should be read by anyone seeking a true understanding of the fire service in urban America. Although much has changed in firefighting since 1972, *Report From Engine Co. 82* contains eternal "insider" truths about firefighting.

On the wide screen, the 1970s brought images of the tremendous bravery of firefighters, and nowhere was this portrayed better than in the film *The Towering Inferno* (1974). In this Irwin Allen disaster-thriller, action hero Steve McQueen portrays rough and tumble Battalion Chief Michael O'Hallorhan of the San Francisco Fire Department. Along with his fellow firefighter, portrayed by Paul Newman, O'Hallorhan and his crew fight a high-rise fire into submission. McQueen's Chief O'Hallorhan was a good role model for the public to see, and the introduction of the concept of firefighting *tactics* (in this case regarding a high-rise building) invited the audience inside a real-world experience.

Another film of considerable interest was *Backdraft* (1991), starring Kurt Russell as Brian McCafferty of the Chicago Fire Department. The final fire in this film, which occurs in a chemical factory, provided a perfect foil for action hero Russell and his crew to battle, employing high-tech tools and advanced firefighting strategies. As well, *Backdraft* portrayed the crusty, gritty underbelly of what it's like to actually be on the inside of a burning building, which was brought about by advances in film technology. Many fire departments reported a surge in applications

after *Backdraft*, and whether this is true or not, it remains a great staple of fire service folklore.

Steve Martin and Darryl Hannah starred in a charming movie, *Roxanne* (1987), a comedic reworking of the seventeenth-century French play *Cyrano de Bergerac*. In this film, Martin plays a Colorado fire chief, C. D. Bales, a man with a huge nose, who meets and falls in love with astronomer Roxanne Kowalski, played by Hannah. Before long the chief discovers that it is one of his firefighters, Chris, who has captured Roxanne's heart, not he—as he had hoped. There are plenty of nose jokes in this movie (twenty-five to be exact) and it is a favorite among fire service fans. Two years later, Steven Spielberg directed *Always*, a fantasy film about a crew of wildland firefighters starring Richard Dreyfuss, Holly Hunter, and John Goodman.

From the 1960s on, there were ample opportunities for the image of real firefighters to be honed in the public's eye. Firefighters found themselves on the frontline during campus revolts, portrayed as military-types next to National Guardsmen. In numerous accounts of major incidents involving civil unrest, firefighters are often seen in the background as witnesses to history, ready to react to the crisis at hand.

It was the traumatic impact of terrorism on United States soil, beginning in the 1990s, that further linked the fire service to high-profile public

Top, left: *Kurt Russell and Robert De Niro star in the 1991 Ron Howard film* Backdraft. *After the death of their firefighter father, older brother Steven (Kurt Russell) follows Dad's footsteps into the Chicago Fire Department. The younger brother Brian eventually winds up back in the Chicago Fire Department, and in brother Steven's fire company. Steven drives Brian out of the department and into arson investigation and Brian ends up working for an arson investigator (Robert De Niro) investigating a series of murders-by-arson. The fire special effects have been described as outstanding and some of the best outside of science fiction films. (Universal Studios)*

Above: Roxanne *is a 1987 film starring Steve Martin as a small-town fire chief. The actual premise of the film is the romantic story* Cyrano de Bergerac. *He falls for the world's most beautiful astronomer (Daryl Hannah), but he is embarrassed by the size of his proboscis and prefers to stay on the sidelines. Like Cyrano, the shy chief instead helps a handsome friend (Rick Rossovich) woo the fair lady by providing flowery sentiments and soulful poetry. (Columbia/Tristar Studios)*

131

Always is a 1989 film by Steven Spielberg that he waited ten years to make. This romantic story follows the adventures of wild-fire air tanker pilots and the love interest of one of them. Richard Dreyfuss plays a dare-devil but competent pilot that "puts the wet stuff on the red stuff." After crashing his plane and dying during a run, he returns as a spirit to do penance for his "wild life" by help-ing out those that he loves as they struggle to carry on without him. (Universal Studios)

events. People no longer had to get their images of the fire service from fictional sources, they could read the newspaper or turn on the news. This shift to a real-world base for assessing firefighters started with the bombing of the Alfred P. Murrah Federal Building in Oklahoma City in 1995. This incident provided Beirut-like images for the American public. In the immediate aftermath, almost every photo-graph of the emergency scene contained images of firefighters and paramedics. Firefighters crawling through debris. Firefighters removing victims, particularly children from the daycare center located in the build-ing. Firefighters slumped in exhaustion. These images were wholly positive for the fire service and served as a wake-up call for the entire nation that our firefighters are indeed first-line soldiers on the emerging terrorist front.

The representations of what happened on September 11, 2001, at the World Trade Center, the Pentagon, and near Shanksville, Pennsylvania, require little formal analysis. The story of the Trade Towers is as much a story of the bravery of FDNY firefighters as anything else. The photograph of Father Mychal Judge being carried from the scene by firefighters is pure emotion, no intellect. The raising of the flags over the debris of the towers within hours of the attacks is reminiscent of the Iwo Jima sculptures at the Marine Corps War Memorial, both riveting testimonials to courage, deter-mination, and stealth bravery.

Images that become icons are often repeated in many forms. The raising of the American flag on Mount Suribachi in 1945, captured by news photographer Joe Rosenthal, became a symbol of American military success and unity. The Pulitzer Prize–winning photograph by Rosenthal became the model for the United States Marine Corps War Memorial in Arlington, Virginia. When firefighters raised the flag over the rubble of the World Trade Center Towers on September 11, 2001, Thomas Franklin captured the image, which was immediately circulated around the world—becoming one of the most defining photos from that day. One reason was its obvious echo of the Iwo Jima photograph. The Franklin photo has appeared reproduced on many items commemorating September 11. But, the image of the flag raising has also been translated into other popular forms, as a way to honor the symbol of unity and triumph. One of the winners of the Marshall, Michigan, 2001 Scarecrow Festival was "Heroes," a tribute to 9-11. (Mt. Suribachi: Associated Press/Joe Rosenthal; Ground Zero Spirit: The Record [Bergen County, NJ]/Thomas E. Franklin; Scarecrows: Susan K. Collins)

There are many images from that day in American history that have been produced in books and films solely dedicated to the FDNY firefighters on September 11th, as well there should be. For no other single experience has galvanized the American public in its love and support for firefighters and the fire service. Not surprisingly, newspaper editorial cartoons surrounding the 9/11 events provided powerful images of the first responders

Since September 11th there has also been an upsurge in pop culture representations of firefighters. Marvel Comics, for instance, has

Opposite, bottom: *Father Mychal Judge (1933–2001) was the first officially recorded fatality at the World Trade Center, indexed as Victim #0001. Judge, age 68, was the New York City Fire Department's (FDNY) most visible and popular chaplain. His white firefighter's helmet was presented to Pope John Paul II when a group of FDNY firefighters visited the Vatican. In France, he was named to the Legion of Honor. (Shannon Stapleton/Reuters)*

THE OTHER TWIN TOWERS OF NEW YORK

NEW YORK POST

CAN I GET YOUR AUTOGRAPH?

NEW YORK POST

WE'VE REACHED THE TOP....

MIKE LUCKOVICH ©2001 AJC.com
ATLANTA CONSTITUTION

Above: *On September 17 and again on September 19, 2001, editorial cartoons by Sean Delonas appeared in the* New York Post. *The first of these shows a firefighter and a police officer from New York City much larger than life, standing in place of the World Trade Center Towers as a tribute and to honor their bravery. The next cartoon shows comic book heroes asking for a firefighter's autograph. The unselfish acts of heroism are honored by these well-known superheroes. (Sean Delonas/*New York Post*)*

Right: *"We've reached the top..." the firefighter radios to his command post. Mike Luckovich of the* Atlanta Journal-Constitution *drew this cartoon envisioning the reward that surely awaited all those New York City police and firefighters that lost their lives in the World Trade Center disaster. Always going higher up the stairs while the occupants were going down to safety, the police and firefighters finally reach the top and are greeted by heaven's gates. (Mike Luckovich/* Atlanta Journal-Constitution*)*

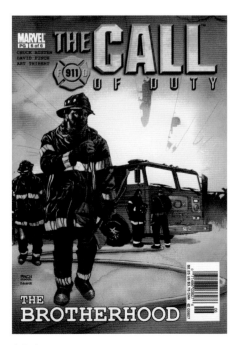

begun a new series, *The Call of Duty*, in its Marvel Heroes sequence. NBC's Peabody-Award–winning drama "Third Watch", which premiered in 2000, fictionalized the Twin Towers incident shortly after the "real" event occurred. This show portrays the personal and work lives of a group of New York City police, paramedics, and firefighters who work the "third shift." Fisher Price has come out with a series of firefighter action figures for children, the most popular of which is Billy Blazes, an FDNY firefighter.

As we look back over the series of images, ranging from the ancient world to the present, we see that firefighting has been a component of popular culture for a very long time. Be they soldiers, saints, clowns, the good-natured guy next door, or today's post 9/11 firefighter-hero, firefighting remains a constant theme in our popular imagination and everyday lives. We give toy fire trucks and helmets to young boys with the coded message, "These are the good guys, you can be one, too." We trust firefighters to establish "safe havens" in their stations for abused and lost children. Communities across the country offer tax breaks and other incentives to volunteer firefighters. Firefighters are the good guys, even if we don't know any personally. Through still images

Above: *Everyone loves a cuddly stuffed bear and with a firefighter's coat and helmet, what could be more precious. Even firefighters have there sensitive and tender side that often shows up when dealing with children in emergency situations. (Collection of Ronald J. Siarnicki/photo by Ronald J. Siarnicki)*

Left: *In the aftermath of September 11, Fisher Price developed a series of FDNY rescue hero toys, such as Firefighter Billy Blazes. Billy is part of a rescue team that includes Mat Medic, Wendy Waters, and Smokey the Firedog. Packaging for the toys includes Fire Safety Tips aimed at young children. Each Rescue Heroes® Series figure sold benefits the FDNY Fire Safety Education Fund. (Christopher H. Kelly. Image used with permission from Fisher-Price)*

and film, we have adopted the firefighter as embodying the best of our collective national character—courageous, brave, intelligent, determined, resourceful, and patriotic.

Left: *NBC television's dramatic series Third Watch profiles the New York City police, paramedics, and firefighters who work the grueling shift between 3 and 11 p.m. Complex interpersonal relationships swerve wildly amidst a steady stream of human tragedies that become just another day's work for these members of New York's Bravest and Finest. Through Third Watch we are able to look into the everyday lives of these everyday heroes. (Warner Brothers Television)*

Opposite, bottom: *This edition of* The Call of Duty *tells the story of Fireman James MacDonald, one of New York's Bravest, and his companions, EMT Jennifer Montez and NYPD Officer Frank "Gunz" Gunzer. In this episode, the "fate of the entire city" rests on their shoulders as they battle the evil drug lord, Halidon, and try to interpret the appearances of a phantom girl who manifests to first responders and warns them of impending doom! (*The Call of Duty, The Brotherhood, *Vol 1., No. 6. January 2003, Marvel Comics)*

Volunteer Firefighters

Volunteer Firefighters: The Ultimate Gift

Stephen P. Austin

Apparatus parades are a staple of summertime activities for volunteer fire departments nationwide. Apparatus representing each participating department is cleaned, polished, and made ready for display. Many parades offer trophies for the sharpest looking piece in the parade. This particular parade is a part of the annual convention of the Maryland State Firemen's Association held in Ocean City, Maryland, each summer. (Leonard King)

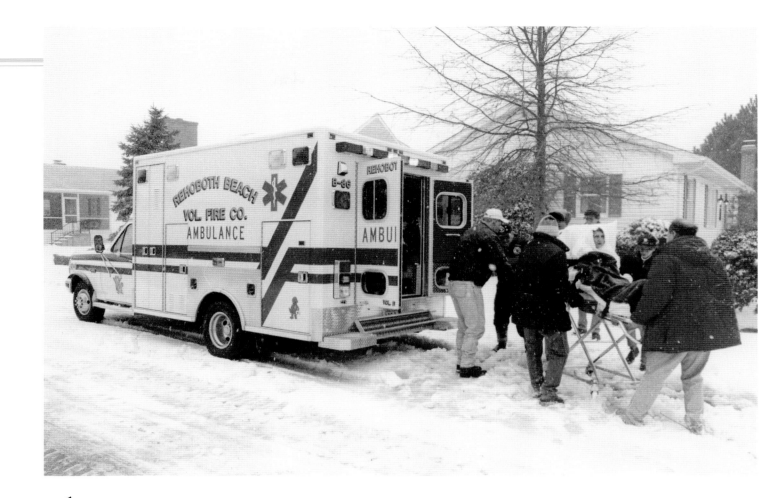

At this very moment, in thousands of communities across the country, from Alaska to the Florida Keys, from the suburbs of great northeastern cities to farming communities in the heart-land of America, an army of volunteers stands ready to respond. At the sound of a siren's wail or the urgent tones of a pager, ordinary men and women immediately set aside whatever they are doing, shift out of the routine of daily life, and become the protectors of their local communities. They are part of one of America's great traditions. They are volunteer firefighters.

These people assume the role of first responders to a range of emergencies that threaten lives and property, routinely risking their own lives to protect others, whether they are friends and neighbors or total strangers. These volunteers are not employees of state or local government, they have no union, and they seek no remuneration. They are motivated by a sense of duty, tradition, and pride to train and prepare themselves and to make themselves available to respond whenever they are called upon, accepting the risks and finding their reward in the simple satisfaction of performing an essential and critical service for their communities.

For most Americans there are no discernable geographical or psychological boundaries separating the career from the volunteer fire service. Americans see all firefighters as unique individuals who are ready to give whatever it takes to protect their fellow citizens. We give very little thought to whether our guardians are paid for their services, or serve voluntarily. When dressed for work in protective clothing and self-contained breathing apparatus, they all look the same and do the same job. There are no volunteer or career fires—the flames are just as hot in a Brooklyn tenement as in a farmhouse in rural Mississippi.

Above: *Battling an unusually harsh winter storm, Rehoboth Beach (DE) Volunteer Fire Company Emergency Medical Technicians prepare to load a patient for transport. (Chuck Snyder)*

Pages 136–137: *College Park, Maryland's, 1971 open cab Peter Pirsch rear mount aerial truck prepares for aerial operations in this dramatic three-alarm blaze that destroyed the Planet X Coffee House and Cafe in the early morning hours of July 18, 1994. This truck is now privately owned by Chief Ron Siarnicki, Executive Director of the National Fallen Firefighters Foundation. (Tom Yeatman, Bowie, Maryland)*

Above: *Volunteer firefighters prepare to load a "packaged" patient who was among the passengers aboard this ill-fated light plane that crashed in dramatic fashion during an aborted takeoff in Bowie, Maryland, in 1995. Amazingly, just one person among the four aircraft passengers was injured in this memorable crash. (Tom Yeatman, Bowie, Maryland)*

139

Above: *This weary crew from the Fish Springs (NV) Volunteer Fire Department takes a rest after fighting a brush fire, on their 1941 International "Brush Queen," which was painted and upholstered by Nevada prison inmates. This department serves a rural high-desert valley located between the High Sierra Mountains to the west and the Pine Nut Mountains to the east, illustrating the diversity of environments served by volunteers. (Linda Monohan, Gardnerville, Nevada)*

A Bowie, Maryland, volunteer firefighter struggles in vain to revive a dog caught in a fire that raced through a Bowie animal hospital. (Tom Yeatman, Bowie, Maryand)

Almost 800,000 Americans call themselves volunteer firefighters. They are our domestic defenders—protecting the homeland from within, just as our military protects us from external attack. This is the most challenging and essential community service provided by volunteers and the most dangerous.

According to the United States Fire Administration, volunteer firefighters comprise 74 percent of the total firefighters in the country and

protect nearly 80 percent of the landmass. Of the 26,350 fire departments in the United States, 87 percent are all or mostly volunteer. More than half of the approximately 100 firefighters who die annually in the line of duty are volunteers. They perform an enormous public service.

A century of volunteer service. The Luray (VA) Volunteer Fire Department celebrates 100 years of service to the community in 2001. (Walter Robertson)

The volunteer fire service is as diversified as America itself. There are volunteer fire companies that have hundreds of members and impressive firehouses filled with the latest and most expensive apparatus and equipment. Their walls are lined with trophies and memorabilia collected over more than a century of proud tradition and service. At the other end of the scale, there are small groups of firefighters in rural communities with the most rudimentary equipment, simply doing their best to protect their communities with the resources they can muster. They are all members of the volunteer fire service and all uniquely bonded by the invaluable mission they perform for their communities.

History

The history and traditions of the volunteer fire service are part of the history of the United States. Volunteer fire companies protected the British colonies in the seventeenth century. George Washington and Benjamin Franklin were volunteer firefighters before they were founding fathers, and the direct descendants of their volunteer fire companies are still in existence. In our largest cities, such as New York, many of today's operational fire companies can trace their origins back to volunteer roots, and their outlying areas are still protected by volunteers.

As America evolved, the volunteer fire service advanced and developed along with it. The earliest settlements relied on volunteer

This statue dedicated to San Francisco volunteer firemen was given to the city by Lillie Hitchcock Coit. She was a firefighting enthusiast whose 1929 bequest to the city was used to build nearby Coit Tower. (© Morton Beebe/Corbis)

141

Members of the Lewes (DE) Fire Company present their lovingly restored 1925 American LaFrance engine at the company's 200th anniversary banquet, making them one of the oldest volunteer fire departments in the nation. This truck restoration took three years. (Chuck Snyder)

Naples, Florida, volunteer firefighters collapse after fighting back wildfires surrounding a home in the Golden Gate neighborhood. The fire forced 200 from their homes. (©Bettmann/Corbis)

bucket brigades to extinguish blazes, years before the first primitive hand pumpers, brass nozzles, and leather hoses were developed. The next generations saw companies of enthusiastic volunteers pulling their hose reels and pumpers to the scene of the fire and taking turns operating the muscle-powered piston pumps to project strong jets of water into the flames. Gradually, and often reluctantly, the volunteers allowed horses to take on the responsibility for pulling larger and heavier apparatus and accepted the superiority of steam-powered pumps. Finally, in the twentieth century, they made the switch to gasoline and then diesel-powered apparatus. In many communities this 300-year evolution from leather buckets to thermal imaging cameras can be traced through the memorabilia of volunteer fire companies that continue to serve with pride and maintain their honored traditions.

The volunteer fire service has also played an important role in the political and institutional life of many communities. Volunteer fire companies were among the first recognized organizations in many areas, and the growing cities of the 1800s often had hundreds of or even thousands of volunteer firefighters. In times of war, whole regiments of soldiers were raised from the ranks of the volunteer fire service.

The volunteers quickly became involved in local politics, supporting various causes and candidates for public office. Many of their leaders became active in local politics and rose to prominent positions. In some cases, the volunteer firefighters became so powerful that they were viewed as a threat by elected officials, who sensed that they could seize control of the local political machine. This hastened the transition to full-time fire departments in several cities where the volunteer forces were abolished and replaced with paid firefighters who could be more easily controlled. This fear of growing political power was clearly a factor when New York City began phasing out volunteers in the 1860s. But, to this day, there are still volunteer fire companies protecting parts of New York City, and hundreds in the surrounding suburban areas.

Above: *Rick Allen (right) and Jeff Allen both of Chenango (NY) Fire Company, using the Hurst "O" cutters to remove the roof of a vehicle at an extrication. (Jeff DeRado, Prospect Terrace Fire Company)*

Taken during a Chenango (NY) Fire Company high-angle rescue training exercise. Jeff DeRado (Prospect Terrace Fire Company) is hanging upside down while Jim "Magoo" Parrotte (Chenango Fire Company) looks on. (Rick Allen, Chenango Fire Company)

Volunteerism in America

Volunteerism has long been recognized as a cherished component of Americanism. Many important functions in our society depend on citizens to perform essential tasks, and millions of Americans routinely give of their time in service to the public, whether it is delivering meals to shut-ins, working at the local library, or raising money to fight a dreaded disease. In a nation where volunteerism has always been valued, volunteer

A Bridgeton, New Jersey, landmark is destroyed in the downtown business district. Over a dozen volunteer fire companies from Cumberland County, New Jersey, fought the blaze in a row of three- and four-story buildings. (Bob Bartosz)

Volunteers are trained for wildland fire fighting in 1942. Straw bosses and foremen get final instructions from the fire boss holding a map at a training camp in Rhinelander, Wisconsin. (© W. J. Forsythe/Corbis)

firefighters are widely recognized as the most skilled, dedicated, self-sacrificing, and enthusiastic to serve.

Campbell County, Wyoming, fire chief Gary Scott, recognizing the tradition of volunteerism, wrote, "One of the longest standing traditions in America is the volunteer firefighter. In Wyoming, volunteering for the fire department is more than a tradition, it is a way of life, and it's about neighbors helping neighbors."

Perhaps this is the backdrop that encourages so many men and women to take the step and actually volunteer to provide a service that may, in the end, take their life. Volunteers do not generally dwell on this aspect of their jobs, but it is no accident that they routinely begin and end all meetings in prayer—for protection as they answer the call of duty. They are willing to give everything to serve their cause, because they know that their primary mission is to save the lives of others.

Who Volunteers?

Volunteer firefighters are a representative cross-section of the American population, young and old, male and female. Individuals join a fire department for a wide variety of reasons. Some join initially for the excitement and adventure; the adrenaline rush of racing to the scene of

"All in the Family." The Chief of Jericho Fire Department of Hicksville, New York and his two sons. (J. Burton Mason, Photo Department, Jericho Fire Department)

an emergency on a 30-ton fire engine with red lights flashing and siren screaming provides a stimulus to the very center of the soul. The thrill of facing danger and conquering the flames may be irresistible. Others join because they are seeking a challenge or simply because they recognize the need and want to serve their communities and help people who are in distress. To some the volunteer fire company provides an apprenticeship on the way to a career in the fire service.

For some families the volunteer fire service is "in the blood" and it is not uncommon to find two or three generations serving in the same company, fighting fires side by side. The active membership roster of a volunteer company often includes husbands and wives, sons and daughters, cousins, uncles, and even grandparents.

Most volunteer companies are continually seeking new members. Recruiting and retention of volunteers have become major concerns in many areas, because the work is so demanding and the fire department has to compete with every other activity and pastime for the time that individual members can devote to it. Active membership in the fire service requires strong dedication and commitment. The initial and ongoing training requirements are extremely demanding and the firefighter must be prepared to respond instantly whenever an alarm is sounded, no matter what is happening at that moment or what else was planned. After every fire and every training session there is equipment to be washed, maintained, and checked to be ready for the next emergency, as well as paperwork to be completed. There is always work to be done and the moments of glory are surrounded by hours of work and effort.

For many young volunteers the first years can be intense and the experience can be overwhelming. The new member wants to attend every training session, respond to every call, and be in the thick of the action whenever and wherever duty calls. But, like any activity, the novelty eventually fades and some drift away, redirecting their time and energy toward earning a living and raising a family. For many others, the passion is transformed into a mature lifelong commitment to remain a firefighter and the adrenaline rush is replaced by the satisfaction of "service for others," a slogan that hangs in many volunteer fire stations across the country.

A volunteer firefighter with the Rockville (MD) Volunteer Fire Department attaches a fire hose to a fire engine during practice. Training for volunteers is a regular activity. They must be ready to meet the challenge of the ever changing emergency situation. (© Richard T. Nowitz/Corbis)

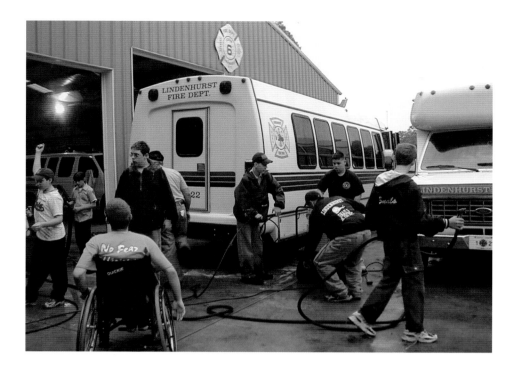

Daytime coverage is often a problem, particularly in suburban communities where a large proportion of the population commutes to a larger city every morning and only returns in time for supper. Shift-workers who are at home during the day become highly valued as volunteers in these areas. Not surprisingly, career firefighters often serve as volunteers during their off-duty hours in the communities where they live, which is often where they first became involved in the fire service.

In communities with colleges and universities, some fire companies offer free room and board to qualified volunteers who commit to being available during certain time periods. Many volunteer companies have evolved into combination departments, staffing their stations with a daytime crew of paid firefighters while continuing to operate as a volunteer organization at night and on weekends. The evolution toward combination staffing is an increasing trend in the areas where call volumes are steadily increasing and fewer volunteers are available to respond.

To maintain a supply of new members, many volunteer fire companies operate Junior Firefighter Programs, Cadets, and Explorer Posts as a feeder system. Recruiting future members at ages as early as twelve or thirteen can yield lifelong members for a fire company. While occupational safety and child labor laws govern the age when young people can become full-fledged firefighters, most departments allow their junior members to learn the ropes by participating in limited training and drills, by cleaning the apparatus, assisting with fund raising, and helping out around the firehouse. The anticipation grows as a junior approaches the age, typically eighteen, at which he or she can qualify to become an active firefighter. Some high schools allow time off from studies to participate in scheduled training sessions or even to respond to alarms if they are qualified and needed.

Vermont holds an annual "boot camp" at the State Fire Training Academy for teenage cadets from volunteer fire companies throughout the state. The experience gives the young trainees an opportunity to learn

147

Above: *Nearly 3,000 people lined the streets for the emotional unveiling of the Brockport (NY) Volunteer Fire Department's lasting tribute to honor the memories of the fallen rescue workers lost in the September 11 attacks. The statue is a life-size interpretation of the famous photo depicting firefighters raising a flag on a leaning pole over "Ground Zero." (Christopher R. Martin, Brockport, New York)*

Top, right: *Deceased firefighter's memorial service, held annually at the town of Babylon, New York, Firefighter's Memorial located at the Babylon Town Hall. (Karen Todd, New York)*

new and valuable skills, lets them experience the values of civic pride and accomplishment, and introduces them to the history and traditions of the fire service. Junior members learn valuable lessons about the fire service and its mission, while structured training sessions focus on developing skills, teamwork, leadership, accountability, and ensuring that the students know how to operate in a safe manner. For many this is their first exposure to a paramilitary organization.

To Be a Member Is Everything

The volunteer fire service in America is much more than teams of individuals who devote their spare time to fighting fires. Volunteer fire departments are the blue-collar country clubs of many communities—institutions in which there is a sense of pride, belonging, fellowship, and shared experiences, as well as an important mission to be performed. Volunteer firefighters treasure their fire company membership just as other Americans value their affiliation with a university or a social club.

The volunteer fire service has long been viewed as a brotherhood, although it is now becoming a sisterhood as well, with the increasing

Red Rock Volunteer Fire Company 1st Assistant Chief Melissa Eigenbrodt, assisted by New York State Office of Fire Prevention and Control Arson Bureau member Michael Knowlton, take a rubbing of the name of a deceased firefighter from the Memorial Wall in Albany, New York, during the New York State Firefighters solemn 2002 Memorial Service, which commemorated the addition of the names of 359 Empire State firefighters who gave their lives in the line of duty, most in the horrors of the September 11 attacks, in 2001. (Richard E. Lindmark, New York)

148

An American flag is hung across a highway in Jericho, New York, between two aerial ladder trucks at the funeral of firefighter John Stahl. (J. Burton Mason, Photo Department Jericho Fire Department)

number of women entering the volunteer ranks. This sense of belonging is reinforced on many symbolic levels. New members can hardly wait to get their company T-shirts, hats, and jackets featuring the fire company logos and station numbers. Special automobile license plates transmit the message "I belong" to the public and to fellow firefighters.

There is a nationwide and worldwide kinship among all firefighters, as well as longstanding friendly rivalries between neighboring companies. Volunteer firefighters are avid travelers and no trip is complete without a stop to visit a fire station along the way. There is strong worldwide affinity among firefighters and the doors of every firehouse swing open when a visiting volunteer stops by to bring greetings and to meet the brothers and sisters who share the same passion. Upon these occasions, fire apparatus is proudly pulled out of the engine bays and onto the apron of the station to allow the visitor to take the traditional three-quarter-view color photographs to memorialize the visit. Upon returning to their home fire station, the pictures will circulate among the members while the traveler reports on the unique features of this station or that apparatus.

The sense of belonging is a powerful incentive to become a volunteer and to stay involved. Benefits are derived from the fraternal atmosphere, which may be as simple as a place to sit down with friends to watch a game on a large-screen TV or shoot a game of pool. Social functions including parades, picnics, and banquets often involve whole families in the activities of the fire company. In our very fragmented society, the bonds of friendship that are nurtured among volunteer firefighters are unique. Many volunteers maintain their social membership in the organi-

In 1928, this group of women firefighters in Silver Spring, Maryland, was part of a women's volunteer fire brigade. Women have long played a roll in the volunteer fire service. (© Bettmann/Corbis)

zation for years after they retire from actively performing emergency duties, continuing to enjoy the fellowship and contributing to the mission by performing administrative and support functions.

For many volunteers the fire service becomes a way of life. The duty schedule may become a central issue in scheduling personal and family activities, particularly during vacation periods when many members want to travel and coverage must be maintained. Family vacations may be scheduled around conventions and training opportunities.

In busy departments, the amount of time devoted to the fire company can easily exceed the hours spent earning a living from a standard forty-hour workweek job. When a sufficient number of volunteers are available, some companies divide their members into squads or platoons to rotate the duty to respond to every call. Some companies assign "sleep-in" crews to remain at the fire station for immediate nighttime response.

Personal Commitment

Active membership in a volunteer fire company requires tremendous personal commitment. In addition to accepting the inherent risks and the inconvenience of responding to other people's emergencies, whenever and wherever they occur, the volunteer has to participate in extensive and regular training to develop and maintain a wide variety of skills. The mandatory training requirements have increased tremendously over the past twenty years and minimum standards have been legally adopted in many states.

The volunteers who want to assume leadership positions and become officers must make an even greater commitment of their time

Below: *Salem, Wisconsin, volunteer firefighters make entry with charged attack lines into heavy smoke conditions during live fire training exercises conducted during the winter of 2001. (Sharon Ditzig, Salem, Wisconsin)*

Bottom, right: *This wintry scene depicts firefighting teams in full turnout gear turning their accountability tags over to their operations officer as they prepare to enter a burning dwelling during live fire training exercises conducted by Gateway Technical College of Kenosha, Wisconsin. Salem, Trevor, and Wilmot (WI) Volunteer Fire Departments, as well as the Silver Lake Volunteer Fire Department, participated in these training exercises. (Sharon Ditzig, Salem, Wisconsin)*

and energy, as well as accepting increased personal responsibility for their actions and decisions. A volunteer company officer or chief is expected to be just as competent and responsible as an individual who receives a full salary for performing the equivalent duties.

Almost to a person, at some point every member of a volunteer fire department dreams of being the chief. It might only be a fleeting wish for some, but for quite a few the desire to be a chief may manifest itself in a drive that is stronger than the need to be excel at one's career. The incentive to command the department, to wear the white helmet—the symbol of a fire chief—may be stronger than the drive to make more money, or to hold a greater title at work. Volunteer chiefs and officers are usually elected by the members from among the qualified candidates, so those who seek the office must prepare themselves and also prove their value to their peers.

The degree of involvement in the fire service may become so important for some individuals that family and personal decisions frequently take into account the availability of volunteer opportunities. A volunteer who has spent years in the same fire company, qualifying and gradually moving up through the ranks, may have to seriously consider the options of a career change that requires relocation versus the opportunity to become fire chief in a year or two. Moving to a new home may not be an option because leaving the fire district would be too great a personal sacrifice.

Members of a New England volunteer fire department pose with a fire engine, ca. 1910. The engine appears to be a hand- or horse-drawn piece with a hand pump. The rig behind it is a hose cart that went with the engine to provide the necessary fire hose for fighting the fire. (© Bettmann/Corbis)

Auxiliaries

Part of the volunteer tradition includes ladies auxiliaries, which give untold hours raising funds and taking care of "their firemen." While the concept of an auxiliary organization composed entirely of the wives, mothers, and daughters of active firefighters is no longer fashionable, many fire compa-

Promoting the public fire safety education message to "Start the New Year Right," this 1949 photo depicts members of Orange County, Florida's, Conway Volunteer Fireman's Association. (Robbie Robertson)

The Capitol Heights Ladies Auxilliary
The First Organized Fire Department Ladies Auxiliary in the United States

On December 1, 1920, the Capitol Heights Volunteer Fire Department Ladies Auxiliary was organized. Mrs. Dora Quill, after arguing with her husband for spending too much time at the firehouse, started the auxiliary after her husband issued this challenge— "start a ladies group," he told her, so you can experience the thrill of firehouse life, too. Responding to the challenge, Mrs. Quill mobilized the women of the community to form what is now the Capitol Heights Volunteer Fire Department Ladies Auxiliary, which holds the distinction of being the first organized fire department ladies auxiliary in the United States. Mrs. Irene Connor served as the auxiliary's first president.

Mrs. Quill managed to convince eleven other ladies to join her. The organization served to support the fire department and to raise funds. Becoming just as active as the men, they arranged their own meeting nights and began holding regular fund-raising events. Some of the activities included lunches, bake sales, card parties, dinners, and assisting the men at the carnivals and meetings. It is not known for sure, but Mr. Quill may have regretted his suggestion once he saw Dora devoting so much time to the auxiliary. Among some of their earliest contributions to the department were funds for the new firehouse building in 1932 and a siren to replace the outdated bell system in 1934.

With the onset of World War II, the department faced a shortage of men when forty members of the Capitol Heights VFD were called up for military duty.

During this period of understaffing, the department recruited junior members and trained the ladies auxiliary to assist in firefighting. After the war, the ladies welcomed their men home with a party in June of 1946—and relinquished their wartime duties.

After the war, the ladies began a capital campaign to once again help the VFD improve its facilities. On September 12, 1948, Mrs. Magdalene Schmidt presented Chief Frank Briguglio with $5,000 in Building Association Stock to put toward the building of the new firehouse. A new firehouse was erected by the volunteers and townspeople, who donated their time, talents, and labor. This new building gave the ladies a larger meeting room and a new modern kitchen to assist them in their preparations for fund-raising and county events.

Throughout the decades, the Ladies of the Capital Heights VFD have continued to donate their time to their community. In 1970, they celebrated their fiftieth anniversary with a gala honoring their achievements. During the 1980s and '90s, several ladies received honors for their years of service to the department and the community through induction into the Prince George's County Fire and Rescue Association-Ladies Auxiliary Hall of Fame.

nies still benefit significantly from the efforts of support groups. Today, many young women choose to become firefighters instead of working in the firehouse kitchen, but there are thousands of men and women who make a valuable contribution by performing important functions that do not include fighting fires and other emergency duties. In many cases, the auxiliaries include older active members who are no longer fit enough to fight fires, but can still perform a wide range of valuable functions and pass on their valuable experience to the younger generation.

Auxiliaries frequently provide canteen service at emergency scenes, serving hot coffee, cold drinks, and sandwiches, along with words of comfort and encouragement to the tired and beleaguered firefighters. Others perform administrative functions, helping to manage the accounting and maintain all of the required records and documentation. Auxiliary members, both ladies and gentlemen, can often be seen marching in parades with their front-line firefighters, demonstrating their pride at belonging to the volunteer fire department.

Funding

The volunteer fire service is no different from any other type of enterprise or organization in its need for money to operate. While salaries can consume more than 90 percent of the budget for most career fire departments, a volunteer fire department has to pay for a firehouse and for all of the apparatus, equipment, fuel, maintenance, supplies, and other services that cannot be performed by the volunteers themselves. It is easy to see that even the basic necessities are expensive.

Almost everything that is needed to fight fires is expensive. A full set of protective clothing costs almost $2,000, and the breathing apparatus that must also be worn inside a burning building costs about the same amount. Add a $1,500 portable radio, and a $10,000 thermal image camera and you have one firefighter ready to go inside to look for victims. It is easy to spend $350,000 for a new pumper or $700,000 for a fully equipped aerial apparatus. Even a basic ambulance costs around $100,000 by the time it is outfitted and ready to roll. Add the ongoing costs associated with keeping everything running properly and the bills for operating the firehouse, and it's easy to see that volunteer companies need money to

Opposite, top: *The Ladies Auxiliary Marching Unit in 1950. Alice Long, now ninety-six years old, is pictured third from the left. Alice is still active in the auxiliary. (From the collection of Jim and Jennifer McClelland)*

Opposite, bottom: *The Capitol Height Volunteer Fire Department Co. No. 1, ca. 1914. (From the collection of Jim and Jennifer McClelland)*

Above: *A "boot drive" in Mulvane, Kansas. Most volunteer fire departments must pursue some form of fund raising. With a "boot drive," they position themselves at strategic intersections throughout the town and solicit donations by having the citizens "fill the boot." These funds allow them to purchase and maintain needed firefighting equipment. (Garry R. Brownlee, Photographer for Mulvane Emergency Services)*

Above: *Volunteer fire companies from coast to coast are often forced, by economic factors, to make do with the apparatus available and affordable to them. The East End Hose Company of Connecticut received and reconditioned this government surplus 1954 Hesse/Reo crash/structure/brush rig in 1972. They painted it yellow long before this color saw widespread application nationally on fire apparatus. (Pasquale Mascolo, Derby, Connecticut)*

Left: *The Red Lodge, Montana, Firefighters 2001 Ski Team: (G. Fox, T. Kuntz, J. Selvey, S. Schilz, J. Ballard). They compete in an annual race event in full gear, carrying a hose line between them as they ski down the hill. (Lee Hauge)*

Suffolk County, New York's, Holtsville Volunteer Fire Department deploys its 102-foot KME Aerialcat ladder truck at the scene of a general alarm fire in May 2000 that burned thousands of discarded tires. (Warren Weiss, Brooklyn, New York)

Volunteer firefighters do it all. On a hot July day in 1971 in Allentown, Pennsylvania, the Hoxie Brothers Circus elephants are hosed-down by members of the Whitehall Volunteer Fire Department. (© Jonathan Blair/Corbis)

do their job. When the volunteers have to go out and raise this amount of money just to make it possible to do their job, the demands on their time can be overwhelming.

Most of America's volunteer fire companies must raise a substantial portion, if not all, of their own operating funds. Some volunteer fire departments are supported by local tax funds, but many others operate entirely on contributions. Even where direct government support is provided, it is often very limited and the volunteers have to solicit additional funds and donations to make ends meet. Bingo games, Christmas tree sales, public dinners, raffles, and carnivals are among the traditional fund-raising tools. Elsewhere, volunteers conduct "boot drives," where they stand at busy intersections, requesting donations from passing motorists by hold a firefighter's boot to car windows and asking the occupants to help fill it.

Many volunteer departments pull their fire apparatus outside the fire station, creating a "hall" that they use for fund-raising events or rent out for every conceivable purpose. Over the years, the members may set up and tear down the tables and chairs thousands of times, transforming the engine bays into a social hall and then back into a firehouse. Some volunteer companies have raised the funds to build impressive meeting rooms and social halls that are specifically designed to be rented out to the public in order to generate operating revenue for the company. Many American brides and grooms begin their married life at a firehouse reception.

Across the nation, volunteer firefighters have come up with many unique and innovative projects to raise additional revenues. Volunteer fire chief and past president of the International Association of Fire Chiefs,

John Buckman, tells of a rural Arkansas volunteer fire department that faced a severe problem when its fire engine jumped out of gear and rolled into a deep lake. To replace it, the company offered an added service to the community to generate the needed funds. For $60 per month, towns-folk could drop off their trash at the fire station and the fire company members would haul it to the dump.

Every July thousands of people travel to Chincoteague, Virginia, for the famed pony drive. The volunteer firefighters round up wild ponies on neighboring Assateague Island and drive them across a narrow channel to be sold at auction. Since 1924, the proceeds from this annual event have gone to support the Chincoteague Volunteer Fire Company.

Chambersburg, Pennsylvania's, ladder tower flows thousands of gallons of water as one of five ladder trucks fighting this massive five-alarm, 1998 fire in Chambersburg's landmark Washington House Hotel. (Denny L. Clopper, Shippensburg, Pennsylvania)

Fire Apparatus

The most visible and treasured icon of the firefighting profession is the fire engine. Across the nation, fire apparatus owned by volunteer fire companies ranks among the most impressive and elaborately decorated vehicles on the highways. Volunteers take tremendous pride in their vehicles and are anxious to take part in any parade. Unique color schemes and markings, chromed accessories, and a deeply polished shine are proud traditions in many volunteer fire departments, where new fire apparatus still comes with gold-leaf lettering and hand-painted decorations. Even in the smallest rural department that has to get by with a twenty-five-year-old second-hand engine, the members take the time to wax and polish their apparatus and are proud to be seen riding on it.

The phenomenon of intricately decorated fire apparatus dates back to the early days, when many companies named their apparatus, just as sailors name their boats, and local artists were commissioned to paint murals on the new apparatus, making them unique works of art. Some companies owned special parade pieces that were never taken to a fire scene. While the parade vehicles were fully equipped and functional, they were far too delicate and valuable to be used to fight fires. A second, more durable vehicle was always available to do the real work. To this day many volunteer companies maintain a fully restored antique vehicle as their "parade piece."

Members of the Valley Stream (NY) Fire Department gather at the rear step of their new 2001 Seagrave pumper after their first working house fire. (Top Left: Bill Schaefer, Jr.; Top Right: Ex-Chief Ron Mastrangelo; Middle Left: John Beck, Jr., and Right: Joe Paese; Bottom Left: Bill Croak, Jr.; Michael Stella; Ex-Chief Bill Kirkman; Capt. Bill Kirkman, Jr.; Justin Sellas; John Ibrug; Ex-Chief Bill Croak.) (Valley Stream (NY) Fire Department)

Once the Lindenhurst (NY) Fire Department's front line pumper, this 1936 Seagrave was saved from the junk heap and lovingly restored by department members. Nothing less would befit carrying the remains of company member Joesph Angelini, Sr., also a member of the New York City Fire Department's renowned Rescue 1, who was lost in the line of duty at the World Trade Center on September 11, 2001. (Karen Todd, New York)

155

Top and above: Ol' Lil *is a 1914 American* LaFrance *belonging to the Keyser (WV) Fire Department. The driver, William Carpenter, restored and maintains the engine.* Ol' Lil *is still in service as a parade piece. (Harry Alt)*

Interestingly, apparatus was often given a woman's name preceded by "Old." For example, *Ol' Lil*, a 1914 American LaFrance engine with carbide headlamps, is still the pride of the Keyser (WV) Fire Department. Purchased by the department when new, *Ol' Lil* is faithfully maintained and officially still in service, but is now brought out only for parade duty.

The purchase of a new piece of apparatus is a major event for a volunteer fire company, especially when the price can easily be in the $350,000 to $700,000 range. Some departments pride themselves on having more, newer, larger, and better equipped fire apparatus than their neighboring companies and are determined to find as much money as it takes to buy whatever they want, while others are satisfied to have a simple vehicle that will get the job done. Usually one part of the organization is charged with finding the money and a technical committee is appointed to develop the specifications and select the make and model of the new piece. While some departments will only purchase their apparatus from one manufacturer, others publish the specifications and seek the best price from several manufacturers.

Virtually all fire apparatus is built to custom specifications, a practice that is costly, but does allow for companies to meet their local needs

A 1972 parade in Farmingdale, Long Island, is a perfect showcase for the Farmingdale (NY) Fire Department's apparatus. The evolution of the department's fleet can be readily observed. (Lori S. Malkin)

Built in 1923 and listed on the National Register of Historic Places, this photo depicts Station 9, the headquarters station of the Aetna Hose, Hook and Ladder Company of Newark, Delaware. Aetna HH&L operates three stations, protecting the city of Newark and its suburbs, home to 75,000 residents, many mercantile venues, an array of heavy industry and manufacturing, and the state's flagship educational institution, the 20,000 student University of Delaware. The author is a life member of Station 9. (Joe Papariello)

and preferences. When the committee reaches a consensus, their findings and recommendations are presented at the company meeting for ratification. The process is not to be taken lightly, since the new apparatus will probably be in service for twenty years or more. As with most decisions in the volunteer company, the majority must agree that the committee has made a good recommendation. Just as volunteers select their leaders, so they also select their most prized possessions—their fire engines.

Firehouses

Volunteers also pride themselves in the buildings they call fire stations, firehouses, or fire halls, depending on the part of the country in which they are located. Volunteer fire stations most often reflect the age, character, and economic conditions of the communities in which they are situated, generally blending with the architectural style of the neighborhood.

All fire stations contain certain basic elements, beginning with at least one engine bay to house the apparatus. In some communities the firehouse is nothing more than a simple garage that houses the fire apparatus.

The Minneapolis Hook and Ladder Company No. 1 was organized in 1868 from a group of volunteers. Funds raised by the city paid for the ladder truck. Here they assemble in front of the apparatus in 1869. (© Minnesota Historical Society/Corbis)

Members and guests of the Bethany Beach (DE) Volunteer Fire Company participate in a "housing ceremony," a local custom for welcoming a new piece of apparatus. During the ritual, each piece of apparatus owned by the fire company (including the new one) is manually pushed in and out of the station three times—honoring God, country, and the fire department. (Chuck Snyder)

Volunteer firefighter Richard Lucke of the Kitsap Fire District #7, Port Orchard (WA) Fire Department rolls up a 5-inch supply hose after a structure fire in South Kitsap County. (Lynn Johnson, Volunteer Photographer)

A statue honoring volunteer firefighters stands in front of the Union County Courthouse in Elizabeth, New Jersey. (© Lee Snider/Corbis)

Constructed on a shoestring budget, some rural fire stations of the 1950s and 1960s actually featured advertising signs for soft drinks, while the rest of the sign identified the building as the volunteer fire department.

Most volunteer firehouses provide some type of back room that serves as the social quarters for the members, as well as a watch desk or radio room where alarms are received. Traditionally, a roof- or tower-mounted siren was used to alert the volunteers to alarms, but the outside sirens are gradually being replaced by radio and digital text pagers that deliver the message to the volunteers without waking up all of the neighbors. Some stations provide dormitory facilities for members to sleep-in on assigned duty nights.

At the high end of the scale are the large and impressive edifices built by more prosperous volunteer departments, often accommodating impressive fleets of vehicles and separate spaces for training, maintenance, administration, physical fitness, recreation, and socializing. These firehouses often reflect the prominent position of the volunteer fire department within the community as well as the success of their fund-raising activities. Some of these buildings are designed with a bingo or social hall located on one end, with a separate public entrance, to support the fire company's fund-raising efforts.

In the eastern U.S., a number of volunteer fire stations that were built in the late 1800s and early 1900s are listed on the National Register of Historic Places. These tend to be large structures that were easily recognizable in the downtown area of most communities a century ago. Many of them were constructed with horse stalls before the days of motorized fire apparatus and some of these structures are still in service as fire stations, while others have been converted into museums or are used for other purposes.

It is more common today to find a volunteer fire station on the edge of town, outside the "downtown area," where they can provide parking for the members as well as rapid access to major highways or busy connector routes. The effort is usually made to blend the architecture with the surrounding area, particularly if it borders on residential property. A growing number of volunteer departments are operating two or more stations to provide faster response times to expanding coverage areas.

Fire Service Public Education:
Skills for a Lifetime

Chief Dennis Compton

The fire service has a long history of teaching safe behaviors through public education programs delivered in school and other venues. Public education programs designed around improving fire safety practices began more than a century ago. Even before the 1900s, fire departments in parts of the United States realized the value of teaching people how to prevent fires, and how to survive a fire should one occur.

One of the earliest national public education efforts was Fire Prevention Week (FPW), authorized each October through a presidential proclamation. Since 1922, the National Fire Protection Association (NFPA) has been the official national sponsor of Fire Prevention Week. Each year, the NFPA establishes a specific FPW theme—usually a problem that is particularly pertinent to children and families. Recent themes have focused on home escape planning, checking smoke alarms, and techniques to reduce specific fire hazards. Fire departments have used Fire Prevention Week as a platform for community awareness events, media attention, and an opportunity to involve children and adults in activities that reinforce positive behavior changes.

Schools play a key role in teaching children safe behaviors by providing a place for teachers, firefighters, inspectors, and public educators to introduce and reinforce fire safety lessons. A book titled Susan's Neighbors, published by Scott, Foresman and Company in 1937, clearly illustrates examples of fire department members teaching fire safety classroom sessions to children, demonstrating how to report fires to the fire department,

A firefighter teaches fire safety lessons to a classroom of children. (Paul R. Hanna and William S. Gray, *Susan's Neighbors at Work*, Scott, Foresman and Company, Chicago, 1937, Illustrated by Clarence Biers and Story, Hurford Studio. Reprinted by permission of Pearson Education, Inc.)

and telling children about the role of firefighters during scheduled visits to fire stations. These are important lessons—ones which we still teach today.

As years progressed, the alarming loss of life from fires became a major concern within the fire service. In 1973, a presidential commission completed a thorough analysis of the fire problem in the United States. In 1973, more than 12,000 people were dying each year from fires, $11 billion in property was being lost, and 300,000 Americans were being injured by fire annually. The Commission's findings, published as American Burning, included a recommendation for the development of a national fire safety education program. America Burning remains one of the most important documents in the history of the fire service, and it has been twice revisited.

In 1978, the NFPA completed and implemented the school-based Learn Not To Burn (LNTB) program. LNTB has been credited with helping to significantly reduce the loss of life and property from fires in North America. LNTB pioneered positive, non-threatening fire safety messages that involved fire departments as partners with trained educators. LNTB focused the American fire service on fire safety education through the development of a training model that identified specific fire behavior errors common to children. It also identified individuals within fire departments who would act as fire safety education "champions." These champions were firefighters and public educators who would go into the schools to deliver the targeted lessons in the LNTB curriculum.

Since the 1970s, fire departments have significantly expanded their role in the delivery of emergency medical services (EMS). This change in the emergency services delivery model has become the catalyst for change in public education programs. Fire departments found themselves called upon to provide a full range of injury prevention messages, beyond fire safety. Unintentional injuries emerged as the leading cause of death for people under the age of thirty-four. More than 100,000 people die each year from unintentional injuries, injuries that are related to motor vehicle use, fires and other burns, choking, suffocation, poisoning, falls, firearms, bicycle use, pedestrian behaviors, drowning, and natural disasters. Although some fire departments had the foresight and the resources to expand their public education curricula, many did not or could not. It wasn't until 1998 that a national program became available.

The NFPA's Risk Watch program has become the model all-risk public education curriculum and delivery system in North America. The LNTB "champions" were transitioned into Risk Watch "champions," and state and provincial "Champion Management Teams" (CMT's) were formed to guide local communities in the implementation of Risk Watch. In a school-based format, Risk Watch used researched based data to provide lessons that cover the most common ways that children and young adults are injured or killed each year. The curriculum includes fire safety, but is much broader and includes other risks to young people.

Top: A firefighter teaches children how to notify the fire department of a fire. (Paul R. Hanna and William S. Gray, *Susan's Neighbors at Work*, Scott, Foresman and Company, Chicago, 1937, Illustrated by Clarence Biers and Story, Hurford Studio. Reprinted by permission of Pearson Education, Inc.)

Above: Children visit a neighborhood fire station to learn about firefighters and their equipment. (Paul R. Hanna and William S. Gray, *Susan's Neighbors at Work*, Scott, Foresman and Company, Chicago, 1937, Illustrated by Clarence Biers and Story, Hurford Studio. Reprinted by permission of Pearson Education, Inc.)

All-risk life safety education programs have positioned fire safety in the broader context of injury prevention, and have tied the fire service to public health. The result of this important shift has been a significantly expanded public education role for fire departments. This approach brokers the delivery of safety messages between schools, homes, firefighters, and other community agents, while keeping the fire service in a key leadership position.

Interestingly, statistics reveal that a high numbers of fire deaths and injuries occur among people over sixty-five, especially as a result of cooking fires and falls. In response to this, a new focus was needed to counter the specific behavior-related issues presented by seniors. In 2000, the NFPA's Remembering When program became available to fire departments. This program, taught in public forums such as senior housing complexes, helps fire departments more effectively reach this high-risk group.

A perfect example of the life saving power of public education has been the fire safety results achieved through the installation of smoke alarms. Today, most homes in the United States now have smoke alarms installed. Collectively, public education programs, as well as many targeted national awareness campaigns,

have saved lives and billions of dollars in property since their implementation. It is hoped throughout the fire service that recent campaigns, for bicycle helmet safety and correct child-seat installation, can have similar positive effects.

Many other efforts have resulted in a heightened level of respect in the fire service for the importance of effective fire and life safety education programs delivered by fire department personnel. While we can strive to develop inherently safer environments, and enforce safety practices through legislation and custom, only the teaching of fire and life safety information, skills, and behaviors can complete an integrated model of success.

Support from the United States Fire Administration, and advocacy groups such as SafeUSA, the Home Fire Sprinkler Coalition and others, has enhanced awareness throughout the fire service regarding the efficacy of strong, all-risk, targeted public education programs.

For the past fifty years, the message regarding fire safety has never wavered: no one should die or be injured in a fire. Children, especially, have been viewed as an at-risk group with a tremendous potential for success. We will never know how many children have been saved because they have been taught "STOP, DROP, and ROLL," or because a teacher helped them draw a home escape plan. But, we intuitively know there have been many, and each one represents a win for the fire service and society at large.

This is the role of public education in the fire service—to change horrific outcomes into success stories. Public education is one of the key components of a fire and life safety system designed to protect lives and property.

Top: In 2002, this automatic fire sprinkler Mobile Demonstration Unit teaches the public about the life safety value of home fire sprinklers. (Rick Montemorra/Mesa, Arizona Fire Department)

Above: Sparky, teachers, and firefighters form a perfect team to teach children fire and life safety behaviors. Fire and life safety education is a key to our success in the future. (Rick Montemorra/Mesa, Arizona Fire Department)

Above: *Typical of the community relations activities of many fire companies throughout the U.S., Santa Claus excites children and spreads Christmas cheer during his annual tour through the community of Pennsburg, Pennsylvania, on the platform of Pennsburg's ladder truck. (Michael Weider, Stillwater, Oklahoma)*

Right: *Jeff Benach of the Wagontown, Pennsylvania, Fire Department teaches elementary school children about firefighter gear during "fire safety week." (Bill Murray)*

Far right: *Bill Murray of the Wagontown, Pennsylvania, Fire Department explains that, in the event of a fire, children need not fear "the friendly monster." (Jeff Benach)*

Above: *TV cameras roll as rescuers from the Laurel (DE) Fire Department participate in a "Prom Promise" drill for students of Laurel High School. The firefighters prepare to take the roof off an accident vehicle, to vividly illustrate the hazards of drinking and driving. (Mike Lowe, Delaware)*

Right: *Members of the Rehoboth Beach (DE) Volunteer Fire Company presenting a public fire safety education program to enthusiastic youngsters in the engine bay of the fire station. (Chuck Snyder)*

The Role of the Volunteer Fire Company in the Community

Wherever they are located, volunteer fire stations are still the center of social life in many small or rural communities. Volunteer firehouses are favorite polling places for elections. President George W. Bush casts his ballot at the Crawford (TX) Volunteer Fire Department. Although the President is not a member of the department, he has frequently been seen clearing brush on his ranch while wearing a Crawford VFD T-shirt.

In large suburban areas, where population growth and government restructuring have all but obliterated many political jurisdictions, the volunteer fire department may provide the only identification that a small town once existed. These volunteer fire companies are often the anchors that distinguish a local community from a vast suburban sprawl.

Because of their very nature of being at the center (sometimes literally) of the communities they serve, volunteer fire company members

eventually gain an understanding of how their local government works. Volunteer chiefs have become adept at budget preparation, in the hopes that some portion of their needs will be met through grants or property taxes, relieving the burden of having to raise their own funds to provide a valuable public service.

Volunteer fire chiefs are frequently being asked to "sit at the table" in communities that are now faced with increased responsibilities for emergency preparedness. Over and over again, they have to remind government officials that the local fire department will be the first to arrive and the first to take action during any disaster—be it natural or the result of a terrorist attack. As such, local fire departments must be adequately trained and prepared, regardless of whether these departments are paid or volunteer.

Volunteer firefighters are widely recognized as citizens involved in their communities, a fact not lost on political candidates. An elected official who provides funding and services to a volunteer fire department is making a smart investment. Strong volunteer fire companies make it less likely that the community will have to hire paid career firefighters, the cost of which often requires additional tax revenue. Additionally, a photo of an elected official beside the fire truck he helped to obtain for the community is a powerful vote-getter in the next election. In his successful campaign for governor, Ed Rendell courted the volunteers in the commonwealth of Pennsylvania, the home of at least 2,300 volunteer fire companies, by talking about the critical role that volunteer fire companies play in the community, particularly in a "post-9/11" environment.

Volunteer fire companies themselves are democratic institutions and it has been said that the elections to select the officers of volunteer fire companies are tougher than general political elections. Not surprisingly, many elected officials in America cut their teeth on politics by testing the waters seeking leadership positions in firehouse elections.

Highly contested elections give a sense of continuous renewal, with the injection of new blood into the volunteer leadership, but they are often difficult for the loser. Potential comebacks in future years are measured on how the loser reacts. Licking one's wounds and returning to the firehouse in a lesser role is a humbling experience, but those who survive the agony of defeat as good losers may come back as viable candidates at a later time.

Top, left: A student member of the Stillwater, Oklahoma, Fire Department developed the "Smoky Joe" puppet in 1947 as part of an early public fire safety education effort. (Robbie Robertson)

Top, center: Although having lost some of their popularity today, "Fire Queen" contests were among the early hallmarks of fire prevention efforts, which fire companies eagerly looked forward to every year. Fully bedecked in her gown and displaying her winner's trophy, this photo features Takoma Park, Maryland's, "Mrs. Fire Prevention 1965." (Robbie Robertson)

Top, right: Merchants at one time took great pride in store-front displays that helped their local fire departments promote a public fire safety education message, as evidenced by this 1950s-era photo of an award-winning florist's window display along Reisterstown Road in Baltimore, Maryland, featuring safety messages and firefighting gear from the Pikesville, Maryland, Volunteer Fire Company. (Robbie Robertson)

Volunteer fire companies have a long history of serving the public, not just by responding to emergency calls, but also by promoting public fire safety education. Citing a number of fire reporting system statistics, this dramatic 1960s-era display by the Takoma Park, Maryland, Volunteer Fire Department offers a very stark and powerful message to "Be Safe, Not Sorry." (Robbie Robertson)

163

A pioneer in public fire safety education, the late E. Wade Thomas, of the Keyser, West Virginia, Fire Department and a past president of the Cumberland Valley Volunteer Firemen's Association, demonstrates effective use of a fire extinguisher in an early simulator unit in this 1950s-era photo. (Robbie Robertson)

Volunteer Fire Service Organizations

Fraternalism and strength in numbers have allowed volunteer firefighters to become a powerful political force in many communities and at least a few states.

Early records show that firefighters traveled long distances, sometimes by horse or rail, to attend firefighter conventions hundreds of miles from home. This dates back to an era when travel was difficult and most people lived their lives not far from their place of birth. By the late 1800s, fire companies had organized local, state, and regional associations to advance their political agenda. Sadly, in some cases, one of their priorities was to purchase insurance to bury and honor members who died in the line of duty.

Today an impressive number of local, state, regional, and national associations represent the interests of volunteer firefighters, fire companies, fire districts and fire chiefs. While they deal with current issues and the latest technology, some of these organizations have roots that extend back more than 100 years and their meetings and conventions still retain honored traditions.

All firefighters love a good convention and modern firefighter gatherings echo the past. To this day, they feature musters and contests of firefighter skills, solemn memorial services to honor those who have died, spirited meetings to guide the future course of the association, and elections, banquets, and grand parades featuring uniformed firefighters and shiny fire apparatus. All official activities are followed by gallons of beer, the traditional and still-preferred drink of firefighters worldwide. These conventions are important as they bond firefighters together in a publicly unified manner.

Challenges

When all the fun and excitement settles, it is an unfortunate fact that the rates of volunteering in local fire departments are declining. According to the National Volunteer Fire Council (NVFC), since the early 1980s, the total number of volunteer firefighters in the United States has declined by 12.5 percent. During the same period the population has increased steadily, the number of emergency calls has increased rapidly, and the training requirements for volunteers have expanded dramatically. Many volunteer departments are facing a huge and looming problem, simply because they are unable to attract and retain the number of volunteers that are needed now and will be needed in the coming years.

While some blame the increased training demands as taking too much time and effort, others point to modern family life and other real-word demands as the major deterrents to joining and staying. Others look at the time that must be devoted to fund-raising as a disincentive; new recruits join because they want to fight fires, not raise money. Older members, who have worked hard to build the volunteer organization, often have a deeper appreciation of the need for a steady source of funding to

George Spears of the Harrods Creek Fire Protection District, Kentucky, ascends the aerial ladder with hose and nozzle during a drill. (Melanie Hilliard/Harrods Creek FPD)

improve fire protection in a community. Most of the younger members are more interested in riding on fire apparatus than calling numbers at the weekly bingo session. The never-ending cycle of raising money can either keep volunteers tied very closely to their company or drive them away.

The other huge and increasing demand on volunteers is for training time. The time spent on the fire ground or the emergency scene is minor

Steve Kohr of Mulvane (KS) Emergency Services is silhouetted against a rural structure fire. As he battles the blaze, smoke curls back toward him. A roof ladder used earlier to gain access to the upper level is now highlighted by the flames. (Garry R. Brownlee, Photographer, Mulvane Emergency Services)

The task of the volunteer firefighter isn't always to ensure that fire goes out. This is proved by a photo of a New Tazewell, Tennessee, Fire Department chief officer overseeing a controlled burn operation. Strategically placed hose lines ensure that the flames from the burning structure do not impinge on any exposures. (Sara Kennedy, Tazewell, Tennessee)

165

in comparison to the commitment each volunteer must make to attend classes and training sessions to acquire and retain the required certifications. While most volunteers love to learn and practice the skills of the trade, more and more are having difficulty finding the time to attend all of the required sessions at the times and places they are offered.

Retention of volunteers has become a major concern in many areas, particularly as the demands of raising a young family often require two incomes and the fire service must compete with every other family priority. It has become popular in some areas to offer small incentives to volunteer firefighters, such as special reductions in state or local taxes or length of service award programs (LOSAP) that provide a small "pension" to a volunteer after many years of service to the community. While the benefits of these programs are usually very small, the symbolic recognition of an individual's service is often as important as the monetary value.

When community leaders look at the tremendous donation of time, effort, and commitment that is given to the public by volunteer firefighters, particularly when compared with the cost of replacing them with fully paid employees, the cost of efforts to support and retain volunteers is easily justified. While it is evident that virtually all volunteer firefighters serve because they truly want to be volunteer firefighters, anything that can be done to make volunteering easier and more attractive is a good investment.

Volunteers from Simsbury (CT) Volunteer Fire Department conduct a mountain rescue drill twice a year. Hikers and hang gliders are among those who are rescued from the rocky slopes. Using ropes and a Stokes Basket, two crewmembers pull the mock victim to safety. (Frederick Arnold/Simsbury Volunteer Fire Department Photo Unit)

Opposite: *Steve Kohr and John Benson of the Mulvane (KS) Emergency Services man a hand line in an attempt to save the Kansas Tourist Information Center. (Garry R. Brownlee, Photographer, Mulvane Emergency Services)*

Firefighters participate in a live fire training exercise, sponsored by Oregon Department of Public Safety Standards and Training, at Mid-Columbia Fire and Rescue in The Dalles, Oregon. Students in the photo are learning the proper techniques to safely and effectively attack a flammable liquid fire. In this scene, the fire is simulated by introducing propane (from a remote source) in a fire pan filled with water. (Paul Halliday)

The Future

One hundred years ago, great fires destroying a business district or a manufacturing facility were often the impetus for a local community to establish a volunteer fire department. Today virtually every American community has a fire department, but few, if any, new volunteer departments are forming. Most new communities are willing to shoulder the tax burden for career fire departments because they do not see the establishment of a new volunteer force as a viable option.

In newly developed exurbs, where there are no classic downtown areas and enclosed shopping malls are the community hubs, the citizens expect to have the services of a fire department, but few are prepared to organize one. It is simply expected that local government will provide this service. Many people in these communities hardly know their neighbors—a climate that does not encourage or sustain the life of a volunteer fire service. Even where there are existing volunteer fire departments the demand for services spurred by a growth in population often leads to more paid personnel and fewer volunteers.

This does not mean that the volunteer fire service will fade into the sunset. Much of this nation will never demand, nor ever be able to afford, a career fire department. Those citizens are satisfied with the feeling of security that comes from hearing the house siren wail, followed by the sound of neighbors rushing from the fire station on their way to the alarm. There will be more career fire departments, but volunteers will

The Western Taney County, Missouri, Fire Protection District Water Rescue Team performs swift water rescue training at Silver Dollar City Amusement Park's "Lost River of the Ozarks" ride in Branson, Missouri. (Dana Aumiller)

continue to protect at least 80 percent of the landmass and most of the smaller communities in the United States. The volunteer fire service still remains a vibrant part of the American landscape.

Harry Carter, a well-known fire service consultant and past chief of his volunteer department in New Jersey, reflected, "We are what America is all about: people stepping forward to help their neighbors in time of crisis. We are the heart and soul of America."

Above: *Volunteering is just in the blood. On March 23, 1982, Pasquale "Patsy" Planatamura, who turned 100 that year, "rides" on the side of a fire truck. When the sirens sound to alert volunteer firemen, he is the first man to respond. A Hewlett, New York, volunteer fireman since 1921, the four-foot, eleven-inch Planatamura was the oldest active volunteer in New York State. (© Bettmann/Corbis)*

Left: *Around 1964, the all-women volunteer firefighters of District 11, Snohomish County, Washington, fight a blaze in a rural town. Rural house fires are frequently devastating due to distances from the fire department and the lack of an unlimited continuous water supply. (© Josef Scaylea/Corbis)*

The author is indebted to Howard Cohen, Esquire, of the Aetna Hose, Hook and Ladder Company of Newark Delaware, for his assistance in the research and preparation of this article.

169

Metropolitan City and County Fire Departments

Metropolitan City and County Fire Departments

Chief Charlie Dickinson

Battling heat intensity of 1,500 degrees, billowing smoke plumes 100 feet high, and zero visibility, Toledo firefighters fought a persistent four-alarm fire that raged through a 100-year-old historic apartment building occupied by senior citizens and people with disabilities. Heavy fireseen through the third floor windows indicates roof structure failure. This required the use of multiple master stream devices from aerial ladders. (Linda Timpe Baker/Toledo Fire and Rescue Operations)

The roots of the American fire service can be traced back to colonial settlements, where local people worked together to extinguish fires. Their spontaneous efforts led to the organization of the volunteer fire companies that protected the nation's growing communities, including all of the major cities that developed during the years that followed the American Revolution. But, as the nation grew, urban populations became magnets for industry and immigration, and complex hubs of transportation. For most of these centers of people and commerce, reliance on citizen-based fire protection proved unworkable. The densely built cities required reliable and well-equipped firefighting forces that could respond immediately to control any fire before it grew too large to be contained. The need for full-time firefighters became evident.

The Cincinnati Fire Department, the first fully paid career fire department in the United States, was established on April 1, 1853. Within the next twenty years most of the major cities established similar forces to supplement or take the place of their volunteer fire companies. To this day, the United States is protected by a mixture of career and volunteer fire forces and many communities rely on a combination of both types.

Above: In continuous service since August 4, 1820, Boston Fire Department Ladder Co. 1 is shown here with a hook-and-ladder-type truck that was typical of Boston ladder trucks before the introduction of aerial ladders. Captain Edward Shallow, later Deputy Chief, stands forward over the front wheel with the rest of his company. An assortment of "rakes" (Boston pull down hooks) are visible on the rear side as is a brass Bresnan cellar pipe. (Boston Fire Department)

Pages 170–171: A Bronx fourth-alarm fire on Box 2251 at Third Avenue and 152nd Street in the Melrose section of the Bronx, New York. The fire in a drug store had burned for four hours when this picture was taken and had burned through the roof. (Steve Spak)

Below: The Great Fire of Boston, 1872, occurred in the commercial area that is known today as Boston's business district. A total of 775 buildings were destroyed and millions of dollars in damage were done. It is said that an epizootic disease (affected horses) was rampant in the city at the time and this caused a delay in the response of the fire department. (The J. Paul Getty Museum, Los Angeles/James Wallace Black, Boston After the Great Fire, 1872, Albumen, 10¼ x 39 in.)

According to the United States Fire Administration, there are approximately 26,000 fire departments in the United States. Approximately 6,000 of these departments are all-career organizations, while the rest are fully or partially served by volunteers. Due to the concentration of population in urban areas, it is estimated that 80 percent of the U.S. population is protected by career firefighters.

Above: *After success with a factory rebuild of the former horse-drawn Deluge Wagon in 1923, Pittsburgh Bureau of Fire had American LaFrance build two more of these Type 31 battlewagons in 1927. This engine was assigned to Engine 1, the other to Engine 46. Deluge wagons sported two Morse deck turrets with Morse 1,100-gallon-per-minute nozzles on a thirty-two-foot tower mast. (Pittsburgh Bureau of Fire)*

A Dallas four-alarm fire on Main Street in 1960 requires "all hands." Depending on the size of the fire and the construction of the building, certain conditions require that fires be fought defensively from the outside. This is done to protect the lives of the firefighters as well as prevent the spread of the fire to other structures. Firefighters are shown directing at least three hose streams into the building from this location. All still in full protective gear, they prepare for any eventuality. (Dallas Firefighters Museum)

Metropolitan Fire Departments

The largest U.S. fire departments are the approximately 100 metropolitan departments that protect the nation's major cities and, in some cases, the surrounding areas. Metro departments serve populations that range from 200,000 citizens to over eight million and protect billions of dollars worth of property.

America's urban centers are magnets for diverse cultural groups and economic activity and present an almost incredible range of challenges for their fire departments. The demand for fire department services increases rapidly with population growth. As the urban areas have concentrated business, industry, and residential developments, the metropolitan fire departments have grown both in size and ranges of capabilities. Today, members of the largest metro departments receive training that prepares them to be the first responders to a broad range of situations, from routine house fires, to hazardous materials accidents, to terrorist attacks.

This is not to say that the metro fire departments have to deal with problems that are totally different from smaller or medium-sized departments. Every community has structures that can burn and people who experience many different types of emergencies. It is the scale, frequency, intensity, and complexity of the problems that set the metros apart. The urban landscape in metropolitan areas is dense and often vertical. Their cores are home to high-rise office buildings, aging industrial districts, warehouses filled with combustible products, and every type of large and crowded structure.

On December 29, 1989, a spectacular gas explosion occurred in the Bronx, New York. The fire at Locust Avenue and 132nd Street went to five alarms. The firefighters in this photo have their work cut out for them as the huge fireballs continue to erupt, endangering them and the structures surrounding the fire. (Steve Spak)

Opposite, top: *Located on the northern slope of Beacon Hill, the Bulfinch Street firehouse was located on an extremely narrow street off Scollay Square. It was built in 1872 and served until 1929. In this 1913 photo, Chief of Department John A. Mullen sits in the back seat of his motorized chiefs car. District Chief Henry A. Fox has the reins in his horse-drawn buggy and (from left to right) Water Tower 1, Engine Co. 4 steamer, and Engine Co. 4 hose wagon stand in the doorways, while Chemical Co. 1 is situated behind the District Chief's buggy. The station remained in service until the famous Bowdoin Square firehouse was opened in 1930. (Boston Fire Department)*

On Thanksgiving Day, November 25, 1982, fire broke out in the Northwestern Bank Building in Minneapolis. The fire started in a department store next to the bank which was in the process of being demolished. This fire went to five alarms and caused $90-million in damage making, it the largest fire in Minneapolis history. The photo shows the fire fully involved at 6:15 p.m. (Minneapolis Fire Department)

From Fire Chief to Modern-Day Manager

P. Lamont Ewell

In years past, the traditional successors chosen to manage the day-to-day operations of governments did not include fire chiefs. Fire chiefs—those from small voluteer companies to very complex metropolitan departments—have had many roles to play in their communities. They were usually not considered to have ambitions to move upward in local government. And, in fact, many chiefs never wanted to leave the departments they nurtured. However, it soon became obvious in many jurisdictions that their fire departments were the best-managed government component, and much of this was attributed to the leadership skills of the fire chief.

Today, more and more, the top echelon of public sector management includes those who began their careers in the fire service, advanced through the ranks to become fire chief, and then ascended to top leadership positions such as city managers and county administrators. So why the change?

In the past two decades, there has been an unprecedented wave of reforms as the traditional model of public administration has come under scrutiny. These reforms originated in communities whose political leaders were under severe pressure to keep down levels of public taxation and expenditure, while simultaneously increasing the quality of government services. Two significant features of the reforms included the belief that government had become completely out of touch with community needs, and that governments were structurally designed to encourage delayed decision-making.

Today, citizens demand that their leaders are honest, competent, forward-looking, and inspiring. They also want people who are credible. In direct response to such expectations, today's elected officials are seeking quality administrators who are capable of taking the collective visions of these officials and translating them into the daily mission. In other words, getting the work force to focus its energy on the achievement of strategically developed goals.

Fire service leaders are uniquely qualified to take on such change management. They are accustomed to working closely with communities to ensure that all programs delivered by the fire department are tailored to meet specific needs. In cities and counties throughout the country, fire chiefs have had to find creative ways to maximize services with limited funds. Having to manage through austere budget years, fire chiefs have emerged as budget wizards. They understand the importance of obtaining grants and finding creative ways to meet facility repairs and improvements, as well as the incredible power garnered through private-public sector relationships. Delivering programs that are on time and within budget is second nature for our best chief fire officers.

Having managed various types of emergency scene situations, chiefs are also comfortable with having to analyze facts quickly and then render immediate decisions in the interest of the public. Equally important, fire chiefs are trained to immediately reassess changing conditions and, where appropriate, adjust their previous decision(s). This concept of shifting priorities based on streaming data was once viewed as indecision; now it is considered one of a leader's greatest abilities.

Above all, fire service professionals are comfortable with being risk takers, an indispensable part of good leadership. Look at any community where leaders are making incredible contributions to the quality of life, and you will find that these leaders have the courage to stare down

2002 Metropolitan Fire Chiefs Conference
Honolulu, Hawaii April 13-18

significant risks. They do not, as a rule, wait for favorable conditions to exist before implementing change. Fire service leaders are more inclined to take risks because they know that being too cautious can kill opportunity.

Our nation's fire chiefs are regarded as competent, credible, and compassionate individuals who place the public's interest first. It is because of all of these traits and values that fire chiefs are being called upon to leave their departments to take on greater roles and responsibilities in managing our communities.

As our communities' needs continue to change, fire marshals and fire protection engineers (FPE) are also looked to for solutions. Fire marshals enforce codes, while FPEs review plans for compliance to federal, state, and local codes.

In both urban areas and suburban regions, "smart growth concepts" are being developed as a preferred development strategy. This is especially true in major cities. Gone are the days of planned suburban sprawl which tolerated severe traffic congestion during rush hour periods. Massive numbers of commuters flowing in and out of urban employment centers is no longer viewed as a sustainable outcome of growth. Increasingly, communities are demanding cleaner air, the preservation of natural habitat, and more open spaces. Fire marshals and FPEs are key to the development of new codes and design features that support these values.

When public expectations are high, we tend to seek solutions from those individuals with enduring values, solid leadership skills, proven capabilities, and credibility. Each of these attributes reflects the essence of the fire service and its best leaders.

Above: The Metro Chiefs are a section of the International Association of Fire Chiefs and the National Fire Protection Association. They consist in cities around the world with career departments of over 400 members or jurisdiction populations of over 200,000. Each year they meet at a conference in the spring. This photo was taken at the April 13–18, 2002, conference in Honolulu, Hawaii. (Honolulu Fire Department)

Left: The bugle has long been a symbol of the rank of a fire officer in the United States. An early form of communication, the bugle was used as a megaphone to give orders to firefighters on the emergency scene. Today, modern two-way communications make that unnecessary. However, the bugle is a continuing symbol of rank: from one bugle signifying a lieutenant to five bugles for the rank of chief of department. (Collection of Ron Siarnicki)

On November 25, 2000, the Philadelphia Fire Department worked a four-alarm fire on Box 8199 at Emerald and York Streets. A firefighter from Engine 25 trains a "deck gun" on the fire amid many electric transmission and telephone lines. Such hazards are always a possibility at a fire scene and firefighters are aware of the steps necessary to minimize them—ranging from avoiding them if possible to having the current disconnected during operations. (Courtesy Fire Department Museum, Fireman's Hall)

A Brooklyn, New York, third alarm fire on Box 881 at Reid Avenue and Madison Street destroys a church. This fully involved, total structural loss was made all the more devastating by the fact that the church was on the eve of celebrating its 125th anniversary on November 10, 1984. (Steve Spak)

Opposite: A four-alarm fire broke out on Riefert Street in Pittsburgh, January of 1966. On the second alarm, members of Truck 24 moved up the ladder into the building to search for downed firefighters trapped by a flashover. All of the firefighters made it out safely. Several ground ladders can be seen up against the building for search, rescue, ventilation, and extinguishment purposes. The aerial ladder allows several firefighters to quickly enter the structure to do the urgent search after the flashover. (Pittsburgh Bureau of Fire)

The cities also provide accommodations for huge numbers of residents, in every type of dwelling from high-rise condos to tenements, row houses, rooming houses, nursing homes, or no houses at all. Fire departments have to be ready to respond to every type of dwelling and any situation that might occur.

Transportation is also a vital issue for big-city fire departments, because emergency apparatus has to respond within the maze of city streets and traffic. Everything in the city is connected to everything else by complex networks of streets, bridges, tunnels, freeways, railways, and subways. They have busy airports and seaports teeming with imports and exports. Eventually, it all comes together and the fire department has to be prepared to confront every conceivable emergency.

All of the nation's big cities are protected around the clock by career fire departments, or in some instances, combination staffed fire departments, including several that have more than 1,000 full-time employees. Most of them operate fleets of ambulances as well as fire apparatus and respond to many more emergency medical incidents than fires. The largest, the Fire Department of New York City, widely known as the FDNY, has more than 15,000 members to protect its eight million citizens. This one organization is almost three times as large as any other fire department in the U.S. and has more resources than the armies of several nations.

The FDNY is also the busiest fire department in the country, responding to nearly 1.4 million calls in 2001. The Los Angeles Fire Department was the next busiest, responding to 327,782 calls. According to *Firehouse Magazine*'s Annual Run Survey (2001) these were followed by: Washington, D.C. (303,085); Houston (283,144); Los Angeles County (260,271); Dallas (249,883); Chicago (215,200); Detroit (214,428); Miami-Dade (192,255); and Baltimore City (190,489). The busiest fire station in the U.S. was Station 2 in Columbus, Ohio, where the units responded to 20,528 calls. The busiest individual companies were San Francisco Engine 1 and Miami-Dade Squad 2.

Protectors of the Nation's Capital

Ken Cox, Sr.

On September 23, 1871, the Washington City Fire Department officially became the District of Columbia Fire Department. This transition from a volunteer service to an all-paid department followed trends around the nation, as cities, teeming with new immigrants and fledgling industries, grew.

During the observance of its 100th anniversary as an organized department, then D.C. Fire Chief Joseph Mattare wrote, "While the creation of the department was created by the stroke of an official's pen, the evolutionary process and the transition from groups of volunteer firefighters to a paid agency of government has spanned a far greater period of time. But throughout all the interval of change, one factor remained unchanged, and that was the desire of certain men to become the trustees for the community's fire safety."

The objectives of those first paid firefighters closely parallels the desires of today's career firefighters—safety, a decent wage, and the improvement of our working conditions.

Realizing the need to speak as one voice, in 1901 a small group of D.C. firefighters requested, and were granted, a charter of organization by the American Federation of Labor, becoming the first organized firefighters in the nation.

Although this group was short lived, it served long enough to set an example for other firefighters to follow. Between 1903 and 1916, as additional cities made the transition from volunteer to paid departments, more than seventeen departments became organized. After a long hiatus, on August 16, 1913, 289 District firefighters formed the Firemen's Association of the District of Columbia. The dues were $1.00 per year, and the salary of a back-step firefighter was $1,080 per annum. The following year they joined forces with the National Firemen's Association of the United States.

Working conditions during this period were deplorable. Firefighters were required to work twenty-one hours per day, with three hours allowed for meals. Every fifth day was given off provided no members of the station were on sick leave. In that case, no one received a day off until the firefighter on sick leave returned to duty.

During this timeframe the government of the District of Columbia consisted of three commissioners who were appointed by the President of the United States. The annual Fire Department budget, including firefighter pay raises and pension benefits came as a result of legislation passed by the House/Senate District of Columbia Sub-Committee on Appropriations, and would be signed into law by the President. In 1916, Congress authorized the salaries for the chief engineer at $3,675, captain at $1,610, lieutenant at $1,389, driver at $1,322, and private at $1,242 per year.

It was during the 1917 Convention of the AFL, that the delegates adopted the resolution authorizing the formation of an International Union of Firefighters. AFL president Samuel Gompers issued a call to all firemens' unions, then chartered by the AFL, to send delegates to a convention to be held on February 26, 1918, in Washington, D.C., for the purpose of "organizing an International Union of Firefighters." Attending the convention, hosted by the District of Columbia Firemen's Union, were thirty-six delegates representing twenty-four unions.

The first resolution adopted by the convention was introduced by D.C. delegate W. A. Smith and "resolved that this convention of delegates of City Firefighters Local Unions form an International Organization of these Unions properly coming under its jurisdictions, and that said International organization become affiliated to, and remain a part of, The American Federation of Labor."

ANNUAL BANQUET
CITY FIRE FIGHTERS ASSOCIATION
EBBITT HOUSE. JUNE, 4, 1924.

After considerable discussion of several names, the delegates were deadlocked between "International Association of Fire Fighters" and "International Brotherhood of Fire Fighters." The chairman pro-tem, Brother R. E. Odem, would break the tie by voting for the former. Local union numbers were assigned following the chronological order in which they became affiliated with the American Federation of Labor prior to the formation of the International Association of Fire Fighters.

As a result of the convention action, the new name would be City Fire Fighters Union, No. 36, International Association of Fire Fighters. As the time approached for the second convention, the number of departments becoming organized had grown to over 200 and included Canada. The International Association of Fire Fighters had truly become "international." Little did the thirty-six delegates who gathered together on February 26–28, 1918, realize the long-range effect this historic gathering would have on the American and Canadian Fire Service. Today, eighty-five years later, General President Harold Schaitberger presides over an organization of 255,000 members across the United States and Canada who proudly wear the logo of the International Association of Fire Fighters.

And what became of the City Fire Fighters Union, Local 36? After undergoing several name changes, the official name became Fire Fighters Association District of Columbia, Local No. 36, of The International Association of Fire Fighters, AFL-CIO.

Above: The Annual Banquet of the City Firefighters Association at the Ebbitt House, Washington, D.C., June 4, 1924. (Collection of Ken Cox Sr.)

Interior view of members of Engine Co. 26 and Engine Co. 35 responding at the Mason Street firehouse. Engine 35, known as "The Hog," was one of two self-propelled steam fire engines that served in Boston for over thirty-five years. Engine 26 has a conventional horse-drawn steamer. Located on a small street in downtown Boston, parallel to the Boston Common, the Mason Street firehouse also served as night quarters for the Chief of Department. (Boston Fire Department)

Above: Boston Ladder Co. 13 with its three-horse hitch is in full gallop responding to an alarm. The tillerman is barely visible seated beneath the aerial ladder. The officer, standing coatless, is Captain Patrick W. Lanegan, who was killed in the line of duty at a four-alarm fire in the Boston Elevated Railway property in 1910. (Boston Fire Department)

Transition from Volunteer to Career Fire Departments

Typically, every fire department in the United States has developed its own history, culture, and traditions. Many of the metro fire departments have documented their histories in books, which are full of interesting facts and stories, and several operate their own museums. They reveal that most of the metropolitan departments evolved from the independent volunteer fire companies that were organized to protect their local neighborhoods. As the cities grew and the demands became too great for the volunteers, they were forced to hire full-time firefighters to augment their capabilities.

In the late 1940s and early 1950s, Pitts-burgh purchased seven Reo Trucks called "Little Mo's." These were deluge wagons. Shown here with their drivers and crews along with fire department officials, the main purpose of these vehicles was to place a large amount of water on a fire in a short period of time. (Pittsburgh Bureau of Fire)

Today, there are hundreds of combination departments across the United States, some of them quite large, such as in Fairfax County, Virginia, or Prince George's County, Maryland, where the service is provided by a mixture of fully paid and volunteer members. These combination departments can provide the best of both worlds—they provide full-time protection are responsive to economic considerations, and allow citizens to still volunteer to keep their communities safe.

Lieutenant Martin J. Dunn with Pompier belted members of Drill Class pose for class picture at Bristol Street fire headquarters. In the foreground is an assortment of contemporary fire fighting appliances including, Pompier ladders, Lowry chucks, a life gun, life net, Siamese connection, distributor nozzle, spanner belts, and a variety of play pipes. (Boston Fire Department)

On June 19, 1959, Box 1754 was sounded for Delaware Avenue and Race Streets in Philadelphia. The fire went to the level of six alarms. Several pumpers are providing at least five hose streams into the front of the building as two firefighters are seen on the roof of the adjacent structure, having gotten there by way of the aerial ladder at that position. In the foreground, "SS-99" prepares to go into operation as other hose lines are laid around it to provide water supply for its 2,250-gallon-per-minute pump. (Courtesy Fire Department Museum, Fireman's Hall)

183

Fire Inspectors & Fire Investigators

William E. Barnard

Effective fire prevention programs include all activities that reduce the incidents of unwanted and uncontrolled fire while also ensuring a reasonable degree of fire and life safety for the occupants of structures should a fire occur. Two key elements of any effective fire prevention effort are fire inspections and fire investigations.

Fire inspectors and fire investigators are often referred to by the generic term "fire marshal." In reality, the duties and responsibilities performed by fire inspectors differ significantly from that of fire investigators. Each of these challenging jobs requires thorough knowledge, applicable fire safety laws, codes, regulations, and standards coupled with their own specific skill set and specialized training.

As an example, in addition to having a significant amount of technical knowledge, an effective fire inspector must be a good educator and salesperson. Fire inspectors provide appropriate assistance to building owners and occupants with the goal of achieving voluntary compliance with applicable fire safety laws, codes, regulations, and standards. Educated and informed building owners and occupants are much more likely to maintain fire safety levels and conditions between formal fire safety inspections. On the other hand, should building owners or managers not comply with the applicable fire safety laws and codes as directed, the fire inspector must be fully prepared to effectively address these issues, including testifying at hearings or court proceedings. Fire inspectors must be fair and impartial in the performance of their duties and the application of fire laws, codes, regulations, and standards.

A fire inspector's duties typically include the assessment of buildings, facilities, and fire safety systems to determine compliance with applicable fire safety laws, codes, regulations, and standards. During the inspection,

many experienced fire inspectors will take time to educate and inform building owners and occupants about fire and life safety matters, thereby increasing their awareness and understanding. Upon conclusion of the fire inspection, building, facility owners, or managers are informed of any code violations and recommended corrective actions to be taken. All fire code violations must be clearly documented and maintained as part of the building or facility record maintained by the department or agency conducting the inspection.

All identified fire code violations must be corrected in a timely manner. Fire code violations that are considered critical to the safety of the building occupants require immediate attention, such as locked or blocked exits in occupied theaters or restaurants, while others are given specific time frames for compliance and reinspection.

In some departments and agencies, fire inspectors are also responsible for performing plan reviews related to new construction, additions, renovations, and fire safety systems. All fire inspectors must be proficient at reading building and fire safety system plans. Fire inspectors conduct preconstruction meetings to establish appropriate inspection points and timetables, while answering questions and advising contractors of inspection expectations. It is much easier and less expensive to make changes to plans while still on paper, before the structure or fire safety system nears completion.

When unwanted or uncontrolled fires do occur, the local fire department responds and takes appropriate action to address the situation. If the origin and cause of the fire cannot be readily determined by the fire company officer, or it appears the fire may have been intentionally set, the services of a fire investigator are normally requested. In smaller departments and agencies, fire inspections and fire investigations

may be performed by the same individual or group of individuals. In larger departments and agencies, these duties and responsibilities are usually divided into separate divisions or bureaus.

At every fire, determining the fire origin and cause is important, regardless of whether the fire was intentionally set or deemed to be accidental in nature. Understanding fire origin and cause can have a significant impact on the community and public education efforts as well as identifying the need to change fire safety laws, codes, regulations, and standards.

Most fire investigators are experienced fire officials with significant specialized training and education. Formal training includes everything from reconstructing a fire scene to interviewing techniques. Every fire investigator needs to have some degree of knowledge about chemistry and physics, including a keen understanding of fire behavior. They also receive appropriate instruction in legal matters related to fire investigation, evidence collection, documentation, criminal prosecution, and a host of other issues.

Fire investigators approach each fire scene using a systematic approach, methodically eliminating each potential fire cause until a determination of the origin and cause of the fire can be identified. Today's fire investigators use a number of techniques and tools to assist them, including canine accelerant detection dogs and sophisticated laboratory testing. Fires determined to have been intentionally set are criminal acts, often

requiring many additional hours and sometimes weeks of criminal investigation in order to achieve a successful prosecution of the responsible person or persons.

Several years ago, fire chiefs gave fire little thought to personnel they assigned as fire inspectors or fire investigators. Far too often, injured firefighters or others unable to fight fires were placed in these positions. In recent years this situation has changed dramatically. The development of nationally recognized certification processes allows fire inspectors and fire investigators to receive appropriate recognition of their education, training, and experience.

Although the organization and operation of fire prevention programs vary significantly depending upon a number of factors, well-trained and experienced fire inspectors and fire investigators are essential elements of any effective fire prevention program. These fire safety professionals are dedicated to preventing fires and helping to ensure that reasonable life safety conditions are maintained in the communities they serve.

Top: A K-9 Accelerant Detection Team work at the scene of a house fire. (Maryland State Fire Marshal's Office)

Below: Fire investigators collect evidence samples for laboratory analysis. (Maryland State Fire Marshal's Office)

Conflagrations

It was the experience of large fires that drove most cities to rationalize fire resources and begin the transition to paid departments. Most of these cities were constructed with little regard for fire protection and provided the potential for huge fires to develop. Almost all of the major cities that developed prior to 1900 experienced at least one notable conflagration, with flames jumping from street to street and consuming dozens or hundreds of buildings. Some of these fires also killed scores of citizens. Lower Manhattan was devastated by a fire in 1835. Ten years later a major portion of Pittsburgh was consumed by flames. In 1849 a fire that originated on a ship in the Mississippi River burned the St. Louis waterfront. San Francisco experienced six conflagrations between 1849 and 1851 during the "Gold Rush" period of its history.

The infamous Great Chicago Fire of 1871 burned for three days, destroyed 18,000 buildings, and left more than 100,000 residents homeless. The next year Boston's downtown business district was ravaged by flames. Downtown Seattle burned in 1889, and in 1901 Jacksonville, Florida, suffered a similar fate. Three years later, in 1904, a large section of downtown Baltimore was consumed by a fire so massive that New York City firefighters and their horse-drawn apparatus were loaded onto rail cars and dispatched to assist the Baltimore Fire Department in gaining control. Two years later, following an earthquake, San Francisco was once again devastated by flames.

Reports issued by the United States Fire Administration and the National Fire Protection Association grimly remind us that urban America is still highly combustible and must be protected by well-trained and well-equipped firefighters, ready to respond immediately when a fire occurs. In spite of many advances, including tremendous improvements in fire suppression capability, modern building codes, and fire codes, the threat of urban conflagrations continues to this day. For example, in 1991, a wind-driven hillside brush fire swept into a residential area of Oakland, California, destroying more than 2,500 buildings and claiming twenty-five lives. America's cities are still vulnerable and firefighters are still an essential defense force to prevent their destruction.

In Bayonne, New Jersey, on November 23, 1987, FDNY's Marine Companies #9 and #1 responded for mutual aid to the Gordon tank farm complex across the Kill Van Kull. Marine Company #9 saved the day by protecting the exposed tanks. On the right side of the photo you can see the massive multiple streams aimed at the endangered storage tanks. (Steve Spak)

Opposite, bottom: As Boston firefighters make their approach to the base of a fire, a flashover occurs. Prior to this, there would have been a great deal of thick smoke coming across the ceiling level of this structure. Super heated by the fire below and the increasing temperatures inside, the smoke reaches its ignition point and "flashes" or suddenly ignites. This condition is one of the possibilities at any structure fire with heavy smoke and fire conditions. (John Cetrino/Code Red)

A Manhattan fourth alarm fire on Box 1789 occurred on July 28, 2002. This fire at 199 Dyckman Street in the Inwood section of Manhattan was a stubborn one. All totaled, six stores were destroyed by the time this fire was extinguished. (Steve Spak)

Major Fires Timeline

Paul Hashagen

Chicago, Illinois. October 8, 1871

October was unusually warm in tinder-dry Chicago. The entire Midwest was in the grips of a serious drought. On October 7, one of the worst fires in Chicago's history blazed through a Canal Street planing mill and burned four blocks of buildings including a large coal yard. Seventeen hours of fire duty had destroyed a ladder truck and taken its toll on the firefighters. Weary men trudged home, many unfit for further duty due to heat and smoke injuries. At about 9 p.m. on October 8, a fire started in the O'Leary barn on DeKoven Street. Sent to the wrong location, firemen lost precious time. Equipment broke down as the exhausted department struggled against a growing wall of flames. The fire tore a flaming path northeasterly across the city. Thirty hours of fire destroyed one-third of the city. The death toll was estimated at 300. In 1922, on the anniversary of the fire, the observance of National Fire Prevention Week began.

Great Chicago Fire. (© Bettmann/Corbis)

Brooklyn, New York. December 5, 1876

The stage play The Two Orphans *attracted more than 1,000 people per show to the Brooklyn Theater. As a large painted backdrop was being lowered into place it brushed against a boarder lamp and ignited. Within seconds the entire mass of scenery backstage was ablaze.*

Actors remained onstage imploring the crowd to exit calmly as flames raced across the ceilings behind them. The audience stampeded toward the main entrance, jamming doors closed. Flames claimed the lives of 296 persons; more than 100 could not be identified and were buried in a common grave in Greenwood Cemetery.

Shocked city officials immediately called for the inspection of all theaters and places of public assembly to ensure that adequate exits were provided.

Milwaukee, Wisconsin. January 9, 1883

Three hundred guests were checked into the Newhall Hotel when a fire in a ground floor elevator raced up the shaft and burst onto all six of the hotel's floors. Thick smoke and fire cut off both the elevators and the stairs, trapping the guests on the upper floors. Forced out onto the window ledges, people cried for help into the frigid night air. The fire department arrived and shot their extension ladder to its full reach only to fall short of many trapped above. Undaunted, two firemen laid a ladder across a twenty-foot span between buildings and began an amazing series of rescues over the ladder bridge. When the flames were quelled, seventy-one guests had perished in the fire. This fire would remain the worst American hotel fire for sixty-three years.

Chicago, Illinois. December 30, 1903

The Iroquois Theater was advertised as "absolutely fire-proof." Rushing to open for holiday audiences the hall's fire-fighting equipment was yet to be installed. A floodlight accidentally ignited a section of drapery fifteen feet above the rear of the stage. Comedian Eddie Foy rushed on stage attempting to keep control of the huge

Iroquois Theater Fire. (© Bettmann/Corbis)

notorious sweatshop. Six hundred girls were packed into tightly spaced rows of sewing machines and cutting tables. There were no sprinklers. Exit doors opened inward, and the only fire escape led to the roof. The only unlocked exit was narrowed to allow the workers to be searched as they left.

Triangle Shirtwaist Fire.
(© Underwood and Underwood/Corbis)

audience as flames shot over the stage. His eyebrows singed and his wig in flames, he was forced to dash out a back door.

Few exits were marked and others were locked or frozen shut. Bodies seven and eight deep blocked the balcony staircase trapping those behind them. Within fifteen minutes the flames were quelled. As the smoke cleared the horror was revealed—602 people were dead. The Iroquois Theater fire directly led to the adoption of the first national fire codes for places of public assembly.

Cleveland Ohio, March 8, 1908

A fire discovered in the cellar of the 2-1/2 story Collingwood Elementary School raced upstairs cutting off the exits and trapping 325 students and teachers before the alarm could be transmitted. With the only known exit from the structure blocked by flames, students panicked and trampled each other. Volunteer firemen arrived quickly but were completely overwhelmed by the volume of fire and the number of students inside the blazing school. Despite the valiant efforts of firemen, parents and citizens 173 students and two teachers perished.

New York City. March 25, 1911

The top floors of a ten-story loft known as the Asch Building housed the Triangle Shirtwaist Company, a

A fire broke out in a pile of scrap material and raced across the open floor area and roared upward. Pressed to the windows by the extreme smoke and heat dozens of women jumped to their deaths to avoid the flames. The fire claimed 145 victims. As a result of this fire legislation was passed nationwide requiring all doors to swing outward in places of public assembly.

Columbus, Ohio. April 21, 1930

The overcrowded Ohio State Penitentiary was under construction to provide more room for the 4,300 inmates. Just after evening meal, flames broke out in the work

Ohio State Penetentiary Fire.
(© Bettmann/Corbis)

area and spread to a six-story-high scaffold along the northwest side of the prison. Fanned by a steady breeze the flames leaped across the prison's upper tier. Fearing the danger of escaped prisoners more than the fire, the National Guard was called before the fire department. Some of the trapped men would be saved from the fire, but 320 men, trapped behind bars, perished as the flames and smoke closed in.

Ringling Brothers Fire. (© Bettmann/Corbis)

Boston, Massachusetts. November 28, 1942

A holiday weekend crowd, about twice the legal limit of 500, packed the tropically decorated Coconut Grove nightclub. The flammable decorations and numerous locked doors would result in chaos as flames flashed across the cloth-covered ceiling. Panicked patrons attempting to flee the growing fire broke the revolving front door. A mass of people rushed toward the remaining exits only to wedge themselves in. Flames then exploded across the upstairs ballroom and thick noxious smoke pressed to the floors. Firemen extinguishing an auto fire outside heard the screams in the club, but could not get through the blocked doors. Several persons jumped into firemen's arms from second floor windows, but in a matter of minutes 491 lives were taken by the smoke and flames. Hundreds were saved by prompt and expert medical care.

Cocoanut Grove Fire. (© Bettmann/Corbis)

Hartford, Connecticut. July 9, 1944

The huge 520-foot-long tent of the Ringling Brothers-Barnum and Bailey Circus was jammed packed with 7,000 people for a make-up second matinee. The circus train had arrived late the prior day, causing a cancelled performance. As the Flying Wallendas made their way up from the sawdust floor to the high wire above the band broke into Stars and Stripes Forever. *The climbing stopped, and the circus crew sprang into action, recognizing the traditional circus musical disaster warning.*

Clowns began to lead the audience to safety when a gust of wind drove a sheet of flame across the paraffin wax coated Big Top, the world's largest single piece of canvas. In seconds the audience was in a panic and the tent and rigging were a flaming death trap. In less than ten minutes, 168 people, one-third of them children, were dead. Within the decade the Big Top-era ended as the large circuses moved performances to auditorium type venues.

Chicago, Illinois. December 1, 1958

Shortly before the end of the day for the 1,250 students of Our Lady of the Angels School, a fire of incendiary origin at the base of the north wing stairs began to fill the building with smoke. Many children were safely led from the school while flames and heavy smoke raced up the stairs, trapping students and teachers in the classrooms above. Despite the quick thinking of teachers and the valiant efforts of firemen, three nuns and ninety-two students perished in third-floor classrooms.

Our Lady of the Angels School Fire
(© Bettmann/Corbis)

McCormack Place Fire, Chicago, January 16, 1967

On January 16, 1967, workers were busy inside the enormous concrete and steel McCormack Place lakefront convention hall complex in Chicago preparing for a huge show. At 2:05 a.m. workers noticed smoke behind

McCormack Place Fire. (© Bettmann/Corbis)

a large display. They saw a small fire and attempted to extinguish it until driven back by the extending flames. Six minutes later the fire department was notified by phone and responded with a full, first alarm assignment. Firefighters arrived at the gigantic structure and were faced with visible fire inside the central glass doors, and a twenty-five-m.p.h. wind from the lake and temperatures a frigid thirteen degrees. Firefighters immediately moved towards the main body of fire with a hand line. They were quickly surrounded by fire and were forced to retreat. A second interior attack was unsuccessful and outside operations were hampered by weather conditions and low water pressure. Five hundred firefighters manning ninety-seven fire apparatus and three fire boats battled the raging flames until it was declared "struck out" at 9:46 a.m. Only one fatality was reported in the $52-million loss.

Beverly Hills Supper Club Fire, Southgate, Kentucky. May 28 1977

A Memorial Day Weekend crowd of more than 2,400 filled the hilltop entertainment complex in the suburbs of Cincinnati when an electrical fire was discovered shortly before 9 p.m. Flames raced through the huge unprotected structure that contained dining areas, lounges, reception halls, and banquet halls. In the panic that followed, 165 lives were lost and hundreds were injured.

Most of the fatalities occurred in the large show lounge at the rear of the complex, where a capacity crowd was being entertained by nationally recognized performers. Without warning the entire room was suddenly enveloped in black smoke as the fire moved from the front to the rear of the building. Many of the survivors described the horror of crawling on the floor,

searching for an exit in complete darkness, feeling the heat of flames moving across the ceiling.

MGM Grand Fire, Las Vegas, Nevada. November 21, 1980

On the morning of November 21, 1980, wiring behind a wall in the MGM Grand's deli smoldered and burned undetected for hours. Just after 7 a.m. a flash fire erupted and roared through the casino. Inside the smoke-filled resort 5,000 tourists and employees scrambled for their lives as thick noxious smoke pushed through the air-circulation system trapping victims in hallways, rooms, and stairwells above. No fire alarm sounded. There were no sprinklers to check the fire's spread as the supposedly smoke-free stairwells and laundry chutes filled with

deadly smoke. Firefighters struggled to extinguish the flames and search the massive resort. When the smoke finally cleared eighty-four persons were dead. Three more victims succumbed in the hospital. The hotel's management paid $223 million in legal settlements.

MGM Grand Fire. (© Bettmann/Corbis)

Happy Land Social Club Fire, Bronx, New York. March 25, 1990

In the early morning hours of March 25, 1990, eighty-five people lost their lives in a matter of minutes when a deranged man ignited gasoline near the entrance to the second floor of a Bronx social club known as The Happy Land. First due units pushed in, quickly knocking down the fire and began venting the thick smoke from the building. Two victims were found, then two more, and two more. Stairs to a mezzanine were located and firefighters pressed up into the oppressive heat and smoke and located a sea of victims. Unsure of the situation, they quickly checked person after person only to realize they had at least fifty additional victims. In one 24-by-50-foot area dazed firefighters found sixty-nine unburned bodies,

Happyland Social Club Fire. (© Bettmann/Corbis)

all killed by smoke. The airports were called to supply the large number of body bags required. Firefighters reverently packaged each victim until removal operations were completed. Medical officers and counselors descended upon the firehouses to remind the firefighters that they didn't lose eighty-five people—someone killed them.

East Bay Hills Fire, Oakland-Berkeley, California. October 19–22, 1991

Twenty-five lives were lost and more than 3,000 structures were destroyed by a wildland-urban interface fire that threatened to consume the entire City of Oakland. The property loss exceeding one billion dollars was the

East Bay Hills Fire. (© George Hall/Corbis)

largest in United States history. It was a fire that demonstrates how natural forces are beyond the control of human intervention, completely overwhelming a combined force of more than 400 engine companies. Control was only achieved when the extreme wind conditions abated.

Large areas of California are known to be critically vulnerable to wildland-urban interface fires due to the development of urban areas in locations that are subject to extreme fire hazards created by climate, terrain, and natural fuels. Several major fires have occurred over the years, including one in 1970 that involved a large portion of the area burned in this incident. The warnings

of local fire officials had gone unheeded and measures that could have reduced the risks were not implemented.

The Station Fire, West Warwick, Rhode Island. February 20, 2003

100 people lost their lives in a popular West Warwick nightclub. The structure was an older, one-story building that had been renovated a number of times and recently passed a fire inspection. During the opening number of the band for the evening, a display of pyrotechnics was lit. After the pyrotechnics stopped burning, fire was still evident on the walls. Some patrons thought that it was still part of the show and continued cheering. However, others and a film crew that was on the scene at the time realized that this was not normal and encouraged those who could, to leave.

The fire spread rapidly up the walls and across the ceiling on what was believed to be a flammable sound insulating material. As people tried to leave en masse, the rapid spread of the fire and the crowding at the exits prevented many from getting out. Very soon the entire structure was aflame.

Many of the dead were caught by the smoke and heat and never got out of the building. Some others that did escape, later died of their injuries. As a result, various issues were being investigated. These included improper use of pyrotechnics, unsuitable insulation material, and local codes that might need to be strengthened.

The Station Fire. (© Reuters NewMedia Inc./Corbis)

Culture and Traditions

One of the most fascinating aspects of metropolitan fire departments is the unique character that can be clearly experienced within each organization. While all of the metro departments perform very similar tasks, each one has been shaped by local history, circumstances, and internal leaders to develop its own culture and traditions. Between departments, the fire apparatus is likely to be painted, marked, and configured differently and the firefighters often wear distinctive uniforms that are unique to their service. Local terminology that is completely oblique to the outsider is

Boston's first rescue company was established June 15, 1917, at the Fort Hill Square firehouse in downtown Boston. In this photo members of Rescue Co. 1, in front of a 1911 American LaFrance wagon, show off some of their equipment. Lieutenant Daniel Hurley, far right, displays an oxy-acetylene cutting torch, while other rescue equipment of the day is on display: screw jack and wedges, an E & J Pulmotor, life line, and Draeger smoke and gas masks. (Boston Fire Department)

Left: Photographed in 1888, Ladder Co. 15, a 1888 Babcock 85-foot aerial ladder with tiller, shown with three-horse hitch, and Engine Co. 33 have occupied this firehouse continuously for the last 114 years. The brownstone firehouse was designed by H. H. Richardson, architect of Trinity Church in Boston's Copley Square. Adjoining it and identical in design was Boston Police Department Station 16. During winter months, the three-horse hitch was supplemented by two additional horses to help maneuver the ladder truck through snow. (Boston Fire Department)

Pages 194–195: A Bronx, New York, third alarm fire on box 2797 burns at Mount Eden Avenue and Weeks Avenue. This fire occurred on July 30, 2000. Many pieces of apparatus have converged on the scene with master streams in operation including an aerial platform. (Steve Spak)

*District Chief Edwin Perkins and Captain
Stephen Ryder with crew of Engine Co. 38,
a self-propelled 1897 Amoskeag 1350 gpm
steamer. Boston firemen were permitted to
wear straw "skimmers" during the summer
months in 1905. Two brass play pipes
stand at attention behind the driver's seat
and a brass bell adorns the pressure dome.
(Boston Fire Department)*

used within different fire departments. Fire departments pride themselves
on establishing concepts and procedures that fit local circumstances.

In spite of the local traditions and customs, the largest metropolitan
departments are also very large organizations, with budgets to prove it.
The leaders of these organizations have to be as highly educated and
highly trained as any business executive. Running a big metro department
is very similar to running a large corporation—with all of the same
demands, stresses, rewards, and satisfactions.

In addition, each of these major fire departments usually influences
many smaller organizations in the surrounding area. If you see an engine
that is painted red with a black roof, you know that it comes from Chicago
or one of the fire departments that has been influenced by the Chicago Fire
Department. Just to be sure, you can check to see if it has a red light on
the left side of the cab and a green light on the right side. If you see firefighters wearing black coats with tails, black turnout pants with pleated
knees, and black leather (or simulated leather) helmets, they are probably
from FDNY and they responded to the alarm on a vehicle that is painted
red, with a white roof, and has white and gold reflective stripes. An all-red
tractor-drawn aerial ladder truck, closely followed by a pumper, is most
likely to be seen on the streets of Los Angeles, and if you see a group of
firefighters wearing helmets that are painted with equal red and white
segments you are almost definitely in San Francisco.

African-American Firefighters: On the Job

Chief Michael P. Bell

In our modern world, where history is occasionally forgotten, and where there is often so much misunderstanding and confusion regarding the participation of blacks in the fire service, it is good to step back and examine the obstacles and triumphs of African-American firefighters in the United States.

In dealing with the participation of blacks in the fire service, there is a belief that affirmative action was the catalyst that brought blacks into this career; but the history of blacks in the fire service actually began prior to the 1800s. In fact, one of the first black rescuers in America was an African-American woman by the name of Molly Williams. In the 1780s, she was a slave bound to a white New York City firefighter at the Oceanus Company No. 11. Although she was a slave at the time, Molly was famous locally for her rescue skills, and was noted for her courageous efforts during a particularly terrible blizzard.

During the early 1830s, a large number of black volunteer companies were organized. Most of these companies were formed in the eastern half of the United States. Black volunteer companies were located in such cities as New Orleans, Louisiana; Philadelphia, Pennsylvania; Savannah, Georgia; Columbia, South Carolina; Richmond, Virginia; and New Bedford, Massachusetts, to name a few.

The key elements of all of these departments were that, in each case, the volunteers were extremely well organized and dedicated to serving the public. Because of their selfless duty, they were also very popular within their communities. These volunteers performed the typical functions of fire suppression, and demonstrated tremendous community loyalty by providing public education to both adults and children at their stations.

Like firefighters everywhere, they would drill and perform their normal duties. When time permitted they further sharpened their skills through participation in volunteer competitive events, games, and trials designed to make them stronger and more agile firefighters. These volunteer events were very similar to the competitions that you can find today throughout the United States in firefighter "Iron Man" contests. These games would test their abilities to handle hose lines and firefighting tools within tremendously competitive time frames. Although we do not have much documentation regarding early firefighter competitions, we do know that they were generally segregated, even though skill levels were reported to be roughly equivalent. Photographs from the era, however, record that the crowds who attended these competitions were mixed, with blacks and whites sitting together enjoying the day.

During the mid- to late 1800s, there were also a number of volunteer companies that were fairly well-integrated with both black and white firefighters. It is interesting to note that the blacks within the fire service were well-known for their ability to handle horse-drawn fire engines—at a very high rate of speed. Typical of the fire service, they were more than aware that the faster they were able to get to the fire, the better chance they had of saving life and property. While blacks who served in the volunteer companies were not given the prestigious jobs, they still performed their jobs admirably and gained respect within their communities.

Considering the wide diversity that existed early in the fire service, you might wonder why there was ever a need to initiate affirmative action. I believe the answer lies in the destructive social policies that developed within fire departments during the Reconstruction period and into the twentieth century. Although all-black firefighting companies continued to form and to gain respect, the incidence of integrated departments closely followed the "color line" of general society.

Throughout the early decades of the twentieth century, the stature of fire departments within communities continued to increase, but so did white resistance to letting black "firemen" enjoy the same benefits. As urban fire departments began to shift from volunteer to paid firefighters, white firefighters further distanced themselves from their black counterparts. This was a disturbing development, one which was not based on either lack of intelligence or skills; skin color seemed to be the only determining factor.

Segregation hurt black communities in inestimable ways, but few have considered the impact it had on firefighting. In fact, a number of the original black volunteer companies disbanded because they were not funded like their white counterpart organizations. Without tools and equipment, and unable to compete financially, these black volunteer organizations eventually folded.

There are even examples of black firefighters gradually losing the professional courtesy normally extended among all firefighters. One powerful and particularly sad example involved two all-black fire companies, the

Vigilant Fire Company and the Enterprise Fire Company, of Columbia, South Carolina. On December 21, 1892, both fire companies successfully extinguished a fire in Columbia. After the fire, two African-American firefighters entered the building to investigate. Shortly after entering the building, they were ordered out by a white police officer. Because they refused to leave, they were arrested, fined, and then later released by the Mayor's Court. One of the firefighters, Don L. Simmons, president of the Vigilant Fire Company, was also a board member of the city's fire masters. The fire masters were an executive board, composed of both black and white firefighters, whose job it was to investigate and establish fire codes. Simons argued that as a member of the Board of Fire Masters he had the right to enter any building during the performance of his duties. In the end, the Vigilant Fire Company and the Enterprise Fire Company severed their ties to the city of Columbia. In a letter published in a local newspaper, they wrote: "Whereas the action of the police Wednesday and the decision of the Mayor's Court this morning indicated that the people of Columbia do not appreciate our efforts. Therefore, be it resolved that we the colored firemen, of the Vigilant and Enterprise Companies, do hereby withdraw our allegiance to the fire department of Columbia, S.C."

Participation of blacks in the fire service declined steadily throughout the first half of the 1900s. Segregation during this time caused a large reduction in the number of black firefighters within the United States. Once again, it had nothing to do with skill or ability, but the uncontrollable factor of race.

The influx of blacks back into the fire service started as a trickle in the early 1950s. The key component that allowed for the significant increase of blacks within the service was Title VII of the Civil Rights Act. Although enacted in 1964, the effects of Title VII were not apparent until the mid 1970s, when court cases started appearing which challenged the minority hiring practices of the fire services throughout the United States. Through successful litigation, city after city established aggressive hiring policies to increase the number of minorities within their fire service ranks.

As anyone who has been around the fire service for twenty or more years understands, this rapid integration was met with much resistance within the rank and file of the fire service. There was a perception that unqualified blacks were taking jobs away from qualified whites because of court-ordered hirings. Due to this perception, many of the blacks during this time worked within very hostile environments. The hazing of black firefighters was not limited to verbal confrontation; actions were designed to demoralize the black firefighter. For example, black firefighters were not allowed to use breathing apparatus that was also utilized by white firefighters; prohibitions were placed on co-sharing dining utensils; and sleeping facilities were segregated. If a black firefighter were to utilize the mattress and bed of a white firefighter, the mattress would often disappear or be destroyed.

Overt behaviors that jeopardized the safety of black firefighters and other minority groups greatly threatened their future in the fire service. So did quotas. Many times during this period of integration, there were quotas that determined the number of blacks that were assigned to any particular station, usually no more than one or two per company. Promotions during this period of time, from the 1940s into the early 1970s, were extremely limited for black firefighters, and black officers were usually promoted and put in all-black stations. Because black firefighters were not represented in the mainstream unions (even though they were required to be paying members) black firefighters formulated their own organization, the International Association of Black Professional Firefighters in 1970. This organization not only defended the rights of black firefighters, but often took on the defense of other poorly represented groups within the fire service.

If it had not been for the strength of these black firefighters, both morally and physically, the ranks of the fire service could still be very much segregated. Perhaps it would have made a difference to white firefighters if they had known that blacks and whites had served side-by-side in the early years of the fire service. This is why it is important for people to know their history.

Unfortunately, even today, there is an impression that blacks or minorities who enter the fire service are not always qualified to do the job. I believe that this kind of thinking, in the long run, will deter and undermine firefighting in diverse American communities across our country. The heart of firefighting is teamwork. If our "two" teams cannot become one, we will not be able to provide excellent services to our citizens. It is now up to us to determine the future success of our fire service.

The color of our skin has nothing to do with the quality of our work. Everything depends on being given a chance and an opportunity to succeed. Dedication, courage, and a desire to help are the universal qualities all firefighters must bring to the job. Loyalty, fairness, and trust are the qualities all firefighters are entitled to receive from the communities they serve.

I would like to thank Mr. Chuck Milligan and Reverend Ron Ballew, two men I have never met, but have to come to respect and admire for the information provided in this section. It is hoped that this brief section on the contributions of black firefighters in America will increase your own curiosity to find the truth. - MB

Opposite: To commemorate the opening of the paid fire department, a photo was taken of the Independent Number One in Columbia, South Carolina. (Courtesy of Columbia Fire Department Museum)

Above: Excelsior Hook and Ladder Company, Durham, North Carolina,: Bart Barber (standing, right) is foreman and holds the trumpet of his office under his left arm. (Collection of Chuck Milligan)

A Firechief's Daring Slide to Safety

From the Minneapolis Tribune, February 3, 1977: "A fireman and a paid daredevil. Ben Faus can't command headlines the way Evel Knievel can, Faus is a Minneapolis acting Deputy Fire Chief whose job is public safety; Knievel is a stunt man who is paid outlandish sums to do death-defying stunts, often on television.

Such, at times, is the irony in human affairs that this week Faus and Knievel were involved in separate happenings, which invite comparison. In Chicago, Knievel was injured in a practice motorcycle leap only hours before he was scheduled to jump over a pool full of sharks—a stunt that would have been shown live on television and would have earned him thousands of dollars. That same day in Minneapolis Faus jumped, out of necessity, from a burning building to save his life.

Knievel's motorcycle jump was badly bungled; instead of landing smoothly after clearing a ninety-foot pool, his machine skidded out of control and slammed into a retainer wall. In the crash Knievel suffered arm fractures that required surgery.

By contrast, spectators say that Faus's leap was a thing of beauty. Straddling a window sill in a burning building four stories above railroad tracks, Faus had to jump, without looking down, to a hand supported ladder ten feet below him and less than twenty inches wide. He hooked a leg onto a rung of the ladder to break his fall, then righted himself and slid down by his gloved hands. He could have been killed, but except for smoke inhalation and burns on his legs, he left the scene intact.

We think it fortunate that a public servant devoted to promoting safety for others should be able to rescue himself with such skill and courage. Unlike Knievel, acting Deputy Fire Chief Faus deserves praise from us all."

(Photos Minneapolis Fire Department)

As different as they may appear on the outside, the metropolitan fire departments share many of the same challenges and problems. Fighting fires is the most obvious commonality, but there are many more complicated issues. In almost every major city, the fire department is also the primary provider of emergency medical services and the demand for this service in urban areas greatly exceeds the number of fires and all other types of emergencies. Metro fire department firefighters are also the heavy rescue specialists, hazardous materials specialists, decontamination

specialists, and every other kind of specialist one can become. And then they have to be specialists of the unknown—prepared to react and respond to the unimaginable. Metropolitan regions are the places where anything can happen—above ground, below-ground, on the streets, in the water, or anywhere else.

As agencies of local government, these fire departments must compete with other agencies for limited funds. A large fire department is like any other type of large organization, dealing with issues of recruiting, staffing, training, promotions, and cultural diversity. A metro fire department has to maintain a collection of fire stations that are located throughout the city, keep a fleet of large vehicles in service, and figure out how to keep aging equipment working while planning a seamless introduction of new technology. The department has to figure out how to keep the firefighters as safe as possible while they perform a mission that is inherently dangerous. Health and safety programs within fire departments are no longer viewed as nice things to have; they are essential to keep members alive.

This response to a fifth alarm fire has resulted in the use of master stream devices and large attack lines. The firefighters in the foreground are using two large-diameter hose lines while the operator of the ladder truck behind them directs the water from the ladder pipe high over the fire. (George Hall/Code Red)

All of this must be done in an environment where consistently excellent performance is required to meet or exceed public expectations. The fact is that citizens have extremely high expectations for their firefighters—they trust firefighters with their lives and property. Firefighters have told people to call them first when they have an emergency, and firefighters strive daily to live up to that commitment. Within metropolitan environments, this covenant between citizens and the fire department requires an amazing level of organizational skill and integrity.

For the firefighters who work in metropolitan departments, the scale and intensity of what they face during every working shift is remarkable. They are asked to meet the toughest challenges, recover, and then do it again. They are expected to respond to an array of fires and other emergencies that may become legendary. Their work is consistently difficult, dangerous, and challenging. But, for the men and women who comprise the firefighting forces in American cities, difficult, dangerous, and challenging are all in a day's work. They are asked to rise to the occasion, to never say no, to search, to rescue, and to save lives in extraordinarily hazardous and perilous environments.

A large wood-framed structure is fully involved with flame. Dwarfed by the engulfed building, the firefighter stands his ground and waits for water from the pumper in order to make his attack. (John Cetrino/Code Red)

201

Industrial Firefighters

David White

"Five Injured in Fire at Oil Refinery."
"Witnesses Describe Blaze at Factory."
"Contaminants Feared Released."

Headlines such as these about industrial fires and emergencies always stir concern for both the public and the managers of industrial facilities. Across the United States, materials are processed in immense quantities that, in raw form, are toxic, flammable, and potentially explosive. Given the vast scale and inherent risks associated with American industrial production, the incidence of death and injury is remarkably low. And even though zero is the only casualty figure acceptable to industry experts, as one prominent industrial firefighter often remarks, "These folks aren't making cake batter."

Of the approximately 60,000 industrial facilities operating in the United States, at least 18,000 have their own fire brigades or emergency response teams. Industrial emergencies include firefighting, hazardous material response, and rescuing trapped or injured employees. The amount of fire protection provided is a management decision based on the level of risk the company is willing to accept. Some facilities have full-fledged fire departments complete with station houses and heavy apparatus. Others provide very elemental equipment and training. How the brigade is staffed also varies from plant to plant. In some places, firefighters are hired as full-time employees. Others contract with outside companies. Some make it mandatory that employees hired for certain jobs also train with the fire brigade to provide support in an emergency. Still other facilities back employee efforts to maintain volunteer plant brigades, much like small-town volunteer fire departments.

Industry became proactive on the issue of fire and its associated hazards early in American history. Textile mills, for instance, inherently carried a heavy fuel load. Devastating fires were common throughout early America,. In the mid-1800s, in fact, intuitive efforts were made to deal with the fire problem in factories. In textile mills, perforated pipes installed above the heads of the workers were the first prototype for industrial sprinkler systems.

However, these systems were not automatic, and these early efforts were as destructive as they were effective. Barrels filled with water and waterproofed dynamite were suspended from the roof of the factory. Fuses leading to the dynamite dangled beneath the barrels. As the theory goes, any fire on the factory floor would ignite the fuse and detonate the explosives. Water from the burst barrel would rain down and douse the fire. But what tended to happen was that the blast would also knock out the factory windows, giving the spreading fire a dangerous supply of oxygen to draw upon. Something packing a little less punch was needed to activate a steady stream of water from above.

Of all people, a piano maker from Connecticut came up with a better solution. Henry S. Parmalee, owner of a New Haven piano factory, designed the first practical automatic sprinkler head in 1775. An improvement on early automatic sprinkler systems, the Parmalee design remains very similar to what is used today. A pipe pressurized with water is blocked with a sprinkler head, the only release for the water. A fusible link keeps that sprinkler head closed until it is needed. In case of fire, the fusible link melts and the sprinkler head releases the water.

Throughout their 150-year history, sprinkler systems remain the greatest lifesaving measure for protecting property and safeguarding life. Although he is little remembered, Henry S. Parmalee is an important figure in the history of fire safety in the U.S.

As we shall see in subsequent examples, the invention of a life-saving technique does not always assure its use. Sprinklers provide a good example. When it was discovered that eight-inch diameter pipe would douse fires more effectively than the six-inch system widely used

Clockwise from left: Even in the early days of Underwriters Laboratories a wide variety of fire protection sprinklers were on the market and required testing. A researcher tests fire extinguishers. This historic photo shows an engine fire test being conducted by Underwriters Laboratories. Two researchers test a fire extinguisher. (All photos courtesy of Underwriters Laboratory)

with the Parmalee heads, it was assumed that the larger pipe would become the industry standard. But eight-inch pipe was determined to be cost ineffective. Six-inch pipe was determined to be good enough given the fact that factory and industrial fires were relatively infrequent. This economy of scale also affected the chemical and petrochemical businesses, which would also fall victim to short-range planning.

Petroleum refineries were the setting for tremendous industrial fires in the late nineteenth and early twentieth centuries. In those early days of refining, it was discovered that the best way to protect against fire spreading through the entire complex was to space the individual processing units and storage tanks apart. Since there was no effective way to extinguish a burning flammable liquid storage tank, the refining industries learned from gunpowder manufacturers to spread their assets across many acres. However, the vast distances needed to accommodate this strategy became very expensive, and over time, tanks and process units were brought closer together on less and less land.

Economics of a crueler kind, and just plain irresponsibility, were to blame for the worst industrial catastrophe of the early 1900s. On March 25, 1911, in New York City, fire swept through the Triangle Shirtwaist Company, killing 145 female employees. The garment factory was located on the top three floors of a ten-story "fireproof"

building. There was no sprinkler system, an obvious danger considering the tremendous fire load of fabric and finished garments that were present. The tallest ladders available to the fire department of New York were too short to reach the victims. Adequate fire exits might have saved many lives, but many were not marked, and those that were had been locked by the employer to keep the women from leaving work early.

Throughout the twentieth century, industrial fires and explosions shook their communities and focused our nation's attention on the potential hazards. Some of these events are famous and some are relatively forgotten. All were important to the victims and survivors; some inspired reforms. Some of the worst included:

1944 — Cleveland, Ohio: Oct. 20, 1944. A ruptured storage tank at the local gas works spilled 6,000 cubic meters of liquefied natural gas into the streets and storm drains. The resulting flames destroyed seventy-nine homes, eight retail stores, and two factories; 133 people died. Regulations requiring the frequent inspection of industrial piping resulted from the disaster.

1953 — Livonia, Michigan: A 1,500,000-square-foot automatic transmission plant burned to the ground. Fumes from heated tar in the plant's composition roof spread the flames through the entire length of the building in twenty minutes. Three plant brigade firefighters died. In 1953 dollars, the loss totaled $80 million. The fire served as a wake-up call regarding the necessity of fire walls and sprinklers.

1955 — Whiting, Indiana: An explosion at a 1,600-acre Indiana refinery tore apart a 252-foot-tall process unit, flinging molten chunks of metal across a quarter-mile radius. Flames spread through a nearby tank farm, destroying sixty-seven tanks over the next two days. Numerous storage tank boilovers were reported.

1956 — Amarillo, Texas: A 500,000-gallon sphere-shaped storage tank containing pentane and hexane caught fire and exploded at a refinery near Amarillo, Texas, killing nineteen workers. All but two of those killed were firefighters battling the blaze.

1975 — New York, New York: Seven hundred firefighters labored sixteen hours to extinguish the fire inside the city's one-block-long, eleven-stories-tall telephone exchange building. A heavy fire load of PVC coated wiring and cables produced toxic fumes. More than 60 percent of firefighters responding to later surveys reported persistent medical problems as a result.

1982 — Falls Township, Pennsylvania: In Pennsylvania, a twenty-seven-acre distribution center was destroyed by a fire that flashed to life when a forklift punctured a pallet of aerosol cans. The flames ignited flammable propellant in the cans and sent them rocketing across the warehouse, spreading the fire too quickly for the sprinkler system to handle. The fire still stands as the largest involving a warehouse in American history.

1984 — Romeoville, Indiana: A rupture in a mono-ethanolamine absorber column resulted in a $127 million fire. Ten refinery firefighters and seven other employees died when a pressure vessel failed and released a vapor cloud that ignited.

1989 — Houston, Texas: A vapor cloud release at a chemical refinery ignited into a monster fireball, triggering a continuing series of explosions that consumed all process units within a 700-foot area. Twenty-three workers were killed and more than 185 injured.

1989 — Baton Rouge, Louisiana: A Christmas eve fire spread through sixteen storage tanks at a petrochemical refinery. Hampering efforts to bring the fire under control were abnormal sub-freezing temperatures that had turned the water supply in aboveground mains to ice.

Top: On Oct. 23, 1989, industrial fire consultant and publisher David White played a key role in extinguishing the fire after a massive explosion at a chemical plant complex in Pasadena, Texas, near Houston. White was conducting safety training at a neighboring plant when the blast occurred. (David White)

Above: A refinery in Baton Rouge, Louisiana, on Dec. 24, 1989, involved sixteen storage tanks filled with heating oil, diesel, and lube oil, as well as two process units, two buildings, 151 rail cars, and seventeen pipelines. Twelve acres were covered by ground spills. (David White)

Disasters reported in other countries would also have a direct impact on industrial fire protection in the U.S. These include:

1983 — Milford Haven, United Kingdom: In South Wales, U.K., a 250-foot-diameter crude oil tank caught fire. Twelve and a half hours later radiant heat from the surface reached a layer of water beneath the crude oil, triggering a boilover that spread flames over a four-acre area. Only minor injuries were reported.

1984 — Mexico City, Mexico: Flames rising from an LPG storage facility brought Mexico City residents living nearby out of their homes to watch. A tremendous fireball erupted, engulfing the homes on both sides of the surrounding valley in flames. At least 500 people died.

1985 — Caracas, Venezuela: A boilover in a burning fuel storage tank killed 135 people, including seventy firefighters.

One industrial incident, however, dwarfs all of these in its magnitude. On April 16, 1947, two freighters loaded with ammonium nitrate fertilizer were moored at the docks in Texas City, Texas. Fire broke out in the cargo hold of one ship, the SS Grandcamp, *producing billowing pink smoke. Municipal firefighters responded and were at work fighting the blaze when, at 9:12 a.m., the freighter exploded with a force that knocked people to the ground ten miles away. Shrapnel and blast overpressure scythed through dock workers and firefighters. All twenty-seven volunteer firefighters who responded were officially listed as missing after the blast, since no trace of them was ever found. Across the dock, 145 employees of Monsanto Chemical Company were either killed outright or burned to death as tanks of butadiene and styrene burst into flame. Many who survived the fire drowned when a receding wall of water forced inland by the blast carried them out to sea. Fifteen hours after the first blast set it ablaze, the second freighter exploded with equal force. The final death toll stood at 581, with another 3,500 injured. Property loses reached an estimated $70 million, or almost $700 million in today's dollars.*

These fires, and many countless others, did inspire reform. To protect key assets and maintain the goodwill of employees and the surrounding communities, industrial complexes such as plants and refineries must make a major commitment to fire protection.

Industrial firefighting, like the rest of the fire service, evolved from simple and basic technology. The first motorized pumpers replaced the old horse-drawn vehicles. Then came diesel engines and large-capacity pumps. As little as fifteen years ago, the normal-sized pump found on an industrial fire truck was only 1,000 gallons per minute. As for hose, in general, 2 1/2-inch outlets fed by 6- to 8-inch fire mains were standard.

To catch up, many plants today are enlarging their fire mains to 10 to 24 inches and installing large-capacity fire water manifolds that flow from 3,000 to 10,000 gallons per minute each. With larger mains and new fixed fire pumps, plants can avail themselves of such alternative water supplies as ship channels, waste water ponds, city fire hydrants, and fire boats. Today, hose has increased from 2 1/2 inches to 5 inches and bigger. And while municipal fire trucks are becoming smaller and more specialized, multipurpose industrial fire trucks are growing larger and more expensive. Standard equipment on industrial fire trucks are 2,000-gallon foam tanks, 500-gallon water tanks, 3,000-gallons-per-minute pump systems with preconnects, plenty of 5- and 6-inch hose, and even a full compliment of EMS equipment. The price tag is $500,000 and up.

At 9:12 a.m. on April 16, 1947, the S.S. *Grandcamp* exploded with tremendous force, knocking people to the ground ten miles away in Galveston, rattling windows in Houston, and registering on a seismograph in Denver. (Moore Library in Texas City, Texas)

One of the most important innovations emanating from the aforementioned landmark disasters came in the development of firefighting foam. The use of foam was a tremendous boon for industrial firefighters, and has migrated to other settings, such as airport firefighting. When foam is applied to flames, water is slowly released as it breaks down. This water increases in temperature, absorbing heat as it turns to steam. This robs the fire of energy and extinguishes it. Since the water is released at a slower rate than directly applying it to the fire, none of it is lost as runoff.

As a firefighting agent, foam did not become effective until the advent of protein foam in the 1940s, created from hoof and horn meal, chicken feathers, or fish meal. Bubbles made from protein foams are highly stable and resistant to heat. In a hydrocarbon fire at a petroleum refinery, protein bubbles applied to the surface resists absorption by the fuel. Since vapors cannot reach the heat to ignite, the fire is smothered. Although the application of foam was not yet foolproof, it was a giant step forward in industrial fire fighting.

In the 1960s, the National Foam Company of Lionville, Pennsylvania, invented fluoroprotein foam. By adding fluorinated surfactant to protein foam, the result was a stronger bubble even more resistant to hydrocarbon breakdown. The next hurdle was speed. It took time to build the mass of bubbles before it could be pushed through the burning hydrocarbon surface. In an emergency operation such as aircraft crash rescue, time is critically short.

Aqueous Film Forming Foam (AFFF), containing flourinated synthetic chemicals instead of protein-based materials, revolutionized aircraft crash rescue. In the 1960s, the U.S. Navy wanted a foam capable of knocking down fire fast enough to save burning aircraft and the occupants inside. 3M Corporation came up with the first of its foams, dubbed AFFF. Rather than large bubbles typical of protein foams, this low-expansion foam produced a thin film from the bubbles. Whereas aircraft fires in the past had usually meant loss of life and destruction of the airplane, AFFF could be used to extinguish the fire and give the passengers inside enough time to escape. Unlike protein or mechanical foams, which had to be aspirated by the device used to apply it, AFFF could be used through standard fog nozzles. Also, there were no shelf life problems as with protein foam.

Today, one crash truck equipped with AFFF arriving at an aircraft disaster is usually capable of bringing the entire situation under control. Likewise, that same technology was applied to large-volume flammable liquid fires. Foam could now be subsurface injected into large-diameter storage tanks and survive to rise to the surface. Also, foam could be projected by ground-based manual application such as large-volume nozzles.

Even with good foam, flammable liquids are inherently difficult to extinguish. Water alone provides for good cooling and reach, but offers no vapor suppression. Foam provides all three, but, like water, is limited to flat, two-dimensional fires such as fuel spills. Chemicals such as dry powder often must be used to extinguish fires involving pressurized gases such as propane. In 1991, Les Williams and his son, Dwight, two of the best-known names in industrial firefighting, devised a way to combine water, foam, and dry powder.

The U.S. Navy had tried a similar approach with its portable twin-agent units in the 1960s and 1970s by using separate nozzles—one for foam and water, and one for dry chemical. This worked pretty well, but a more efficient marriage was made possible with the Williams' Hydro-Chem™ technology. Already marketing a foam-water combination known as Hydro-Foam™, they added a port in the center of the nozzle through which dry chemical could be discharged. To clearly identify the white dry chemical from the water and foam, all of which blends into the same color in the fire-fighting stream, Williams Fire & Hazard Control developed a special formulation of Ansul's Purple K dry chemical known as PKW. The dry chemical is an unmistakable bright purple and easier to track as it is used against the fire. Hydro-Chem made it possible to project dry chemical as far as the water/foam stream. The Hydro-Chem nozzle is not only effective against storage tank fires but against fires on towers and vessels up to 10 to 150 feet high. It can also be mounted on an aerial ladder and shot as high as 200 feet and higher.

Another important innovation attributed to the Williams family was the volume of water and foam it could

The photo shows the largest portable water/foam monitor in the world, capable of 15,000 gallons per minute. The monitor is manufactured by Williams Fire & Hazard Control. This monitor is owned by Exxon and Marathon Oil companies. (David White)

introduce at a fire. For the average municipal firefighter, a nozzle producing 500 gallons per minute is considered large. The Williams line of heavy-caliber firefighting nozzles range from 2,000 gpm to 15,000 gpm. In an October 1996 demonstration, an array of Williams nozzles produced an arc of 29,567 gallons per minute covering a distance of nearly 400 feet. To supply the volume these giant nozzles require, many plants and refineries have invested in bigger mains and ready access to water storage. The American Petroleum Institute recommends a firefighting capacity of 8,000–10,000 gallons per minute be available to apply within the first ten minutes of a fire.

Given all of the tremendous steps forward in industrial firefighting, coupled with federal oversight and regulations, major fires in plants and refineries have been greatly reduced. But, such occurrences are still a part of the plant and factory life, as evidenced by the Houston and Baton Rouge refinery fires of 1989, which stand as the largest refinery fire and the biggest chemical plant explosion on record, respectively. The 1990s saw an increased reliance on fixed systems (such as detectors and sprinklers) to provide fire protection, thus eliminating many industrial firefighting positions. This may be short-sighted, for although the incidence of fires has been reduced, the potential for major fires and explosions continues. Trained firefighters

remain an important element in industrial fire protection.

Texas A&M University, the University of Nevada, Reno, and other educational institutes have become closely identified with industrial fire training. These schools offer full-size simulations of industrial facilities where live fire exercises can be conducted.

Most recently, Tropical Storm Allison, in July 2001, set the stage for one of the seminal events in modern industrial fire fighting—the successful extinguishment of a burning jumbo storage tank with substantial product saved. Dwight Williams, of Williams Fire & Hazard Control, was contracted to extinguish a 270-foot-diameter storage tank in Norco, Louisiana, containing about 10 million gallons of burning gasoline. Heavy rains sank the floating roof on the storage tank, making the exposed contents vulnerable to a lightning strike. Disregarding the accepted "surround and drown" philosophy of indiscriminately throwing as much water and foam as possible into the tank, Williams concentrated a massive foam attack on a single spot, gaining a foothold and expanding extinguishment from there. This is known as "The Footprint," a methodology patented by Williams F&HC.

Applying the "Footprint" methodology in Norco, Williams F&HC saved half the contents in the jumbo storage tank. The successful extinguishment of that size tank ranks as the biggest in history, nearly 100 feet bigger in diameter than any other such containment. For years to come the Norco storage tank fire will be written about as an enormous breakthrough, an event that proved all the theories and set a new standard for industrial fire fighting.

Industrial firefighters should not be overlooked in our recent national conversation on firefighting. They have performed heroically for over 300 years, as this country grew through the Industrial Revolution into the world's greatest producer nation. What we produce, sometimes, is very dangerous to those who have chosen to work in high-risk industrial environments. Through the provision of safer environments and innovative technology, industrial firefighters not only protect workers in these factories and plants, they also contribute greatly to our continuing positive economic future.

AMERICA'S
Federal and
Military
Firefighters

AMERICA'S
Federal and
Military
Firefighters

William D. Killen

Often overlooked in discussions of firefighting in the United States, federal and military firefighters provide fire protection to several thousand domestic facilities and installations in all fifty states and more than twenty foreign countries. In addition to fire suppression, federal firefighters also provide emergency medical treatment, respond to hazardous materials situations, and inspect our military bases and other federal facilities. They were among the first rescuers on the scene when the Alfred P. Murrah Federal Building in Oklahoma City was bombed on April 19, 1995, and when the Pentagon was attacked on September 11, 2001.

Products and services of U.S. Department of Defense (DOD) fire departments include fire prevention instruction, public fire education, structural fire suppression, aircraft rescue firefighting, hazardous materials emergency response, wildland firefighting, and rescue operations. They also respond to both natural and man-made disasters, including threats of terrorism and weapons of mass destruction. Rescue operations involve confined-space rescue in structures, ships, aircraft, and trench collapse. High-angle and water-rescue operations are performed in high-rise buildings, towers, mountainous terrain, rivers, lakes, and during floods.

The history of the federal and military fire services can be traced to the founding of the United States in 1776. Although fire protection was a long-standing duty within every colonial settlement, the earliest specifically trained firefighters in the United States were military personnel. With a new country came new federal facilities and forts that required fire protection. These early installations were typically protected by volunteer bucket brigades consisting of soldiers, sailors, and, in some cases, civilians. In the more densely populated areas, the bucket brigades also

Above: *A C-130 Hercules from Colorado's 302nd Airlift Wing releases Phoscheck, a chemical fire retardant, on one of many firefighting missions. (U.S. Department of Defense)*

Pages 208–209: *On board the ammunition ship USNS* Kilauea *(T-AE 26), a firefighting team practices hose handling skills during a general quarters drill in the Persian Gulf in support of the Southwest Asia buildup during Operation Enduring Freedom. (U.S. Navy)*

Opposite: *A tracked firefighting vehicle stands by as a 7th Military Airlift Squadron C-141B Starlifter aircraft is unloaded at McMurdo Station, Antarctica. (U.S. Air Force)*

Above: *A left-side view of an Air Force O-11A aircraft firefighting truck. Aircraft firefighting apparatus are able to dispense firefighting foam from the turret mounted on the top of the cab. This can be done while stationary or while in motion. Often a runway will receive a coating of foam before an aircraft in trouble lands to reduce friction and sparks. (U.S. Air Force)*

The Seal of the Fire and Emergency Services of the United States Department of Defense. (From the collection of William D. Killen)

provided fire suppression for commercial and private property. Federal facilities are protected by federal fire departments who are often assisted by local departments through mutual aid agreements.

Today, federal agencies operate and maintain career fire departments to protect federal facilities throughout the United States and in foreign countries around the world. These agencies include the Departments of Agriculture, Commerce, Defense, Energy, Interior, State, Transportation, and the Veterans Administration. In addition to cabinet level departments, four independent agencies maintain fire departments. These include the Federal Emergency Management Agency (FEMA), National Aeronautics and Space Administration (NASA), National Institutes of Health (NIH), and the National Institute of Standards and Technology (NIST). Prior to Congress establishing "home rule" for the city of Washington, D.C., in 1973, the District of Columbia Fire Department was a federal fire department.

Over 25,000 men and women serve in the federal and military fire service, protecting government office buildings, industrial plants, hospitals, schools, nuclear power plants, dams, bridges, aircraft, ships, vehicles, forests, museums, and the national parks system, whose combined value approaches many trillions of dollars. The majority of federal firefighters work for the Department of Defense (DOD), protecting the nation's military installations; the Department of Veterans Affairs (VA), protecting its hospital complexes; and the Department of Agriculture (DOA), whose Forest Service employs both full-time and seasonal firefighters throughout the wildland regions of the United States.

The DOD includes the Army, Navy, Marine Corps, Air Force, and several defense agencies, with over 16,000 military, civil service, contractor, and foreign national firefighters. There are approximately 450 DOD fire departments protecting in excess of 1,000 DOD installations in the United States and around the world. These installations alone are valued at more than $1 trillion dollars. The history of the military fire service is long and respected within the fire service, although remarkably little of its history has been recorded for posterity.

We do know that after the Revolutionary War, Army forts and Navy shipyards employed bucket brigades manned by soldiers, sailors, and civilians for fire suppression. These firefighters fought fires by passing buckets of water man to man, from the source of water to the conflagration. The development of the hand-tub, or hand engine, increased firefighting capabilities at Army and Navy installations, and elsewhere throughout the new nation. A hand tub was a tub on wheels with a single-action cylinder with a copper air chamber in front of the cylinder, drafting from stern and discharging water from the front of the engine. These hand tub fire engines could draft and discharge water through hoses and nozzles.

William C. Hunneman, an apprentice under Paul Revere, purchased patents on the hand engine and began the manufacture of Hunneman Fire Engines in Massachusetts, delivering his first engine in 1792. The Hunneman Company manufactured several engines for the Army and Navy during the early years of the nineteenth century. Hunneman delivered Engine #5 to Fort Independence in Boston Harbor on January 1, 1805, and in 1818, Engine #56 was delivered to the U.S. Military Academy

Marines of the 5th Marine Regiment from Camp Pendleton, California, stand in formation while awaiting assignment to one of several firefighting efforts within Yellowstone National Park. (U.S. Department of Defense)

Left and above: *Hunneman Engine #168 is the oldest known surviving fire engine used by the Navy and is probably the oldest known surviving fire engine to serve the Federal Military fire service. (From the collection of William D. Killen)*

A fireman in St. Paul, Minnesota, sits on the front of his fire engine, knitting a sock for a soldier during World War I in 1917. His skill level is being monitored by the woman on the left. (© Minnesota Historical Society/Corbis)

at West Point. Hunneman's company also delivered four engines to the District of Columbia between 1817 and 1819.

During the opening years of the nineteenth century, fire suppression at Navy shipyards also consisted of bucket brigades manned by shipyard workers and sailors. Bucket brigades were the first line of defense for firefighting on ships as well. On October 28, 1812, Hunneman Engine #28, *The United States*, was assigned to USS *United States*, a 44-gun Frigate built in Philadelphia in 1797. From December 1812, through October, 1814, Hunneman built and delivered Engine #31 *The Chesapeake* for USS *Chesapeake*, Engine #35, *The Independence*, for USS *Independence*, and Engine #37 *The Washington*, for USS *Washington*. The USS *Independence* and USS *Washington* were both 74-gun ships built in Charlestown, Massachusetts, and Portsmouth, New Hampshire. Hunneman #168, delivered to the Charlestown Navy Yard, Boston, Massachusetts, on March 7, 1836, for $700.00, and later sold to Boothbay Harbor, Maine, is on display at the Railroad Museum, Boothbay Harbor. In 1849, Hunneman Engine #361, *Sally Blythe*, was delivered to the U.S. Naval Academy in Annapolis, Maryland.

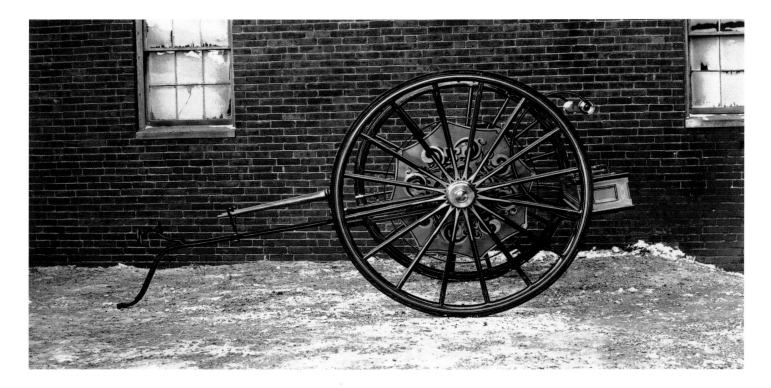

Historically, soldiers, sailors, and Marines performed firefighting duties at Army forts, Navy shipyards, and aboard ships until the start of the Civil War. The cornerstone of the federal fire service was laid in 1862, when Secretary of War Edwin M. Stanton issued an executive order to Mayor George Opdyke, mayor of New York City, to provide fire protection assistance on behalf of the Federal (Union) Army.

New York's assistant chief fire engineer, John Baulch, was tasked to fulfill the secretary's order. Baulch responded amazingly fast, and within six hours departed for Fort Monroe, Virginia, with two of New York City's most powerful engines, Mohawk Engine No. 16 and Peterson Engine No. 31, along with four experienced firefighters. When he arrived at Fort Monroe, a considerable task was laid out before Baulch and his firefighters. He was charged with setting up the foundation that we recognize today as the federal fire service. The first thing he did was to organize several companies from the ranks of the volunteer regiments already stationed at Monroe. In fact, many of the soldier-firemen stationed there already knew of Baulch, since they served under him New York prior to military service. These hearty veterans of previous fire duty were divided up between the engine and hose carriage companies. Baulch was further assigned the duty of developing written policies that would eventually become the foundation of federal fire service procedures for years to come.

Baulch was appointed as the chief engineer of the fire department of the southern division of the federal Army. He was the equivalent of a two-star general in the overall supervision of the fire department. Since he realized that a large operation in the theatre of war was about to take place, he requested apparatus from Philadelphia, Baltimore, and other major cities. Soon Fort Monroe was established as the headquarters of the Army's firefighting detachments.

A typical firefighting battalion consisted of two engine companies, two hose companies, a supply company, sometimes a light ladder or

service truck, and a headquarters/administrative company. Bringing up the rear of the federal Army's southern division, the fire department's mission was to follow the main military body and take charge of all the fire apparatus in southern towns and cities. When the federal Army occupied southern towns, Baulch reorganized as many of the southern fire companies as he could utilizing his forward-thinking policies.

Baulch saw that repairs were made to southern fire apparatus and critical items such as extra nozzles, axes, pike poles, ladders, and hose

The Union Army's hose companies used hand-drawn hose carriages similar to this 1875 Ryan Brothers hose carriage. This was the third of three hose carriages delivered to the U.S. Naval Academy. (From the collection of William D. Killen)

Above: *The Navy Yard in Portsmouth, New Hampshire, Fire Department's old hose wagon and Dupont Fire Steam Engine with Marine Corps crews in front of Old Quarters, Building No. 64, November 1, 1933. (From the collection of William D. Killen)*

were supplied as needed to bolster items lost or damaged in the war effort. Baulch received many complimentary letters from the southern fire companies and their governing bodies, recognizing the fact the federal firefighters did something positive for their southern counterparts in the midst of the war.

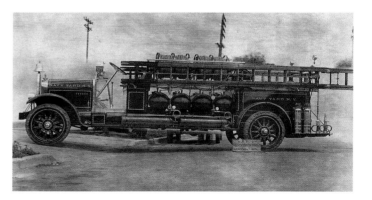

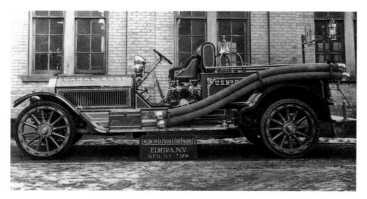

Documented written history of the federal fire service between the end of the Civil War and World War II is limited, and consists mostly of photographs. We do know that trends of modernization of military fire apparatus began during World War I, when motorized fire engines and ladder trucks were placed in service. Tradition was as strong in the military fire service as on the civilian side—horse-drawn fire apparatus remained in service at military installations well into the 1930s.

The entry of the United States into World War II immediately impacted local fire departments when both volunteer and professional firemen enlisted. The desire to do one's military service precipitated havoc in communities, which had relied upon these same men to provide local fire and emergency services. Likewise, machinery and equipment that had been designed and sold to municipal fire departments were appropriated on a regular basis by the federal government for the war effort. This was not an unusual practice; during the Civil War, cities in both the north and the south were left vulnerable to fires due to the flight of volunteers into the armies.

The cover of *Fire Engineering* magazine's January 1942 edition featured the fire station at the U.S. Army's Hickam Field (Hawaii), which suffered heavy damage when Japan attacked Pearl Harbor. Both of its fire engines had been destroyed, thus effectively putting the base's fire department out of service. Reflecting upon this, *Fire Engineering* editor Fred Sheppard suggested that "strengthening American fire departments to the extent that those in Great Britain were augmented would not be justified. But, fire departments should be brought up to full peacetime strength and a reasonable supply of auxiliary equipment should be provided; also, a force of auxiliary firefighters should be trained and maintained." Unlike the British experience, where all local fire brigades were unified into a

The Fire Station at Hickam Field, Hawaii, took heavy punishment when Pearl Harbor was attacked. Both fire trucks were destroyed. (Honolulu Fire Department)

national service from 1941 to 1948, a cry for a nationalized fire service in the United States was not forthcoming.

The mobilization of America's resources for World War II had a direct impact on the delivery of fire services, not only in the local municipalities, but also in the industrial plants, Army forts, and Navy installations across the United States. The War Department's need for firefighting

This unique 1941 Model 21 Peter Pirsch 500 gpm midship pumper was equipped with railroad wheels and ran on rails at the Naval Ammunition Depot, Hawthorne, Nevada. Pirsch delivered a Model 21 with railroad wheels to the Lualualei Ammunition Depot in Hawaii in 1934. (From the collection of William D. Killen)

This 1942 Seagrave Model 80E 750 gpm pumper carried 200 gallons of water and served the Naval Station in Dutch Harbor, Alaska. (From the collection of William D. Killen)

By direction of President Franklin D. Roosevelt and the Secretary of the War Department, this 1942 Mack was turned over to the Navy and placed in service at the Portsmouth Naval Shipyard on March 9, 1942, in Kitterey, Maine. This engine is preserved in the Portsmouth Naval Shipyard Museum and is regularly used for public fire safety education programs. (From the collection of William D. Killen)

vehicles, soldiers, sailors, and Marines directly affected municipal and industrial fire departments in terms of equipment and personnel available for domestic purposes.

For instance, in 1942, the local fire department in Manchester, New Hampshire, had ordered a new Mack 1000 gpm pumper for the enormous sum of $10,376. Just before it was delivered, Manchester was notified that the unit was being appropriated by the War Department and was being placed in service at the Portsmouth Naval Shipyard, Kittery, Maine. Throughout the Second World War, hundreds of fire trucks ordered by municipalities were redirected to the federal government to support the war effort.

The number of municipal firefighters who either volunteered or who were drafted for military service between 1942 and 1945 created a serious drain on municipal fire departments across the country. In 1942, Arthur F. Bell, former chief of the Camp Upton (New York) Fire Department was named inspector of Army fire departments for the First Corps (England), Second Corps (Algiers), and Third Corps (Pacific) areas. Chief Bell supervised the instruction of all Army fire department personnel in

During World War II, fire departments, paid and volunteer, realized a loss of personnel due to the war effort. As members were drafted into the military or their reserve units activated, departments had to do more with less. This V-Mail was sent by such a member to a magazine, The Fireman's Grapevine, *in 1943. The magazine was produced by the Los Angeles Fire Department. (Courtesy* The Fireman's Grapevine*)*

The Army deployed hundreds of the Class 525 4x4 500 gpm pumpers during World War II. (From the collection of William D. Killen)

BUCKET
BRIGADE
1942

FIRST
CRASH
CREW

This watercolor titled "Bucket Brigade 1942 First Crash Crew" depicts the basic fire-fighting in the early months of World War II. (From the collection of William D. Killen)

The aircraft carrier USS Intrepid's *(CV 11) firefighters battle the fires caused by a kamikaze strike during the battle for Leyte Gulf in the Philippines on November 25, 1944. (© Barrett Gallagher/Corbis)*

that large territory. He had served as supervising instructor of the Nassau County (New York) Fire Department for five years prior to being named fire chief at Camp Upton, and was deemed qualified to conduct the Army's firefighter induction and training programs.

All throughout the War, but especially in the early months, towns and urban areas across the United States feared the loss of firemen, a fear that was not without merit. It must have been with considerable ambivalence that some communities requested the deferment of their volunteer and paid firefighters for on-going domestic protection. In early 1942, in a letter to the International Association of Fire Chiefs, relative to the deferment of professional firemen, Major G. H. Baker, Office of the Director, Selective Service, Washington, D.C., wrote: "Selective Service Regulations make provisions for the deferment of any registrant who is found to be a necessary man in any service, the maintenance of which is necessary to the National health, safety or interest. Each case must be considered on its own merits at the time of classification. In addition to establishing the qualification of this individual, by reason of his training and experience, it must also be shown that there is a shortage of available men with the required training, qualifications of skill, and that if the registrant were removed he could not be replaced, and further, that if he were removed and his occupation left vacant his removal would cause a serious loss of effectiveness in such activity."

In other words, it was possible to appeal the induction of a paid fireman if the criteria laid out in this letter were met. Reluctantly, many communities did file appeals for deferment on behalf of firemen who, if removed for the war, would cause the "serious loss of effectiveness" noted in Major Baker's directive.

The experiences of the vast majority of fire departments in requesting deferment for skilled firefighters proved unsatisfactory. When summoned, most firefighters answered their nation's call, leaving their local communities to train teenagers, women, and, in many cases, older citizens to take their place as firefighters, drivers, and pump operators. Several municipal fire departments lost senior personnel to Army and Navy fire departments simply because the pay was better. Retired firemen and chiefs, who could have staffed and managed the domestic departments, were lured out of retirement to manage new military operations.

In the end, hundreds of municipal fire chiefs continued to submit reports in letters to the editor of *Fire Engineering* expressing frustration that all through the war the federal government repeatedly raided the local fire departments as soon as new recruits were trained. This drain on domestic fire departments was seen by these chiefs as unfair and putting American lives in jeopardy. They may have been right.

One significant effect on local communities was the decrease in fire watches and fire wardens who had routinely patrolled areas that were subject to fires. During the period, "blackouts" in major cities created delays in the discovery and reporting of fires, a situation exacerbated by the absence of the wardens. A typical example of this occurred in 1942 when a department store in Seattle was virtually destroyed when a fire went undetected due to blacked-out windows and the absence of a local fire patrol. The extent of damage caused by this fire was determined to have been directly influenced by the blackout provisions. Thereafter, Seattle's Fire Department discouraged the blackout of windows unless directly ordered for security purposes.

During World War II, the Army and Marine Corps used commercial and military vehicles modified with firefighting pumps and agents for fighting aircraft fires. The Army's standard airfield crash truck was a 1 ton, 4 x 4 manufactured by the Chevrolet Motor Division of General Motors. Carbon dioxide was used extensively for airfield crash firefighting and was delivered to the fire scene in wheeled carts, commercial trucks, and motorcycles. High octane aircraft fuel was highly volatile and rapid

USS West Virginia *(BB 48) aflame in Pearl Harbor in 1941. The U.S. Naval Fleet was surprised during the Japanese aerial attack. Sailors fight the fires from small launches and a larger fireboat. (© Bettmann/Corbis)*

"Accident or Sabotage?" asks a war effort poster from 1943. Citizens were asked to be alert to suspicious fires and report anything unusual. It was thought that the enemy could be inside the U.S. attempting to disrupt daily life by such actions. (© Corbis)

A FFN-1 crash truck at the scene of an aircraft accident where the landing gear collapsed on landing used high pressure fog as an extinguishing agent. (From the collection of William D. Killen)

This ca. 1940s Indian motorcycle carried a two-man crew and a hose reel to discharge carbon dioxide from cylinders. The firefighters, dressed in asbestos crash suits, would position the motorcycle close to the aircraft and advance the carbon-dioxide-fed hose line into the fire area. (From the collection of William D. Killen)

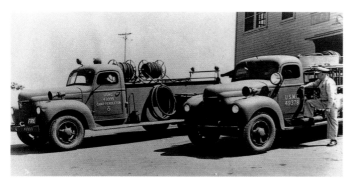

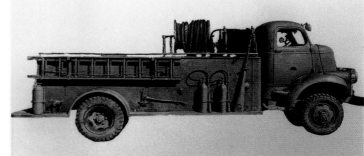

Above: *Marine Corps Base Camp Pendleton, California, used these 1941 International Harvester Model K5s, hose wagon with two top-mounted hose reels (left), and the pumper (right) in service during World War II and the Korean War. (From the collection of William D. Killen)*

Above, right: *The Marine Corps used this 1939 cab over engine Chevrolet equipped with carbon dioxide discharged through hose lines with the large nozzle mounted on the running board. (From the collection of William D. Killen)*

response to aircraft crashes was extremely critical. The Navy had used motorcycles equipped with carbon dioxide extinguishing systems starting in the early 1930s to respond to aircraft fires. The FFN-1 crash truck was a major improvement over the standard truck.

The two-piece engine company concept consisting of a pumping engine and a hose wagon or hose tender to carry hose and appliances was developed as a firefighting strategy in municipal fire departments prior to World War I. The two-piece engine company concept adopted by the military during World War II is no longer used in the federal fire service and has been phased out in most municipal fire departments, but it its day it was a revolutionary step forward.

Shipboard firefighting is a function of every sailor from seaman apprentice to the captain of the ship. This was true during the war years, as it is today. Shipboard firefighting is a collateral duty for all Navy personnel, and includes damage control operations as well as the control and extinguishment of fires. Dedicated firefighting crews or shipboard fire departments are an important segment of the ship's crew on aircraft carriers. Navy enlisted personnel are trained in shipboard firefighting techniques at the Navy Fire Fighting School in Pensacola, Florida. The Navy MB-5 crash truck was the first crash truck designed for use on board aircraft carriers and Naval air stations. American LaFrance and Oshkosh truck manufactured the MB-5 series of crash trucks.

During the Korean War years, the Army, Marine Corps, and Air Force provided limited structural firefighting capability within the various divisions, regiments, and squadrons utilizing military personnel as firefighters.

This period did, however, see some solid steps forward in military firefighting. The Air Force and Marine Corps crash crews, and shipboard firefighting units fought aircraft fires with protein foam and water. Navy research developed a hydrolyzed protein liquid that was unaffected by carbonates, chlorides, and sulfates. This hydrolyzed protein was manufactured from soybean oil, animal blood, hoof and horn meal, and even fish scales. It was found to have properties that when added to water increased the surface tension greatly. Produced as foam liquid, it was

This MB-5 crash truck served Naval Air Station Pensacola, Florida, for several years. The MB-5 crash truck was designed for use on aircraft carriers as well as shore installations. (From the collection of William D. Killen)

In 1951 International Harvester supplied the Army in Korea with 500 gpm pumpers. (From the collection of William D. Killen)

Airborne soldier firefighters tumble from a troop carrier command plane over the scene of a forest fire in Pendleton, Oregon, in September 1945. Using similar jump tactics to those developed in the great WWII paratroop operations at Normandy, Holland, and over the Rhine, these African-American paratroopers of the Airborne Infantry assisted the U.S. Forest Service in a peace mission. (© Bettmann/Corbis)

nicknamed "Navy Bean Soup." Aircraft fires often resulted when aircraft damaged during combat missions landed on ships and airfields with damaged landing gear, wings, and aircraft operating systems.

Following World War II and Korea, many of the retired municipal fire officers who had joined the federal service remained in the employment of the Army and Navy as district fire marshals and inspectors. The residual effect of having these municipal fire officers—many of them worked for the military fire departments into the 1960s—was quite important in terms of how the structure of the modern military fire services would evolve.

In general, the infusion of these retired officers greatly improved the effectiveness and the efficiency of the military fire departments. For instance, the U.S. Navy's district fire marshals' annual inspection of Navy fire departments required the departments to evaluate the proficiency of their personnel in structural firefighting skills, readiness, and the condition of firefighting vehicles, tools, and equipment. Fire prevention, for the first time in military consciousness, was considered to be the most effective tool in preserving and protecting Navy property.

One of the major differences of military firefighting in the combat zone is the added danger of working while under fire, and the risk of exposure to explosives and toxic materials. Many fires are started as a

TRUCK, ADVANCED BASE FIRE PUMPER
U.S. NAVY YDXP-2

Curb Weight (Gross) . . .	28000 lbs.	
Water Capacity	200 gal.	
Foam Capacity	30 gal.	
Wet Water Capacity	30 gal.	
Pump Capacity	750 gpm.	
Hose Body Capacity:		

2½" Double Jacket . . 1200 ft.
1¼" Double Jacket . . . 400 ft.

Dimensions O/A:

Length . . . . 295 in.
Width . . . . 96 in.
Height . . . . 131½ in.
Wheelbase . . . . 156 in.
Ground Clearance . . . . . 13 in.

Engine:

R6602, 223 BHP @ 2800 RPM
505 lb-ft torque @ 1400 RPM
6 cyl, in-line, overhead valve
602 cu. in. displacement

Transmission:
Spicer Military No. 6352
5 Forward Speeds - 1 Reverse

1st gear . . . . . 7.31 to 1
2nd gear . . . . . 4.09 to 1
3rd gear . . . . . 2.41 to 1
4th gear . . . . . 1.44 to 1
5th gear . . . . . 1.00 to 1
Reverse . . . . . 7.33 to 1

Transfer Case: Timken Model T-138

Direct . . . . . . 1.000 to 1
Underdrive . . . . 2.024 to 1

Axles: Timken Five Ton Military
6.443 to 1
Suspension: Semi-elliptical
spring radius rod drive
Steering . . Ross Hydraulic P720
Tires . . . . 14:00 x 20 - 16 ply
Brakes . . . . . . Air/Hydraulic
Gradeability 60%

B2558 _____ 8 ABERDEEN PROVING GROUND 8   5 October 1954

This pumper was produced for the U.S. Navy at the Aberdeen Proving Ground in Maryland in 1954. This list of specifications shows all of the vital information regarding this piece of apparatus. The items listed would have been the specifications required by the government contract signed with the vendor. (From the collection of William D. Killen)

consequence of enemy action, so military firefighters must often be exposed to crossfire and other battle threats even prior to fighting fires. Mass casualty situations are also common in war, often requiring that military firefighters be diverted to attend the needs of the wounded prior to extinguishment duties. In many instances, this trade-off results in bigger fires of longer duration. War forces the reprioritizing of firefighting goals, which sometimes calls for decisions that would not be made on the civilian side. This form of firefighting triage, were combat assets are given the highest priority, exposes firefighters to dangers equal to that of any other infantry soldier. Unlike their civilian counter parts, military firefighters don't go home at the end of their shift; a 24/7 work week is not unusual, but rather the norm in combat zones.

At the Naval Air Station in Brunswick, Maine, civilian and military firefighters conduct hot fire training evolutions on July 28, 1955. In this simulated aircraft fire, the crews attack a burning fuel spill on the ground with the turret gun mounted on the top of the pumper. (From the collection of William D. Killen)

Naval Powder Factory firefighters administer oxygen to one of their own during firefighting operations at the Naval Powder Factory, Indian Head, Maryland, ca. 1950s. (From the collection of William D. Killen)

A right underside view of an HH-43B Huskie helicopter lifting a fire suppression kit to a fire battle site. The aircraft is assigned to Detachment 8, 38th Aerospace Rescue and Recovery Squadron. (U.S. Air Force)

After Korea, change came rapidly to the military fire service. Beginning in 1958, USAF firefighters were assigned to the Kaman HH-43 Huskie helicopter. It was found that this unique sync-copter (side-by-side intermeshing blades) had the ability to assist in combating aircraft fires by using the aircraft's rotor wash. Firefighters used a sling-mounted Fire Suppression Kit (FSK) nicknamed the "Sputnik"(because of its shape) to create a rescue path through the flames to rescue pilots. The HH-43's rotor wash would reduce the height of the flames, push away smoke, increasing visibility, limit the heat impinging on the firefighters and assist in spreading the aerated foam concentrate. Besides their firefighting duties, these Airborne Rescue soldiers (ABR) were trained to operate the rescue hoist, attach sling loads, and ride the hoist down to assist and remove victims.

This shift to air rescue apparatus called for a rethinking in air crew management. A standard Local Base Rescue (LBR) aircrew consisted of a

The Model 530-C Crash truck was one of the major airfield crash trucks used by the Army, Air Force, and Marine Corps in Vietnam. (From the collection of William D. Killen)

A U.S. Marine Corps 1960s-era 530 B 750 gpm pumper with a 500-gallon tank manufactured by Ward LaFrance on a Reo chassis. (From the collection of William D. Killen)

pilot, copilot, medical technician (firefighters were trained in advanced first aid) and two ABRs. On hot days, when the lift capacity was limited, the copilot was sometimes left on the ground to reduce the overall aircraft weight. The USAF established fifty Air Rescue LBR detachments in the continental U.S., fifteen in the Pacific Theater, sixteen in Europe, two in Turkey, and one each in Canada, Bermuda, the Azores, and Libya.

During the Vietnam War, air crews continued to play a critical role. In all, fourteen LBR detachments were strategically placed across South Vietnam and Thailand. Airborne Rescue men/firefighters participated in many aircrew recoveries, and on more than one occasion were lowered to crashed aircraft to pry or cut out trapped victims. The HH-43 was the first USAF rescue helicopter in Vietnam, and was the last to leave. It has more combat saves than all other types of rescue helicopters combined. The HH-43 was the little helicopter with "Blades of Wood" flown by "Men of Steel."

In May 1961, President John F. Kennedy announced a national goal to land men on the moon and return them safely by the end of the decade. NASA began acquiring land immediately, and construction at the Kennedy Space Center (KSC) commenced rapidly in 1962. The KSC industrial area was completed during the years 1962 through 1964. Its first fire department was established in March 1964, when W. F. Eldredge (retired district chief from Miami) was appointed its first fire chief. Three assistant chiefs reported in mid-March, and thirty additional personnel from municipal fire departments in Florida and Georgia reported on March 30.

Marine Corps Base Quantico, Virginia's, 1967 Kaiser 6x6 American Air Filter 530 C crash truck. Firefighting foam was discharged through the roof turret from a 500 gpm midship-mounted fire pump. The 530C carried 400 gallons of water and 40 gallons of Aqueous Film Forming Foam concentrate. (From the collection of William D. Killen)

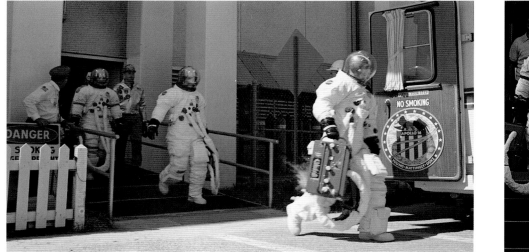

KSC fire department personnel participated in extensive training programs in support of the early Gemini and Apollo moon missions.

The Kennedy Space Center fire department suffered a terrible blow on January 27, 1967, when the Apollo One flight crew died in a tragic fire on Launch Pad 37 during preliminary tests. After months of investigation, the Apollo Space Program was put back on track with major changes in hardware, procedures, flight tests, and on-site fire-rescue operations.

The KSC fire department established the Astronaut Rescue Team in October 1968, in preparation for the Apollo 8 launch to the moon in December. Eleven members of the KSC fire department were selected from among 120 candidates, and these men immediately began intensive physical training that included calisthenics and long-distance running. Astronaut

Below: *Overall scene of fire at Crawler Transporter 2 on August 13, 1965. The Kennedy Space Center Fire Department responded to and extinguished a fire during the construction and assembly of the Crawler Transporter. The Crawler Transporter is used to transport the Launch Umbilical Tower and Saturn V rocket to the launch pad. Two crawler transporters built to support the Apollo program are still in service transporting the Space Shuttle to the launch pad. (From the collection of William D. Killen)*

Rescue firefighters familiarized themselves with the multitude of life-support systems, explosives, fuels, and safety devices incorporated in the Apollo Command Module and the Saturn V rocket. Special procedures were developed to extract the astronauts from the command module, and from the 320-foot level of the Launch Umbilical Tower (LUT). Saturn V rockets were assembled on LUTs in the vehicle assembly building, and safely transported to the launch pad on one of two crawler transporters.

KSC fire department personnel supported numerous missions where fuels and oxidizers were off-loaded from barges, railroad cars, and highway tankers into specialized storage vessels. In addition to the unique duties associated with the space program, KSC firefighters responded to structural fires, motor vehicle accidents, wildland fires, snakes bites, and even delivered a baby or two!

The Saturn V rocket, with the Apollo 11 command module, along with astronauts Neil Armstrong, Michael Collins, and Edwin Aldrin, Jr., on board, lifted off from Kennedy Space Center July 16, 1969. It was with tremendous pride that the staff of the Kennedy Space Center fire department watched four days later, on July 20, when Neil Armstrong took his great leap into history.

The Navy's district fire marshal concept evolved into the area fire marshals in the early 1970s, and the process of annual fire department inspections continued in use until 1998. In that year, the Chief of Naval Operations (CNO) adopted the Commission on Fire Accreditation International's self-assessment and accreditation concept to assess capabilities and readiness of Navy fire departments.

The Navy's Fire and Emergency Services (F&ES) program was realigned in April 2002, with the disestablishment of the area fire marshal assessment protocols. The Navy F&ES program is managed by the director, Navy Fire and Emergency Services, and a six-member staff consisting of a deputy director, four assistant directors, and one contract employee. CNO established the Navy Fire and Emergency Services Advisory Board in April 2001 to advise the director Navy F&ES on fire service issues and new technology. The advisory board membership consists of fire chiefs

Chaplain (Capt.) Thomas C. Marsden speaks during a burial at sea service aboard the aircraft carrier USS John F. Kennedy *(CV 67). The service is being held for Chief Specialist (Firefighter) John A. Powers, USNR, and Patrick C. Moran, son of Lt. Cmdr. Thomas J. Moran, Medical Corps, USN. (U.S. Navy)*

115th Airlift Squadron loadmasters lower the Modular Airborne Firefighting System (MAFFS) discharge tubes prior to making an airdrop of Phoscheck. (U.S. Department of Defense)

Top: *Firefighters wearing protective suits and oxygen breathing apparatus (OBA) work their way down a passageway during a firefighting drill on board the nuclear-powered aircraft carrier USS* Abraham Lincoln *(CVN 72). Lincoln's crew is receiving refresher training under the supervision of personnel from Fleet Training Group, Guantanamo Bay, Cuba. (U.S. Navy)*

Above: *SRA David Bryant, U.S. Air Force fire-fighter, takes a break with a fellow firefighter at Rhein-Main Air Base, Germany. As with all aspects of modern military life, women have entered the world of military firefighting alongside their male counterparts. (U.S. Air Force)*

representing regional commands in the U.S., Europe, and Japan. There are eighty Navy fire departments that protect approximately 71,000 buildings occupying more than 2.2 million acres of land valued at more than $160 billion.

The U.S. Navy—forward deployed around the globe—has 383,500 active-duty officers and enlisted personnel, 160,300 ready reservists, and 4,281 midshipmen in training, and 185,184 civil service employees. Nearly half of the 309 ships and 4,000-plus aircraft are underway (away from homeports) manned with 41,092 personnel.

The U.S. Marine Corps structural fire departments are staffed by approximately 900 civil service firefighters who protect over 9,900 facilities at fifteen Marine Corps installations in the United States and the Pacific. Airfield rescue firefighting services at Marine Corps air stations and bases in North Carolina, Virginia, California, Arizona, Hawaii, and in the Pacific are provided by Marines (military personnel). The Marine crash crews (fewer than 1,000 personnel) are part of the Marine Expeditionary Forces that are forward deployed and provide airfield fire protection in combat zones and remote areas.

The Army Air Force of World War II became the United States Air Force on September 10, 1947, and became a component of the Department of Defense. The Air Force established a firefighting school at Lowry

Air Force Base, which was later moved to Greenville Air Force Base in Greenville, Mississippi, and moved to Chanute Air Force Base in Rantoul, Illinois, in 1964.

The U.S. Air Force firefighting school provided basic training for Air Force firefighters and advanced training for senior enlisted personnel and civil service Air Force fire chiefs. The Air Force school became the DOD fire school in 1980, tasked to train all DOD firefighters in basic and advanced firefighting techniques. The school was relocated to Goodfellow Air Force Base in San Angelo, Texas, with the closure of Chanute Air Force Base and today is known as the Louis F. Garland Fire Academy. Many ideas and concepts developed at the school were later employed in firefighting operations and firefighting vehicle design. These ideas and

A firefighter stands by in a P-16 firefighting and rescue truck aboard the aircraft carrier USS Constellation *(CV 64) during an exercise in the Pacific. (U.S. Navy)*

A right-side view of an Air Force A/S32P-15 large-capacity firefighting vehicle. This firefighting truck was designed to combat aircraft fires in all weather conditions. Its main function is to discharge foam agent on a crash site and to extinguish the fire within seconds of a plane's arrival. (U.S. Air Force)

concepts included nozzles designed to penetrate aircraft fuselage struc-tures to discharge foam and water, airfield rescue firefighting vehicles with pump and roll capability to traverse the terrain around a burning aircraft discharging agent, and automated bumper and roof turrets capa-ble of discharging agent over, above, and below aircraft components to reach burning fuels.

An example of innovation emanating from the military fire service can be found in Department of Defense research in the field of firefighting chemical agents and concepts that have led to new and better firefighting agents and airfield rescue firefighting vehicles, including the Oshkosh P-15, the largest fire truck built for airfield firefighting. Many of the things taken for granted in today's civilian fire departments were developed by the military. Case in point was the dedicated rescue vehicle and trained rescue crew. This began in the 1950s with the Air Force deployment of the R2 rescue truck, forerunner to today's Squad, and was later followed by the R2A, P-10 rescue vehicle, the P-28 heavy rescue and the P-30 medium rescue vehicles.. A specialized advanced rescue man course was offered at the Air Force Fire School to train personnel manning these vehicles.

In the early 1960s, Dr. Richard Tuve of the Naval Research Labora-tory in Washington, D.C., developed the twinned agent concept of firefight-ing by discharging dry chemical extinguishing agent and foam through

U.S. Air Force Airman First Class Jovon Stafford, a firefighter from the 1st Civil Engineering Squadron, Langley Air Force Base, Virginia, is dressed in a full proximity suit as she sprays water from a hose during an aircraft fire scenario for the 1st Fighter Wing's Operation Readiness Inspection. (U.S. Air Force)

A firefighter uses a gas-powered saw to cut a trench in the roof of the Lockheed building during a fire training exercise. (U.S. Department of Defense)

twin nozzles. The twinned agent concept was widely received and is still employed at many commercial airports and military installations around the world today in rapid response vehicles equipped with water, foam, and dry chemical. Virtually every commercial airport in the world today utilizes this technology.

One of the most successful military-civilian technology transfers occurred in airborne firefighting concepts with the development of the U.S. Air Force HH-43B helicopter manufactured by Kamen Aircraft Corporation in Bloomfield, Connecticut. The helicopter was used for aerial pickup of survivors, fire control and suppression, crash entry, survivor removal, and immediate first aid. This firefighting package consisted of 83 gallons of foam and water mixture, yielding 690 gallons of expanding foam with fifty seconds of continued use and could reach up to fifty feet on full stream. This proved to be ample time because of the "rotor wash." The objective was not to extinguish the fire, but to cut a path to the burning aircraft and hold the path until the other firefighter could accomplish the rescue. The Air Force used the HH-43B to support the Kennedy Space Center fire department's astronaut rescue team during the Apollo missions to the moon from 1968 to 1972. After fourteen years of devoted service, the HH-43 "Huskie" was retired from use in April 1973.

The U.S. Air Force firefighting school at Chanute Air Force Base, in Rantoul, Illinois, provided basic training for Air Force firefighters and advanced training for senior enlisted personnel and civil service Air Force fire chiefs. The Air Force school became the DOD fire school in 1980, tasked to train all DOD firefighters in basic and advance firefighting techniques. The school was relocated to Goodfellow AFB in San Angelo, Texas, with the closure of Chanute AFB and today is known as the Louis F. Garland Fire Academy.

The DOD fire academy curriculum is accredited by the International Fire Service Accreditation Congress (IFSAC). Accredited courses taught at the DOD fire academy range from Firefighter I to Fire Officer IV, and include Rescue Technician, Hazardous Materials Technician, and Weapons of Mass Destruction Technician, as well as three levels of Fire Inspector and Fire Instructor. Several DOD fire academy courses are recognized by the Community College of the Air Force and other institutions of higher learning for college credit.

The Air Force developed and maintains the Department of Defense Firefighter Certification Program for all DOD Components. The Department of Defense Firefighter Certification Program was accredited by IFSAC in 1993 for firefighter I, II, airport firefighter, fire officer I and II. IFSAC accredited fire officer III and IV, fire instructor III and fire inspector III, Hazmat Incident Command in June 1997. Today, the Department of Defense Firefighter Certification Program is approved to award certifications for more NFPA professional qualifications standards than any other entity accredited by IFSAC or the Professional Qualifications Board.

The Navy adopted the Commission on Fire Accreditation International's self assessment program for all Navy fire departments in 1998. The Department of Defense mandated the CFAI self assessment and accreditation program for all DOD fire departments in 2000. The DOD

Fire Department Accreditation Program is managed by the Naval Facilities Engineering Command for all DOD fire departments. The first fire departments accredited in DOD were Naval Air Station Jacksonville, Florida; Naval Air Station Keflavik, Iceland; and U.S. Air Force Academy Fire Department, Colorado Springs, Colorado. Over 100 DOD fire departments throughout the United States and overseas are currently enrolled in the self-assessment process.

The Commission on Chief Fire Officer Designation was established to review and validate the professional accomplishments and experience of fire chiefs and chief fire officers. Similar to the professional registration accorded certified public accountants, certified safety professionals, and professional engineers, the designation of "chief fire officer" is awarded after peer review of the candidate's portfolio. The candidate portfolio documents the experience, training, education, professional achievements, and community services of the individual candidate and is reviewed by peer reviewers who have been designated chief fire officers. The first DOD fire officers to achieve chief fire officer designation were formally recognized by the Commission on Fire Designation in Kansas City, Kansas, in August 2002. More than fifty DOD chief fire officers are working on chief fire officer candidate portfolios.

Today, approximately 450 Department of Defense fire departments protect more than 700 military installations across the United States and abroad, providing every emergency service routinely found in modern municipal and industrial fire departments.

In recent years, DOD firefighters responded to assist municipal and state governments in rescue and recovery operations ranging from hurricanes and tornadoes in Florida, Georgia, North and South Carolina, Virginia, and Maryland, to earthquakes in California and Washington. They are at the forefront of emergency operations in any scenario involving terrorist attacks, and proudly responded to the bombings in Oklahoma City on April 19, 1995, as well as to the September 11, 2001, tragedies.

Naval Support Facility Thurmont's 2002 Pierce-International custom designed mini-pumper has a Waterous 500 gpm CL VK pump, a FoamPro 1600 foam system with a 25-gallon foam cell, and seating for five. The unit is equipped with Xplore Technologies GeneSys II Tablet on board computer and Bendix X Vision infrared camera with back-up camera and is assigned to the Presidential Retreat at Camp David. (From the collection of William D. Killen)

Firefighters from the Boots and Coots Oil Well Firefighting Company use a crane to cap a blazing well in the aftermath of Operation Desert Storm. The well, situated in the Ahman Oil Fields, is one of many set afire by Iraqi forces prior to their retreat from Kuwait. (U.S. Department of Defense)

Wildland Firefighting
in the American West

Wildland Firefighting
in the American West

Steve Robinson

The history of wildland fire in the American West has been colorful, devastating, and instructional. As the settlers, trappers, and miners headed west to explore and conquer, they found everything from the scorching temperatures of the Southwest to the frigid winters of the Rockies. And each new horizon had one thing in common: wildfire.

From the beginning of our country's settlement, farmers were using wildfire as a tool to clear vegetation to plant crops. While agricultural fire could be an ally, it was also the leading cause of wildfire when many of these fires escaped their set boundaries. Huge fires around the

Above: *A DC-3 tanker plane makes a slurry drop on the Little Valley Fire in 1981. (Mike Cassidy)*

Pages 236–237: *The raging flames of the Little Valley Fire light up the night sky in 1981. (Mike Cassidy)*

Left: *A brilliant display of lightning such as this is often unaccompanied by a downpour during fire season. As such, this is a natural combination of poor fire conditions: dry timber, no rain, and a cloud-to-ground lightning strike. Many wildland fires occur from these natural causes. (Nevada Division of Forestry)*

Opposite: *A crew of five firefighters moves slowly yet purposefully toward their objective. Bringing with them shovels, chain saws, and other tools, they will be engaged in clearing a fire line to prevent the fire from advancing. The hills are steep, the distances never short, and the equipment is heavy. (Nevada Division of Forestry)*

turn of the century wrought havoc in the Great Lakes states and the west. The Peshtigo Fire in October 1871 burned nearly 1.25 million acres and killed 1,200 people in Wisconsin and northern Michigan. Most of the timber had been "cut over" in these areas; the Peshtigo burned much of the remaining stands.

Wildfire struck again with a vengeance in 1902. The Yacolt Fire in Washington and Oregon killed thirty-eight people and burned nearly a million acres as it swept through communities and onto nearby ridges. Large-scale fires such as Yacolt awakened the public, who began to demand governmental action for both human safety and timber resource conservation.

Changes to land management in the early twentieth century demanded changes in the need for fire suppression forces. The main thrust of organizing fire suppression forces was to protect the valuable stands of timber and the watersheds vital to a clean water source. Many of the most precious watersheds and vast expanses of forested lands were pulled into the public domain as the National Forest System was created by Congress in the late 1800s and early 1900s. Around the same time that many national parks were created, National Park Service employees were hired. Along with Army soldiers at nearby outposts, these new federal employees were expected to fight the wildfires that threatened the pristine wilderness. The administration of President Theodore Roosevelt remains a watershed in the history of the national parks system and the role of the federal government in natural resources management. Under Roosevelt, Gifford Pinchot, chief of the U.S. Forest Service, greatly expanded the acreage of the National Forest System. President Roosevelt himself created numerous national parks and monuments. All this expansion of the federal domain led to increased federal responsibility for fire suppression.

When the Bureau of Forestry was moved from the U.S. Department of the Interior's General Land Office into the U.S. Department of Agriculture in 1905, the USDA Forest Service (commonly referred to as the

Above: *This firefighter shows how dirty and demanding wildland firefighting is. A sooty face and firefighting gear indicate that she has been involved in this operation for some time. Evidenced by the ever-present two-way radio, communications are a vital aspect of being able to control a changing situation. (Nevada Division of Forestry)*

Opposite: *Silhouetted against a brilliant fire scene, a firefighter surveys the current situation. Outfitted with fire gear, backpack, and one of several firefighting tools available, he is ever mindful of the potential for changing conditions. Each wildland firefighter must know how to anticipate fire behavior for survival. (Paul Ramirez/Phoenix Fire Department)*

Left: *This image was captured late in the afternoon of Sunday August 6, 2000, from a bridge over the East Fork of the Bitterroot River just north of Sula, Montana. These elk sought refuge in the river bottom during what may have been the most extreme day of fire behavior on the Bitterroot in more than seventy years. Animals are forced to leave areas that they use for food, water, and shelter. Besides being displaced, many are killed each year when trapped in fires. (John McColgan/Bureau of Land Management Alaska Fire Service)*

Modern-day wildland firefighters are equipped to handle the job. Helmets and goggles, fire-retardant clothing, gloves, canteen, boots, two-way radios, and other equipment are at their disposal. Notable here is the "Pulaski Tool" that the firefighter carries. This tool was invented by Edward Pulaski at the beginning of the twentieth century. Still in use today, the "Pulaski Tool" is a staple of wildland firefighters a century later. (Loretta Smith)

Many firefighters battle smoldering fires in residential areas around Los Alamos, New Mexico. This firefighter is ready and willing to accomplish that objective. This is an example of the serious concern for life safety and the preservation of property that is caused by the positioning of structures in close proximity to wildland areas. (Andrea Booher/ FEMA News Photo)

USFS) was created. Protecting and enhancing the land for clean water and timber production was the central mission of the new agency. Quickly, the USFS codified its own series of guidelines and policies in the *USFS Use Book* (1905), which read, in part, "Probably the greatest single benefit derived by the community and nation from forest reserves is insurance against the destruction of property, timber resources and water supply by fire." The *Use Book* predicted that "the burden of adequate protection cannot well be borne by the State or by its citizens, much as they have to gain, for it requires money to support, train, and equip a force, as well as to meet emergencies."

The *Use Book* guided the early park rangers in patrolling and controlling forest fires. It gave them tips and information on the value of posting signs prohibiting fire, and for working with citizens on the formation of civilian fire brigades. Camping safety was emphasized, as the western national parks quickly became camping havens for American families and sportsmen. The *Use Book* also contained practical fiscal advice regarding timber slash practices, fire cost tracking, and suggested penalties for set (arson) fires.

Several of the earliest mutual aid agreements in the fire service were forged in the Pacific Northwest, when the USFS and the states realized that they had to work cooperatively to put out fires. Most of these early alliances were primarily funded by the wealthy timber companies, entities who had a lot at stake. Despite these cooperative agreements, the Big Blowup of 1910 demonstrated nature's ability to disregard the best laid plans. It only took two days in August for fires to burn three million acres in western Montana and northern Idaho. The Big Blowup killed eighty-five people, an enormous and tragic loss.

Many stories of tragedy and heroism emerged in the wake of this devastation. In one recorded account, the 1910 fire swept over USFS Park Ranger Edward Pulaski and his firefighting crew of forty-five men, who found themselves cut off from escape by the walls of flame. As Pulaski watched fear take over his men, he decided the only chance they had was to take shelter in a mineshaft he recalled from his backcountry treks. Because of the mens' fear of the firestorm outside, Pulaski allegedly held them in the mineshaft at gunpoint, while single handedly fighting the fire at the mine entrance until he too passed out. One man died beneath a falling tree as he ran his own way, and five were burned and died in the mineshaft, but the remaining thirty-nine men, including Ranger Pulaski, lived through the ordeal. Pulaski continued serving with the USFS and created a tool that is still used by wildland firefighters. The Pulaski tool combines an ax with a sharpened hoe, an implement that greatly aids in fire line construction.

The first USFS African-American firefighters also worked on the Big Blowup. The 6th Company, 25th Infantry was stationed near Avery, Idaho, when the fires began. They were called on to help fight the fire and, later, bury the dead.

After an assessment of the Big Blowup and three million acres of timberland lost, the powerful timber companies of the Northwest made their voices heard in Washington, D.C. Quickly, the Weeks Law was passed, which allowed the federal government to purchase private land and add these lands to the National Forest System, thus giving them federal fire protection. Congress appropriated more funding throughout 1910, and the word soon came down to the five-year-old Forest Service that fire *control* was its new priority. This shift from *fire suppression* to *fire control* was extremely important and illustrates the forward-thinking of early USFS and Congressional leadership.

After 1910, things began to change on the wildland firefighting landscape. Lookout towers were built and staffed for the early detection and reporting of fires, fire access roads were constructed, fireguard stations were built for bunker crews who could readily respond to remote fires, and radio and telephone communications were vastly improved. The science of understanding wildland fire was also developing. New tools to take fuel moisture readings greatly helped the park rangers, as did an enhanced understanding of weather patterns on fire behavior. The automobile allowed fire patrols to cover more ground, and some were even converted to run on existing railroad tracks.

The states remained primarily responsible for fire protection on industrial and nonindustrial state and private lands. With the landmark Clarke-McNary Act (1924), Congress allowed the USFS to assist with the cost of state fire protection services, creating a partnership and some consistency in quality regarding fighting wildfires on federal, state, and private lands. During the Great Depression, Civilian Conservation Crews were also trained as wildland firefighters.

Edward Pulaski (on the right) briefs a firefighter prior to heading out for a wildland fire. The firefighter carries the "Pulaski Tool," which Edward Pulaski invented for the forest service. This tool is a combination of ax and grubbing tool and is still in use today. (U.S. Forest Service, Region 1, Missoula, Montana)

Edward Pulaski, inventor of the "Pulaski Tool," was a forest ranger in Idaho in the early part of the twentieth century. Here he sits near the entrance to a cave where he is credited with saving thirty-nine of his forty-five-man crew during "The Big Burn" of 1910 in Wallace, Idaho. Trapped by fire from both sides, he led his crew into the cave and waited out the fire. One died in the fire because he lagged behind and five were burned and died in the cave. (U.S. Forest Service, Region 1, Missoula, Montana)

FIRE LOOKOUTS PAST AND PRESENT

Below are a collection of fire lookouts past and present. At one time, they dotted the entire country North to South and East to West. They have held a prominent role in the protection of America's forests with the ability of the attendant to give early warning of a developing wildland fire. For many, they are a symbol of protection and conservation, and once were the primary means for detection of forest fires in remote, unpopulated area. Today many still perform the function of fire lookout, but others have either become abandoned and fallen into disrepair or no longer exist. Some lookouts are available as overnight camping accommodations. Lookouts varied from being perched on the tops of treeless mountains, to sitting at the top of tall towers in flat country.

All photos courtesy of Sierraville Ranger District (U.S. Fire Service)

In the 1930s, it became apparent that professional fire crews would be necessary to augment the firefighters of the USFS and volunteers from the separate state forestry agencies. Montana took the lead in hiring and training permanent twenty-person crews. These crews were trained with military precision and stayed together for many years, truly perfecting their roles as professional wildland firefighters.

The Ninemile Remount Depot, a local staging and replenishment station, was established during the Great Depression to supply the huge numbers of mules needed to supply fire guard stations and camps. These mules, and others involved with wildland firefighting, quickly became indispensable partners in the West's firefighting history. Because of their great strength and ability to traverse terrain beyond a horse's ability, the

Nothing more than a charred landscape of West Washoe Valley, Nevada, is left in the aftermath of the Little Valley Fire. (Ronan Thornhill)

animals were and remain today a staple of backcountry movement by federal, state, and private packers where motorized vehicles are prohibited or limited. Many rangers of the early twentieth century credited the stubborn but reliable mule with saving lives and acres during fires.

The next large fire was the 1933 Tillamook Fire in Oregon. This fire is well-remembered, but it consumed only about a third (one million) of the Big Blowup acres. It appeared that the dedication and organization expended between 1910 and 1933 was having the desired effect in terms of land protection. Tillamook gained national attention and solidified the policy of aggressive suppression of all wildfire as the primary approach.

The Bureau of Land Management (BLM) was created in 1946 through a merger between the General Land Office and the Grazing

SMOKEY BEAR

On May 6, 1950, a lookout in a tower north of the Capitan Mountains in New Mexico spotted smoke on the Lincoln National Forest and called the nearest ranger station. Crews responded and fought the Capitan Gap Fire, finally gaining control of the 17,000-acre fire a few days later. During one of the lulls in firefighting, reports came in of a lone bear cub wandering near the fireline. The men left him alone thinking the mother bear might return.

During the firefighting, twenty-four people were caught directly in the path of the flames, but escaped by laying face down until the fire had burned past them. The firefighters were safe except for a few scorches and some burned holes in their clothes.

Nearby, the little cub had been caught in the path of the fire and taken refuge in a tree that was now a charred smoking snag. The climb saved his life but left him badly burned on the paws and hind legs. The firefighters removed the little bear cub from the burned tree, and a rancher who had been helping the firefighters agreed to take the cub home. A New Mexico Department of Game and Fish warden, Ray Bell, heard about the cub and drove to the rancher's home to get the bear. The cub needed veterinary aid and was flown to Santa Fe where the burns were treated and bandaged. Bell cared for the bear during his recovery.

News about the little bear spread swiftly throughout New Mexico and the nation. Many people wrote or called to inquire about the little bear's progress. Warden Bell wrote an official letter to the chief of the Forest Service, presenting the cub to the agency with the understanding that the small bear would be dedicated to a publicity program of fire prevention and conservation. The bear was sent to Washington, D.C., where he found a home at the National Zoo, becoming the living symbol of Smokey Bear. The original bear died in 1975, and was buried in his home forest in New Mexico

In the year 2000, the nation celebrated the fiftieth anniversary of Smokey. He remains a beloved symbol of wildland fire safety to the nation.

remember—
only you can PREVENT FOREST FIRES

Opposite, top: An air tanker drops its load of fire-retardant material on an unburned area of the forest in advance of the actual fire. By doing this, it is hoped that they can create an area that will either stop or slow down the spread of the fire and give fire crews on the ground a chance to effect extinguishment. (Nevada Division of Forestry)

Service, both of the United States Department of the Interior. Whereas the General Land Office and the Grazing Service had been charged with land disposal, the new agency's mission was to focus on land conservation. Fire protection was now part of its responsibilities also, particularly focusing on the rangelands it managed. Without direct funding for fire suppression, the BLM relied on cooperative agreements between other federal agencies and the states. With the majority of the BLM-managed lands in the Great Basin states (a specific area lying in parts of Nevada, Idaho, Wyoming, Oregon, California, and Utah), the BLM fire program grew around smaller, more mobile crews who could be moved within the large region swiftly.

These small crews performed excellently, but severe rangeland fires in 1957 and 1964 highlighted the need for larger, well-funded fire suppression forces as well. By the mid 1960s, the BLM had beefed up its engine and "helitack" (helicopter) crews to a more appropriate size. It had also built additional lookouts, augmented the fire guards program, begun aerial fire detection flights, and adopted advances in radio communications.

Aviation

The earliest use of aircraft for wildfire detection was in California by the USFS in 1917, when they began patrolling wildlands in a surveillance capacity. During the 1920s, various attempts at trying to find ways for aircraft to drop water on fires failed, although many creative ideas were tried. For instance, wooden beer kegs and five-gallon cans filled with water were attached to parachutes and dropped on fires—with limited success. In 1935, the USFS established the Aerial Fire Control Experimental Project in California, which researched and developed techniques for dropping fire retardant and water on wildfires. Most of these efforts were ineffective, however, so much of the USFS aviation efforts in the 1930s stayed focused on fire detection, with the government hiring private contractors to do the scientific work on chemical retardants. In 1939, the USFS took delivery of its first agency-owned detection airplane, a Stinson Reliant SR-10FM.

In 1954, Operation Firestop—a consortium of the USFS, the California Division of Forestry, the Los Angeles Fire Department, the Federal Civil Defense Administration, the U.S. Marine Corps, the U.S. Weather Service, and the University of California—united to address aerial firefighting issues. This partnership produced a successful water dropping system from a TBM-1C bomber with a modified bomb bay to hold the water. On September 1, 1954, the TBM-1C made the first operational water drops on the Jamison Fire near San Diego in southern California. The first use

When roads are scarce and locations are remote, the only way to get to the fire is to jump from aircraft. This firefighter parachutes into a predetermined rally point where he will join up with his fellow "smoke jumpers" and proceed to the fire. Equipment is also parachuted to these firefighters after they are on the ground. (Nevada Division of Forestry)

Above: *Wildland firefighters often have to gain access to areas of the country that are not readily accessible. One method is to parachute into an area from a fixed-wing aircraft. Another way is to rappel from a helicopter from a relatively low altitude. Here firefighters demonstrate rappelling from both sides of the aircraft. (Nevada Division of Forestry)*

Top, right: *A type-1 heavy air tanker takes off from air command to fight the Hayman, Colorado, fire southwest of Denver on June 6, 2002. Tankers such as this provide invaluable sources of water and fire retardant materials to slow and extinguish massive wildland fires. They are able to rapidly deploy to inaccessible areas and assist firefighters on the ground with their extinguishment efforts. The hose hanging below the tanker allows it to fill its tank with water from a source without actually having to land. (Michael Rieger/FEMA News Photo)*

Center: *Helicopters perform many functions in wildland firefighting. They can transport crews and equipment to the scene of a fire and perform rescue operations. They can be used for reconnaissance missions to track the progress of fires. Here, a Sikorsky helitanker is taking on a load of water from a lake. Once full, the helicopter will proceed to a predetermined drop point in the fire. These efforts not only help slow the spread of the fire, but may be necessary to rescue trapped firefighters. (Nevada Division of Forestry)*

of a "helitanker," a 1,200-pound sling held by a Marine Corps Sikorsky helicopter, also occurred in 1954.

In 1955, concepts borrowed from agricultural spraying were engineered into what we now call Single Engine Air Tankers (SEATs). SEATS were a significant improvement in that they were able to drop 125 gallons of water on active fires. A SEAT became *Air Tanker #1* in California. These single-engine units remain a vital and expanding component of the air arsenal to this day. Capacity of load continues to expand, along with maneuverability.

In 1956, helicopters had been in use for large-fire support for about a decade, primarily transporting equipment and ferrying ground crews. That year, the first "heli-rapellers" were incorporated into wildland firefighting. These helicopters allow firefighters to climb down (rappel) to the fire area to serve as effective initial attack forces. There are currently over thirty-five heli-rappel bases in the western United States.

In 1959, surplus military aircraft were used as airtankers for the first time throughout the western United States. The first fleet consisted of one B-25 (1,000 gallons), one PB4Y-2 (200 gallons), and several F7Fs (750 gallons) tankers. In 1960, the Douglas B-26 (1,200 gallons) and the Lockheed P2V (1,000 gallons) were added to the fleet. In this same year, use of the B-25s was discontinued after a fatal accident in which wildland firefighters were killed.

Use of airtankers spread from the western coastal states to South Dakota in 1961, and to the northeastern states in 1963. They remain an important initial attack tool. All airtankers are owned by private companies who bid competitively for state contracts.

Many of the aircraft initially put into service are still in use. Aircraft used in western wildfire suppression work also include a King Air B90, a Super King Air 200, and a Cessna Citation used for infrared detection. Other components of the fleet also now include Barons used

A type-1 Helicopter picks up 1,000 gallons of water as it works on the north side of the Hayman Fire, near Castle Rock, Colorado, on June 13, 2002. Helicopters add a level versatility to the arsenal of wildland firefighting equipment. Along with fixed wing aircraft, they are able to make drops of water on critical points of fires to slow their spread. (Michael Rieger/FEMA News Photo)

Helicopters perform many tasks in wildland firefighting. One operation is forward fire spotting, as conducted here during the Indian Creek Fire in Douglas County, Nevada. (Ronan Thornhill)

An aerial photo shows the massive one-half mile of flame front on Fred's Mountain Fire, north of Reno, Nevada. (Ronan Thornhill)

Opposite, bottom: *Fighting a wildland fire is a constant battle—day and night. Here, night operations take place on the Little Valley Fire in West Washoe Valley, Nevada. (Ronan Thornhill)*

as aerial fire detection and lead planes, DC-3s, Sherpas, and Twin Otters used by the smokejumpers. USFS aircraft oversight is managed by the USFS Aviation staff. Other federal agency aircraft are managed by the U.S. Department of the Interior's Office of Aircraft Safety (OAS), established in 1973. Safety of this aging fleet has become an issue of national attention with several fatal crashes in the last decade. Congress, federal, and state governments are considering measures to address the problem and update the fleet.

An offshoot of the early failed water bomber experiments was the focus on parachuting as a way to combat wildland fires. During the summer of 1939, some sixty experimental jumps were made into the forests of northern Washington from the base in Winthrop, Washington. In 1940, the Forest Service Smokejumper Project became operational with six smokejumpers based at Winthrop, and seven at the Moose Creek Ranger Station in Idaho. On July 12, 1940, two smokejumpers from Moose Creek made the first operational attack jump on a fire in the Nez Perce National Forest in Idaho. Eight more fires were jumped that first year. The purpose of the smokejumpers was to have a firefighting force that could be delivered quickly to areas that were inaccessible by vehicle. They are initial attack resources used to immediately respond to fires, and to hopefully extinguish them before they become unmanageable.

In 1941, the whole smokejumper program, (consisting of twenty-six men) moved to Missoula, Montana. Missoula was picked because it was home to the Johnson Flying Service, the company who supplied the smokejumper's aircraft and pilots. In short order, due to World War II, fewer experienced firefighters were available to become jumpers. In 1943, seventy members of the Civilian Public Service, conscientious objectors to the military draft, were trained as smokejumpers. In 1944, the USFS officially adopted the smokejumper program and it rapidly expanded.

By 1958, there were 398 USFS smokejumpers operating from new bases in Grangeville, Idaho; West Yellowstone, Montana; Silver City, New Mexico; and Redding, California. Today, the Silver City base is no longer an active smokejumper base, having been replaced by one at the original jump site in Winthrop. In 1981, the first woman smokejumper joined the ranks at the base in McCall, Idaho.

The Bureau of Land Management (BLM) started a smokejumper program in 1959 by establishing a base at Fairbanks, Alaska, with fifteen new jumper/firefighters. They were soon a major part of Alaska fire suppression. In 1987, the BLM established a second base in Boise, Idaho.

A Nevada Division of Forestry Engine Captain receives a briefing from the Operations Section Chief. Constant communication and situation assessments enable firefighters to better gauge the fire's status as well as to protect the safety of the crews fighting the fire. (Ronan Thornhill)

Hotshots

USFS "hotshot crews" were started in southern California in the late 1940s. The name was a reference to their being elite crews who were dropped or mobilized into the hottest part of wildfires. Their specialty is wildfire suppression, but they are sometimes assigned other jobs, including search and rescue and disaster response assistance. These crews may be sent anywhere in the United States, and have been deployed to Mexico and Canada as well. As with smokejumpers, these elite firefighters can safely and efficiently use all fire tools including Pulaskis, chainsaws, blasting fuses, pumps, and generators. They are also trained to offer emergency medical services. In national emergencies the crews are assigned to floods, earthquakes, and to manage events requiring interagency efforts.

Above: A "fire boss" assesses the ever-changing situation of an wildland fire. Armed with a two-way radio, he is able to report developments to his headquarters and request additional assistance as required. Also, his whistle allows him to communicate quickly with his crew as they go about their suppression activities. (Nevada Division of Forestry)

"Hot Shot" members from Zuni, New Mexico, take a well-deserved break from their efforts to control the raging fires around Los Alamos in May 2000. As with their structural firefighting counterparts, wildland firefighters can suffer from exhaustion, smoke inhalation, and burn injuries. Rest and hydration are critical to survival in these long firefighting campaigns of the wildland fire season. (Andrea Booher/FEMA News Photo)

In 1981, the National Park Service created the first Department of the Interior hotshot crews. The Bureau of Land Management followed with a California crew in 1983, and an Alaska-based hotshot crew in 1984. In 1986, the Bureau of Indian Affairs (BIA), which is responsible for fire protection on Native American lands, established the Mescalero Apache hotshot crew in New Mexico.

Coordinated Response

As firefighting efforts became more organized and efficient, the country saw a drop in the number of acres burned. During the decade of the 1940s, an average of nearly 23 million acres burned. During the 1950s, the number had dropped to about 9.5 million. The 1960s brought further reductions with the average yearly number of acres burned reported at 4.5 million.

The 1960s also brought great changes to wildland firefighting. The Boise Interagency Fire Center (BIFC) was established in 1965, evolving from separate efforts by the Bureau of Land Management and USFS to improve fire and aviation support throughout much of the Great Basin

Opposite, top, left: A Santo Domigo (New Mexico) Indian firefighter in action in June 1956, in Sitgreaves National Forest, Arizona. Removing the unburned material by shoveling it into the burning area is one way to prevent the forward progress of a wildland fire. By doing this, fuel sources are removed, and the fire is not able make progress in a particular direction. (National Agricultural Library/Special Collections)

and Intermountain West. The Weather Bureau soon contributed its fire weather forecasting capability to this unique interagency mission.

Efforts to pool fire and aviation resources proved so successful that three more land management agencies—the National Park Service, the Bureau of Indian Affairs, and U.S. Fish and Wildlife Service (USFWS)—brought their fire leadership to operate from the BIFC in the 1970s. The USFWS, which formally instituted a fire program in 1978, is the youngest of the five federal land management agencies to have a fire program. In early 1993, the BIFC name was changed to the National Interagency Fire Center (NIFC) to more accurately reflect its national mission. In 2002, the National Association of State Foresters (NASF) established a full-time fire director position at NIFC.

State forestry organizations form the basis for state and private lands protection and are an equal partner with federal fire agencies. The mandate for state-federal coordination at NIFC influenced the formation of the National Wildfire Coordinating Group (NWCG) in the early 1970s. The publication by a federal commission of *America Burning* (1973) also brought some pressure for integrated national firefighting concepts. Wildland fire programs also became interesting to the aerospace industry, which had just been drastically reduced in defense missions. An finally, the escalating costs associated with wildland firefighting argued for cost-sharing among the states, private industries, and the federal government.

Top, right: *In the August 1961 Sleeping Child Fire in the Bitterroot National Forest, Montana, the fuel was heavy lodgepole pine. Massive trees full of pine sap are a potent fuel source for a large fire. The crew seen here has been in the process of cutting down trees in the way of the fire. Not only does ground cover need to be cleared, but in the event of a crown fire that races across the tops of the trees, removing the entire tree may become necessary. (National Agricultural Library/Special Collections/W. E. Steuerwald)*

Above, left: *Flames are beginning to climb into the tops of trees on the McKnight Fire in Gila National Forest, New Mexico, in 1951. This 41,000-acre fire crowned out continually, often sweeping over back-fired areas and across the line into virgin territory. Wildfires are sometimes unpredictable and change directions at a moment's notice. (National Agricultural Library/Special Collections/E. L. Perry)*

Above, right: *Mescalero Apache Indians from New Mexico fighting a forest fire on the Mendocino National Forest, California, in August 1951. They were flown in by the Air Force from their reservation and are the crack "Red Hat" group trained by the Indian Service to fight fire on their reservation. (National Agricultural Library/Special Collections/Chester Shields)*

Above: *A bulldozer draws a "fire-line"—a line that firefighters hope will stop the fire. Heavy equipment is often necessary to create a fire break to deprive the fire of the fuel that it needs to continue to burn. Once cleared, this line will provide a chance for firefighters to get the upper hand on a deteriorating fire spread situation. (Liz Roll/FEMA News Photo)*

Right: *A fire crew utilizes two booster lines to extinguish a small fire in low brush before it has a chance to grow larger. Women and men work side by side (as seen here) to combat wildland fires across the country. Stopping a small fire early means they won't have to deal with a larger incident later. (Nevada Division of Forestry)*

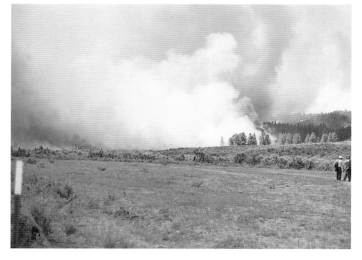

Two of the first major actions of NWCG were to promulgate a charter outlining its organization and functions, and to add a representative from the National Association of State Foresters (NASF). The first state forester added was the chair of their NASF's Fire Committee and a past president, Ralph Winkworth, of North Carolina.

Under the NWCG umbrella, all the federal firefighting agencies and their state counterparts have the same training materials and requirements. In order to participate, agencies have to agree to specific qualifications for each firefighting position, the consistent use of personal protective equipment (PPE), and an integrated Incident Command System. Also, the coordinated "closest forces" approach to dispatching firefighting resources must be adhered to. The most important element of the NWCG cooperation, however, has to do with its commitment to firefighter safety.

Safety

Fighting wildfires is dangerous—extremely dangerous. In 1937, fifteen USFS firefighters were killed on the Shoshone National Forest in Wyoming. In 1943, eleven firefighters were killed on the Hauser Creek Fire in the Cleveland National Forest in California. Tragedy struck the USFS smoke-jumper community in 1949, when thirteen jumpers were overcome on the Mann Gulch Fire on the Helena National Forest in Montana. In 1953, fifteen firefighters died on the Rattlesnake Fire on the Mendocino National Forest in California; and in 1956, eleven more perished in the Inaja Fire on the Cleveland National Forest in Pine Valley, California. Many other wildland firefighters from federal, state, and local agencies also suffered fatal injuries during these same years.

In 1957, chief of the USFS, Richard McCardle, chartered a group to study ways in which the Forest Service could strengthen efforts to prevent firefighter fatalities. In the late 1950s, federal agencies commissioned a group of experts to study firefighter fatalities and to recommend improvements. The report identified common characteristics in fatal fires, the most significant of which were: the widespread use of "flashy" fuels capable of quick ignition and rapid spread; the misidentification of a "rapid change" period during a wildland fire wherein remedial action was not taken; and lack of understanding of fire behavior due to changing weather conditions, or the phenomenon of a fire actually creating weather within its influence. Key to the findings was the conclusion that although a dangerous endeavor, wildland firefighting could be much safer, and fatalities could be greatly reduced.

From the recommendations in this report came the seeds of firefighter safety training as we recognize them today. First, ties to the National Weather Service were greatly strengthened in recognition of the importance weather accuracy plays in firefighter survivability. Second, training materials were standardized and distributed to all federal, state, and private wildland firefighters. This material concentrated on safety and included fire behavior models. Firefighters were encouraged to use their radio communication equipment much more frequently, and improved

Forest fires resulted from extreme drought in Florida in June 1988. Some were caused by lightning strikes and others were believed to be arson. This fire rages in an area ripe for rapid advancement. The material is dry and there is a great deal of underbrush. The pine trees provide a high fuel content and burn rapidly under these conditions. (Liz Roll/ FEMA News Photo)

Opposite, bottom, left: *Mitchell Canyon Fire (northwest of Reno, Nevada) races toward Highway 395. In preparation, the Nevada Highway Patrol closes the road. (Ronan Thornhill)*

Opposite, bottom, right: *Fire mop-up duties are carried out by the Nevada Division of Forestry handcrews on the Mitchell Canyon Fire that burned northwest of Reno, Nevada. (Ronan Thornhill)*

Helen Dowe watches for fires from the Devil's Head Fire Lookout in Pike National Forest, Colorado, in 1919. An Osborne Fire Finder is on the table. Spotting small fires from elevated lookouts was once the primary means of early warning. (© F.E. Colburn/ Corbis)

255

A wildland firefighter takes a much needed break from the obvious strain of working in the brush. This will be short lived, however, as the fire behind her will not take the same respite. Women serve all over the country in wildland fire crews. (Nevada Division of Forestry)

communication techniques were called for. Finally, the report recognized the pivotal role of the "crew boss" in the survival scenario.

In 1959, the USFS Missoula Technology and Development Center (MTDC) began working on a fire shelter, and exploring fire-resistant clothing for additional firefighter safety. The fire shelter was developed in 1967, and made mandatory in 1977. The shelter is a part of the standard issue of personal protective equipment carried by all wildland firefighters, and fits the body like a snug sleeping bag. It is utilized only as a last resort when overcome by a fire and is capable of protection in excess of 500

The Arkansas River 31 wildland fire crew works on putting out hot spots on the southern flank of this Hayman, Colorado, fire in June 2002. Once the major portion of the fire is extinguished, crews must revisit areas of smoldering wood and brush to prevent a rekindle. (Michael Rieger/FEMA News Photo)

A major wildland fire works its way up a hillside. Wildland fires generally move quickly in an uphill direction and are difficult to stop until they reach the top of a ridge. Positions above this fire on the ridge top are especially dangerous and difficult to defend. However, getting ahead of the fire at some point is critical to slowing or stopping its progress. (Nevada Division of Forestry)

degrees. Extensive use of flame-resistant treated cotton shirts and the testing of pants began in 1962. In 1973 and 1974, due to work done by the MTDC, the Forest Service adopted Nomex flame resistant shirts and pants. Over the next few years, all the federal firefighters and most state firefighters adopted the Personal Protective Equipment ensemble of hardhat, gloves, goggles, flame-resistant clothing, and boots.

Through federal grant programs administered by the states, rural and volunteer firefighters receive assistance to outfit their firefighters as well. A redesigned fire shelter offering improved protection was approved for issue in June 2003. The current fire shelter has saved over 250 lives, but is still no substitute for following the Ten Standard Fire Orders, and avoiding entrapment.

Lessons about entrapment avoidance, and adherence to the Fire Orders, were tragically reinforced after nine Princeville Hotshots, three smokejumpers from McCall, Idaho, and two helitack firefighters died on the South Canyon Fire in Colorado in 1994 (also commonly known as the Storm King Fire). South Canyon was a wakeup call to the wildland firefighting community that even experienced professionals could forget the basics with tragic results. As a result of this one event, the approach to wildland firefighting safety would never be the same. All agencies resolved that firefighter safety would not simply be an element of fire suppression, but the first priority.

Firefighting safety training programs now stress each individual's responsibility and the right to a safe work environment. Wildland firefighters receive lessons to help them correctly identify breaches in safety practices, and to demonstrate appropriate responses to unsafe conditions. They are taught risk management practices, fire behavior science, improved communication skills, and entrapment avoidance. Field drills, to simulate wildfire behavior and suppression techniques, are widely used.

FEMA coordinated closely with emergency services to battle this Los Alamos, New Mexico, blaze more effectively. The jobs of a wildland firefighter are many and varied. They can be actively fighting a fire with hoses, clearing a fire break, felling large trees, starting backfires, or wetting down hot spots to prevent rekindles. All are necessary and all are important. (Andrea Booher/FEMA News Photo)

The danger of living in the forest. This house shows the risks that are taken when building homes and businesses near woodlands that are prone to wildland fires. Such a situation becomes a priority for the firefighters to save the lives and property as well as concentrating on the fire looming behind. (Nevada Division of Forestry)

Firefighters battle flames along State Road #11 in Bunnel, Florida, in June 1998. Wildland fires occur in areas with easy access as well as regions remote to any organized road system. Roads such as this may act as a man-made fire break and slow the spread of a wildland fire. (Liz Roll/FEMA News Photo)

Urban Interface

In 1970, 382 homes burned in one wildland fire in Laguna, California. It wasn't until 1991, when over 2,000 homes burned in the famous Malibu fires, that urban interface issues began to garner public attention. With more and more homes built in or near wildlands, more homes are burning. The technique called "defensible space," wherein homeowners protect their property through the proper placement and type of landscaping, began to focus homeowners on their responsibilities. In 1996, the USFS developed FIREWISE, a wildland fire prevention program used by fire departments and wildland firefighters throughout the West.

Recently, wildfires have become larger and the firefighting season prolonged. Partially because fire suppression worked so well during the years since the 1910, a buildup of fuel sources in our national wildlands have contributed to record loss years for 2000 and 2002. This unintended consequence of fire suppression—fewer fires allowing the accumulation of fuel sources—and the growth of unhealthy forests and range conditions have created the dangerous environment of the last two decades.

For example, in 1988, the fires in Yellowstone National Park caught the nation off-guard. Almost completely due to the problem of undergrowth buildup, over a million and a half acres burned in Yellowstone and adjacent forests during that fateful summer. Although the land management agencies had been quietly burning undergrowth for many years, public resistance regarding this practice was intense and had kept controlled-fires to a minimum. Media coverage of wildfires in Yellowstone, however, has helped spread the message that these large fires feed on the fuel load created by the avoidance of controlled fire and mechanical

treatment measures. As a result, "prescribed" fires are increasingly used as tools to reduce overgrown forests and rangelands. As these measures are used safely, public acceptance should increase.

Much of the history of the American West, natural and human, has been shaped by fire. That's not likely to change in years to come. The record fire season of 2000 brought unprecedented funding to the federal agencies and states, not only for suppression, but for research, and a better understanding of the fuel build-up issues. In 2002, the administration of President George W. Bush (a Texan) and the governors of the western states, signed a ten-year comprehensive strategy to address the problems of forest health and fuel load, while pledging to a long-range commitment to new and better suppression controls.

Top, left: Miami-Dade firefighters from Squirt 29 work on extinguishing a wildfire in South Florida. Florida has been susceptible in recent years to large wildfires. A long period of drought and ample fuel are a lethal combination. Firefighters from metropolitan areas are often called upon to respond to wildland fires when favorable fire conditions and frequency are high. (Miami-Dade Fire Rescue)

Top, right, and above: Firefighting equipment stands ready for use in battling raging fires in the Oakland and Berkeley areas at the Naval Air Station in Alameda, California, on October 1, 1991. Active duty and reserve naval units also provided equipment, airlift support, and medical assistance to help combat the blaze, which was being labeled as one of the worst residential fires in U.S. history. The second photo, above, shows an aerial view of the massive amount of apparatus. (U.S. Air Force)

There is a great appreciation for the work that wildland firefighters do. As depicted in this makeshift sign, the citizens of this particular area are indeed grateful for the efforts of these fire crews. (Nevada Division of Forestry)

Rose Davis, USDA Forest Service, Public Affairs Specialist, contributed substantially to the writing and research of this chapter. Also of significant assistance were Jo Simpson, Bureau of Land Management, Chief of Communications; Dylan Rader, Bureau of Land Management, Firefighter (Engine Module Leader); and Loretta Smith, Nevada Division of Forestry, Administrative Assistant.

Fire Departments and Emergency Medical Services

Fire Departments and Emergency Medical Services

Chief Mary Beth Michos

According to a survey conducted by the International Association of Fire Chiefs (IAFC) in 2002, an estimated 94 percent of fire departments in the United States provide some level of out-of-hospital Emergency Medical Services (EMS). But it wasn't always this way. While the fire service has delivered emergency medical care for over seventy years, their participation in EMS has evolved over the years, and sometimes somewhat reluctantly. This evolution was almost a natural occurrence, since traditionally fire departments have been strategically located in communities and have the resources for rapid response to citizens in crisis.

As early as 1928, a few fire departments began providing first aid services to citizens suffering from heart attack symptoms or who had trouble breathing. These services were provided with the respirator equipment the firefighters carried to treat other firefighters who were overcome with smoke. Later during the 1930s, fire departments began developing special vehicles to render assistance to citizens in their communities who were ill or injured.

During the 1940s and 1950s, more fire departments started providing ambulance services, which consisted primarily of basic first aid and sometimes transport services, too. In many communities this was out of necessity as funeral home directors, the traditional providers of ambulance services, began to give up this practice.

Above: Different incidents present different challenges. A minor cut, burn, or fracture can be easily handled by a few rescuers. Other responses require many hands. This call required the full attention of paramedics and firefighters. CPR is performed, intravenous fluids and medications are administered, special monitoring equipment is employed, and all of this needs to be moved toward the transport vehicle as quickly as possible while still performing all rescue functions effectively. (Paul Ramirez/Phoenix Fire Department)

Pages 260–261: Having located, immobilized, treated, and packaged this patient for transport, this fire and EMS crew load him into the transport vehicle. In some jurisdictions the treatment and transport vehicles are two separate units. In others the paramedics arrive in the same vehicle in which they will eventually transport the patient to the hospital. (Craig Hacker)

Opposite: Even the rescuers can be the victim. Here is an incident where the vehicle responding to the emergency became the emergency. Crew members access the victims through the front window of the vehicle while others work to remove the metal structural members with a hydraulic spreading and cutting device to free their fellow workers. (Montgomery County (MD) Fire and Rescue Service)

Above: *Early emergency medical services were provided by funeral homes. They had the vehicles appropriate to carry a patient and an attendant. When fire departments took over EMS, they initially used similar vehicles. Above is a 1937 Buick hearse belonging to the Beall Funeral Home. When the Damascus, Maryland, Fire Department began their EMS service they used this vehicle to get started and co-owned it with the Beall Funeral Home. (Olin Molesworth/Collection of Leonard King)*

Top, right: *In 1949, the FDNY purchased this 1949 Flexible as Ambulance 1. It was utilized as a mobile emergency room. While today's concept of EMS is to treat the patient in the field and bring them to the emergency room, this was more of an attempt to bring the emergency room to the patient. (Jack Lerch)*

Right: *This 1957 Desoto Ambulance is an example of standard vehicles adapted for EMS roles. Initially, many funeral homes provided ambulance services. Once the fire departments started emergency medical response, they adapted the vehicles used by the funeral homes for EMS. Manufacturers such as Cadillac, Oldsmobile, and Desoto were used for these vehicles. (John A. Calderone)*

In the early days before EMS services were a part of fire departments, fire apparatus carried basic first aid equipment. This particular unit was a metal kit mounted on the running board or side of the fire truck in the 1940s. Initially the kit was to be used for treating firefighters and the occasional civilian injury. (Craig Hacker)

By the mid 1960s, it was becoming obvious to agencies within the federal government and medical profession that deaths from traffic injuries were increasing annually, and that a better system of caring for trauma victims was needed. In 1966, the National Research Council published a document titled *Accidental Death and Disability: The Neglected Disease of Modern Society*, which cited a lack of training, standards, and a systems approach as the contributing factors to the loss of lives outside the hospital from trauma. This report set into motion the wheels of change that greatly transformed the medical approach to caring for accident victims. But, most importantly, it also laid the foundation for a nationwide movement to improve out-of-hospital emergency procedures and created a systems approach to trauma care.

One of the most important developments in understanding the "chain of survival" occurred in 1967, when an Irish cardiologist, Dr. J. Frank Pantridge, published the results of his research on the benefits of taking advanced life support to the victims of heart attacks and sudden cardiac arrest. Prior to this, the standard of care for such patients was to get them to the hospital for care. The results of Pantridge's trials demonstrated that the mortality from cardiac disease could be reduced by early administration of advanced life support on scene, a true revolution in victim survivability. In several locations throughout the United States, the medical profession took note of this and initiated pilot programs based on the success of the Irish studies. Physician groups in university medical centers and Heart Association chapters in Seattle, Washington, Columbus, Ohio, Jacksonville, Florida, and Montgomery County, Maryland, partnered

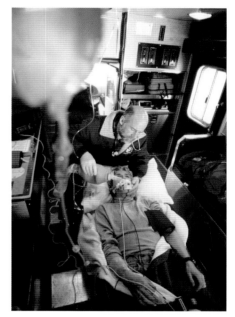

Above: Modern paramedics have many tools at their disposal. As this paramedic assists the patient's breathing, the heart is monitored, the oxygen saturation level is kept track of, and the blood pressure is checked regularly. Many other pieces of equipment are available in the cabinets of the emergency vehicle for any eventuality. (© Tom Stewart/ Corbis)

with the local fire departments to implement the first paramedic advanced life support programs in the country.

In 1972, a television show called "Emergency!," based on the Los Angeles County Fire Department Paramedic Service, became a huge hit. The program educated the public as to who paramedics were, what they did, and even more importantly, set an expectation in communities across the country for fire departments to provide similar services. The public, as well as local government and fire service leaders, became more aware of the value-added characteristics of the EMS which, in turn, led to its

Left: In the earlier days of fire departments, EMS vehicles were adapted from standard vehicles. This FDNY Ambulance 4, 1975 Dodge/Yankee is one example. Taking a standard, commercial full-sized van, the roof is raised by adding a fiberglass addition. This allowed more room in the rear for patient care. (John A. Calderone)

265

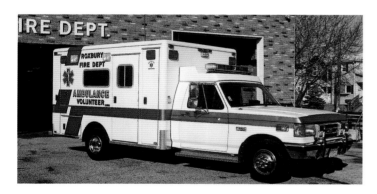

Above: *Ansonia, Connecticut, Civil Defense uses this 1989 GMC/Emergency One vehicle to transport emergency equipment and supplies to mass casualty scenes. It also pulls an EMS All-terrain vehicle (above, right). This adaptation of an ATV is similar to the Gator used by the New York City Fire Department. This ATV would carry paramedics and equipment to an incident that would be difficult for larger vehicles to access. Once the patient was treated, they could be taken back to a transport vehicle or, if necessary, lifted by helicopter using the Stokes Basket attached to the side. (John A. Calderone)*

integration into many fire departments. Aside from media attention, there really were many characteristics of fire departments that made the adoption of EMS a natural fit. Several of these included:

- The existence of staff who were already trained in basic medical support services;
- Proximity and access to the public from fire stations strategically located in the community;
- In-place communication systems;
- An understanding of command and control structures;
- Administrative and managerial support;

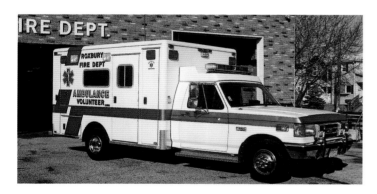

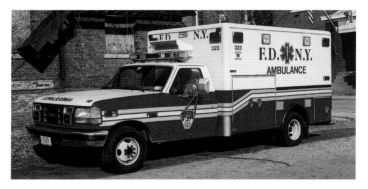

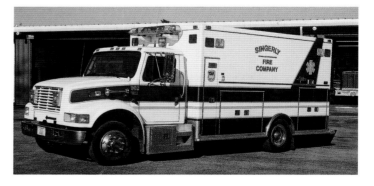

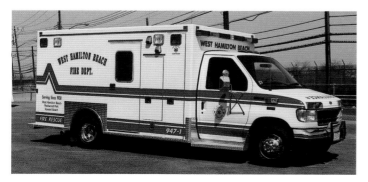

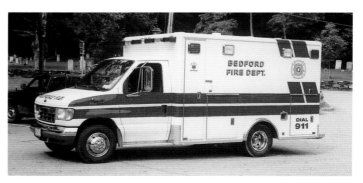

- Existing public relations and public education programs;
- Capacity for additional services (in some fire departments) due to a decline in fire suppression activities.

Throughout the 1970s, more fire departments throughout the United States became involved in providing EMS. The interest the federal government and Congress had in EMS resulted in the Emergency Medical Services Systems Act of 1973. Along with this legislation, nearly $200 million was authorized to be spent on improving EMS. This funding was motivation for many fire services to get involved in this aspect of public safety. In future years, many fire departments would come to view entering EMS as an excellent business decision.

With the increase of fire departments offering EMS, it became apparent that there needed to be some guidance for fire services in EMS program design and operations. In late 1979, the United States Fire Administration (USFA) sponsored the "Rockville Conference" in Rockville, Maryland. The report from the conference laid the foundation for fire-based EMS programs, and provided guidance for the development of programs in alignment with the federal guidelines for prehospital EMS. The result of this widely read report was an increase in the number of fire department EMS programs. There was still reluctance, however, among some fire service leaders to fully embrace EMS.

In 1991, Olin L. Greene, Jr., USFA administrator, along with Wallace E. Stickney, director of the Federal Emergency Management Agency (FEMA), signed a mission statement, stating, "The nation's fire service is recognized as the first responders to medical and other emergencies." This was on the tail of a joint statement between the International Association of Fire Chiefs (IAFC) and International Association of Fire Fighters (IAFF), recognizing the role of the fire service as a major provider of prehospital EMS. After years of perseverance by many fire services and EMS leaders, EMS was finally being accepted as a primary component of the fire service. With the recognition, support, and encouragement of national organizations such as the IAFF, the IAFC, and the National Fire Protection Association (NFPA), every year more fire services are getting into EMS or increasing their involvement.

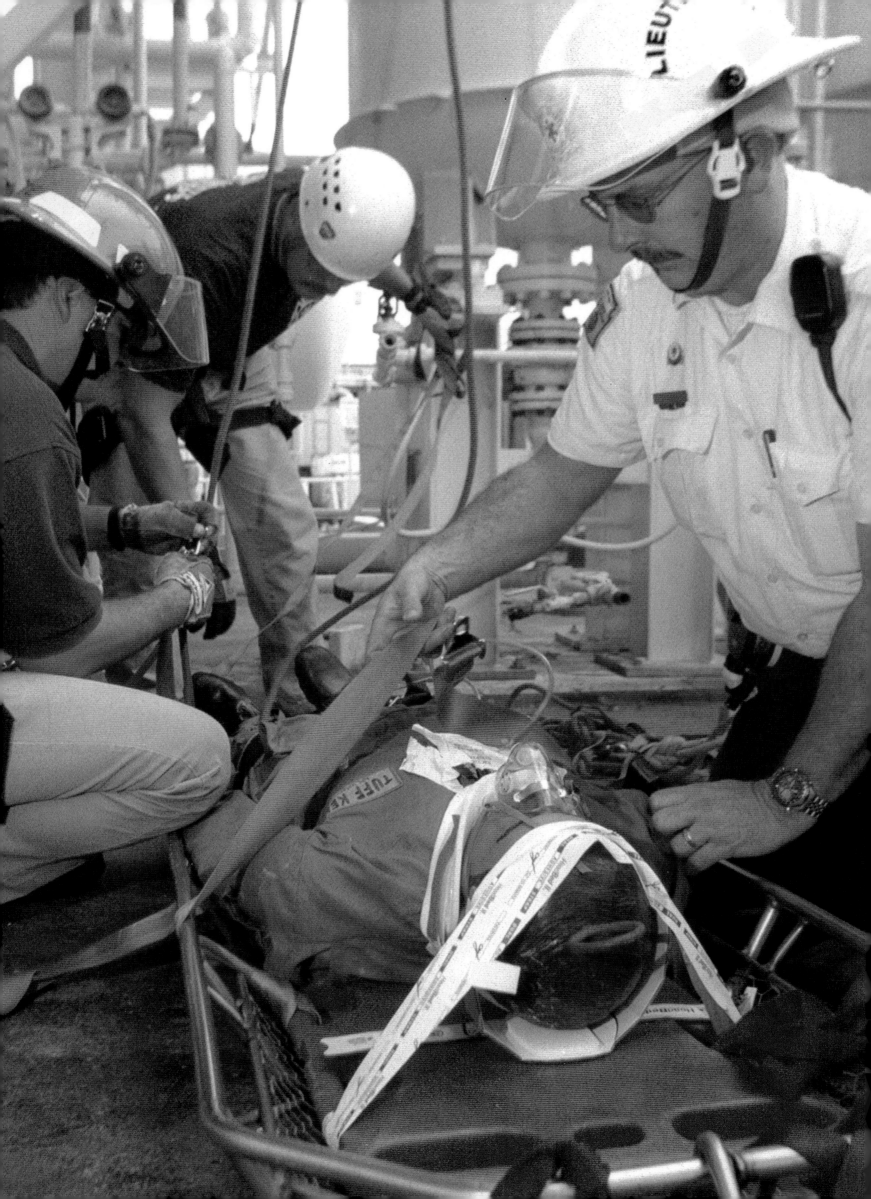

While there are numerous people who played a significant role in developing and promoting fire-based EMS programs, there is one person who has been there since the beginning of "modern EMS" and who is still influential today. James O. Page has been an innovator and crusader of Fire-EMS since the 1960s. Jim participated in the early Rockville Conference, and was responsible for many of the early publications that guided the formative years of fire-based EMS. He knows the fire service well, having worked his way up the ranks to the position of fire chief in Carlsbad, California. From serving as a consultant on the set of "Emergency!," to being an attorney specializing in EMS, and the publisher emeritus of an EMS publication (*JEMS*), Jim has kept his finger on the pulse and the state of EMS, and has provided guidance to support its growth and increasing levels of sophistication.

James O. Page, shown here in 1959 driving Los Angeles County's Rescue 11, has been a visionary for the fire service in general and EMS in particular. The author of fire service books and the founder of the Journal of Emergency Medical Services, James O. Page now works as a consultant and legal advisor in California. Both firefighters and paramedics are grateful to him for his contributions to the service. (Courtesy of James O. Page)

Fire-based EMS Today

The level of involvement in EMS varies from fire department to fire department, and according to the region of the country. A *Fire Service/EMS Program Management Guide*, published by FEMA and the Acute Coronary Treatment Foundation in the early 1980s, described twenty-eight different EMS Program profiles. These profiles still hold true today. The fire-based EMS models consist of different levels of treatment capabilities, ranging from First Responder, Emergency Medical Technician, to Paramedic.

The service treatment levels are primarily categorized as to transporting or nontransporting. Whether a department is a career, volunteer or combination service will also influence the EMS service model. The large variety of configurations sometimes leads to frustration between the fire departments and the communities they serve. With populations being so mobile, and as citizens change communities, they bring with them certain expectations for prehospital service. In particular, they have ideas about appropriate levels of service and response times, which may not be met in their new community.

A standardization of programs still does not exist. While there are national educational curricula for the various levels of providers, profound

Opposite: Firefighters and paramedics prepare this patient for removal from the location where he was injured. Industrial sites such as this do not often allow a simple way to get the patient to the transport vehicle. A preponderance of equipment or narrow passageways make it difficult to move a patient who has been immobilized. Here the Stokes Basket is being prepared for lifting. (Craig Hacker)

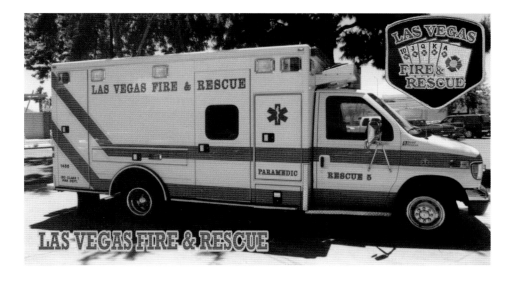

Rescue 5 of Las Vegas Fire and Rescue stands ready to respond. Las Vegas has a tremendous transient population in its tourist areas due to the large number of hotel/casinos that house thousands of people. This, along with the resident population, presents a unique challenge to EMS personnel. (Las Vegas Fire Department)

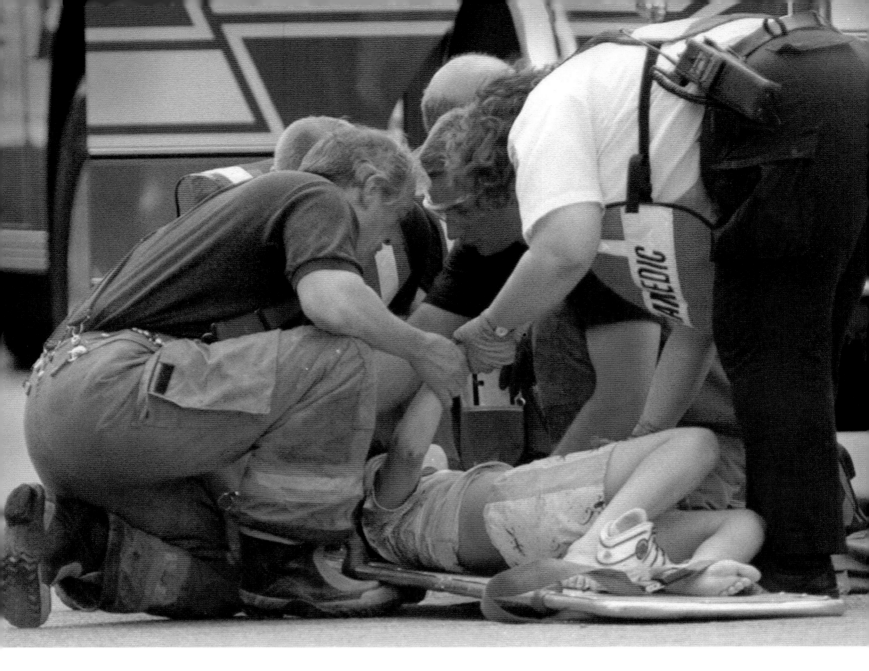

Paramedics and firefighters work to treat and reassure this young patient. Children are a particular challenge for EMS personnel. Because they are strangers to the child, it is important to gain the child's trust as soon as possible. This is made all the more difficult because the child has just suffered an unexpected trauma and may be in extreme pain. (Craig Hacker)

differences still exist. An obvious area of difference is the training, certification, and recertification of advanced life support providers. Most of the differences occur state-to-state. There are various levels of advanced life support personnel, with some states addressing them as Paramedic I, Paramedic II, and so forth. Other states call their advanced life support personnel Cardiac Rescue Technicians, Cardiac Technicians, Shock Trauma Technicians, and Intermediate Paramedics. These differences are a result of programs that were developed before standard curricula were developed and that have become widespread within specific states.

A national *EMS Education and Practice Blueprint* was developed and distributed in 1993. The *Blueprint* has guided development of national curricula by the U.S. Department of Transportation (DOT). Updates of the *Blueprint* have also guided the certification process of the National Registry of Emergency Medical Technicians (NREMT). Use of the NREMT for testing and certification over the past thirty years has made significant impact on standardization of EMS testing and certification programs at the state level. A more recent publication, *EMS Education Agenda for the Future* (2000), was developed under the auspices of the DOT National Highway Traffic Safety Administration. It establishes goals for accreditation of EMS training programs and a national EMS certifying agency. These goals offer a significant challenge to fire departments, but

they can be addressed through planning. Fire departments providing EMS services today face many challenges, including changes in community demographics, an aging population, budget constraints, the demands for new technology, and even medicine itself.

EMS in the fire service brought many new relationships and issues that are new to fire department culture. With EMS came oversight by the medical community. Today, all levels of EMS are required to have medical control and direction. This requires fire administration dealing with a new group in the community that sometimes speaks a different professional language. The coordination of the medical aspects, with the operational-delivery aspects of the fire service, has required the forging of partnerships between the fire departments and medical communities—both individual physicians and hospitals. Larger fire departments have found the need to hire their own medical directors, either on a part-time or full-time basis. The duties and responsibilities of the physician are broad and frequently defined in state legislation or local regulations.

One primary area of medical director responsibility is the oversight of quality assurance programs for the training and practice of EMS personnel. This internal auditing of emergency medical services is labor and resource intensive, but is necessarily part of the cost of doing business for an EMS program. In times when resources are limited, it takes a coordinated effort between the fire administration and medical director to ensure that high-quality programs are available to the community.

A paramedic bends over a trauma patient and stabilizes his head prior to immobilization. Obvious bleeding wounds make it necessary for the caregiver to don gloves and glasses to prevent his exposure to any unknown medical condition. Still, the utilization of these precautions does not delay the treatment of the patient. (Paul Ramirez/Phoenix Fire Department)

Teams of bicycle paramedics allow emergency care to reach patients in areas not easily accessible by motorized vehicles. Here, the Phoenix Fire Department bike team patrols at the Sky Harbor International Airport. Airports, malls, pedestrian shopping areas, festivals, and sports events are a few of the situations that lend themselves well to this type of response. (Paul Ramirez/Phoenix Fire Department)

271

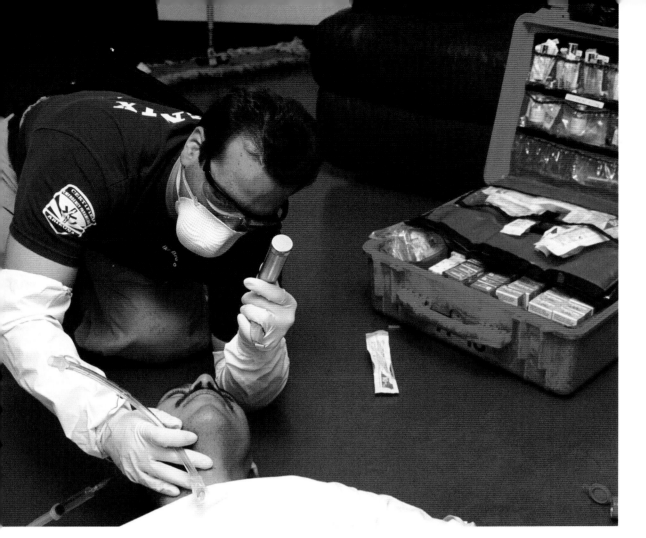

Training is as important in EMS as it is in firefighting. This series of photos shows a paramedic crew involved in a mock incident. Not only do they have to treat the patient; they need to be wary that there are inherent hazards to themselves in patient care. To minimize these hazards, they are outfitted with masks, gloves, and glasses to prevent the patients bodily fluids from coming in contact with them. These photos illustrate key points in the treatment: a) the airway is secured by the placement of an endotracheal tube; b) an intravenous catheter is inserted for fluid replacement; c) Cardio-Pulmonary Resuscitation (CPR) is in progress. (All photos courtesy of Paul Ramirez/Phoenix Fire Department)

Opposite, bottom: FDNY Battalion 58 Gator is a 1999 Deere/Chief Equipment. This is used for major events, parades, and New Years Eve at Times Square. Able to access tight, crowded areas and traverse rough terrain, this vehicle, or other configurations, is used to allow EMS teams access to unusual areas. These were workhorses at the World Trade Center in New York City in September 2001. (John A. Calderone)

Initially fire departments embraced EMS programs when the grant funds were plentiful. In the mid-1980s, when the federal funding sources disappeared, fire departments explored other means of funding their EMS programs. Private ambulance providers charged a fee for service, which in the majority of cases was paid by third-party payment from either insurance providers or Medicare-Medicaid. Many fire departments saw this as a means of generating a revenue stream to supplement public funding of their EMS programs. So, fee-for-service programs were implemented by fire departments throughout the country. The range of charges varied considerably, from a nominal fee to rates competitive with the private sector. Collection rates varied according to the aggressiveness of the jurisdiction. Generally a collection rate of 60 to 75 percent was considered very good.

Today EMS is seeing changes in the reimbursement from Medicare and the insurance industry. These changes will impact the amount of reimbursement for treatment and transportation services. Fire departments, as well as other EMS providers, will have to explore other means of supporting their programs, or ways of being more cost effective.

In 2000, federal funding became available to the fire service in the form of the Assistance to Firefighters Grant Program. Initially, the grant categories were very specific for fire operations, equipment, training, and health and safety. Recently EMS was added as a category, and funds became available for fire departments to advance the level of EMS care they provided. At this time, it is still too early to determine the impact of this funding on fire-based EMS.

Another challenge faced by fire departments nationwide is the shortage of paramedics. Fire departments have had to implement changes to

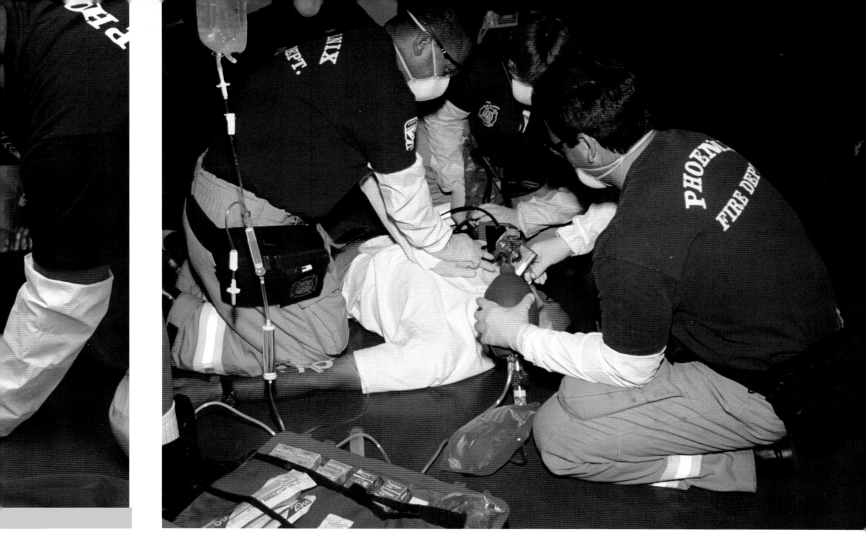

their operations to manage the shortage. Several departments, like the Dallas Fire Department, provide paramedic training as part of their recruit firefighter training program. Others like the Prince George's County Fire/Rescue Department in suburban Maryland, require all newly hired personnel to obtain their paramedic certification by their fourth year of service, or risk losing their job.

While many industry experts cite the increase in EMS training requirements as a disincentive, the problem is broader and has to do with the status of the profession. When asked what they want to be when they grow up, children will mention being a firefighter, and others interested in health care will say they want to be a nurse or physician. Children generally do not view being an Emergency Medical Technician or Paramedic as career options. Fire departments faced with EMS provider shortages need to present EMS opportunities as part of their career public education programs and recruiting efforts.

Fire-based EMS faces the same challenge today as do other emergency services, especially due to the increased threat from terrorism and weapons of mass destruction. By the nature of the threat to health and safety, the role of EMS is vital for the welfare of the general public and other emergency response personnel. Fire/EMS programs are providing response training and protection for providers. Triage and disaster management skills, along with hazardous materials response practices, are being packaged into training programs to protect all first responders, as well as to prepare them for dealing with mass casualty incidents resulting from terrorist acts.

Since their early proclamations regarding EMS as being an integral part of the fire service, the USFA, the IAFC, and the IAFF have taken

A U.S. Army medic tries to help a wounded soldier in Vietnam in 1966. War has traditionally led to advances in medicine that benefit the public at a later time. After the Vietnam War, some trained medics joined fire departments and eventually became part of the new EMS systems in those departments. (© Bettmann/Corbis)

Captain Mahner and the Search and Rescue Squad. The Honolulu Fire Department began to respond to rescue calls in 1932 and the rescue squad was given its first apparatus in January 1934; a modified 1923 Model "T" Ford Truck, christened "Rescue Wagon." Most of the squad's equipment was bought with private funds. (Honolulu Fire Department)

EMS crews are called to a variety of incidents in many varied locations. Here a worker was injured during a land clearing operation. Because of the injuries it was necessary to immobilize the patient to prevent further injury and start intravenous fluid replacement to prevent shock. Due to some remote locations, removing the patient to the transport vehicle can also be a challenge. (Prince William County [VA] Department of Fire and Rescue)

steps to demonstrate their commitment in this area. The IAFC has a very active EMS section, which recently was approved to have a representative on their board of directors. The IAFF has a very active EMS program promoting and supporting EMS among their membership. Both organizations conduct an annual conference focused on fire-based EMS.

The USFA National Fire Academy (NFA) has an EMS program and offers several courses focusing on the development of EMS leadership in the fire service, and educates thousands of fire service leaders annually about issues impacting fire-based EMS. The NFPA has supported the development of numerous standards that address EMS operations associated with fire department response. In addition, NFPA currently has an EMS committee that is developing guidelines for EMS programs.

Fire Service— EMS and Specialty Services

In the fire service, EMS has become a vital component of special and tactical operations. In the early 1980s, hazardous materials emergency response became more defined and regulated. As the level of involvement of the fire service advanced, the need for on-scene oversight of personnel became apparent. Fire departments with EMS programs saw the need to

Severely crushed vehicles require that specialized tools be used in order to extricate the patient in the least amount of time while not further jeopardizing the patient or rescue crew. Hydraulic spreaders and cutters have been a welcome addition to this process. They are able to exert tremendous pressures at their tips to either cut through metal or spread the metal members apart to gain access to the trapped victim. (Prince William County [VA] Department of Fire and Rescue)

Confined space rescues are a particular challenge for firefighters and paramedics. Often these spaces are very limited in size and make it difficult to access and treat the patient. In this case the crews were able to descend into the space to treat and immobilize the patient before removal. He has been secured to a Stokes Basket and removed from the space using a crane with the cable attached to on end of the Stokes. (Courtesy Las Vegas Fire Department)

275

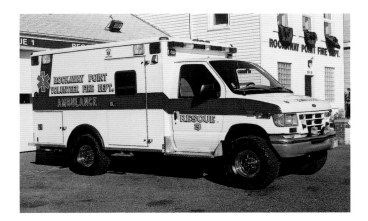

Rockaway Point Volunteer Fire Department in Queens, New York, Rescue 3, shows off their 1997 Ford/Wheeled Coach four-wheel-drive unit. Rockaway uses this configuration because they are a beach community with the need to access patients through sandy terrain. (John A. Calderone)

The Ansonia, Connecticut, Civil Defense Mass Casualty Unit is a 1978 Mercedes. These vehicles are stocked with supplies and equipment that might be required after catastrophic events including disastrous fires, floods, and storms. Initial responses would be handled by local fire departments with a unit such as this called in once the magnitude of the event was determined. (John A. Calderone)

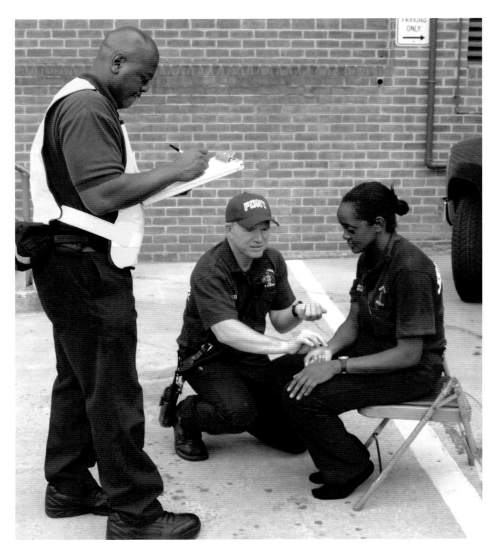

Part of the function of EMS in the fire service is the continued care of their own. Firefighters as well as the citizens they serve become injured and exposed to hazards of all kinds. Here a firefighter is monitored after working on a Hazardous Material Incident. While the firefighter may not be exhibiting signs of exposure at this point, and may not at all, it is important to develop a baseline of information to determine if there are changes later. (Prince William County [VA] Department of Fire and Rescue)

utilize their EMS staff to provide medical monitoring of their hazardous materials personnel to ensure their safety. In many areas, EMS staff assumed the responsibility for decontamination. As the NFPA developed standards and competencies for hazardous materials response, it also developed NFPA 473, which addresses the EMS response to hazardous materials incidents.

Within the development of Urban Search and Rescue (USAR) teams, an EMS sector was considered vital right up front. USAR teams all contain an EMS component to provide for the health, safety, and care of their response personnel.

The Role of Women in the Fire Service

Chief Debra J. Jarvis

The role of women in the fire service has evolved in much the same way as the role of women throughout American history—slowly, with great courage and much perseverance. Elizabeth Blackwell, the first U.S. woman physician once said, "It is not easy to be a pioneer—but oh, it is fascinating! I would not trade one moment, even the worst moment, for all the riches in the world."

Women entered the fire service, as they have many other professions, where there was a need to volunteer and serve the community. Like their male counterparts, they came from a variety of backgrounds, had an overwhelming desire to serve and help people, and often their family or friends were already involved in the fire service. This desire to serve and help people is a common bond that all firefighters share with each other in the United States. Women now serve as volunteer firefighters, career firefighters, emergency medical technicians, paramedics, dispatchers, public safety educators, wildland firefighters, and more. In many cases, after having been denied fire service opportunities, women have had to prove their abilities every step of the way. In other cases, they have had to fight to overcome barriers to employment.

There is no question that the fire service requires the hard physical labor that many other jobs have since eliminated with machinery. The women who have chosen to become firefighters have had to prove their way into this field, and continue to do so on a day-to-day basis. Mary Lou Retton, Olympic gold-medal gymnast, described the fire and passion that is necessary for all significant triumphs when she said, "Heat is required to forge anything. Every great accomplishment is the story of a flaming heart."

At the turn of the twentieth century, women were characterized as frail, weak, and better able to serve in the home than in a world where workers were referred to as "manpower" and hard, physical labor was the norm in many employment activities. Not until World War II was it proven on a large scale that women were up to the task of doing the physical labor that modern society had excluded them from for so long. To replace men who were sent to war, they labored in the factories and in nontraditional positions like firefighting. At this period in history, women served in many volunteer fire companies.

Interestingly, the first known woman firefighter in U.S. history was not a volunteer or a career firefighter, nor do we know if she chose to fight fires. Molly Williams, an African-American slave owned by a firefighter in the Oceanus Engine Company # 11 in New York City, served in the 1780s and into the 1800s. During the blizzard of 1818 she was reported to have been as good a "fire laddie" as any of the men in the Engine Company 11.

The Cedar Hill, Rhode Island, Fire Department lays claim to having the first woman fire chief in the world. Anne Crawford Allen Holst was the great grandniece of the founder of Factory Mutual. Chief Holst (also known as Nancy) was also a pilot and had an active interest in forest fire management. In the 1930s, the New England Association of Fire Chiefs published some of her work on forest fire weather and the angle for airplanes when fighting fires. Later, as the deputy state fire marshal, Holst developed the first fire control plan for the entire state of Rhode Island.

Following World War II, the first women to be paid for fire suppression work were in the USDA Forest

Amy Allen, a volunteer with the Chenango Fire Company, New York, donning her Self-contained Breathing Apparatus at the scene of a fire. (Rick Allen)

Service and on Bureau of Land Management (BLM) wild-land fire-fighting crews. One woman was actually hired and fired in the same day because she was a woman. In order to discourage her from further interest, she was given the impossible task (they thought) of recruiting twelve other women to do the same work if she wanted to be rehired. She ultimately recruited twenty-four other women to work on an all-women wildland fire-fighting crew in Fairbanks, Alaska, in 1971. The BLM reported the work of these women to be excellent.

Joe Carol Hamilton came from a firefighting family. Both her father and grandfather were firefighters. She started out helping at grass fires in the mid-1960s and ultimately became the first woman fire chief in the state of Arkansas. Before she became chief of the Shirley Volun-

teer Fire Department, she was a fire dispatcher, an apparatus driver, a fire instructor, and writer about women in the fire service. She focused on the importance of technique (for both men and women), rather than brute strength to effectively handle hose lines.

The first known career women firefighters were Sandra Forcier in 1973 in Winston-Salem, North Carolina (currently a battalion chief), and Judith Livers in 1974 in Arlington, Virginia, who retired in 1999 as a battalion chief. By 1975, women were serving on the following fire departments: Fort Wayne, Indiana; Fairborn, Ohio; Houston, Texas; Petersburg, Virginia; and the United States Air Force.

According to their 2001 survey, Women in the Fire Service, Inc., (WFS) estimates that there are approximately 6,100 women career firefighters in the United States (approximately 2 percent), and several thousand more women volunteer firefighters. Of U.S. career fire-

fighters, less than 400 women are officers below the rank of chief officer, less than 80 serve in chief officer ranks, and only 15 females serve at the top fire chief level. Urban fire departments (those with more than 75 career personnel) with the highest percentages of women firefighters include: Minneapolis, Minnesota (16 percent); Madison, Wisconsin (15 percent); San Francisco, California (15 percent); Boulder, Colorado (14 percent); and Miami Dade, Florida (13 percent). The top states in the number of women firefighters are California, Florida, Texas, Maryland, and Virginia.

Notable Women Fire Service Leaders

Women have served as chiefs of volunteer fire departments since the 1930s, and WFS estimates that there are approximately 125 women currently serving as volunteer fire chiefs. Chief Judy Cooper, recently retired, served ten years as the fire chief of Rattlesnake Volunteer Fire Department in Parker, Colorado.

Only in the last few years have women been appointed to career fire chief positions. As of July 2002, there are at least fifteen career or combination fire departments headed by a woman chief. Retired Chief Rosemary Bliss of Tiburon, California, was the first woman to head a career fire department. She went to California in 1973 and served as the Tiburon fire marshal until 1993 when she was appointed fire chief.

The first woman to be named chief of a large metropolitan fire department was Mary Beth Michos in 1994. Chief Michos currently serves as fire chief of the Prince William County Department of Fire and Rescue in Virginia. Chief Michos began her professional career as a critical care nurse before being hired by the Department of Fire and Rescue Services in Montgomery County, Maryland, as the emergency medical services officer. In 1986, she was assigned the position of fire/rescue training officer, and in 1989 was promoted to assistant chief. Chief Michos is one of the co-founders of the Women Chief Fire Officers organization, whose mission is to support, mentor, and educate current and future women chief fire officers.

Carrye B. Brown was the first woman and the first African-American to head the United States Fire Administration, the highest ranking fire service position in the country. Brown had the longest tenure (six years) of any United States Fire Administrator thus far. Fire losses achieved new lows during her administration, largely due to the development of more cooperative relationships between the USFA and state and local fire service organizations. She also initiated the first national public education program in USFA history that targeted reducing fire and life losses in high-risk groups. A native of Texas, she was appointed in 1994 by President Bill Clinton.

In 2002 in East Point, Georgia, Rosemary Cloud became the first African-American woman in the United States to become fire chief. Prior to that, Chief Cloud worked in the Atlanta Fire Department for twenty-two years, where she served in the ranks of firefighter, driver, lieutenant, captain, chief officer, and as assistant chief of Hartsfield International Airport Operations. Chief Cloud is a community activist involved in programs that promote improved educational opportunities. She is currently working with young girls in a mentoring program sponsored by WOMEN, INC.

One woman firefighter who has opened the hearts and minds of many to fire fighting as a career option for women is Olympic silver medalist Lea Ann Parsley. Ms. Parsley was a member of the 2002 U.S. Olympic Team in the head-first sliding sport of skeleton. Lea Ann, age thirty-three, has also been a career firefighter with the Plain Township Fire Department in New Albany, Ohio, since 1995. As a teenager she followed in the footsteps of her two older brothers, who were volunteer firefighters in her hometown of Granville, Ohio. Since the age of sixteen, she has been, and continues to be, a Granville volunteer firefighter. In addition to working toward a doctoral degree in nursing from Ohio State University, she is also a member of the Ohio Interagency Wildfire Crew that is part of the Federal Forestry Service. She has also been involved with a program through the Ohio Fire Academy that helps introduce young women to the fire service.

One of the most significant contributions for nurturing and linking women together has been Women in the Service, Inc. (WFS). Formed in 1982 by Terese M. Floren, an Ohio firefighter, and Linda Willing, a Boulder, Colorado, firefighter, WFS originally had 200 members. Now more than 100 members (male and female) join every year. WFS incorporated in 1984 and since that time has significantly impacted the national fire service with its involvement in fire service policy and standards-making bodies such as the United States Fire Administration and the National Fire Protection Association. Today, over 500 women (and men) routinely attend its biennial Women in the Fire Service conferences.

An offshoot group, the Women Chief Fire Officers Association, formed in 1998 by several women chief officers, focuses on supporting, mentoring, and educating current and future women chief fire officers. Their annual Fire Service Leadership Conference attracts some of the top fire and non-fire-service leadership speakers, and seeks to send the consistent message to women and men at all levels of the fire service that inclusion is an essential organizational value the fire service must embrace in order to continue to effectively serve our communities.

While women have not been invited into the fire service in most instances, they have earned their way in by demonstrating their passion, skill, strength, courage, dedication, and ability to do the job. In September 2002, the First Annual New York State Women Firefighters seminar was attended by 150 women from 101 fire departments. In her keynote statements, Battalion Chief Rochelle "Rocky" Jones, a veteran of the New York City Fire Department since 1982, summed up the sentiments of many women in the fire service when she said, "If you give it your all, you will succeed. Of course, not everyone will accept you, or give you credit you are due, but you can succeed. I have weathered the storms, but now all I see are the rainbows."

City of East Point, Georgia, Mayor Patsy Jo Hilliard and Fire Chief Rosemary Cloud at an event in Chief Cloud's honor, June 7, 2002. Chief Cloud was named on March 14, 2002, as the new chief of the East Point Fire Department. She became the first African-American woman, anywhere, ever to hold the position of fire chief. (Photo courtesy of Women in the Fire Service, Inc.)

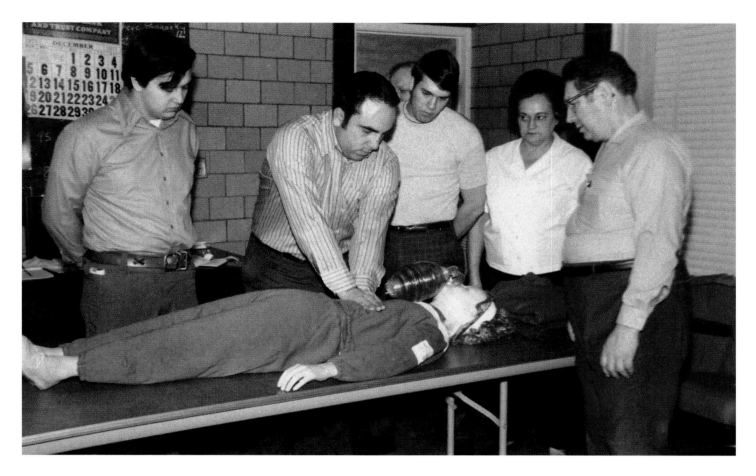

Fire-based EMS Public Education and Prevention Programs

Fire service involvement in EMS extends beyond emergency response. One of the components of an EMS system is public education and prevention, both areas where the fire service has a successful history. Using the framework and structure they had in place, fire departments have expanded their programs into the medical areas associated with their

An early CPR class at the Monessen (PA) Volunteer Fire Department Hose House #2. In early 1960, Drs. Kouwenhoven, Knickerbocker, and Jude discovered the benefit of chest compression to achieve a small amount of artificial circulation. Later in 1960, mouth-to-mouth and chest compression were combined to form CPR similar to the way it is practiced today. First used by doctors and then EMS personnel, it soon became evident that citizen-based CPR would buy valuable time for a patient in cardiac arrest until advanced care arrived. (Collection of Ronald J. Siarnicki).

Taking time to treat an injury of a child is never a chore for a firefighter or a paramedic. Here a young man receives treatment to cool the pain of a small burn injury on his arm. (Paul Ramirez/Phoenix Fire Department)

281

delivery services. Early on in the 1970s, departments started offering blood pressure checks at their stations and expanded to teaching citizen cardio-pulmonary resuscitation (CPR) classes for the public.

Fire prevention programs have evolved into injury prevention programs, with fire and burn prevention being an important component. The NFPA has expanded its prevention programs from the *Learn Not to Burn* program, targeted to third graders, to a more comprehensive injury prevention program. Their new *Risk Watch* program is a kindergarten-to-eighth-grade program with a curriculum addressing eight areas for risk prevention. They include fire and burn prevention, bike and pedestrian safety, choking, suffocation and strangulation prevention, motor vehicle safety, fall prevention, firearms, and water safety.

Fire departments throughout the country offer a variety of programs for their communities as part of their EMS prevention services. Many fire departments host or are active members of local "Safe Kids Coalitions." With this comes involvement in programs to promote bicycle helmet use, child passenger restraint projects, poison prevention, and child safety programs customized to meet the needs of the local community. Several departments have implemented a program for innoculating children, which was first developed and implemented by the Phoenix Fire Department.

Emergency Medical Dispatch

The rapid growth of EMS over the years has redefined the role of the various players who provide the service. As the level of sophistication of the emergency medical service increased, the role of the communications dispatcher (the entry point to the service), became more critical. In 1979, Dr. Jeff Clawson, of the Salt Lake City Fire Department, identified the medical dispatcher as the "weak link" in the chain of EMS response. Dr. Clawson became the pioneer in advancing the training and protocols for emergency medical dispatching.

Children who are victims of fire or injury have always been the focus of firefighters throughout the centuries. These innocent victims of situations beyond their control are given the full attention of all who respond. This child, a victim of a fire in a dwelling, is rushed to immediate care by a paramedic. (Craig Hacker)

Another example of the bicycle paramedic team. Las Vegas Fire and Rescue employs these teams for many events and in many areas that are not easily accessible to larger vehicles. In this manner the paramedics can be patrolling and respond very quickly to an incident. Once on the scene they can provide quick assessment and treatment before more formal transportation arrives. (Las Vegas Fire Department)

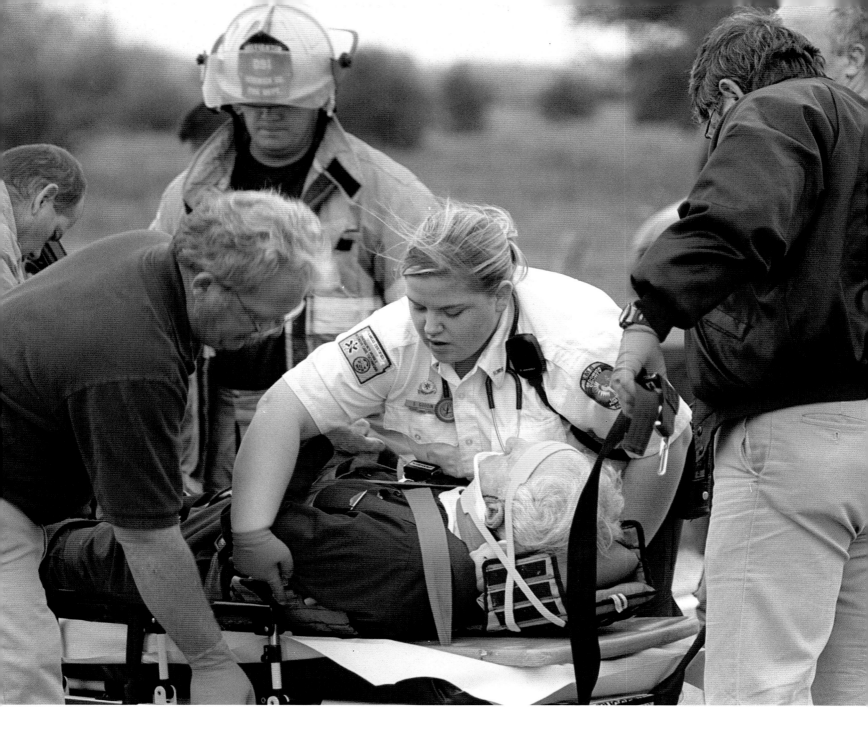

Dr. Clawson and others recognized the importance of the dispatcher as a vital player in the prehospital scenario. Dispatchers must screen calls to obtain enough information to set into motion the most appropriate apparatus and level of care. Triaging, or the prioritizing of calls, includes providing prearrival instructions to the caller, as well as providing responding units with vital information regarding the status of each patient. This has resulted in standardized training programs for communications call-takers and dispatchers. Courses for communication personnel now range from twenty-four to over forty hours, with certification as Emergency Medical Dispatcher (EMD) available through several sources.

Like other EMS personnel, medical dispatchers have to participate in continuing education. Always, their services should be under the auspices of the EMS system medical director. As with other components of an EMS system, there are quality assurance processes associated with EMD programs to ensure review of the processes as revisions are determined necessary.

When EMD programs were initially established, there were concerns expressed about the liability potential with screening of calls, triaging, and

"Many hands make light work." However, those hands need to be able to work together and trained for the task. Firefighters and paramedics work together as a team to ensure proper patient care. There are also different levels of cross training. In some jurisdictions, firefighters are capable of performing basic paramedic skills to assist in setting up intravenous solutions, starting of IV's, as well as the basic skills learned as Emergency Medical Technicians. (Craig Hacker)

283

As with most victims of trauma, stabilization must occur where the patient lies prior to transportation. The one exception to this would be if the conditions of the scene were hazardous to the patient or the rescuer. Paramedics perform an initial assessment and prepare to immobilize the cervical spine before proceeding further. (Craig Hacker)

Many patients in automobile collisions must be treated initially in the vehicle itself. Once the scene is determined safe, the paramedic assesses the patient for an open airway, adequate breathing, and adequate pulse. When that is assured, any obvious bleeding must be attended to, spinal immobilization accomplished, and obvious fractures splinted if possible. Intravenous fluids may be administered. All of this is done prior to moving the patient from the vehicle. (Montgomery County [MD] Fire and Rescue Service)

prearrival instructions by dispatchers. In many areas these concerns served as a significant barrier to implementation of EMD programs. Over the years, these programs have proven their worth and life-saving capabilities. Dispatchers routinely save lives by coaching callers through CPR, the Heimlich maneuver for relief of obstructed airways, and control of bleeding. Human interest stories about dispatchers helping in the delivery of babies are still viewed as newsworthy. A program that was once feared as a liability is now viewed as a great community asset. Dispatchers are indispensable partners in fire-based EMS programs.

Throughout its history, the fire service has responded to needs in the community. The provision of EMS was one of these needs, and the fire service over the past eighty years has made significant advancements in this area. In departments providing such service, EMS calls compose the majority of their emergency responses. No matter how reluctant initially, the fire service has taken up the challenges of providing emergency medical service, and has done so magnificently. EMS has transformed the fire service—it has become part of its culture, and a significant part of its future.

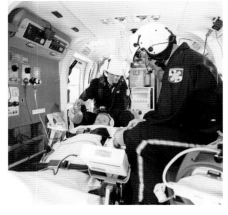

Hazardous Materials and Firefighters

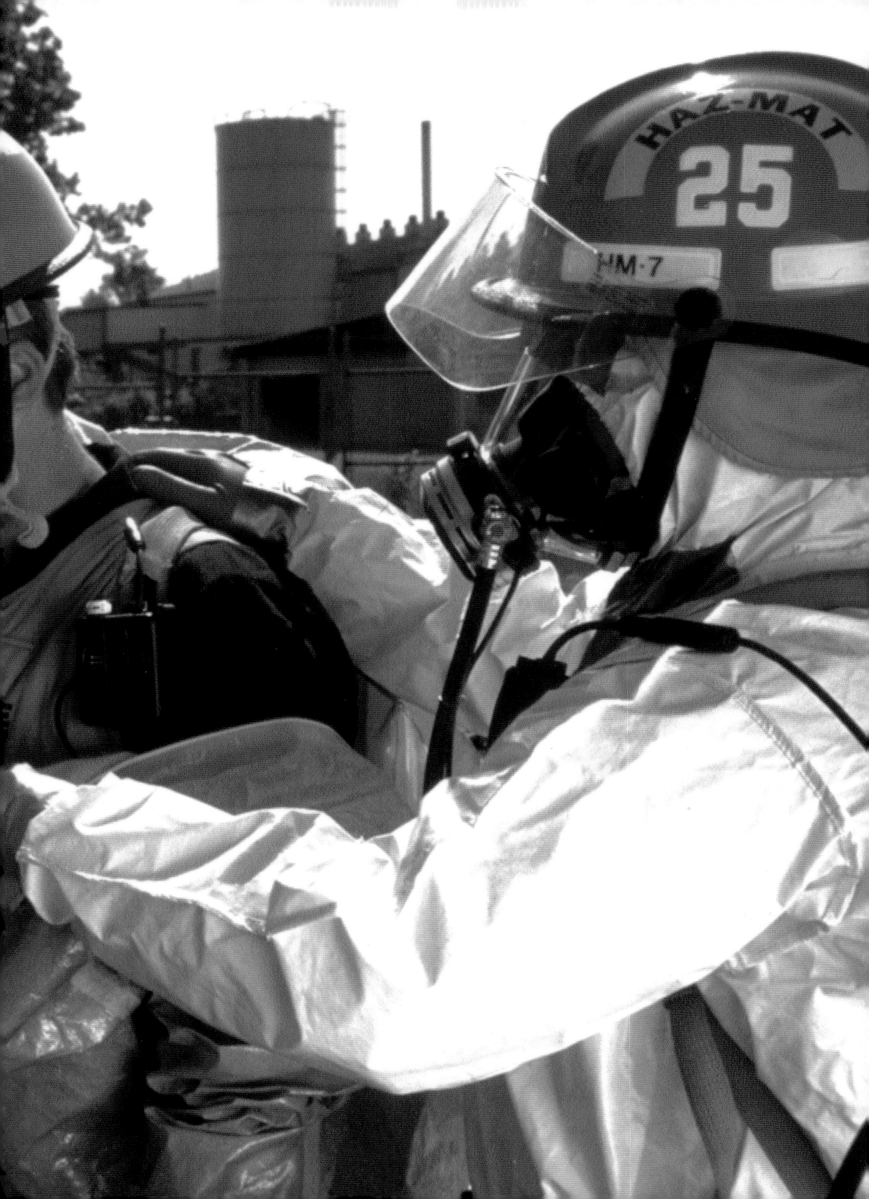

Hazardous Materials and Firefighters

Chief John M. Eversole (Ret)

irefighters today have an important role as the nation's first responders to a wide range of emergencies that extend far beyond the traditional role of fighting fires. The fire service has the important added responsibility for protecting the public in all types of emergency situations that involve hazardous materials. This is an increasingly complex area of responsibility and has expanded even further to place firefighters on the front lines of homeland defense, facing a whole new range of real and potential threats.

A broad definition of hazardous materials includes everything from ordinary fuel oil and gasoline to exotic chemicals, radioactive materials, and biological agents. Thousands of these substances are in common use for all kinds of purposes and are stored and transported across the United States in quantities ranging from a few grams to millions of gallons at a time. It is almost inevitable that these substances occasionally will be spilled, escape, or leak from their containers, explode, react with each other, become involved in fires, or in some other manner become involved in dangerous situations. The possibility that terrorists could use chemical, biological, or nuclear materials as weapons has added previously unanticipated risks to the hazardous materials agenda.

Above: *Members of a recruit class in Jacksonville, Florida, move in on a 500-gallon horizontal liquid propane bulk storage tank training prop with 1¾-inch fog lines to cool the tank. Once this is accomplished, they will be able to shut off the flow of fuel at the tank valve and extinguish the fire. (Steve Gerbert/ Jacksonville, Florida, Fire and Rescue Department)*

Pages 286–287: *After the completion of the decontamination process, a firefighter is assisted with the removal of his gear by other team members. As difficult as it is to properly don HazMat protective clothing, it can be even more difficult to remove after a long incident in gear that can become very hot and exhausting. (Hildebrand and Noll Associates, Inc.)*

Opposite: *Members of the Jacksonville, Florida, Fire and Rescue Department train on a new Fire Training Academy prop simulating a heat exchanger pressure fire that can be found at a petroleum chemical processing facility. In the first photo there are two covering hose streams on the right and one attack line advancing up the steps. In the second photo the officer and crew have been able to make the platform to effect an extinguishment. (Steve Gerbert/Jacksonville, Florida, Fire and Rescue Department)*

Below, left and right: This accident on a Jacksonville, Florida, highway involved a Sports Utility Vehicle and a gasoline tanker. Arriving on the scene, members of the Jacksonville, Florida, Fire and Rescue Department are greeted with a fully involved flammable liquid incident. The second photo shows fire crews approaching the burning vehicle with full protective gear and self-contained breathing apparatus. They are putting down a layer of foam to cover the flammable liquid and extinguish the fire. (Jacksonville, Florida, Fire and Rescue Department)

In most communities the fire service is the only agency that has the training and resources that are essential to respond and take immediate action when "HazMat" incidents create an imminent hazard to people or the environment. To fulfill this responsibility the fire service must be prepared for an almost limitless variety of potential situations and may have to face tremendous risks. One of the greatest challenges is that emergency responders must be prepared to deal with whatever goes wrong in technologically complex situations, even if the problem is a rare and unanticipated occurrence.

Above: *A training officer controls the level of flammable liquid going to a simulated propane tank fire. At the tank, a fire officer is leading two coordinated hose streams to provide protection for the crew and to ascertain whether or not the fire can be controlled by turning off a valve. (Hildebrand and Noll Associates, Inc.)*

Left: *Members of the Jacksonville, Florida, Fire and Rescue Department train on a Fire Training Academy prop simulating a liquid and vapor fire involving a 3,000-gallon liquid propane bobtail delivery truck. Approaching from the side of the vehicle, they are able to avoid being caught in an explosion should the end of the tank fail. (Steve Gerbert/ Jacksonville, Florida, Fire and Rescue Department)*

First Responders

Ordinary firefighters are usually the first to respond to any type of emergency incident and must be prepared to face whatever hazards are presented to them, whether the situation involves leaking containers of highly toxic chemicals, an overturned gasoline tanker in the middle of a busy intersection, a fire in a building where explosives are manufactured, or an envelope containing suspicious white powder delivered to someone's mailbox. Wherever and whenever an incident occurs, it is the local fire company that provides the critical first response and those firefighters must

Opposite, top: *Industrial areas close to city centers have constantly changing HazMat potential. A train yard is a combination of ordinary and hazardous cargo. If an incident were to occur at this location, the HazMat crews would need to know the contents of all of the containers that might become involved very quickly. They depend on shipping manifests carried by the train crews and railroad yard workers. (Hildebrand and Noll Associates, Inc.)*

Above: *Controlling the flow of hazardous materials is an early priority. This firefighter takes a quick and simple measure to keep any runoff from entering a stream. He has shoveled clean soil from around this outflow and blocked the possible path of any fluids. (Hildebrand and Noll Associates, Inc.)*

Top, right, and middle row: *Hazardous Materials incidents require a great deal of specialized equipment, material, and knowledge. Specialized units, as shown top, have been developed to respond to these emergencies. The first photo shows the exterior of two such vehicles. The unit in the front is designed to carry supplies needed for the incident while the unit to the rear carries not only supplies, but also the equipment for the emergency. This equipment includes specialized HazMat suits for the team, self-contained breathing apparatus, and extra air cylinders, the decontamination stations, monitoring equipment, and much more. (Hildebrand and Noll Associates, Inc.)*

Above: *Each individual in this command post has a specific responsibility as indicated by their vests. Here information from data collected at the scene and from outside resources will be assembled and analyzed. While it is important to correct the emergency situation as soon as possible, careful thought and the creating of an appropriate plan are critical. (Hildebrand and Noll Associates, Inc.)*

Right: *Miami-Dade Fire Rescue firefighters enter Miami International Airport in HazMat suits after a Hazardous Materials scare at a security checkpoint closed terminal in 2002. Thirty-six passengers were treated for respiratory distress when something got into the air. Whether or not the incident is finally determined to be real, all due precautions must be taken when assessing the potential danger. (REUTERS/Marc Serota/Corbis)*

know what to do and what not to do to protect lives and property. In some cases this may be limited to identifying the problem, removing unprotected individuals from the immediate danger area and isolating the hazard.

Specialized HazMat teams have been developed in most parts of the country to provide highly trained personnel with advanced equipment and operational capabilities to reinforce the initial response to hazardous materials incidents. In most cases these teams are comprised of firefighters

This crew is at the location of a hazardous materials incident. They have determined that it is safe to approach this close and make any repairs or adjustment necessary to mitigate the situation. If they determine that they are unable to stop the leak with what they have available to them, action may need to be taken at a remote location, such as shutting a valve somewhere else in the plant. (Hildebrand and Noll Associates, Inc.)

who have advanced training, special protective clothing and equipment, monitoring instruments, and reference materials, as well as the tools and equipment that are essential to safely stop the leak, contain the spill, extinguish the fire, neutralize the chemical reaction, clean up the residue or to do whatever is required to control the problem. In many cases they work closely with the local, state, and federal agencies that are directly responsible for public health, environmental protection, and law enforcement, as well as a variety of private sector organizations and contractors. Their work is highly technical and demands precise planning and coordination of efforts to manage the hazards.

A modern mobile command post has the equipment necessary to maintain communications, collect data, and access resources necessary for the analysis of a HazMat incident. Technicians may consult stored and online resources as well as agencies and companies around the country for the information they need. (Hildebrand and Noll Associates, Inc.)

A little HazMat humor. Hear no evil, smell no evil, see no evil. This cartoon provides a light-hearted comment for those who do not take proper HazMat procedures seriously. Standing in the midst of a hazardous liquid, these fellows seem to feel that if it explodes, cover your ears; if it is poisonous, cover your mouth and nose and hope the bird doesn't die; and if it isn't flammable, the match won't ignite it. (Hildebrand and Noll Associates, Inc.)

An overturned tractor trailer presents several causes for concern. First, the access to the trailer is impeded by the fact that it is on its side. Doors must be opened carefully and kept open to gain access and prevent injury to the crew. Next, the contents of the trailer have been subjected to possible damage and some may be combining with others, creating a compound that is not listed on the driver's manifest. (Hildebrand and Noll Associates, Inc.)

HazMat team members gain access to the rear of a tractor-trailer involved in a hazardous materials incident. Among other information available, the placards on the outside of the left door indicate that the material within is flammable and poisonous. While this may be the obvious hazard indication, the responding crew must be ever watchful for the unknown and unexpected. (Hildebrand and Noll Associates, Inc.)

Historical Perspective

Firefighters became involved with responding to hazardous materials incidents long before the term *HazMat* was even invented. The first encounters with hazardous materials probably occurred when they were called to extinguish fires involving very basic chemicals, such as gunpowder. They quickly learned that situations become much more dangerous and complicated when even small quantities of simple hazardous materials are involved.

In subsequent years people called the fire department whenever there was a chemical spill or a release of something hazardous, because they had come to expect that firefighters could fix just about anything and because firefighters were always willing to face the risks that everyone else wanted to avoid. Fire departments had the first primitive breathing apparatus and protective clothing and, even if it was only designed for ordinary firefighting, it was generally better than nothing. In the days when there was no other organization that knew what to do or had the resources to deal with hazardous materials emergencies, firefighters would always do whatever they could to save lives in any situation.

Over the years responses to HazMat incidents proved to be very costly to the fire service. Firefighters went bravely and blindly into situations where they did not have an adequate understanding of the hazards they might encounter and certainly lacked the essential equipment to protect themselves. Incident after incident resulted in deaths and permanent injuries to firefighters. It was a fearful, yet exciting time when there were neither rules nor regulations to direct personnel on proper procedures and few places to go for training or direction. Firefighters had to rely on their basic instincts and ingenuity and whatever advice they could obtain from "local experts" to survive; those who were smart and lucky lived to fight another day. The fire service gradually learned how to deal with hazmat situations, but the lessons came with the results of bad experiences.

Milestone Incidents

The path toward safety in hazmat responses was marked with incident after incident of injury, death, and destruction. Following are a few of the incidents from which important lessons have been learned.

In 1964 a truck loaded with explosives developed a tire fire. The driver parked the vehicle and removed the warning placards, then left to call for assistance. The Marshalls Creek, Pennsylvania, Fire Department arrived on the scene and began to fight the fire, not realizing that the burning truck could explode at any second. Three firefighters and three bystanders were killed when a massive explosion occurred moments later. The importance of proper warning placards on vehicles transporting hazardous materials was a lesson that came at a costly price.

In the predawn hours of November 29, 1988, two Kansas City Fire Department engine companies responded to a routine call for a late-night vehicle fire in a remote area of the city. Upon arrival they found that a storage trailer had been set on fire at a construction site. The trailer, which was being used to store twenty tons of explosives, exploded without warning, instantly killing six firefighters. At that time the Bureau of Alcohol, Tobacco, and Firearms did not require warning signs on the trailer, because the risk of theft of explosives was considered to be more critical than warning firefighters of the imminent danger in the event of a fire.

Most firefighters had never heard the term BLEVE (Boiling Liquid Expanding Vapor Explosion) before a series of massive explosions destroyed the business district of Crescent City, Illinois, on June 21, 1970.

A tank farm has a number of hazards inherent in its layout, not the least of which is the exposure of one tank to another if a fire starts. The tank on the left has already reached the point of collapse from the heat its sides were subjected to. Now the tank on the right is on fire due to exposure to the once intense fire of its neighbor. (Hildebrand and Noll Associates, Inc.)

A massive detonation occurs in a train yard. Situations such as this require that responding fire crews be sure of what the potential is given the contents of the train cars and their condition on arrival. This is not an incident to be rushed into. Obviously, if there were crews operating close to this scene, their survival would be doubtful. (Hildebrand and Noll Associates, Inc.)

A gasoline tanker and an automobile collide on a major suburban highway. The resulting fire now presents a hazard to the surrounding community and environment. Fire crews will strive to contain the fire spread, stop the flow of any flammable liquid into the local storm water drainage system, and extinguish the flames. (Hildebrand and Noll Associates, Inc.)

HazMat incidents can occur anywhere at any time. A petroleum-hauling tanker ship is engulfed in flames as a fireboat attempts to cool what is left of the ship's hull. Incidents such as this not only create the obvious flammable hazard, but also have an impact on the environment. Smoke rising from the flames is an irritant and the unburned fuel contaminates the water, flora, and fauna in the area. (Hildebrand and Noll Associates, Inc.)

They had no idea of the physics involved in such an incident or the magnitude of the explosion that could occur if a tank of liquefied propane gas was exposed to a fire.

When several tank cars loaded with LP gas derailed and a fire was ignited in the wreckage, Crescent City firefighters responded in the highest tradition of the fire service to protect their community, supported by mutual aid assistance from several neighboring fire departments. The train wreck also destroyed the town's pumping station, leaving them without an adequate water supply to fight the flames. Forced to withdraw, they witnessed a series of huge fireballs as the individual tank cars ruptured and released clouds of highly flammable vapors. Although more than sixty firefighters were injured in this incident, no deaths occurred. Unfortunately this was only the first of a series of very similar incidents involving railroad tank cars.

On July 5, 1973, the Kingman, Arizona, Fire Department responded to a burning railroad tank car at an offloading facility on the edge of their community. Twelve firefighters and one civilian died when the tank car ruptured.

A train wreck in Oneonta, New York, in February 1974 resulted in a major fire that exposed several tank cars filled with LP gas. There were no hydrants in this remote area and firefighting operations were limited to the supply that could be delivered by tanker apparatus. Nevertheless, firefighters made a valiant attack on the fire until a tremendous explosion occurred, injuring more than fifty of them. This incident demonstrated one of the basic lessons of risk management; evaluating how much we should be willing to risk versus what we can possibly save.

When several LP tankers derailed in the town of Waverly, Tennessee, in 1978 there was no fire initially, but local firefighters wisely evacuated the local area. They were still standing by two days later as railroad crews were in the process of untangling the wreckage. Without warning, one of the damaged tankers ruptured and released another huge cloud of highly flammable vapor, which ignited seconds later in a huge explosion that claimed sixteen lives, including the local fire chief. The subsequent investigation determined that several circumstances contributed to this disaster, but one of the major factors was that no one recognized the danger of increasing internal pressure in a damaged pressure vessel as the ambient temperature increased.

The New York City Telephone Exchange Fire occurred on February 27, 1975, in a large telephone switching facility in lower Manhattan. Fire traveled through miles and miles of plastic-coated wiring in the basement and on several floors of the building, enveloping it in clouds of highly toxic smoke for over sixteen hours. More than 200 firefighters suffered respiratory injuries, partly because the culture of the times did not require the strict use of self-contained breathing apparatus. In subsequent years dozens of firefighters were forced to retire and several premature deaths from cancer and respiratory diseases were linked to this incident.

As the world became more highly industrialized and technologically advanced, there was a tremendous increase in the use of all types of chemicals for thousands of different purposes. This trend inevitably resulted in more and more incidents involving dangerous products and substances and, correspondingly, the role of the fire service in dealing with these situations also expanded and became more sophisticated. The training of firefighters improved and their protective equipment advanced, although many of the changes only occurred in response to bad experiences.

For many years the basic plan for a chemical spill in most communities was to wash the problem down the drain, no matter what it was. Flushing the bad stuff into a storm drain or directly into a river usually got rid of the immediate problem and a two-and-a-half inch hose line could deliver copious quantities of water to get the job done. The spilled material on the ground was the fire department's problem, but flushing it into a sewer made it the sewer department's problem. Unfortunately this strategy caused many other types of problems downstream.

Changing Expectations

The advent of the U.S. Environmental Protection Agency (EPA) and various state agencies in the 1960s and 1970s meant that those old attitudes for handling chemical incidents had to change. Environmental concerns would no longer permit reckless disposal of hazardous materials and demanded that every trace of a spilled product must be picked up and removed to an approved disposal site; then the incident scene must be carefully decontaminated. Dealing with HazMat incidents was suddenly much more complex and highly regulated.

Also, a strong factor bringing about change was the formation of the Occupational Safety and Health Administration (OSHA) and the adoption

Opposite, top: An urban gas station is a potential HazMat environment. Many safeguards have been incorporated into gas pumps, tanks, and electrical systems in these installations. However, these can fail or become ineffective depending on their proper maintenance and the conditions at the time of the incident. (Hildebrand and Noll Associates, Inc.)

Once a HazMat incident has been contained, it is necessary to package and remove the material for safe disposal. Here the HazMat crew is preparing to seal a fifty-five-gallon steel drum for such a disposal. In the background fire crews keep an ever-watchful eye on the situation and train a charged hose line at the drum in the event that it is needed. (Hildebrand and Noll Associates, Inc.)

A modern tank farm has many safety precautions built into the design. Dikes surround each tank in the event of leakage to contain the liquid to a specific area. The tanks are equipped with lightning arresting devices to help prevent damage from lightning strikes. Water deluge piping and nozzles are installed for use on site prior to the arrival of the fire department. (Hildebrand and Noll Associates, Inc.)

297

Above: *A burning petroleum product involves a massive area along this highway and additional tanks are being exposed to the conflagration. The crews on the scene need to be constantly aware of the potential for change in conditions. Should the wind shift, the smoke and flames could create an immediate hazard to those in close proximity. (Hildebrand and Noll Associates, Inc.)*

Above: *A beautiful view of a petroleum processing plant at dusk. All industrial facilities present some level of concern for hazardous materials incident potential. HazMat teams depend on many sources of information to be prepared. Plant managers and crews, electronic and printed resources, and monitoring devices information are all part of the larger picture that is developed during an emergency. (Hildebrand and Noll Associates, Inc.)*

of stringent worker safety regulations. The number of firefighter deaths and injuries attributed to hazardous materials incidents was finally recognized and new regulations and procedures were adopted to manage the risks. Fire departments rapidly adopted new strategies for handling hazardous materials incidents, provided much more training for their firefighters, and purchased new equipment to deal with a wide range of potential situations. During the same period very significant advances were made in the design and use of respiratory protection and protective clothing for both fire suppression and HazMat operations.

The responsibility for responding to HazMat incidents became recognized as an official component of the fire service mission during the 1970s, and the first specialized HazMat teams were established during this decade. The dedicated efforts of many individuals within the fire service led the way in making the transition from dealing with HazMat problems as an unofficial sideline activity to adopting HazMat as a mainstream component of professional practice for the fire service. A wide range of individuals and organizations from outside the fire service also made important contributions to help create our current level of sophistication and preparedness for many different types of situations.

Early Leaders in Hazardous Materials

Many individuals and organizations made important contributions to the development of hazardous materials capabilities in the fire service; however, some of them will certainly be remembered because of their important and lasting contributions.

Ludwig Benner was a pioneer in the field of investigating hazardous materials incidents and developed many of the basic principles that have become cornerstones of modern-day risk management in the fire service. For many years Benner was the chief investigator for the U.S. National Transportation Safety Board (NTSB) and in that capacity he was responsible for examining the circumstances and outcomes of hundreds of hazardous materials incidents. His detailed analysis of those real experiences led to the development of many major safety recommendations.

Benner is best known for the DECIDE method of analyzing an emergency situation and then determining the best course of action for emergency responders. First published in 1975, DECIDE is a simple, yet systematic process that can be used by emergency responders, even if they are dealing with a specific type of incident for the first time.

THE "D.E.C.I.D.E." PROCESS
1. Detecting Hazardous Materials Presence
2. Estimating Likely Harm Without Intervention
3. Choosing Response Objectives
4. Identifying Action Options
5. "Doing" The Best Option
6. Evaluating Progress

Deputy Chief Charles W. Bahme had a long and rewarding career with the Los Angeles Fire Department and was also a captain in the U.S. Naval Reserve. He was a prolific author who wrote several books that became standard references, including *Fire Officer's Guide to Dangerous Chemicals*, *Fire Officer's Guide to Emergency Actions*, *Fire Officers Guide to Disaster Control*, and *Fire Service and the Law*.

As fire chief of South San Francisco during the Korean War era, Chief James H. Meidl's response area included a large defense complex that was full of exotic hazardous materials. He was very concerned that the firefighters needed to have more knowledge of the hazards they would have to face when they responded to emergencies at these facilities. When he was still a captain, Meidl wrote several books including *Flammable Hazardous Materials*, and *Explosive and Toxic Hazardous Material*. He was way ahead of his time and provided education that was available nowhere else.

Chief Warren Isman, who was the chief of Fire Rescue Department for Fairfax County, Virginia, was also chairman of the Hazardous Materials Committee and later president of the International Association of Fire Chiefs. He led the effort to develop the National Fire Protection Association's (NFPA) first Standard for Professional Competencies for Responders to Hazardous Materials Incidents, and was relentless in pursuing legislation and regulations to reduce the hazardous materials risks throughout the United States. Along with his colleague Gene Carlson, of Oklahoma State University, Chief Isman traveled tirelessly across the country to teach classes for firefighters, bringing about a new level of hazardous materials awareness that will be long remembered.

As captain with the Jacksonville, Florida, Fire Department, Ron Gore is generally credited with creating the first specialized hazardous

Opposite, top: Petroleum and chemical processing plants are a very complicated combination of pipes, valves, and tanks. It is critical that HazMat crews know about these installations prior to any emergency. Therefore, fire departments make regular visits to such facilities in order to "pre-plan" for any eventuality. (Hildebrand and Noll Associates, Inc.)

Members of a HazMat team stand in a staging area prior to donning additional protective gear near an entrance to the U.S. Post Office and regional mail sorting facility in Bellmawr, New Jersey, October 31, 2001. One case of skin anthrax was traced to this facility that handles mail from 159 local post offices in southern New Jersey and employs more than 1,000 workers. The HazMat team gathered samples for analysis. (AFP Photo/Tom Mihalek)

Above: This fire in the tank on the left on the interior of this tank farm is a very difficult one to access. Because of its distance from the roadway, hose streams have a hard time reaching the fire. Fire crews are now positioned on the tops of adjacent tanks to get water closer to the flames. (Hildebrand and Noll Associates, Inc.)

Protection of HazMat crews and civilians is of highest importance on any emergency incident. The incident is divided into zones around the hazard based upon the severity of the hazard and current weather conditions. Obvious from this explosion is the fact that a very large exclusion zone would have been necessary to provide protection for the local population. (Hildebrand and Noll Associates, Inc.)

Opposite, top: Even an ordinary citizen can create a HazMat incident. This small truck was not large enough, nor appropriate, for the transport of drums of hazardous materials. The HazMat crew applies a compression patch to a leaking drum to stop the flow of these materials, which are labeled poisonous and corrosive. (Hildebrand and Noll Associates, Inc.)

Fully encapsulated and briefed on the situation ahead of them, this crew prepares to advance on the reported hazard. As they survey the scene, they will take readings with monitoring devices and report that information to the command post. With what they are able to glean from visual and objective observations, they can then develop a plan for mitigation. (Hildebrand and Noll Associates, Inc.)

materials team within the fire service. He is also credited with establishing several important protocols and developing a number of specialty tools to handle specific situations. He also spent many years teaching his "hands-on" program to thousands of emergency responders throughout the country.

Chief Max McRae is credited with being the "grandfather" of the big city hazardous materials teams. His area of responsibility in Houston contained dozens of massive chemical production, processing, and storage facilities. Chief McRae established a highly competent response organization within the Houston Fire Department and is also credited with being a pioneer in developing a strong cooperative relationship between the local industries and the fire service.

Continuing advances in technology have allowed the fire service to become more sophisticated in dealing with HazMat situations, while new challenges have continually demanded greater efforts and dedication. The most recent emphasis has been directed toward preparations to deal with chemical, biological, and nuclear agents, in case they are ever used as weapons of terror, which has prompted fire departments to work closely with military and law enforcement agencies to plan and train for joint operations.

Regulations and Standards

The term "Hazardous Materials" was actually coined by the U.S. Department of Transportation (DOT) in 1968. This marked the real beginning of a new regulatory era as the chemical and transportation industries were required to develop better shipping methods, meet minimum standards, and better identify the hazards of what was being shipped. The abbreviated version "HazMat" was soon adopted by the fire service.

The Research and Special Programs Division of DOT was charged with the development of the regulations for transporting hazardous materials. The new regulations required minimum shipping container standards

and also included the placarding and labeling system that was designed to quickly make first responders aware of the hazards they might encounter at an incident.

As the fire service responded to more and more chemical incidents it was apparent that there were no standards on how these incidents were supposed to be handled. The NFPA was petitioned to form committees of experts to establish recommended practices and professional qualifications standards for responders to hazardous materials incidents. The NFPA established a technical committee to develop the responder standards and a parallel committee to develop standards for chemical protective clothing. Through the efforts of these committees the documents titled Recommended Practice and Professional Competencies of Responders to Hazardous Materials Incidents, commonly referred to as NFPA 471 and 472, were developed, followed by NFPA 473, which specifically addresses Competencies of EMS Personnel Responding to Hazardous Materials Incidents. These documents are widely accepted as the cornerstones of emergency response to hazardous materials incidents. Aside from operational and procedural concerns, these standards also address the respiratory and protective clothing concerns of firefighters.

Hazardous materials incidents can be spectacular and they can be the result of ordinary events. A truck loses its load of HazMat drums either as a result of an accident or lack of proper containment. This crew has several drums that are creating a potential hazard. They will talk to the driver, if available, look over any manifests, and check the labeling on the drums. Finally, because all or some of this information may be inaccurate, they will also approach in full protection and take readings from all of the material to determine the actual hazard. (Hildebrand and Noll Associates, Inc.)

Respiratory Protection

Today every firefighter routinely uses self-contained breathing apparatus (SCBA) that must meet the exacting standards of the National Institutes for Occupational Safety and Health (NIOSH) as well as NFPA. This level of respiratory protection is considered to be an essential safety measure for fire suppression as well as HazMat operations. The SCBA only became standard equipment in the fire service during the 1950s and 1960s and, even after most fire departments had acquired SCBA, it took years to implement comprehensive departmental policies for their use. The fire service can be a difficult place to make changes; after all, we were the land of "iron men and wooden ladders."

Respiratory injuries took a tremendous toll during the decades when "leather lungs" were a proud sign of manhood. It was necessary for the fire service to go through a very difficult and sometimes costly learning curve. Firefighters like to push the envelope and one common practice was to build a "cheater mask" from miscellaneous parts—a canister-type filter, a connecting tube, and an aviator's mask that covered only the nose and mouth all taped together. Sometimes these homemade masks worked very well and sometimes failed miserably. If there was an insufficient

amount of oxygen in the atmosphere or toxic gases that the canister could not filter out, the results could be fatal. Firefighters wanted to see just how far and how fast they could go, and with a canister-type mask they often went too far, too fast, and paid the price.

Protective Clothing

For many years firefighters had little choice in the type of protective clothing they wore, and many wore very little at all. The big choices were rubber or canvas for coats, and leather or aluminum for helmets. Usually the engine crews wore rubber coats and those on the hook and ladder and squads wore canvas. We were all satisfied because there was nothing else available, and we did not know any better. As time progressed we tried a number of new experimental fabrics—some worked well, and some melted off our backs.

Today we have advanced to space age technology and more encapsulating-type garments. These ensembles certainly protect us better, but they require greater user knowledge and much closer monitoring to ensure safe operations.

After leaving a hazardous materials environment, the firefighter must be decontaminated by a very specific process. The first photo is an overview of the decontamination (Decon) equipment set up at every HazMat incident. First the firefighter enters the Decon area on his own and thoroughly showers off. Next his boot bottoms are cleaned in a boot wash. Next, he is assisted by other team members in HazMat gear who scrub him down and rinse thoroughly. Finally, he can be assisted off with his gear by the other team members. (Hildebrand and Noll Associates, Inc.)

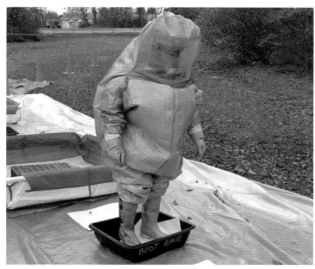

Hazardous materials can be as close as our kitchen sinks, basements, or garages. Each year hazardous materials handlers collect cans and buckets of household hazardous waste for safe disposal and recycling on Earth Day. While these are ordinary home products, they can be deadly if used improperly or mixed with other products. (© Tom Bean/Corbis)

Gloves have always been a challenge to the firefighter. For years the single layer canvas glove was the standard for many departments. The Salvation Army passed them out free with a hot cup of coffee at fires and firefighters were happy to get them. Later on we progressed to the orange "fireball" gloves, which were great until you grabbed something hot and then they melted on your hands. We have come a long way and now realize that special jobs such a hazardous materials response require specific hand protection for a particular chemical.

Firefighters learned early on that they could provide some skin protection from some chemicals by coating their exposed skin with Vaseline. Sometimes it worked and sometimes it didn't.

The only people who seemed to have any practical knowledge of what type of clothing should be required for chemical incidents were the industrial chemical people who worked around these products all the time. We quickly learned that these people had some very good ideas, but their expertise was generally limited to a particular chemical group, while we had to be prepared for any type of chemical exposure. We also learned that there were no standards for the manufacturing or testing of chemical suits. In those days we simply bought a suit from a manufacturer, then put it on and went into whatever kind of incident we encountered. We just assumed that the suit would work because the manufacturer said it was made for chemicals.

Early testing of chemical protective clothing by the Chicago Fire Department and others showed that these garments, both new and used, leaked extensively. The various systems used in sealing the seams and zippers were faulty at best. Although the base materials were tested, there were no tests to ensure that all of the materials used in the construction of the suits had the same chemical resistance. This was made very apparent in an incident at Benicia, California, where the suit material resisted the chemical adequately, but the face piece lenses failed in a few seconds. A great amount of research and testing was conducted by the National Fire Protection Association and the protective clothing manufacturers, in cooperation with several fire departments. The result is that we now have chemical protective clothing that is much more resistant, more wearable, and in many cases, more cost efficient.

Conclusion

The role of the fire service has changed dramatically during the past thirty years. Some may say that the heroic days of the firefighter are gone, because fire prevention has done such a good job in reducing fires. The truth is that our workload has changed and we are responding to more emergency incidents than ever before. Today we rely less on muscle and more on brains. We are able to provide far more competent responses to much more complicated incidents, because we have the training, tools and equipment to do the job. We have moved hazardous materials response up to a well-organized systematic and safe approach.

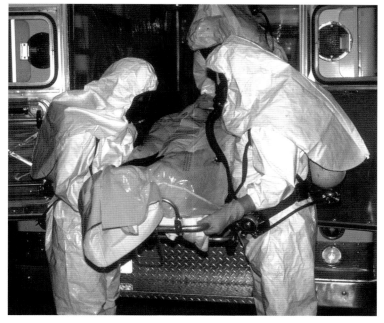

The Fire Service and Emergency Preparedness

George W. Buck, Jr., Ph.D.

The fire service has a long history in this successful experiment called "The United States of America." For many years, the fire service has responded to disasters above and beyond the call of duty. With the establishment of the first settlement in the early 1600s, the fledgling field of emergency management planted its roots solidly in the foundation of the fire service. When fire swept through the village of Portsmouth, New Hampshire, in 1803, local and state resources were overwhelmed. This led to congressional legislation making federal resources available to assist local and state governments in the recovery phase of disasters. This single congressional act in 1803, was to become the first of a series of national disaster legislation designed to protect the United States from catastrophic events.

For most of the twentieth century, emergency management was known as civil defense, with responsibilities shared among many state and federal agencies. This was true during World Wars I and II and the Cold War. But, by the early 1970s, it became clear that a separate agency was necessary to coordinate the complexities of the field that would soon come to be known as Emergency Management.

In 1979, the federal government established a new combined agency, FEMA (Federal Emergency Management Agency), which would be separate from other federal public safety agencies and departments. FEMA's main objective during the period from 1979 to 1992 was to protect the civilian population in the event of enemy attack. However, with the landfall of Hurricane Andrew in August 1992, (eventually rated as a Category 5 Hurricane), FEMA was thrust into the position of substantially rethinking its mission. Hurricane Andrew, along with pressure from the American people and the media, prompted FEMA to redefine itself from a recovery and response agency, to one that focuses on mitigation and preparation in addition to recovery and response. Most importantly, under the leadership of Director James Lee Witt (1993–2001), FEMA came to understand its role as an all-hazards (natural and man-made) agency, not one which was just focused on wartime scenarios. FEMA, under Director Witt, answered the call and firmly established itself as a respected partner in federal government. In 2003, FEMA became an agency within the newly created Department of Homeland Security.

FEMA coordinates federal, state, and local efforts to protect citizens during national emergencies and to improve the nation's capability to respond to an emergency when it does occur. FEMA also provides ongoing guidance and support for state and local emergency management teams for a Comprehensive Emergency Management (CEM) system throughout the United States. After the global events of the 1990s and September 11, 2001, the focus on events of terrorism on home soil of America has increased. But, it would be wrong to think that emergency management was invented in 1979 with the establishment of FEMA.

In the United States, modern concepts of emergency management were forged during the Truman presidency, especially the years 1948–1950. This was the period that the USSR exploded its first nuclear device and Americans

---

Top: Copy of the Emergency Management bill from 1803. (George W. Buck, Jr. Ph.D)

faced yet another war, this time in Korea. In 1949, the Truman administration established the Federal Civil Defense Act, and in 1950, the Defense Production Act. The Disaster Relief Act, which outlined response strategies for natural and man-made disasters, was also passed in 1950. Today we refer to the Disaster Relief Act as the Stafford Act.

In 1958, the Federal Civil Defense Act was amended to include federal matching funds (50/50) for personnel and administrative expenditures for civil defense preparedness. During the Cuban missile crisis in 1962, civil defense was elevated to a national perspective and concern as Americans waited to see if missiles would be launched from Cuba into the United States.

In the 1970s, the civil defense program was expanded to include natural disasters. Through an executive order, President Jimmy Carter directed that a new federal agency, FEMA, be organized to assist state and local governments in responding to disasters, both natural and man-made. During the 1980s, the idea of "Comprehensive Emergency Management" (whereby all hazards are analyzed and assigned "phase-management" risk level) was clearly articulated by FEMA as its primary mission. FEMA's Project Impact, a community-based approach to all-hazards preparedness, is a reflection of comprehensive management thinking.

Although federal officials may devise and guide the broadest issues regarding emergency management, the day-to-day, hands-on responsibility rests locally. Both FEMA and the American people rely heavily on the local

fire and rescue departments to make the integrated and comprehensive risk management plans work. Due to organizational values that stress preparation and cooperation, and an emphasis on training, fire services across the United States have met this challenge by developing outstanding local programs for hazard mitigation and management.

Over the years, fire service departments have assumed numerous roles and responsibilities for their communities. Some of these are emergency medical services, hazardous materials containment, and, in many jurisdictions, com-  *prehensive emergency management. The fire service's role in emergency management is a focal point for leadership and resources in many communities across the United States. By the late 1980s, over one-third of part-time emergency management directors*

Top: Rescue crews work to find additional victims at the Murrah building in Oklahoma City after the bombing on April 19, 1995. (Ralf-Finn Hestoft/Corbis SABA)

Above: Tomorrow's firefighter helps today. A young boy fills sandbags in an effort to stop the flood from causing further damage in the Midwest during June 1994. (George W. Buck, Jr., Ph.D)

worked full time for the local fire department. According to the Emergency Management Institute (EMI), by 2000 that number was considerably higher.

Today, fire services are increasingly involved in all aspects of hazard management, including responses to weapons of mass destruction (WMD). Although this challenge is growing, it is not really new to the fire service. Emergency management has, in fact, borrowed many management techniques of the fire service, such as command-and-control and the concept of the incident command system. In addition, the fire service has benefited from this relationship with emergency management also, particularly in the development of emergency management concepts such as Comprehensive Emergency Management and the Integrated Emergency Management Systems (IEMS), two valuable tools in disasters planning.

The fire service and emergency management focus on two basic tasks: preparing the organization to manage emergencies or disasters today, and preparing for such situations tomorrow. The fire department leader who promotes knowledge of emergency management techniques helps determine his community's capacity to survive a serious event. By doing so, improvements in the management of day-to-day operations also occur. If emergency service personnel are not functioning as part of an integrated emergency management system, the response capability of all first responders (fire, police, and EMS) is greatly diminished. Interagency cooperation (the sharing of data) and communication are absolute prerequisites for successful mitigation planning and emergency response.

Emergency management systems are useful at all locations, for all types of situations, and for all types of fire organizations. To be effective, emergency management systems must be suitable for use regardless of the type of jurisdiction or agency involved. This may include single jurisdiction/single agency, single jurisdiction/multiagency, and multijurisdiction/multiagency involvement. The organizational structure must be adaptable to any disaster applicable and acceptable to users throughout a community or region. End-users of these systems must be readily adaptable to a new technology and capable of logical expansion from the initial response to the complexities of a major emer-

Rescuers helping the injured during a June 1994, Midwest flood. (George W. Buck, Jr., Ph.D)

gency. Emergency management and firefighting is carried out in a constantly changing environment—although the situation may get better or worse, it seldom stays the same.

To demonstrate the importance of the role of the fire service in emergency management, as of July 28, 2002, the restructure of the National Emergency Training Center in Emmitsburg, Maryland, has reorganized the Emergency Management Institute under the control of the United States Fire Administration located at the center in Emmitsburg, Maryland.

EMI serves as the national focal point for the development and delivery of emergency management training to enhance the capabilities of federal, state, and local government officials, volunteer organizations, and the private sector to minimize the impact of disasters on the American public. EMI curricula are structured to meet the needs of this diverse audience, with an emphasis on how the various elements work together in emergencies to save lives and protect property. Approximately 4,000 students attend resident courses each year, while 100,000 individuals participate in nonresident programs sponsored by EMI and conducted by state emergency management agencies. Instruction focuses on the four phases of emergency management; mitigation, preparedness, response, and recovery.

Any way you look at it, emergency preparedness is a cooperative venture. No jurisdiction can go it alone. As such, coordinated planning is essential for the management of mutual aid from local, state and federal sources. So interconnected is the system at present that almost any jurisdiction in the United States (under attack or from a natural disaster) will receive federal assistance. Soon after the Alfred P. Murrah Federal Building explosion in April of 1995, multiple agencies arrived on the scene to assist, even though the Oklahoma City Fire Department (OCFD) never requested mutual aid. Personnel and equipment from surrounding cities, counties, state, and federal agencies started to arrive en masse, and they had to be organized quickly. Because the fire department had an advanced planning system, it rapidly designated a department command vehicle and gave its crew the responsibility of organizing a command post with a mutual-aid coordinator. This coordinator from the OCFD was able to staff the incident as requests were made from the site of the explosion. Thus, unrequested resources were quickly integrated with maximum results by the OCFD because it was prepared to do so.

History repeats itself, and on September 11, 2001, agencies from all over the mid-Atlantic region (and, in short order, the rest of the country) came to Ground Zero and the Pentagon with amazing speed. But what was more important was that most of these responders came with a working knowledge of the integrated command system and its central goal of maintaining order within chaos. By all accounts, America's emergency services "did it right" on September 11th, due in large part to the many years of planning and preparation that supported these responders' efforts.

September 11, 2001—it was a day we witnessed, in stunned disbelief, the unthinkable horror of the destruction of the World Trade Center towers, the attack on the Pentagon, and the tragic plane crash in Pennsylvania. It was a day when our sense of security was shaken, our freedoms challenged, and our national spirit renewed. It was a day

we mourned the loss of thousands of lives taken by senseless acts of terror by named and unnamed adversaries. We remember September 11th as a day we were overjoyed by those who miraculously made it through alive; and as a day we waited and hoped for signs of more survivors. It is a day that changed the world, America, and our emergency services.

This book contains photographs from the day of September 11th that highlight many of the heroes, personnel both at and behind the scenes—members of the fire service, emergency medical services, and emergency management who, along with a host of others, served above and beyond the call. It was widely publicized on September 11th that New York City's Emergency Operations Center located in the World Trade Center complex was destroyed. What is less widely known is that within hours emergency planners had established a replacement center that was up and running at Pier 92 of the passenger ship terminal on Manhattan's West Side. This served as NYC's EOC until February 2002. This was a remarkable tribute to the American "can do" spirit in the face of a tremendous catastrophe. God Bless America—our first responders and emergency planners, past, present, and future.

Left: Expressing thanks near Ground Zero. (George W. Buck, Jr., Ph.D)

Top, right: Montgomery County, Maryland, Fire and Rescue assist in clean up after a tornado. (George W. Buck, Jr., Ph.D)

Technical Rescue and Special Operations

Technical Rescue and Special Operations

Fire Lieutenant Fred Endrikat

Firefighters trained in special operations make up the highly skilled teams that are prepared to face almost any difficult and dangerous situation—anywhere, anytime. Whenever things go seriously wrong, particularly in a way that puts lives at risk, people rely on their fire departments to respond quickly and to know what to do to successfully resolve the problem, particularly if it is unusual, complex, and dangerous. These firefighters must be trained and equipped to immediately respond to these situations.

Today most large cities have at least one heavy rescue company and many fire departments have additional special operations companies or teams that are trained to perform a range of increasingly complex functions. Special Operations has evolved from the concept of a fire department heavy-rescue squad that originated during the first part of the twentieth century. Rescue companies were created as elite groups of highly trained firefighters who would be ready to respond with special equipment for the most challenging fire situations and difficult rescue operations. In addition to extensive training and great determination, they would respond with the most advanced equipment and the ingenuity to use it.

An article from a 1947 edition of the Philadelphia *Inquirer* describes the duties of firefighters at that time and an account of a confined space rescue operation assigned to one of the city's four heavy rescue companies:

Above: *Several Search and Rescue Teams operate in close proximity to each other requiring coordination of effort and communication. If one team decides to move a particular structural member as a part of their search effort, it could affect other teams and victims close by. (Michael Rieger/FEMA News Photo)*

Pages 310–311: *Members of FDNY remove debris at the World Trade Center site and continue to search for survivors among the wreckage. Masses of steel and rubble combined with many rescuers and the potential for many victims creates a hazardous environment. The removal of tons of small and large debris is a painstaking process. (Andrea Booher/FEMA News Photo)*

Opposite: *Search and Rescue Teams use different tools and methods to attempt to access victims at the Murrah Building in Oklahoma City. Pneumatic jack hammers and drills, acetylene torches, sledge hammers, buckets, and shovels, are the tools used most often by rescuers during collapses and other special rescues. (FEMA News Photo)*

While Urban Search and Rescue teams work to find survivors, firefighters from the San Francisco Fire Department join in to remove the wreckage of the World Trade Center. The response from other departments around the country reinforced the concept of "the fire service family." (Andrea Booher/FEMA News Photo)

Members of the South Florida Urban Search and Rescue Team/Florida Task Force 2 search for survivors at the World Trade Center. Concealed spaces, tangled steel, and hazardous dust present their own problems for the rescuers. Efforts must be purposeful and well thought out. (Andrea Booher/FEMA News Photo)

Two workmen had been emptying a tank car of transformer oil—tricky stuff that can give off dangerous fumes. A few inches remained, and one of the pair dropped inside to clean the car. The railroad siding was only slightly cooler than Death Valley at high noon; inside the car, the heat and fumes were literally unbearable. The workman looked blank and fell on his face in the oil. His companion yelled for help and went to his aid. In proof of a point Captain Joseph F. Meskill of Rescue 1 was trying to make—that rescue is for professionals—he passed out beside his mate. Somebody ran for firemen from a fireboat moored nearby. The first fireman went in without a gas mask. Now there were three in the oil, which was deep enough to drown a fallen man. A second fireman donned a mask, but it was the wrong kind or got knocked askew. He added himself to the stack.

Rescue 1 got there with the proper masks, but, as usual, there were unusual complications. The breathing bag and canister on the chest made a man too bulky to go through the hatch. Time was everything; four men were in imminent peril of drowning or suffocating. One of the rescuers made a lasso. Another seized a ceiling hook, carried to pull down plaster and lathe in getting at fires. He used it now to fish for prisoners. As he raised one of their arms or legs, his mate dropped the loop over it. Head first or feet first, the four were hauled out. Put under resuscitators and drained of oil, all four came around fairly quickly.

More than fifty years after this article appeared, citizens rely more than ever on fire departments to successfully resolve technical rescue incidents. Firefighters continue to assume the primary responsibility for rescuing citizens who are in peril from a wide range of incidents and scenarios. Firefighters are called upon to rescue victims from a variety of dangerous situations, from dramatic helicopter rescue operations in communities impacted by floodwaters, to extricating an industrial worker who has an arm entangled in heavy machinery, to removing injured victims from the thousands of automobile accidents that occur daily on our highways and streets. They use their ingenuity, training, experience, and specialized tools and equipment to get the job done.

Picture the stranded window-washer dangling precariously from the fifty-seventh floor of a high-rise office building after the cable on a scaffold platform has snapped. The fire department is expected to come to the rescue. Whether it is a single-victim accident or a mass casualty incident with dozens of victims trapped in the debris of a building collapsed by a terrorist attack, the response of firefighters trained in rescue operations is literally the difference between life and death.

FDNY members (the one with the orange helmet shield is a probationary member) assist as a member of the Washington State Task Force 1 Urban Search and Rescue Team enters a concealed space at the World Trade Center. Rescuers must work in teams for their own safety. (Andrea Booher/FEMA News Photo)

FDNY Rescue 1

When did fire departments begin to examine the concept of providing specialized rescue services in addition to basic firefighting capability? At the turn of the twentieth century, fire chiefs in cities across the country realized they were facing increasingly difficult and dangerous situations while fighting fires, particularly in underground structures and confined spaces, such as subway tunnels, ships, and the basements and sub-basements under commercial buildings. At a time when most firefighters had never even

Charter members of Rescue Company 1 FDNY pose with some of their specialized equipment as the company is placed into service March 8, 1915. (Courtesy of Paul Hashagen)

heard of breathing apparatus, they often had to make entry into areas where ventilation was extremely limited. They also faced extremely difficult forcible entry situations in order to rescue occupants or attack a fire.

One such fire occurred at the Equitable Building in New York City in 1912, where firefighters had to use hacksaws to cut through steel bars covering the windows. It took an hour and fifteen minutes to remove the bars in order to rescue two employees who were trapped inside the building. Then in 1915, a subway train caught fire between two stations in

Manhattan creating a heavy smoke condition. Hundreds of civilians were overcome by smoke and almost 200 were sent to hospitals for treatment. It took hours for firefighters to reach the burning train and control the fire. During this time period, other large cities were experiencing similar challenging situations.

The Fire Department of New York (FDNY) recognized the need for a specialized unit that would have uniquely trained firefighters assigned to it, and would carry a complement of special rescue tools and equipment. The first specialized rescue company in the United States was FDNY Rescue Company 1, which was placed in service on March 8, 1915. The primary mission was to provide for the safety and rescue of trapped firefighters, however Rescue 1 was trained and equipped to handle any emergency.

Rescue Company 1's first captain, John J. McElligott, was given the task of selecting the members for this new unit. Many veteran members volunteered, but preference was given to experienced firefighters who had knowledge of mechanics, engineering, rigging, welding, electrical work and other special trades. The members that were selected were then given extensive physical examinations. Eight firefighters and one lieutenant were chosen and detailed to the training school, where they received training in using specialized rescue tools and first aid, as well as the Draeger smoke helmet, which was the only breathing apparatus available at that time. Captain McElligott, who later became chief of the department, was the first firefighter to test this new device.

Rescue 1's first firehouse was in the densely populated area of lower Manhattan and the first apparatus was a 1914 Cadillac touring car adapted for their special mission. The equipment carried by Rescue 1 included a Lyle lifeline gun, rigging equipment, life belts, a cutting torch, jacks, an extensive tool kit, a first aid kit, and a pulmotor.

On September 22, 1915, Rescue Company 1 operated at one of its first major technical rescue incidents. A subway tunnel under construction caved in, causing numerous deaths and injuries to the workers. The cave-in also caused the street surface to collapse and a passing trolley car to plummet into the void.

In his book, *A Distant Fire: A History of FDNY Heroes*, FDNY historian Paul Hashagen notes, "The men of Rescue 1 operated in some of the most hazardous situations firemen had ever operated in. They would venture into areas that were untenable to others without the benefit of the smoke helmets. They would routinely handle ammonia leaks, sub-cellar

Below, left: *Outfitted with smoke helmets, members of Rescue 1 pose with their new 1924 chain-driven Mack Bulldog. This rig, larger than their previous two trucks, reflected the growing number of tools carried by the company. (Courtesy of Paul Hashagen)*

Below, right: *Breathing protection in the 1940s consisted of hose masks (with hand-cranked air pump), filter masks, and smoke helmets. The rescue companies were still the only firemen who had access to breathing apparatus. (Courtesy of Paul Hashagen)*

Top: *The first Rescue 1 apparatus was a
1914 Cadillac touring car, rebuilt by the
department shops. It featured a right-hand
steering wheel and a huge bell mounted on
the center of the dashboard. In the rear, space
for storage was found beneath the two bench
seats and inside a center compartment.
(Courtesy of Paul Hashagen)*

Above, left: *Mayor Hyland inspects smoke
helmeted fireman in the quarters of Engine
33 and Rescue 1 on Great Jones Street, Manhattan, spring of 1919. (Courtesy of Paul
Hashagen)*

Above, right: *Original members of Rescue 1
spring into action from their 1914 Cadillac
rig. (Courtesy of Paul Hashagen)*

fires, ship fires, and building collapses. They handled these fires and
emergencies with flawless precision. Their special tools and training gave
them a decided advantage over the average firefighter. The company was
continually placed in the most perilous situations."

Rescue 1 continued to be a proving ground for innovative firefighting
and specialized rescue tools and techniques. In 1939, Ward LaFrance constructed the first apparatus that was specifically designed for technical rescue service. In 1943, Rescue 1 received the first portable fireground radios
issued to firefighting units. These radios earned the name "handi-talkie"
because of the ease of communication they allowed at a fire or technical
rescue operation. In 1946, Rescue 1 was assigned six self-contained
breathing apparatus as a pilot program to test this new equipment.

In 1946, Rescue 1 participated in the rescue of several firefighters who were trapped in a tunnel beneath a building that was involved in fire. Pavement breakers were used to gain access to the trapped firefighters. These specialized tools were an early version of the modern hydraulic-powered concrete breaching equipment carried by fire department rescue teams today. In subsequent years, Rescue 1 pioneered the use of many more new power tools that are used for cutting, boring, bending, prying, and lifting, including the Hurst Tool, also known as the "Jaws of Life." This hydraulically powered tool system was designed for auto extrication, subway accidents, and other emergencies. Today, Rescue 1 continues to be a proving ground in the field-testing and development of new technical rescue equipment and procedures.

Members of Urban Search and Rescue Teams from the San Diego Fire Department as well as the Santee Fire Department and FDNY work together in the World Trade Center search effort. Hand-over-hand methods of removing debris are performed to gain access to suspected areas of survivors. (Amanda Bricknell/FEMA News Photo)

Heavy Rescue Companies Today

Most U.S. cities now have dedicated heavy rescue companies that respond to working fires and also specialize in technical rescue operations. Other cities and towns rely on regionally based technical rescue or specialty teams. These rescue companies and specialty teams are staffed by firefighters who have advanced training in one or more technical rescue disciplines. Today, most firefighters receive basic awareness-level training in the various types of rescue operations, but only a small percentage receive the extensive additional training to become certified in specialized rescue operations. They spend many hours training and practicing their trade with modern tools and equipment designed specifically for rescue applications.

There are nine major categories of technical or specialized rescue operations: building collapse, confined space, rope rescue, water rescue, vehicle extrication, mass transit extrication, industrial extrication, trench/excavation collapse, and fireground operations with specialized rescue considerations. Each specific category involves unique hazards to the rescuers and requires specialized equipment and training.

Actual rescue incidents frequently entail more than one category of rescue operations. For example, firefighters responding to a call for a trench collapse may encounter a broken water main flowing freely into a twenty-foot-deep excavation with workers trapped at the bottom. The rescuers may have to utilize a variety of technical rescue skills including trench rescue, water rescue, confined space entry, and rope rescue operations at this one incident. The rescuers must be comfortable with their

Opposite: A member of Florida Task Force 1 prepares to initiate a search with special equipment. Slung across his back is a "SearchCam" with a camera lens and microphone that can be placed through a small access hole to search for victims. The telescoping probe can reach to the depths of suspected trapped victims before digging takes place. (Michael Rieger/FEMA News Photo)

knowledge of all of the tools, equipment, and specific procedures that are unique to each different type of operation in order to successfully resolve this type of complex incident.

Rescue incidents can involve a tremendous range of unusual and unanticipated situations. Some examples are the collapse of a construction elevator at a high-rise office building project that has punctured the roofs and pinned the occupants of neighboring buildings, while leaving heavy sections swaying in the wind forty stories above the street, or the rescue of a burglar who became wedged in a chimney while trying to evade capture by the police.

Firefighters responding to a building collapse can expect to be confronted with a wide variety of situations. Whether it is a wood frame single-family dwelling flattened by hurricane-force winds, a four-story row-house in a densely populated inner-city neighborhood that has crumbled due to age and neglect, or a steel-frame and reinforced concrete office building destroyed by a terrorist's bomb, firefighters must use specialized equipment and tactics to rescue trapped and entombed survivors.

One of the most challenging aspects of collapse rescue operations is the task of accurately locating buried victims. Modern technical search equipment in the form of fiber-optic cameras and electronic listening devices helps firefighters pinpoint the exact location of victims buried in

Above: *The Salt Lake City Utah Task Force 1 crew works at the World Trade Center along with heavy equipment operators to search for victims. Hand work as well as heavy equipment work must be coordinated in order to effectively search for victims and ensure the safety of everyone involved. (FEMA News Photo)*

collapse voids. Search dogs may also be used to locate trapped victims. Once they have been located, various types of power saws, drills, and hammers are utilized to cut through or breach wood, steel, brick, and concrete to gain access to buried victims.

Wood and mechanical shoring systems are used to temporarily stabilize parts of a damaged or partly collapsed structure or section of a building. This reduces the risk to firefighters and victims by preventing a secondary collapse as the debris is removed. While some shoring may be required during the search phase, the shoring operations will increase in complexity as breaching and tunneling operations are conducted to reach the victims and extricate them.

Heavy-duty equipment is often required to reach victims who are trapped under collapsed structural components. Oxy-acetylene and exothermic cutting torches are used to cut through metal beams and columns. Inflatable airbags are utilized to gently lift heavy debris, allowing victims to be removed from void spaces. Powder-actuated tools are used to fasten anchor bolts into large concrete pieces so that cables can be attached to allow for removal by cranes or other types of heavy equipment. Firefighters often must work in conjunction with structural engineers, architects, utility companies, demolition contractors, and various technical advisors to successfully resolve these incidents.

Above: *Rescue crews work at night to rescue a man who fell over a cliff at Point Ferman, California. Searchlights from the helicopter illuminate the scene for the workers on the ground. The helicopter may also be used to evacuate the injured victim. (© Layne Kennedy/Corbis)*

The United States Park Service Mountain Rescue Team teaches fellow rangers rescue techniques in the rugged mountains of Montana's Glacier National Park. Here a ranger simulates a crevasse rescue mission. (© Lowell Georgia/Corbis)

Confined spaces are enclosed areas with limited entry or egress, such as sewers, industrial tanks and processing units, caves, and the cargo-holds of ships. Rescue operations in confined spaces can be extremely dangerous because, in many cases, the atmosphere inside these spaces is oxygen-deficient, explosive, or toxic. Workers may have been overcome by an unknown substance while working deep inside a tunnel that is accessible only through a manhole. Firefighters are trained in the use of atmospheric monitors and metering devices, and intrinsically safe

hardwire communications systems that have been designed specifically for confined space rescue. Specialized supplied air systems can deliver a virtually unlimited supply of breathing air to the rescuers while operating in these dangerous spaces. Special patient packaging devices are used in conjunction with tripod hoists and rope rescue systems to remove victims from confined spaces.

A variety of situations require the application of rope rescue systems. Firefighters rig anchor systems and rope hauling systems to reach victims who are stranded on water towers, communication towers, bridges, cliffs, mountainous areas, or on the outside of high-rise buildings. High-angle and low-angle rope rescues can occur in any elevated or below-grade areas. Water rescue and confined-space operations also rely extensively on rope rescue systems.

Vehicle extrication operations are the most frequent technical rescue incidents. Firefighters use hand tools, air-powered tools, or hydraulically powered rescue systems with a variety of tools and attachments to cut, bend, push, or pull the metal components of a vehicle in order to free trapped occupants. Overturned automobiles can be stabilized using a combination of step chocks, wood box-cribbing,

A "long-line" rescue is being performed by Phoenix Fire Technical Rescue Team members. Team members on the ground access the victim and stabilize him. A helicopter is called to extract the victim and rapidly evacuate to the appropriate level of medical care. (Jack Jordan/Phoenix Fire Department)

325

Phoenix Fire Technical Rescue Team members involved in a swift water rescue training scenario. The team member in the water depends on those on the shore to provide security as he attempts to reach and retrieve the victim. Using hand signs, the rescuer is able to communicate with other team members. (Jack Jordan/Phoenix Fire Department)

A Chicago fireman rescues an unconscious four-year-old, and leaps from the roof of a garage to the ground, after rescuing the youngster from a burning building. Suffering from smoke inhalation, the child was taken to the hospital in critical condition. (© Bettmann/Corbis)

Camden, New Jersey, firefighters practice catching a fellow firefighter as he jumps from a training tower. This rescue technique of the 1930s, while spectacular, was not always successful. Not only was it difficult to position the net, but it took no less than fourteen firefighters to hold it. Victims often missed the net or bounced off, and even firefighters suffered injuries for the effort. (© Bettmann/ Corbis)

high-pressure air bags, and high-lift jacks. Similar techniques are employed by firefighters operating at mass transit extrication operations that can result from accidents involving subway trains, railroads, buses, and aircraft.

Water rescue operations require planning, regular training, special equipment, and the ability to quickly deploy personnel to rescue potential victims. These incidents may involve the surface rescue of a drowning person or someone who has fallen through the ice into frigid water or a person with traumatic injuries from a pleasure boating accident. Divers may be required to rescue the occupants from a submerged vehicle or to free a SCUBA diver who has become trapped under water. Firefighters also respond to rescue victims trapped in their homes by floodwaters or swept downstream by a flash flood. Most water rescue incidents involve only one or two victims, although it is not hard to imagine an incident involving dozens of victims from a capsized water taxi on a busy urban waterway, or hundreds of victims in the water following the collapse of an aging pier that had been transformed into a nightclub or recreation facility.

Across the country every day, hundreds of trenches are opened to facilitate the placement of underground piping or utility cables, to repair underground utilities or to construct tunnels. When the walls of a trench are not properly shored the ground can become extremely unstable. Fire departments have been called to hundreds of incidents where construction workers have been buried alive. Firefighters trained in technical rescue can quickly stabilize a trench collapse using a combination of mechanical shoring, special panels, and 6 x 6 in. wood cross bracing. Once the walls have been secured they can safely dig down to remove the trapped workers.

Industrial rescue incidents may involve a worker who has become entangled in a commercial meat-grinder or a printing press or a mechanic who has fallen from scaffolding and is suspended over a thirty-story elevator shaft, barely hanging on to a metal railing. These are just two examples of the diverse nature of industrial extrications that firefighters must be prepared to resolve.

Special rescue techniques may also be required at fire incidents. Rescue companies are often given the most complex and challenging assignments at fires, such as carefully removing the glass from a window of a high-rise building to provide ventilation or cutting through a concrete floor to reach a fire in an underground vault. Team-search operations may be required to locate firefighters who are trapped or missing in high-rise office buildings or large commercial basement fires. These searches require the use of specialized rope techniques and thermal imaging cameras that allow the user to see the heat of a body or a fire through blinding smoke conditions.

Fireground building collapses are the fourth leading cause of firefighter fatalities. A building collapse is always a complex situation, but the added complication of a heavy fire condition creates an even more challenging problem. Firefighters must be prepared to utilize all of their technical rescue training and equipment under the worst circumstances.

Fire Dogs

JoEllen Kelly

Dogs have served long and well in the fire service. They have earned and deserve our admiration and loyalty. Of course, the Dalmatian is the most recognized breed associated with the fire service, and they are still found in firehouses today as companions and guard dogs. But these dogs were bred to work with horses, and work they did in almost every firehouse in the nation prior to the mass adoption of motorized vehicles. Dalmatians were bred to be serious work dogs; they have been utilized as sentinels, draft dogs, hunting dogs, and retrievers. In their native Dalmatia and Croatia, they were valued for their speed, endurance, and lack of fear of horses.

In America, these were the qualities that made them superb "carriage dogs," who would run alongside the horse-drawn apparatus, keeping the horses calm and focused. They were able to run along with the horses for as much as twenty to thirty miles a day. Firemen loved their dogs, and many early photos of fire companies capture dogs as part of the "team." After motorization, fire dogs (except as mascots) and fire horses virtually disappeared from the fire station.

But, today, dogs are back in the fire service, contributing in ways that would have seemed unimaginable seventy-five years ago. In fact, it is rare that a community does not have at least one canine working as a public safety partner. Search and accelerant-detection dogs are integral in today's fire service. Several breeds have proven to be excellent working dogs, including Labrador and golden retrievers, German shepherds, collies, rottweilers, schnauzers, some mixed-breeds, and even the Dalmatian. These dogs are particularly adapted to solving arson crimes as accelerant-detective canines. Dogs also assist the fire service in wilderness searches, trailing, human remains recovery, water search, rescue, and as bomb dogs. They work in all conditions, and in remote locations. Canine first responders have been trained to work on aerial ladders, boats, helicopters, and at collapsed building sites.

On September 11, FEMA deployed twenty-five of its nationwide Urban Search and Rescue Task Forces to the World Trade Center and the Pentagon, including 80 FEMA-certified dogs. Over 300 canine search and rescue dogs worked at both sites after the terrorist attacks. They worked around the clock and were absolutely critical in the search and recovery efforts. One dog, a Port Authority Police dog, Sirius (Badge 17), died on duty on September 11. Four months later, under full honors, with a prayer and a salute, his body was removed from the wreckage. All machinery and action on "the pile" stopped, and he was given the same honors accorded to police officers and firefighters.

Below, left: A canine member of the Arizona Urban Search and Rescue Task Force 1 takes a minute to rest from searching the wreckage at the World Trade Center crash site. (Michael Reiger/FEMA News Photo)

Right, top: French Search and Rescue team search for survivors among the wreckage of the World Trade Center. (Andrea Booher/ FEMA News Photo)

Right, bottom: FEMA's Urban Search and Rescue teams search for survivors amongst the wreckage of the World Trade Center. (Andrea Booher/ FEMA News Photo)

Thanks to Mitch Mendler for his history of fire dogs and fire horses.

Urban Search and Rescue Team efforts require planning and coordination. Here a safety officer reviews plans and progress with a team member. All incidents require a safety officer to allow one individual to be alert to unanticipated hazards that come with all search and rescue operations. (Andrea Booher/FEMA News Photo)

A structural engineer from Virginia Task Force 1 provides a structural damage assessment for buildings damaged in the November 1999 earthquake in the town of Düzce, Turkey. Structural assessments are necessary to ensure rescuer as well as victim safety during the rescue attempt. (Fairfax County Fire and Rescue Department)

National Urban Search & Rescue Response System

Similar to the rapid advances and extensive development of emergency medical services and hazardous materials response capabilities during the 1970s and 1980s, the field of technical rescue has seen significant improvement in terms of organization and training during the 1990s through today. New performance standards and accompanying training and legislative initiatives for technical rescue operations have been developed and teams have been assembled with all of the capabilities that are needed for the most complex and challenging incidents. The Federal Emergency Management Agency's Urban Search & Rescue National Response System is the product of these efforts.

In 1990, following the federal government's responses to the disasters of Hurricane Hugo and the Loma Prieta earthquake, Congress tasked the Federal Emergency Management Agency (FEMA) to develop a national civilian urban search and rescue capability. Several advanced urban search and rescue teams had already been developed by individual fire departments and within regions where special risks had been recognized, such as California with its well-known earthquake potential. FEMA, with support from federal, state, and local authorities, fire departments, the nation's top technical rescue specialists, and other interested groups, developed The National Urban Search & Rescue (US&R) Response System.

The primary purpose of this system is to provide a nationwide network of heavy search and rescue teams that can be rapidly deployed to disaster incidents. The individual teams are established at the local jurisdiction level and can be mobilized by FEMA as needed for nationwide response. The US&R teams provide an organized system of resources to locate, extricate, and provide immediate medical treatment to victims trapped in collapsed structures and to conduct other life-saving operations. They can be called upon for any situation where victims are savable but inaccessible through other rescue techniques. The Nationwide US&R Response System is responsible for the coordination, development, and maintenance of the federal effort in providing these resources to augment state and local resources in disaster situations.

The twenty-eight US&R Task Forces are the fundamental units of FEMA's national response system. Each task force is sponsored by a state or local government jurisdiction and is comprised of at least seventy technical specialists, who are divided into management and operational elements. A significant number of the sponsoring agencies are municipal fire departments, and firefighters comprise the largest percentage of the rostered members within the system.

Each task force maintains extensive capabilities within seven major functional elements. Search specialists utilize canines and technical fiber-optic and electronic search equipment to locate trapped victims. Rescue specialists are skilled in cutting, shoring, lifting, and breaching steel and reinforced concrete to extricate trapped victims. Many firefighters are also

Members of Virginia Task Force 1 evaluate a seven-year-old boy who was trapped in the rubble of his home after the devastating earthquake in Izmit, Turkey, in August 1999. He was entombed for over sixty-eight hours before being located and extricated by the search and rescue team. (Fairfax County Fire and Rescue Department)

Members of Virginia Task Force 1 discover and extricate a young woman who was trapped in the ruins of her home for over fifty hours after the Izmit, Turkey, earthquake in August 1999. (Fairfax County Fire and Rescue Department)

Above: *A "recon" team from Virginia Task Force 1 evaluates a building for possibly trapped survivors in the town of Düzce, Turkey, in November 1999. A "recon" team is comprised of a structural engineer, a hazardous materials specialist, a search specialist, a canine team, a medical specialist, and a rescue specialist. (Fairfax County Fire and Rescue Department)*

Above, right: *U.S. Search and Rescue base camp located in Izmit, Turkey, site of the first devastating earthquake in August 1999. Two teams from the United States (Fairfax County Fire and Rescue, VA-TF1; and Miami-Dade Fire Rescue Department, FL-TF1) worked for two weeks in Turkey. Both teams are funded by the United States Agency for International Development (USAID) Office of Foreign Disaster Assistance (OFDA). (Fairfax County Fire and Rescue Department)*

Opposite, top: *The tragedy of the Murrah Building and its occupants in Oklahoma City was the result of a domestic terrorism detonation of a large explosive device on April 19, 1995. The results are evident here of the power of this action. While some of the building is still standing, much of it has been destroyed and other areas are unstable. The challenge is to search for victims without causing further hazard to them or the rescuers. (© AFP/Corbis)*

Opposite, bottom: *Emergency vehicles surround the twin towers of the World Trade Center after a blast ripped through the world's second tallest office complex (February 26, 1993), killing two people and injuring 200. This 1993 bombing preceded the tragedy of September 11, 2001. (© Mike Segar/Reuters NewMedia Inc./Corbis)*

trained as rigging specialists to work in conjunction with heavy equipment, such as large hydraulic cranes, to remove heavy debris. Physicians and medical specialists (at the paramedic or equivalent level) provide advanced life support capability and prehospital and emergency care for the task force members as well as crush syndrome and confined space medicine for the rescued victims.

Structural engineers provide structural integrity assessments of structures during rescue operations. Hazardous materials specialists and technical information specialists provide support to the overall search and rescue mission, including planning, hazard evaluation, hazardous materials assessments, and technical documentation. Logistics specialists support the mission by providing supplies, equipment, communications, and transportation for the task force and managing the mobilization and demobilization processes.

The US&R Task Forces have been deployed to natural disasters such as hurricanes and earthquakes in the United States and overseas. The firefighters assigned to temporary duty during these deployments have had many opportunities to put their extensive technical rescue training and experience to use.

Response to Terrorism

As terrorism has become a critical national and international concern, firefighters have also been called upon to deliver technical rescue services in the arena of weapons of mass destruction. Responses to the bombing of the Murrah Federal Building in Oklahoma City in 1995, the bombing at the 1996 Olympic Games in Atlanta, and the bombings of U.S. embassies overseas have increased the urgency for firefighters to continue to improve their skills and develop new technologies to mitigate complicated technical rescue situations.

The most significant response in the history of FEMA's US&R National Response System was triggered on the morning of September 11, 2001,

when terrorists hijacked commercial aircraft and used them as flying weapons of mass destruction to simultaneously attack the World Trade Center complex in New York City and the Pentagon in Arlington, Virginia. The devastating results of these attacks prompted a Presidential Disaster Declaration under the Stafford Act, and the immediate activation of the Federal Response Plan. The government implements the Federal Response Plan during a disaster to provide state and local government with technical expertise, equipment, and other resources. FEMA mobilized the US&R Task Forces to provide their unique technical capabilities and to support the ongoing search and rescue efforts at both sites.

At the World Trade Center site, the firefighters who deployed with US&R Task Forces assisted the FDNY and union ironworkers in the massive steel cutting and heavy equipment rigging operations that were required to remove debris and gain access to voids inside the collapsed structures. They also assisted the FDNY in the physical search of numerous void spaces, while fires continued to burn within the debris. The sixteen-acre site was the largest and most complicated urban search and rescue operation ever conducted.

Extensive confined space operations were conducted to search for victims within the huge debris piles and down into the vast underground infrastructure of the World Trade Center. With six stories below ground level, including miles of corridors and subway tunnels, underground

Above: *Firefighting crews pour water into the Pentagon minutes after a hijacked airliner crashed into the southwest corner of the building. On September 11, 2001, along with the World Trade Center in New York City, the Pentagon, in Arlington, Virginia, was attacked by the deliberate crashing of a hijacked passenger jet into the building. (© Reuters NewMedia Inc./Corbis)*

Opposite, bottom, left: *Sacramento Urban Search and Rescue Team members discuss plans and complete calculations in their search for survivors at the World Trade Center. Size and construction of the structure prior to its destruction is part of the process of determining where victims might be and how they might be rescued. (Andrea Booher/FEMA News Photo)*

Opposite, bottom, right: *A seasoned New York City firefighter (middle) flanked by two probationary members work side by side with Urban Search and Rescue Teams from around the country at the World Trade Center. Many "probies" were pressed into service during the incident due to the large loss suffered by the FDNY. (Andrea Booher/FEMA News Photo)*

Right: *Minutes after the dust settles from the outer wall of the Pentagon collapsing as a result of the terrorist-hijacked plane crashing into the building on September 11, 2001, rescue personnel returned to the scene to continue rescue efforts. (© Corbis/ Reuters, U.S. Army Sgt. Carmen L. Burgess)*

stores, parking, mechanical and utilty areas, all buried under mountains of crushing debris, the site was the most complex urban area ever encountered for collapse search activities. Toxic and hazardous flammable atmospheres, as well as the threat of further structural collapse, were constant concerns, demanding the highest levels of accountability and communications.

While this operation was occurring in New York City, there was a simultaneous deployment of US&R task forces to the Pentagon, where

many similar challenges were encountered. During both of these deployments the teams worked with new technology (some of it highly classified) supplied by Department of Defense and Department of Energy experts. Field-testing was conducted by US&R personnel using new state-of-the-art optical, robotics, and pulse radar equipment. It is expected that more highly effective technical search equipment will be developed as a result of this experience.

From the humble, yet visionary, origins of rescue service in New York City in 1915 to the highly trained firefighters that staff many of the positions on the FEMA Urban Search & Rescue Task Forces of today, firefighters in every corner of the United States continue to meet the challenges of complex technical rescue incidents and stand ready to respond whenever and wherever they are needed.

This chapter is dedicated to a mentor, and more importantly a friend, Deputy Chief Ray Downey of the FDNY Special Operations Command, who made the supreme sacrifice in the line of duty at the World Trade Center collapse on September 11, 2001.

Above: *Rescuers in HazMat gear examine the crater on September 11, 2001, at the crash site of United Airlines Flight 93 in Shanksville, Pennsylvania. The plane from Newark, New Jersey, and bound for San Francisco, California, is believed to have been intended to crash in Washington, D.C. The passengers on board took over the plane from the hijackers and foiled the attempt. There were no survivors. (© Gary Tramontina/Corbis Sygma)*

Above: *A battalion chief of FDNY and Urban Search and Rescue teams continue to search for survivors in the World Trade Center wreckage. Teams from all over the country responded to the incident and worked many long hours in the effort. (Andrea Booher/ FEMA News Photo)*

The Firefighter's Sacrifice

THE
Firefighter's
Sacrifice

Marion H. Jordan M.D., Margaret Gunde R.N.,
Kathleen Hollowed R.N., James C. Jeng M.D.

E very year in the United States, firefighters respond to over 20 million incidents. These events include vehicular accidents, explosions, weather-related catastrophes, medical emergencies, and fires of all sizes and locations. Most emergencies are attended to without injury to the responders. Unfortunately, due to the nature of the job, accidents do occur and firefighters suffer an array of injuries. The injuries include, but are not limited to, burns, smoke inhalation, lacerations, broken bones, internal trauma, exhaustion, and, tragically, death. According to the National Fire Protection Association (USFA) the nature of on-the-job fatalities in 2001 (excluding the World Trade Center) included heart attack (40 percent), internal trauma (27 percent) asphyxiation (15 percent), burns (4 percent), crushing (3 percent) and drowning (3 percent).

For some firefighters, a fate almost as tragic as death is a "life and limb altering" burn injury. One such tragedy happened to Firefighter Joe Morgan of Washington, D.C. This is his story.

The evening of May 29, 1999, started as a normal work day for Joe Morgan. He reported to duty at 6:15 PM for an overtime shift at Engine Company #26 in the District of Columbia. While returning from a false call for a motor vehicle accident, a real call came in: house fire on Cherry

Above: A Chicago firefighter, overcome by smoke and near collapse, is carried away from a blazing restaurant in Chicago's West Side in October of 1954. While battling the blaze, ten firefighters were injured and a deputy battalion chief was trapped and presumed dead when the floor of the restaurant collapsed. (© Bettmann/Corbis)

Opposite: As smoke pours out above them, three Boston firefighters gasp for fresh air from the upper window of a Phillips Street dwelling in January of 1972. The firefighters were nearly overcome as they battled a two-alarm blaze in the structure. (© Bettmann/Corbis)

Pages 334–335: On December 12, 1966, two lines of firemen bow their heads and place their helmets on their hearts as one of their comrades is carried from the still burning wreckage of the building. At the time, this was described as "the worst tragedy in Fire Department history," when twelve firemen were killed. (© Bettmann/Corbis)

A Case Study in Safety:
Phoenix Fire Department

Chief Alan V. Brunacini

Structural firefighting is considered by many to be the most dangerous form of firefighting. All firefighters routinely put themselves in hazardous situations, but structural firefighting is particularly dangerous. According to National Fire Protection Association (NFPA) figures, there are over 500,000 structure fires annually in the United States, and each one of these provides an opportunity for firefighter death or injury. Yet, it remains that structural firefighting is what most firefighters do. This is our bread and butter. This is our job. And this is where, in general, we die.

For about two decades, there has been a tremendous interest in firefighter health and safety. Along with industry and government, we have developed and refined protective equipment, tools, systems, standard operating procedures (SOPs), and wellness programs to improve firefighting safety and survivability. The promulgation of health and safety codes, such as the NFPA's controversial 1500 Standards on Fire Department Occupational Safety and Health Program (1987), have made structural firefighting safer—but not safe enough.

In Phoenix, and elsewhere, fire service leaders proclaim that our members are our most valuable resource. This has become a very popular slogan in the fire service, and we are finding out that it is a very challenging way to manage our departments. Safety comes at a price, and in the era of doing more with less, safety is often a casualty in the budget wars.

During the early (and mid) years of my career, we spent a lot more money maintaining our apparatus than we did maintaining our people. I hope this economic model has finally been turned around. More and more often, fire service organizations now try to base their day-to-day operations keeping in mind both the needs of the community, and what is right for the people who deliver emergency services.

It wasn't very long ago that the estimated success of a fire department depended on how many fires it extinguished in a year. Everything we did organizationally was based on controlling and eliminating fires. Our sole reason for existence was to control fire. At any cost, it didn't matter. Whether there were civilian lives at risk or not, we had to get that fire knocked down. Our new way of delivering services says, "Hey, wait a minute!" What do we really accomplish if we save a building, but loose a firefighter? Our emphasis now places a premium on our members conducting quality operations, supported by one constant core value: firefighter survivability.

This new model requires us to analyze the variables that injure and kill firefighters. We do this by collecting and analyzing our own data from Phoenix, and from looking at national trends. One of the best things we in the fire service can do for ourselves is to scientifically study our working environments. Unless we understand what happens to cause a firefighter to be severely burned, for example, we can't implement changes.

Having said that, we do understand many of the factors that lead to firefighter injuries and fatalities at structure fires. These include heart attacks, structural collapse, heat/thermal insult, getting lost/trapped and running out of air. In addition, a large number of firefighters are killed responding to and returning from the incident scene (traffic accidents), and due to the progress of a fire (backdraft or flashover.)

Heart attacks account for half of on-scene firefighter fatalities. We can prevent heart attack deaths as part of a total wellness program. Firefighters must be both physically and mentally fit for duty. Many medical

researchers believe that managing stress is a critical part of maintaining a healthy heart. In Phoenix, we do everything we can to reduce the stress associated with delivering emergency services by providing good training, adequate staffing, and modern equipment. In addition, we believe that procedure-based operations are the safest, and we strive to make fireground procedures as rational as possible. Well-trained, properly equipped companies with clearly defined responsibilities handle the stress of emergency operations much better. Developing this type of organizational culture requires that senior leaders/managers develop sane, non-ego-based management skills.

The other piece of a healthy heart program is physical fitness. The core of this program is achieved through the ongoing relationship between each member and the doctor/medical staff. Here in Phoenix, members must have yearly physical exams that include an evaluation of how well their circulatory system (heart and lung) functions under stress. Lifetime physical fitness

and nutrition programs for each member are essential for maintaining both a healthy body and mind.

Personal protective equipment (PPE) has been a major safety improvement, especially over the past twenty-five years. The development and mandatory use of self-contained breathing apparatus (SCBA) began the revolution in PPE. Prior to SCBA, the cancer rate for firefighters was off the charts due to exposure to smoke and other toxic substances. The PPE ensemble worn by our members today offers an unprecedented level of protection. Improvements in PPE will, hopefully, allow many more members to enjoy healthy retirements.

Structural collapse, heat/thermal insult, and incidents of firefighters getting lost and confused during emergency operations continue to vex our industry. There are no easy answers to these problems, and it is too easy

Top: A Safety Officer patrols the scene of a well-involved two-story condominium fire. One of the Safety Officer's primary functions is to make sure that firefighters stay out of areas or situations where they might be injured or killed. (Paul Ramirez/Phoenix Fire Department)

to say that we must continue to study them. In my department, our safety section and safety officers work diligently every day to educate our members about safer work environments.

Integrating safety consciousness into everything we do (including routine operations) is hard work. It requires a universal commitment from every member of the organization. It must become a prerequisite for everything we do. From training, to the tools, equipment, and apparatus we buy, safety is our preeminent concern. We don't buy from vendors who don't take safety seriously. We don't let our managers allow sloppy fireground operations, and we strive to keep up with the latest developments in fire science.

These commitments represent the major components of any good fire department safety program. We try to go beyond them. We develop and use other concepts such as safety sectors at major incidents, formalized accountability systems, Rapid Intervention Crews (RIC) and, above all else, we have a Risk Management Plan.

Our Risk Management Plan is a vital organizational document. It outlines what risks we will take to save lives (a lot), and what we will risk to just save property (a lot less). We have decided, as a department, that we will not take any risk to protect property that is already lost. Although these statements may appear callous, they reinforce our tactical priorities: save lives, control hazards, and preserve property. We can't meet

our tactical goals if we continue to put firefighters at risk.

We believe deeply that our managers and supervisors must be supported in terms of training and resources. We support them by allowing them to manage the positions and resources assigned to them. This involves building an effective command organization (command team, section chiefs, and support staff).

Technology has made firefighting safer—the safest it has ever been. But we still do structural firefighting in much the same way our ancestor's did—we bring water to fire. Today, though, you may see a structural firefighter doing her job using a thermal imaging camera to locate victims, or you may see a command officer outside locating his firefighters inside a structure using a global positional system. As a fire chief, I can't wait to see what this decade brings to make us safer. I am proud that the Phoenix Fire Department has staked its claim to being an ever-increasingly safe organization.

Top, left: Firefighters face high hazard situations as an everyday part of their job. Fire departments must develop, use, and refine safety and incident management systems as a normal and standard part of the delivering emergency service to the community. (Paul Ramirez/Phoenix Fire Department)

Top, center: The Incident Commander is responsible for determining the correct strategy that firefighters will use when fighting structure fires. When the fire takes possession of most of the building (or in this case, buildings) we fight them from safer and more effective outside positions using lots of water. (Jack Jordan/Phoenix Fire Department)

Top, right: The goal of every incident we respond to has to include us surviving the event. (Paul Ramirez/Phoenix Fire Department)

Above: *Firefighter's turnout gear hangs ready for the next emergency. The best protection a firefighter has against injury is his personal protective clothing. Clean, well-maintained turnout gear, worn properly, along with self-contained breathing apparatus, offers total encapsulation for the firefighter. While all equipment has a point at which it will fail, under extreme or prolonged heat, modern gear provides superior protection. (© Doug Wilson/Corbis)*

Left: *A firefighter rests after fighting a blaze in a Brooklyn warehouse in June of 1988. Firefighting takes its toll from the most fit and most prepared in the ranks. While danger is "a part of the job" the goal is to make exhaustion the worst complication of doing the job. (© Robert Maass/Corbis)*

Road in Northeast D.C. Joe and three of his fellow firefighters rushed to the scene. The owner of the house directed them to his townhouse. Joe assumed the position of layout: taking the hose from the wagon, connecting it to the hydrant and backing up the nozzle. The wagon proceeded to the house a half block away.

Within minutes, a second fire company arrived. Joe hooked up their hose to his to provide additional pressure. He then put on his gear and went to the house to back up his partner, who was the nozzle man. The two entered the smoke-filled home crawling down a hallway to the living room in search of the fire. Joe was advancing in very low visibility when he felt an increase in heat coming from behind him. He looked over his left shoulder and saw a flash of flames coming from the basement door, then extreme heat bellowed up the staircase from the chimney effect of the fire. The room blackened down very quickly and Joe scrambled farther into the building to escape the intense heat. Joe realized instantly that he was in trouble and summoned his partner to get out of the house. He crawled a few feet to the nozzle and directed water to the ceiling to cool down the room and prevent a flashover. He followed his hose line out of the building and told his fellow firefighters where to locate the others inside. The company officer managed to escape with relatively small areas of second-degree burns that healed with medical

In January 1933, a fire officer assists one of two firefighters who were injured in the blaze at the Czechoslovakian Legation in Washington, D.C. (© Bettmann/Corbis)

A Sage IIc (Surface Area Graphic Evaluation © 1987-2002) Burn Diagram is used to calculate the percentage of the body surface that is burned. This value is used to estimate the acute resuscitation fluid requirements, the daily maintenance fluid losses, and the daily nutritional needs. (The Burn Center at Washington Hospital Center, Washington, D.C.)

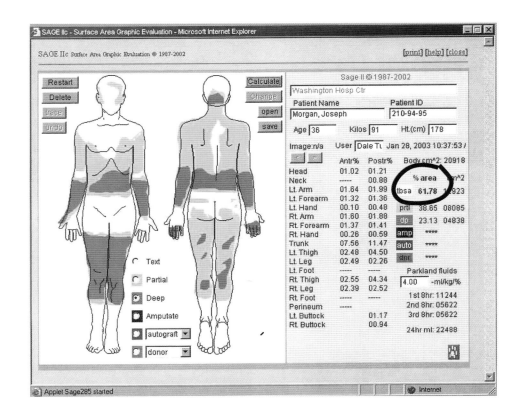

Bottom, left: An incision is made through the inelastic burned skin to relieve the tourniquet effect and allow the healthy, deeper, injured tissues to swell without losing blood flow. (The Burn Center at Washington Hospital Center, Washington, D.C.)

Bottom, right: A plastic tube is inserted through the vocal cords into the trachea to maintain an open airway during the early hours or days when all of the body's tissues, especially injured structures, develop swelling as a normal response to the injury. (The Burn Center at Washington Hospital Center, Washington, D.C.)

treatment within a few days. Unfortunately, Joe's partner and another firefighter were at the top of the stairwell in direct line with the flames and suffered extensive burns that were quickly fatal.

Although Joe had not been in direct contact with flames, he had been exposed to intense heat estimated to be in excess of 1,500 degrees Fahrenheit. Firefighters hosed him down and then, with the paramedics, removed his gear, undressed him, and put him in an ambulance. One paramedic attended to Joe while the other stayed at the scene. A policeman drove the ambulance to the hospital.

Joe could see that his fingers were burned and was very worried that they would stick together. He kept spreading them apart and convinced the paramedic to wrap them individually. He tried to calm down. It was a seven-minute ride to The Burn Center at Washington Hospital Center. There he was assessed as having suffered third-degree burns to almost 62 percent of his body surface. The only areas that were not burned were his feet, parts of his torso, thighs and lower legs, face, and the top of his head.

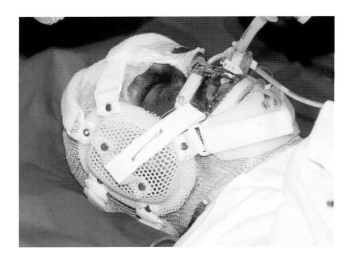

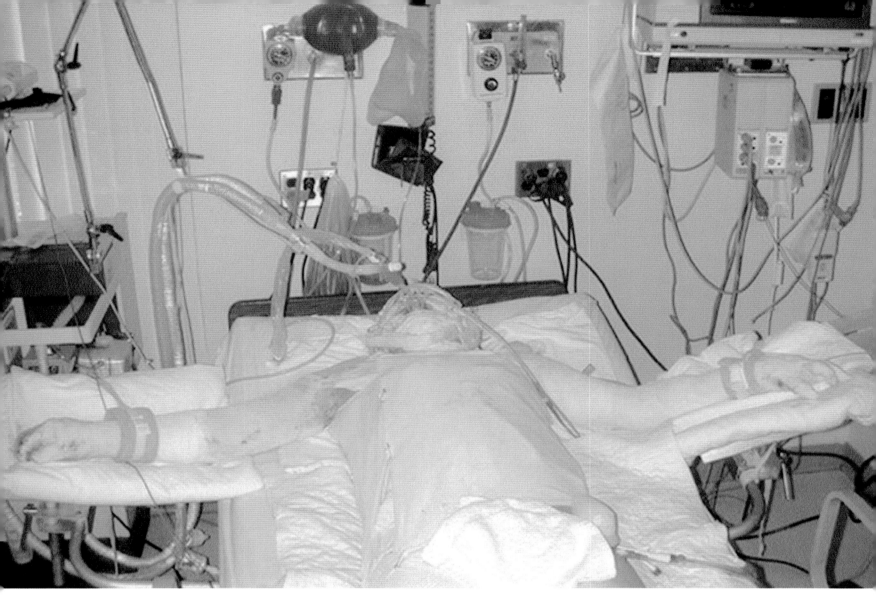

His fluid replacement requirements to prevent shock were calculated to be 22+ liters (more than five gallons) to be given intravenously during the next twenty-four hours. The rapid infusion of intravenous fluids, combined with the burn injury, caused swelling in his extremities and torso which created a tourniquet effect. That pressure essentially cut off blood circulation to these areas. Escharotomies—incisions through the burned skin—were performed to relieve the pressure and restore circulation. A plastic (endotracheal) tube was inserted into his airway because of concern that his airway would swell closed.

Transfer from the trauma admitting unit to the burn intensive care unit occurred within one hour. Once in the burn unit, Joe was immediately weighed and then bathed to remove the blistered, loose skin and adherent burned clothing. Intact burned skin was cleansed with an iodine solution. Twenty minutes later, Joe was in his intensive care unit room surrounded by nurses applying silver sulfadiazine dressings (designed to control infection) to his face, arms, hands, legs, chest, and back. Based upon his age and burn extent, his estimated chance of survival was approximately 5 percent.

Joe's burn wounds were cleansed and bandaged twice a day, every day for two months. For the first few weeks, the extensive dressing changes consumed two hours each. During and between those events, the nurses and rehabilitation therapists coached him to move his extremities frequently to prevent losses of flexibility due to the inevitable scarring. As time passed, the rehabilitation therapy became more intense.

Above: *The burned areas are covered with gauze dressings that contain an antibacterial chemical composed of sulfa drugs and silver molecules. The dressings control the growth of bacteria in the burned skin and thereby control life-threatening infection. (The Burn Center at Washington Hospital Center, Washington, D.C.)*

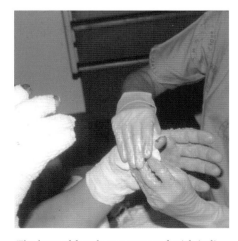

The burned hands are wrapped with individual dressings for each finger to allow the patient to use the hands and reduce the disability from scarring. (The Burn Center at Washington Hospital Center, Washington, D.C.)

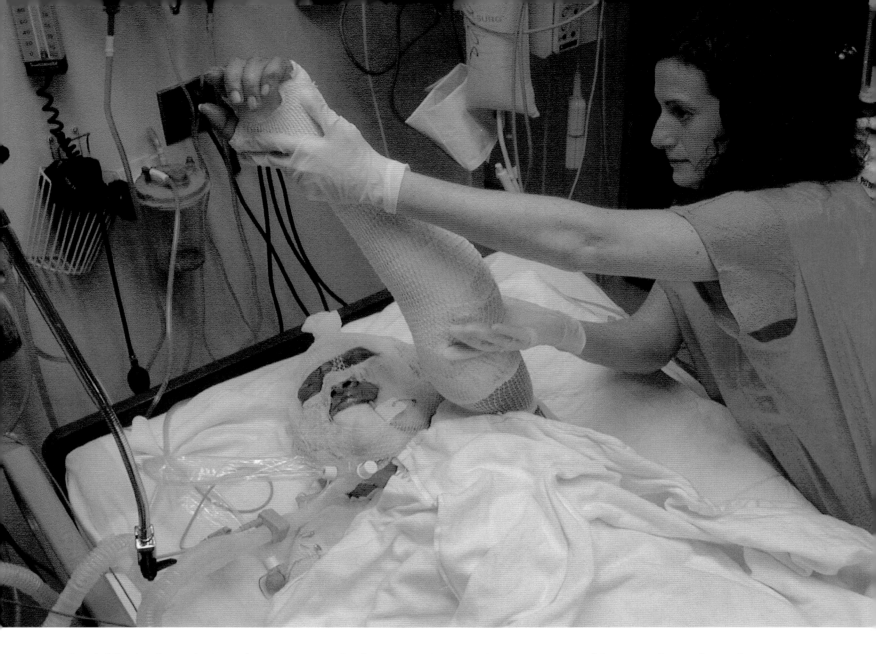

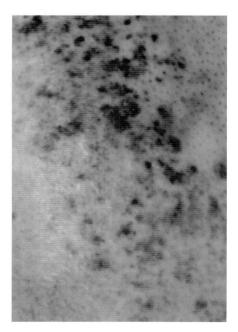

For the first week, his breathing was assisted by a mechanical ventilator, with air delivered through the plastic tube in his trachea. While that tube was in place, his only method of communication was to nod "Yes" or "No" to questions. Fortunately, his lungs and airway had been protected by his SCBA, and the endotracheal tube was able to be removed by June 5. Feeding was accomplished with another tube passed through his nose into his stomach. This remained in place for the first several weeks to ensure that he received the 4,000–4,500 calories daily (equivalent to eating eight Big Macs) that would be necessary for wound healing. His survival was always in question, but the absence of airway and lung injury gave cause for hope.

The first of fifteen surgical procedures began on June 1, 1999, and most of those operations occurred every two to three days during the first month. All of the burned skin had to be removed and serially replaced with skin from his unburned areas—a process called excision and skin grafting. Since the amount of unburned skin on his body was much less than what was burned, temporary skin substitutes were used, including human cadaver skin from a skin bank and a synthetic, bio-engineered product made from cow protein and powdered shark cartilage. The former provided coverage of the raw wounds with a living human skin that would eventually reject and require placement with his own skin. The latter served to protect the wound while providing the

body with a biological "scaffold" to grow new dermis for eventual coverage with his own outer layer of skin cells.

In total, the burned areas requiring skin grafts totaled 12.5 square feet, a surface equal to a tabletop measuring two feet long and six feet

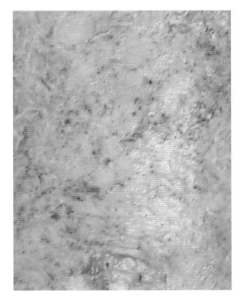

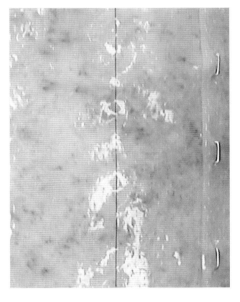

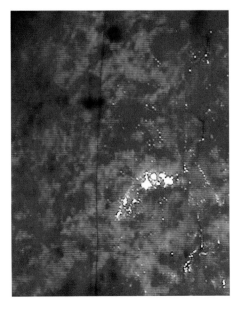

Opposite, bottom: The burned skin is dry, leathery, and has lost its outer layer (epidermis), which contains the pigment for skin color. The exposed, damaged second layer— the dermis—is vulnerable to infection with bacteria. It must be surgically removed for healing to occur. (The Burn Center at Washington Hospital Center, Washington, D.C.)

Top, left: In the operating room, with the patient asleep, the burned areas of skin are shaved off in a series of paper-thin layers with a razor-sharp instrument. (The Burn Center at Washington Hospital Center, Washington, D.C.)

Top, right: The second layer of damaged tissue is removed with the razor knife. The damaged tissue shows staining of the tissue layers from red blood cells leaking from small blood vessels. (The Burn Center at Washington Hospital Center, Washington, D.C.)

Center, left: The wound surface after bleeding has stopped shows yellow fat and healthy dermis mixed with an early thin layer of scar tissue. (The Burn Center at Washington Hospital Center, Washington, D.C.)

Center, right: The delicate deep tissues have been covered with Integra®—a bioengineered material made of cow protein and powdered shark cartilage bonded to a sheet of silicon—which protects the wound and serves as a scaffold for healing cells to create a new dermal layer. (The Burn Center at Washington Hospital Center, Washington, D.C.)

Bottom, left: The burn wound after two weeks shows evidence of red blood circulating in newly developed blood vessels which grow into the Integra® scaffold beneath the shiny silicon sheet. (The Burn Center at Washington Hospital Center, Washington, D.C.)

Bottom, right: The Integra® scaffold must now be covered with an outer layer of skin—the epidermis. This is accomplished by removing a thin sheet (.012" thick) of skin from an unburned area of the body. (The Burn Center at Washington Hospital Center, Washington, D.C.)

345

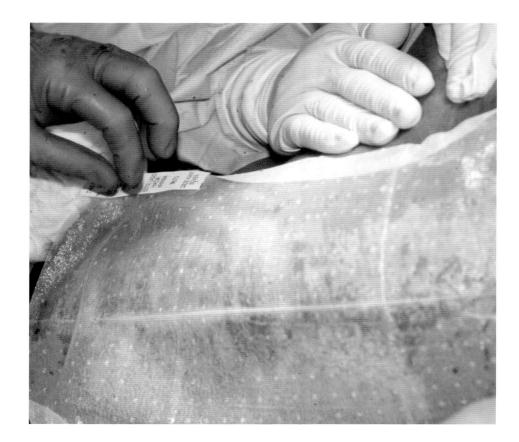

Above: *When the burn injury is extensive, and donor areas are scarce, the skin sheet is perforated with an instrument called a mesher to allow expansion of coverage. (The Burn Center at Washington Hospital Center, Washington, D.C.)*

The meshed skin graft, in this case, was expanded in a 3:1 ratio to allow seeding of epidermal skin cells over a larger wound. The graft is upside-down on the plastic carrier to allow direct application of the underside to the wound surface. (The Burn Center at Washington Hospital Center, Washington, D.C.)

wide. Because virtually all areas were grafted twice—once with temporary skin substitutes and subsequently with Joe's own skin—the total surfaces grafted were double that amount. The last surgery before his discharge from the hospital was August 13.

Joe was discharged from the hospital eighty-five days after the fire. He had lost more than twenty pounds due to loss of tissue and

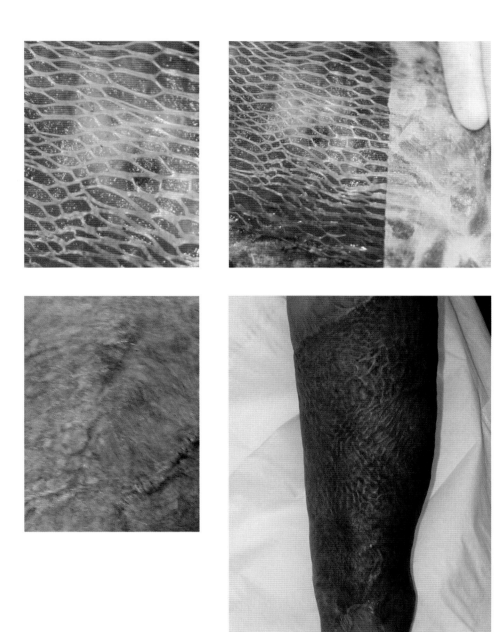

Top, left: *The Integra® silicon layer has been removed, and the skin graft has been placed on the new dermal layer. Within two to three weeks, the skin cells will grow from the edges of the meshed graft and fill in the open, diamond-shaped areas. (The Burn Center at Washington Hospital Center, Washington, D.C.)*

Top, right: *The skin graft is carefully wrapped with a petrolatum gauze to prevent drying and movement and then is covered with multiple layers of cotton gauze and elastic gauze to prevent shearing until the new blood vessels have grown into the epidermal layer. (The Burn Center at Washington Hospital Center, Washington, D.C.)*

Center left: *Several months later, the grafted area still shows a slightly irregular surface, but the pigment has filled in and the grafted skin is a durable covering for an area that suffered a full-thickness burn injury. (The Burn Center at Washington Hospital Center, Washington, D.C.)*

Center, right: *In some areas, because of the urgency for rapid wound closure to prevent life-threatening infection, the grafts were applied in one stage without the intermediate use of the Integra®. These areas also have durable coverage, but exhibit a more visible mesh pattern. Reconstructive surgery after recovery from the acute injury remains an option for an improved, smoother appearance. (The Burn Center at Washington Hospital Center, Washington, D.C.)*

Below, left: *Rehabilitation therapy focused on hand and finger motion as a priority, with early tasks such as stacking cones being difficult at first. (The Burn Center at Washington Hospital Center, Washington, D.C.)*

Below: *As dexterity improved, exercise was prescribed to regain hand and upper extremity strength. (The Burn Center at Washington Hospital Center, Washington, D.C.)*

wasting of muscle mass from the forced inactivity during the critical phase of illness. He faced a long course of rehabilitation therapy and reconstructive surgery.

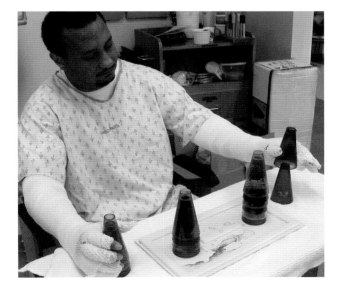

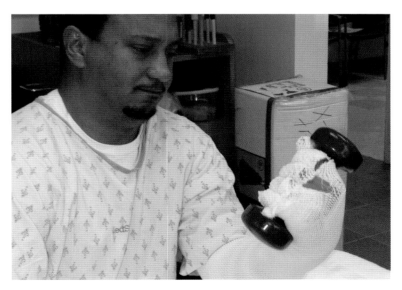

347

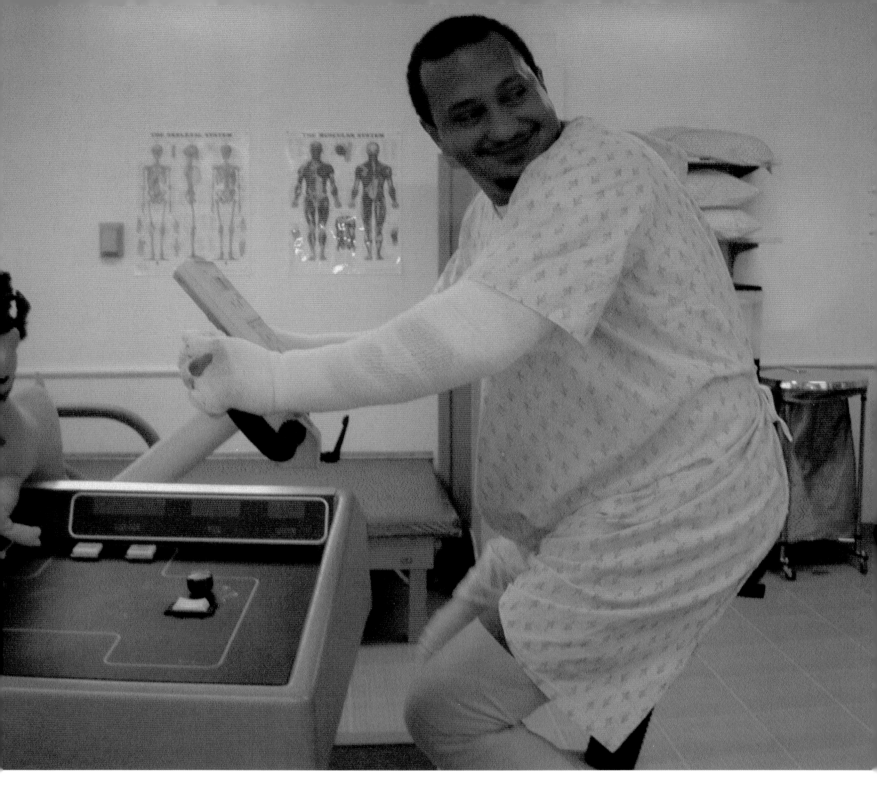

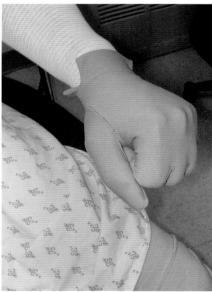

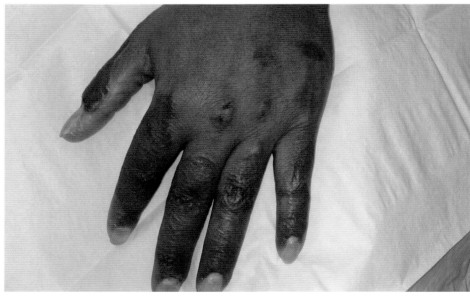

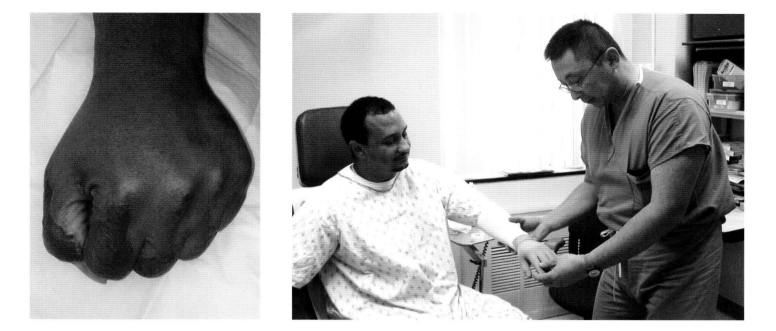

After several months of rehabilitation, Joe Morgan returned to the job full-time, proudly wearing his uniform and performing his duties in a modified role that recognizes his inability to endure extreme heat, but takes advantage of his ability and experience in teaching safety and prevention of injury. He lost one of his battalion brothers and a firefighter from the other responding unit, but he was alive and able to continue his career as a firefighter.

As Joe's story illustrates, all burned firefighters deserve to be transported as quickly as possible to a dedicated burn facility; being brought

Opposite, top: During the critical period of illness, the body's muscles become weak and endurance is lost. As soon as balance and muscle control returned, the treadmill and exercise bike were added to the therapy program. (The Burn Center at Washington Hospital Center, Washington, D.C.)

Opposite, bottom, left: A part of rehabilitation therapy is scar control. All areas with healing wounds were covered with elastic, custom-fitted compression garments to flattened the scars as they matured. The gloves and body suits were required for twelve months, twenty-four hours daily, and needed replacements every six to eight weeks to maintain proper pressure. (The Burn Center at Washington Hospital Center, Washington, D.C.)

Opposite, bottom, right: The desired result of the surgery and the therapy is a strong, fully-functional person. Scar control was successful. (The Burn Center at Washington Hospital Center, Washington, D.C.)

Top, left: This hand regained full motion and strength well before the gloves were discontinued. (The Burn Center at Washington Hospital Center, Washington, D.C.)

Top, right: Regular visits to Burn Clinic and Burn Rehab Therapy are routine for the first twelve months after discharge from the hospital. Measurements of strength and motion were made, and the compression garments were checked for wear and effectiveness. (The Burn Center at Washington Hospital Center, Washington, D.C.)

Left: Burn patients develop a strong bond with the Burn Center staff, as evident by a typical expression of affection between Joe and the head nurse of the Burn Rehab Unit during one of his Burn Clinic visits. (The Burn Center at Washington Hospital Center, Washington, D.C.)

349

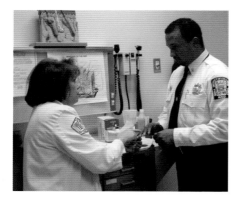

When the patient dons the uniform and returns, the burn team is rewarded for its effort. Here, Joe is receiving final instructions in skin care and activities from the Burn Nurse Practitioner. (The Burn Center at Washington Hospital Center, Washington, D.C.)

This story had a happy ending. A fully recovered firefighter and his daughter visit with his co-workers. (The Burn Center at Washington Hospital Center, Washington, D.C.)

to such a unit is the only guarantee that the firefighter will receive the highest level of medical care available to burn victims. Fire departments who are not within range of a burn unit should make contingency plans to get their firefighters transferred from a emergency unit to a burn center with all due speed. While Joe Morgan was wearing all of his gear and still received life-threatening burns, there is increased risk of injury when firefighters rush into emergencies without taking the time to don their total gear package. According to the National Fire Fighter Burn Study completed in 2002, the absence of any portion of the personal protective gear is a major contributing factor to firefighter burns. In addition, on the opposite end of the spectrum, a firefighter fully encapsulated in gear, and exposed to the danger of rapidly moving fire conditions, does not have the ability to feel the change in environment (heat level increase) until it's too late. Both of these situations are major contributing factors to firefighter thermal injuries.

Joe Morgan's recovery is but one example of courage and heroism that occurs every year in the fire service. Fortunately for the public, there are valiant young men and women who choose to place themselves in harm's way to save others' lives and property. While some injury and loss of life seems inevitable, considering what they do, the progress in burn care and rehabilitation offers hope for survival and recovery of function. Joe's return to duty is a memorial to fallen firefighters, and each day that he contributes is an inspiration to the burn team and his coworkers.

Serving Those Who Serve:
Fire Department Chaplains

Chaplain Ed Stauffer

Fire departments by tradition have had someone in the role of chaplain since organized firefighting began in our country during the early eighteenth century. In many departments, a local clergy person has been appointed chaplain to handle emergency situations within the department, such as serious injury to fire department members, line-of-duty deaths (including notification of family members), and suicides involving fire department members or their families. Chaplains have fulfilled a traditional ceremonial role by giving the invocation at fire department functions and conducting weddings and funerals for fire department family members.

Virtually all fire departments have formalized the role of the chaplain. The pressures of living in a complicated world have an impact on everyone, including emergency workers. Firefighting presents unique aspects of stress not normally associated with other professions.

Firefighters, for example, have to learn to live with high levels of uncertainty. When the alarm sounds, a firefighter responds, never quite sure of what will unfold during the next few minutes or hours.

Interpersonal tensions can create potent sources of conflict within emergency service organizations, primarily due to staffing and scheduling patterns. Often tensions are heightened by long hours spent in the fire station away from their families.

Firefighters are witness to the results of a wide range of human tragedy and carnage. This constant exposure to death, injury, and loss takes its toll on firefighters and paramedics with far-reaching physical and psychological consequences.

All of these issues—uncertainty, interpersonal conflict, physical demands, and emotional strain—make the role of the chaplain even more important in today's fire

service. In these instances, chaplains are called to function as family counselors, psychologists, and spiritual advisors. Caring and compassionate fire department leaders see to it that their chaplain staff is well-trained. Chaplains must be able to recognize the signs of stress affecting personnel, and have the resources available to help firefighters cope with the problems they encounter.

Aside from our role as counselors, fire department chaplains are often found at the scene of emergency events. It is not unusual for chaplains to be issued running gear to offer them some level of protection during an incident. Some chaplains are even volunteers themselves! This on-scene time makes our job more real, and the challenges of helping firefighters more rewarding.

For many reasons, the chaplain of the fire department is one of the most vital and respected positions in the fire service. Not only does the chaplain become the repository of much confidential information regarding individual members, but he or she can also help shape the organization's culture during both good times and bad.

Assists from a higher power from a chaplain during the events of September 2001. Chaplains of many faiths now assist the members of the fire service and their families. They provide support, spiritual guidance, and counseling before, after, and during emergency incidents. (George W. Buck, Jr., Ph.D.)

EPILOGUE:
Firefighting Refocused

Chief Ronald J. Siarnicki
Executive Director, National Fallen Firefighters Foundation

Above: *As honor guards pass in review, a firefighter shows respect for the American flag and honor for those who lost their lives in the line of duty during the previous year. Never an easy task, it is the acknowledged duty of the "fire service family" to pay tribute to the sacrifices of those lost, and to give support to all of the survivors left behind. (Bill Green)*

Left: *The 2002 National Memorial Weekend sponsored by the National Fallen Firefighters Foundation was particularly difficult. Not only were there losses of firefighters from thirty-four states in 2001, but the events of September 11, 2001, touched the lives of firefighters around the world. Crossed aerial ladders suspend an American flag as firefighters from across the nation formed a "sea of blue" joining honor guards and bagpipers to honor not only the fallen, but also their survivors. (Bill Green)*

N o cause is as noble as saving another's life. No sacrifice is greater than giving your own to do it. That's what firefighters do. The face of every firefighter you see illustrated in this book represents a person who has made the same commitment: "I will lay down my life to save another." As we tell the story of firefighting in the United States, we tell the many stories of men and women, of all ages and social backgrounds, who exemplify courage and bravery to a degree most of us will never comprehend.

Every year, an average of 100 firefighters die in the line of duty. In the year 2001, during an unimaginable time, 442 firefighters received a call for help and never hesitated to respond. It happened at the World Trade Center. It happened in the vast western wildfires. It happens in America, on average, every three days. It usually happens during the everyday, routine calls when everyone expects to make it home safe and sound. No matter where our firefighters responded, they were thinking of the job at hand that day. They were not contemplating what fate would hold—if they did, they could not do their job.

The National Fallen Firefighters Foundation helps our country take pause, take notice, and give its humble thanks to the survivors who have lost so much. Immediate survivors include family members, friends, and

Opposite: *Constructed in 1981, and located in Emmitsburg, Maryland, the seven-foot stone monument features a sculptured Maltese Cross, the traditional symbol of the fire service. At the base of the monument, an eternal flame symbolizes the spirit of all firefighters—past, present, and future. Plaques encircling the base list the names of the men and women of the fire service who have died in service to their communities since 1981. Whenever a firefighter dies in the line of duty, fire officials post a notice of the death at the monument and lower flags at the site to half-staff. (Bill Green)*

Honor guards and bagpipe bands have a long history in the fire service. Traditionally "Amazing Grace" is played at the funeral service of a firefighter lost in the line of duty. Here the New York City Fire Department's Emerald Society Pipes and Drums play at the annual memorial service at the National Fire Academy in Emmitsburg, Maryland. (Vina Drennan)

fellow firefighters, who responded side by side with the heroes who we honor. But we are all survivors because firefighters die to protect values we all hold so dear. Because we survive, we hold these men and women as true patriots in every sense of the word.

Each year at the NFFF National Memorial Weekend, we publicly honor those lost and privately help survivors deal with grief. As they learn to live beyond the immediate pain, we offer support for all the years to come. This is a key ingredient that makes the programs offered by the Foundation so meaningful and successful for all who decide to take advantage of our services. We make a commitment to always be there for the emotional support survivors need beyond the first year or two of loss.

It is true that the Foundation offers survivors a wide array of services and support. It is true that corporate donations will help us provide more. But the truth is the National Fallen Firefighters Foundation is nothing without the courageous survivors who join our ranks each year, and who stay with us. I have always known that dignity, compassion, and commitment run deep in firefighting families. I cannot estimate the number of sons and daughters of fallen firefighters who are following in the footsteps of a family member who died in the line of duty. We have often said among ourselves that firefighting is "in the blood." But I think a stronger case can be made that firefighting is "in the values" of the over one million current Americans who have taken the oath, and the many millions more who recognize and salute their efforts.

September 11, 2001, changed the lives of firefighters everywhere. It was the moment our hearts broke, but it was also an instance when the entire world witnessed the unimaginable dedication of the U.S. firefighter. On that day, and for many days after, firefighters responded—first to the immediate crisis of rescuing civilians, and then to the details recovering 347 brothers from the remains of the World Trade Center complex. Along with the ironworkers and construction and demolition crews, FDNY firefighters and firefighters from across the United States attended to the rescue and recovery effort, often again, putting their lives at risk. Our firefighters are the envy of the world's firefighting community and, in my mind, they deserve it.

Every day of every year firefighters put it all on the line so that others may live. That's the mission statement. About 100 times a year, the ultimate sacrifice is made. That is why the National Fallen Firefighters Foundation exists—to help, to serve, to see the journey through. You see, our values are no different from the values of the firefighters we remember.

For our families, Emmitsburg is no longer a remote corner in the rolling hills of Maryland. It is now and forever the place where an entire world can gather and say, "We will always remember and thank you, our fire service heroes."

Survivors of the loss of a firefighter, a mother and her son receive the United States flag and a rose as a tribute to their sacrifice. Each year in Emmitsburg, Maryland, the survivors of line-of-duty deaths are honored along with the memory of their firefighter. (Joe Tecce)

The author would like to thank Hillary Howard, WUSA-TV9, for her insights and contributions to this essay. Her commitment to the NFFF is deeply appreciated.

355

A Survivor's Account

Vina Drennan

I stood as proudly as I could that chilly day in early October at the National Fallen Firefighters Memorial. I had journeyed there to honor his life and to hear the words, "On behalf of a grateful nation." My hand reached out and fingered the fabric of our nation's flag, and I heard his name ring out with all the respect that a name can be spoken: "Captain John J. Drennan, New York City."

I cradled the flag that had been so lovingly folded close to my body. With all my heart I wished the sound of his name would echo forever, never wanting his sacrifice to be forgotten. Later I mingled with the crowd that gathered around the memorial. I knelt near the plaque that bore his name, and let my finger trace the engraved lettering that honors the memory of the brave man I had loved for so many years. It was 1995, and my first trip to the National Fallen Firefighters (NFFF) Memorial Weekend, which is held every October on the campus of the National Emergency Training Center in Emmitsburg, Maryland. The weekend is a special time for family members of fallen firefighters to come to honor and remember their loved ones who have died in the line of duty.

That year, 107 lives were honored; 107 times the color guard rigidly and meticulously presented the tightly folded triangular flag; and 107 times, "On behalf of a grateful nation," was uttered. The 107 families came, often accompanied with representatives from their fire department, all bearing broken hearts, needing to honor a loved one whose life ended too soon and too tragically.

From all over America we journeyed—from Oregon and Arkansas, from Massachusetts and Indiana. This was a pilgrimage from all parts of our nation, representing departments that serve our most rural communities to departments that serve our biggest urban areas. We came to hear their names, to place a rose, to run our fingers across the letters that will always adorn a plaque that honors their heroism. A line of duty death in the fire service represents the highest level of sacrifice. We came hoping that the sacrifice would never be forgotten.

My husband, a fire captain with FDNY, had died on May 7, 1994, after a forty-day struggle to live. He had been burned extensively while battling a residential fire in Manhattan. Even before this weekend, his life had been celebrated at many tributes and memorials and quite frankly, my family was exhausted. So, I came alone to Memorial Weekend in Emmitsburg, a very weary widow, going through the motions, tired of pity. What I did not expect is exactly what happened.

That weekend made a significant difference in my life these last seven years. It certainly was a dignified flag ceremony. The chapel service on Sunday could not have been more inspiring. It warmed my heart to see his face on the giant screen and to honor his image. It was beautiful to hear the bell chime when his red rose joined the others in the bouquet commemorating the nation's loss. All these things were most touching. Yet, there was one significant factor that made Emmitsburg stand apart from the other tributes and memorial services.

At Emmitsburg, they honor the lost firefighter most by helping his or her family. A significant portion of the weekend is dedicated to working with families—adults and children alike—deal with their stage of grief. Qualified and sensitive professionals are on hand to help the families cope with their overwhelming sense of loss. Without making any promises, they provide the support network family members need to begin to put the pieces of their lives back together. Each relationship to the firefighter is honored. Parents, spouses, children,

siblings, and even fellow firefighters can talk about their loss, surrounded by people who have been through the experience. In my mind, this is the key to what makes the Emmitsburg experience so valuable.

I was assigned to a room and had an opportunity to talk with other widows whose pain was as raw as mine. We had ample time to share our stories. We showed our photos and newspaper clippings, and exposed our broken hearts. I wasn't alone: their children hurt, they had trouble cooking, the empty chair at the table made them cry, too. They also worried how they would get through the holidays. They were sometimes disappointed with departments and the bureaucracies, with friends, and even with family members. This was GRIEF in capital letters and neon.

Many times well-meaning people had said they knew what we were going through, but I don't think they really knew how we felt. Every widow in that room understood each other in a completeness I had never felt before. It opened my eyes to the plight of

widows who don't have the financial security my state provides for its line of duty families. When a firefighter dies and leaves a family, that family has ongoing needs that must be met. Truly, states that take up this responsibility respect the life that was lost by taking care of the family left behind.

The Irish have a saying, "No matter how long the road, there comes a turning." Sometimes I would think I had come to the turning, only to be disappointed to find that the sorrow had found a way to creep back inside me. I hadn't been able to find a band aid big enough to fix my pain. There's no root canal for broken hearts. Yet, it was that weekend that I mark as the turning, the first of many that would follow.

That weekend we learned that there was a network in place that would be there for us long after the

A member of an honor guard places a rose in a replica of the medallion, which sits at the top of the National Fallen Firefighters Memorial in Emmitsburg, Maryland. Each rose represents a firefighter lost on-duty during the past year. (Joe Tecce)

public attention had stopped. Indeed, throughout the country, the NFFF provides opportunities for spouses, parents, children, and firefighters to network with each other, helping in ways unique to this support service. As important as the beautiful ceremony was in Emmitsburg, I realized that it is the ongoing care that makes the difference in how a family recovers. Understanding that others had traveled the same road before, and had persevered, made the difference. How comforting it was to know that there were people who that cared about the firefighter's survivors.

Each year, the firefighters in our nation respond to approximately 2 million fires. The National Fire Protection Association reports that, on average, 4,400 Americans die in fires annually, and that over 25,000 suffer severe burns and other injuries. Most years, 100 firefighters die in the line of duty fighting those 2 million fires. Today, our firefighters are at additional risk due to the impact of terrorism. The loss of 347 firefighters from FDNY on September 11, 2001, leaves a deep scar on our hearts.

As part of its mission, the NFFF recognizes firefighter safety as one of the most important issues facing the fire service. We must renew and fund prevention programs that aim to educate the public regarding reckless fire behavior. We must lobby state legislatures to ensure that criminal fire activity is severely punished. The fire service must present a united front whenever fire-related issues are discussed in public forums. Protecting the lives of all present and future firefighters is the greatest tribute we can pay to the names that sit silently on the memorial plaques at Emmitsburg.

Captain
JOHN DRENNAN

As we left that weekend, clutching our flags, we knew that the empty chair at the table would still be there. Our homes were houses now, no matter how we repainted or remodeled. Yet, from our weekend we took heart that there were bridges that had been built, and that there was a place, only a telephone call away, that would be there for us in the future. Returning survivors are always welcome in Emmitsburg.

Firefighting is a dangerous job. Sadly, new names will be added to the plaques each year, and new families will continue to come to grieve. Since my first trip to Emmitsburg, a thousand more names have been honored, a thousand more flags have been presented, and a thousand more families have come. They are grateful for a place to honor their loss, grateful for a place where people truly understand the shorthand and the long trail of grief.

The memorial at Emmitsburg will always be a holy place for those of us who love firefighters and the ideals they represent. Until there are no more deaths, we all stand together, united in a bond that cannot be broken, on a journey that ends in a different place for each person. We will continue to come, searching for answers, wanting to share our loss and needing to hear the words, "On behalf of a grateful nation."

Above: The author's husband, Captain John Drennan, lost his life on May 7, 1994, as the result of catastrophic burn injuries received in a building fire while with the New York City Fire Department. (Vina Drennan)

Opposite: In 2002, the National Memorial Weekend was held in Washington, D.C., due to the impact of the events of September 11, 2001. This "Sea of Blue" was formed by firefighters from all over the country marching in formation and lining the route used by buses carrying the survivors of the fallen to the Memorial. This tribute was in the greatest tradition of the "fire service family." (Bill Green)

Sea of Blue

—Bill Manning, *Fire Engineering*, October 6, 2002

We miss you, fallen heroes,
And time seems to move slower without you;
Yet through the mists of grief
We feel you still, and that is our relief:
For our hearts beat as one.
Your hearts beat within us,
Within the sea of blue.

Long through the day and into the night,
We turn out, leaving behind
Our fire stations and our homes
For a dangerous destination,
A clash with the unknown; but
We are poised, battle-ready, our nerves honed
With steel, and we are not alone:
Your hearts beat within us,
Within the sea of blue.

Our sirens are the heralds of hope-
From those in danger, never far away-
And to the helpless, they say,
"We have made a promise, a sacred trust,
As our forefathers did and as we now must
Fulfill, for we are firefighters true,
And our hearts beat as one
In a sea of blue."

As we push through the smoke,
Advance our line through the door,
As we throw ladders and
Search above the fire floor,
As we take command
And make our stand,
We are one true sea of blue.
As we drop from planes
And cut fire breaks,
As we search through the rubble,
As we do whatever it takes
To rescue those in mortal trouble,
As the sweat drips from our brows,
As our eyes meet in battle
With a recognition and resolve,
As drops of blood in tears dissolve,
As we burn with the flame of life
And reach deep down
To find the courage
And the strength to carry on,
Our hearts are one, and your hearts beat still
Within a sea of blue.

When we say "yes"
To the firefighter's life,
When we say "yes"
To duty, honor, and sacrifice,
We are saying "yes" with you, fallen hero.
You are alive in ways that can't be seen:
We follow our dream
In your footsteps and,
As you emptied your goodness into life's cup,
So will we follow and raise it up-
For our hearts are one
In a sea of blue.

Across our hearts and minds
A spirit blows, throughout time, unceasing:
A virtuous spirit called "sister" and "brother"
That joins us to one another
And fills us with the power
To walk this unforgiving road
And lock arms around the helpless
In a rock-solid wall of human kindness
Between the perilous
And the imperiled.
For we are one, a sea of blue.

We are fire patriots, our flags unfurled,
A sea of blue in a circle of lifegiving
That's everwidening
And transcendent of this world.
Your immortality sings within us
To the beat of the hearts in a sea of blue.

Let us testify, brothers and sisters,
To the families of the fallen whose love
For their heroes is deeper than the sea,
Let this be our solemn vow, our destiny:

May our fallen heroes live on
In our every act of courage,
In every deed of honor,
In every discharge of duty,
In every mark of kindness,
In every expression of compassion,
In our passion for the job,
In our every achievement,
In our every success,
In everything we do:
May you live on, fallen heroes,
In the enduring sea of blue.

*We dedicate this
book to firefighters
everywhere—
past, present, and
future.*

—The Editors and Authors

(George Hall)

Acknowledgments

This book is the work of many hands. Some of them belong to: Paul Hashagan (FDNY), Heather Schafer and Craig Sharman (National Volunteer Fire Council), Barbara King (NFFF), Loretta Smith (Office of the Nevada State Forester), Marc Baron, Scott Currier, Elizabeth Redding Granzow, Pete Piringer (Montgomery County Fire & Rescue Service), The London Fire Brigade, Dolores Granito, Leonard King, Jim Wood (Office of Senator Paul S. Sarbanes), Tom Rockwell, Melissa Hough, Captain Alan Disney, Neil Schreck, Dave Hubert and Blaze, Bill Melemai (Honolulu Fire Department), Rozane Sutherland, Russ Sanders (NFPA), John Calderone (FDNY), Katie Porch (CFSI), Amanda Burbank, Dennis Smith, Nick Brunacini, Battalion Chief Dewey Perks, Captain Larry Schneider, Professor Stephen J. Pyne, Wayne Powell (United States Fire Administration), Sue Collins (Marshall, MI), Chuck Milligan, the New York *Post,* the *Atlanta Journal-Constitution,* and all the many career and volunteer fire departments who submitted photographs for the book. We thank William Webb, Director, Congressional Fire Services Institute for permitting us to use original artwork, commissioned for CFSI, for Senator Sarbanes's Prologue. We thank Chief Ron Siarnicki, Executive Director of the NFFF, for his suggestions and assistance.

A number of independent photographers went far above the call of duty. In the front of the line are Craig Hacker (Wichita, KS), Firefighter/Paramedic Mitch Mendler (San Diego, CA), George Dodson, Joe Tecce, George Hall, Steve Spak, and Bill Green. Two FEMA staff photographers, Michael Rieger and Andrea Booher were generous in allowing their photos to be published; as well, thanks to Lauren Hobart FEMA Photo Desk Specialist for her help. We thank Marvel Comics, Warner Brothers, and Columbia Pictures for allowing photos of their material to be used. A number of federal entities provided material for the book, including the Department of Defense, the Defense Visual Information Center (DVIC), the Department of Agriculture (USFS), the Library of Congress, the National Agricultural Library, and the Department of Homeland Security (FEMA). We thank Amy Yatsuk and Hannah and Christopher Kelly for their support and encouragement for this project.

At Hugh Lauter Levin Associates, we are grateful to Project Editor Jim Muschett, Lori S. Malkin, and Debby Zindell.

360

Authors and Editors

STEPHEN P. AUSTIN is a thirty-two year veteran of the State Farm Insurance Companies, where he advises State Farm on matters impacting the Fire and Emergency Services. He is involved in national fire service issues as the Director of Governmental Relations for the International Association of Arson Investigators. He also serves on committees of the National Fire Protection Association, International Association of Fire Chiefs, and the Congressional Fire Services Institute among others. He is a Past President of the Delaware Volunteer Fire Firemen's Association and the Cumberland Valley Volunteer Firemen's Association. Steve serves as the Vice Chairman of the Fire Service National Professional Qualifications System. He is a member of the Board of Directors of the Burn Foundation and Delaware Crimestoppers. He is a Life member of the Aetna Hose, Hook and Ladder Company of Newark Delaware, where he serves as a fire police.

WILLIAM E. BARNARD Is the Maryland State Fire Marshal. He has been actively involved in the Maryland fire and rescue service for thirty-five years. He began his journey in the fire and rescue service as a volunteer firefighter with the Hyattsville Volunteer Fire Department in Prince George's County, Maryland. He served as a career firefighter and fire officer with the Prince George's County, Maryland, Fire Department for many years, where he progressed through the ranks working in every functional area, retiring as a deputy fire chief. Bill is a Certified Fire Protection Specialist, and has a Bachelor of Business Administration degree from Averett College. He is a member of numerous professional organizations.

CHIEF MICHAEL P. BELL was appointed Fire Chief of the City of Toledo, Department of Fire and Rescue Operations on August 21, 1990. Upon his promotion, Chief Bell became the first African-American to be appointed to the position of Chief in the history of the fire service in the City of Toledo. Chief Bell joined the Department on March 21, 1980. Prior to becoming Chief, Chief Bell worked as a Water Rescue Diver, Fire Recruiter, Paramedic, Paramedic Shift Supervisor, and Training Officer (on both State and National level). His last position before being promoted to Fire Chief was the position of Training Captain in the Department's Training Bureau. He holds a Bachelors of Education Degree from the University of Toledo, graduating in 1978. Among his honors, he was selected to carry the Olympic Torch in June 1996 through the City of Toledo as a community leader.

CHIEF ALAN V. BRUNACINI joined the Phoenix Fire Department in 1958. After serving in every rank he was promoted to the position of Fire Chief in 1978. He earned a degree in Fire Protection Technology from Oklahoma State University, a Bachelors degree in Political Science and a Master of Public Administration from Arizona State University.For the past thirty years Chief Brunacini has taught seminars throughout North America, on topics ranging from firefighting tactics and strategy to customer service. He is the author of the book *Fire Command*, and *The Essentials of Fire Department Customer Service*, and has finished his third book, *Command Safety: The IC's Role in Saving Our Own*. He is the past chairman of the Board of Directors of the NFPA, the former Chairman of the NFPA 1500 committee on Fire Department Occupational Safety and Health and is currently the Chairman of the NFPA 1710 committee on Career Fire Service Deployment. He is the recipient of Governing Magazine Public Official of the Year. He has also been awarded the NFPA'S Paul C. Lamb Award for his leadership in the standard making process. Brunacini has a long-standing relationship with the International Association of Firefighters and is a proud member of Local 493.

HAL BRUNO, Chairman of the National Fallen Firefighters Foundation served over forty years as an active volunteer firefighter. He is a director of the Chevy Chase, Maryland, Fire Department, and a member of the Friendship Fire Association of the District of Columbia Fire & Rescue Service. He has written the monthly "Fire Politics" column for *Firehouse* since the magazine was founded in 1976. Bruno was a professional journalist for fifty years, retiring in 1999 as the Political Director of ABC News. Prior to that he was with *Newsweek* magazine, the *Chicago American* newspaper, the City News Bureau of Chicago, and the DeKalb (Ill.) *Daily Chronicle*. He is a graduate of the University of Illinois, served as an Army intelligence officer during the Korean War, and was a Fulbright Scholar to India. Mr. Bruno has won numerous awards for his work in journalism and the fire-rescue service. In 1995 he was named "Fire Service Person of the Year" by the Congressional Fire Services Institute, and in 1999 received the "President's Award" from the International Association of Fire Chiefs.

GEORGE W. BUCK, JR., PH.D., has been involved in the fire/rescue service and emergency management for more than twenty years. He is presently the Director of Training and Education/Associate Professor at the University of South Florida's Center for Disaster Management and Humanitarian Assistance. He teaches graduate level courses specializing in Emergency/Disaster Management and terrorism. Dr. Buck was previously with St. Petersburg College as Director of the Institute of Emergency Administration and Fire Science and the National Terrorism Preparedness Institute. He has served as a Fire Management Specialist with the United States Fire Administration in Emmitsburg, Maryland. He was a Principal Member of the Technical Committee for "Emergency Management, NFPA 1600" and served on the committee from 1992–2000. Dr. Buck holds a Bachelor of Science degree in Emergency Administration and Planning from the University of North Texas, along with a Masters and Doctorate in Public Administration.

JOHN. A. CALDERONE is a Battalion Chief in New York City. He started his fire service career in 1972 as a member of the New York Fire Patrol and entered the FDNY the following year. He has been assigned to some of the busiest units in New York City as well as serving in assignments at the Research and Development Unit, as an instructor at the Fire Academy, as a member of the Apparatus Design Committee, and in the Safety Division. He has a degree in Fire Protection Technology and is a a student of apparatus design and evolution. He is also the editor of *Fire Apparatus Journal*, has written numerous trade magazine articles, and authored several books about fire apparatus.

CHIEF RONNY J. COLEMAN is currently the President of the Fire & Emergency Training Network, otherwise known as FETN. He also serves as the Senior Consultant for Citygate Corporation, a Management Consulting Firm, and is a Principal in Fireforceone, a website for fire protection services. He formerly served as the Chief Deputy Director, Department of Forestry and Fire Protection and the California State Fire Marshal. He has served in the fire service for forty-one years. Previously he was Fire Chief for the cities of Fullerton and San Clemente, California. He has served in both the United States Forest Service and U.S. Park Service. He has held elected positions in professional organizations, including President, International Association of Fire Chiefs, Vice President, International Committee for Prevention and Control of Fire (CTIF), and President, California League of Cities, Fire Chiefs Department.

CHIEF DENNIS COMPTON is a well-known speaker and the author of the *When In Doubt, Lead!* series of books, as well as many other articles and publications. He is also the Co-Editor of the current edition of the ICMA's textbook titled, *Managing Fire and Rescue Services*. His background includes a significant management, consulting, and teaching history covering a wide variety of disciplines and subjects. He is a national advocate and executive advisor for fire service and emergency management issues and organizations. Dennis served as Fire Chief in Mesa, Arizona, for five years and as Assistant Fire Chief in the Phoenix, Arizona, Fire Department where he served for twenty-seven years. Chief Compton has been an active participant in the international fire service. Among other things, he is the Immediate Past-Chair of the Executive Board of the International Fire Service Training Association (IFSTA), Past Chair of the Congressional Fire Services Institute's National Advisory Committee, and serves on the Board of the NFPA (National Fire Protection Association). Dennis was selected as the American Fire Sprinkler Association's Fire Service Person of the Year 2000 and is a charter member of the Arizona Fire Service Hall of Fame. He was also selected as the Year 2001 Distinguished Alumnus of the Year by the University of Phoenix.

KEN COX is a twenty-nine-year veteran of the Washington, D.C. FD where, during the course of his career, he received several commendations including a Silver Medal for Valor and The American Legion Firefighter of the Year Award. Since 1974, Cox has served as Vice President of IAFF Local 36 where his responsibilities include the preparation of testimony, lobbying the U.S. Congress and the District of Columbia City Council, and Managing Editor of The Capital City *Fire Fighter Magazine*.

CHARLIE DICKINSON served twenty-four years in the Hayward, California, Fire Department working through the ranks to the position of "Staff" Battalion Chief assigned to the Fire Chief's Office. In 1986, he accepted an appointment to the City of Pittsburgh (PA) Fire Bureau as an Assistant Chief responsible for the Operations and Training Divisions. Two years later, he was appointed Fire Chief of the Bureau, serving in that capacity until retiring in August of 1998. He presently holds the position of Deputy U.S. Fire Administrator of the United States Fire Administration (USFA), where he oversees the day-to-day operations of the six divisions that comprise the USFA. He teaches part time at the National Fire Academy in the Command and Control curriculum, and is an active volunteer with the National Fallen Fighters Foundation (NFFF).

VINA DRENNAN has been an advocate for fire prevention since her husband, FDNY Captain John Drennan's death from serious burn injuries in 1994. She has addressed over eighty conferences throughout North America and as far away as Australia. She was appointed to serve on the FEMA's America at Risk Commission. Currently she is an Advisory Board member of the National Fallen Firefighters Foundation and the Silver Shield Foundation in NYC. She is serving on the New York State Task Force to develop a Teacher Training Curriculum. She represented the National Sprinkler Association in Harrisburg, Pennsylvania, to advocate for sprinkler systems in college dormitories. She has authored numerous articles and frequently appears as a media spokesperson for fire safety. Currently she is working on publishing her speeches and journals.

STEVEN T. EDWARDS is the Director of the Maryland Fire and Rescue Institute of the University of Maryland. He is a former Fire Chief of the Prince George's County (MD) Fire Department, where he served for twenty-five years in every position from high school cadet to Fire Chief. Mr. Edwards also serves as Chairman of the Board of Directors of the Safety Equipment Institute, Vice Chair of the Congressional Fire Service Institute National Advisory Committee, among others. In 1997, he was elected as the President of the North American Fire Training Directors. He is a graduate of the University of Maryland University College with a Bachelor's Degree

in Fire Service Management and a Master's Degree in General Administration. He has attended the Harvard University John F. Kennedy School of Government "Program for Senior Executives in State and local Government," the National Fire Academy, and presented at national conference and seminars. Mr. Edwards is currently a member of the adjunct faculty at UMUC, and is the author of the textbook *Fire Service Personnel Management*.

FRED ENDRIKAT is a twenty-eight-year veteran of the Philadelphia Fire Department, serving as a Lieutenant in Rescue Company 1 and as the Lead Technical Rescue Instructor at the Philadelphia Fire Academy. He serves as the National Task Force Leaders Representative for the FEMA Urban Search & Rescue (US&R) National Response System, and for the FEMA US&R System Advisory Committee. Fred is the Senior Task Force Leader for Pennsylvania US&R Task Force 1, and has responded to numerous disasters, acting in various capacities at the local, state, and federal levels. Lieutenant Endrikat was deployed by the FEMA US&R System to the World Trade Center collapse in New York City on September 11, 2001, for forty days, where he was assigned as the Operations Section Chief. He currently serves as a Contributing Editor and instructor for *Firehouse Magazine*.

CHIEF JOHN M. EVERSOLE is the recently retired Chief of Special Functions for Chicago Fire Department. He joined the Department in 1969. He was responsible for the Hazardous Materials HIT Team and coordinated all the Fire Department's units that make up the Hazardous Incident Task Force. Also, under his command was heavy rescue, collapse rescue, air/sea rescue, and the Office of Fire Investigation. He is the Chairman of the Hazardous Materials Committee of the International Association of Fire Chiefs. He is also the Chairman of the Hazardous Materials Professional Competency Standards Committee of the National Fire Protection Association. He is a certified Master Instructor through the Office of the Illinois State Fire Marshal. He has been an instructor teaching Fire Science programs for the Chicago City Wide Colleges and the University of Illinois. He received a Bachelor's Degree in Management at Lewis University.

P. LAMONT EWELL served in the Fire Service for a total of twenty years. He was appointed Fire Chief with the City of Oakland, California, in 1991. In 1995, he was promoted to the position Assistant City Manager. He became City Manager of Durham, North Carolina, from 1997 to 2001. He currently serves as Assistant City Manager of San Diego, California. Ewell holds an undergraduate degree in Business Administration and Masters degree in General Administration.

JOHN A. GRANITO, ED.D, is a consultant in fire-rescue services and emergency management. His clients include federal agencies, national associations, engineering groups, and municipalities in the United States and abroad. He lectures nationally and is the author and editor of numerous articles, books, chapters, and technical papers on the organization and management of emergency response services. Dr. Granito has served as New York State Supervisor of Fire Training and Coordinator of the Urban Fire Forum, composed of the chief executive officers from the fire departments of thirty of the largest cities in the United States, Canada, England, and Germany. He holds a doctoral degree in leadership studies and is Professor emeritus and retired Vice President for Public Service of the State University of New York at Binghamton.

PAUL HASHAGEN joined the fire service in 1976. He worked in the FDNY for twenty-five years, serving in Rescue Company 1 in Manhattan for twenty years until his retirement in 2003. He is also a former chief of the Freeport (NY) Fire Department. Paul is a contributing editor for *Firehouse Magazine* and has written three books on fire history including *The Bravest*, the official history of the FDNY. He is currently finishing a historical novel, and is the president of Firefighter Rescue, Inc., a training group.

CHIEF DEBRA J. JARVIS of the Oak Brook (Illinois) Fire Department has been in the fire and rescue business since 1978, beginning as a firefighter. She has been the Fire Chief in Oak Brook for five years. Prior to Oak Brook, she served in three other career Fire Departments. Chief Jarvis has a Master of Arts in Leadership Studies, a Bachelor of Science degree in Management, an Associate of Science degree in Fire Science Technology, and six Indiana State Master Firefighter certifications. She is also a graduate of the National Fire Academy's Executive Fire Officer Program, as well as an adjunct faculty member for the National Fire Academy. Chief Jarvis is active in several fire service organizations and is the Chairperson of the International Fire Chiefs Diversity Committee and of several co-founders of Women Chief Fire Officers. She also teaches and consults on a wide variety of subjects including leadership and management, diversity, recruitment, promotional testing development, and emergency incident management.

MARION H. JORDAN, M.D., is the Director of The Burn Center at the Washington Hospital Center, Washington, D.C., with twenty-five years in that role. He is the 2002–2003 President of the American Burn Association. Margaret Gunde, R.N., is the Burn Unit Operating Room Nurse, with twenty-four years of burn care experience in the ICU and the operating room. Kathleen Hollowed, R.N., is the Education Coordinator for The Burn Center, with seventeen years of experience in burn nursing and education. Dr. James C. Jeng is the Associate Director of The Burn Center and, with fifteen years of burn care experience, was the burn surgeon with primary responsibility for the firefighters who made the ultimate sacrifice in the event of May 29, 1999.

THE KANSAS FIREFIGHTER'S MUSEUM is located in Wichita in Historic Engine House #6. This building is on the Kansas and National Registers of Historic Places. The Museum offers the public opportunities to view historically significant fire apparatus and equipment, including a 1902 American LaFrance Metropolitan steam pumper. The Museum also maintains an extensive collection of old fire records, photographs, manuals, and books related to firefighting. In June, 2002, the Kansas Fallen Firefighters Memorial Wall and *Final Call* statue were dedicated on the grounds of the Museum.

JOELLEN L. KELLY, PH.D., *(Editor-in-Chief)*, is the president of Greenridge Associates, Inc., a fire service consulting firm, located metropolitan Washington, D.C. She holds a doctorate in American Studies from the University of Maryland. Her fire service career began with the Prince George's County (MD) Fire Department in 1985.

WILLIAM D. KILLEN, CFO, is the Director, Navy Fire and Emergency Services. He started his fire service career as a volunteer, and his career spans forty-seven years, including service with the Kennedy Space Center Fire Department where he was as a member of the Astronaut Rescue Team during the Apollo and Skylab missions. He was also Chief of the Lake Barton Fire District, Orange County, Florida. He was appointed to his present position in 1985. He holds a Bachelor of Science in Fire Department Administration from University College, University of Maryland, and was awarded his Chief Fire Officer Designation in 2002. He was Charter Chairman of the Federal/Military Section of the IAFC, and was awarded the Commission on Fire Accreditation International's Ray Picard Award in 2001, the IAFC President's award in 2000, the Federal Aviation Administration's Special Achievement Award 1982, and the Government of Venezuela's Meritorious Service Medal for service to Venezuelan Civil Aviation Fire Services 1980. He co-authored the history of the Kennedy Space Center Fire Department in 1994.

CHIEF MARY BETH MICHOS leads the Prince William County (VA) Department of Fire and Rescue, a 300-person career department which provides support to twelve volunteer companies within the county. She started her career as a Critical Care Nurse. In 1973, she was hired by the Montgomery County, Maryland, Department of Fire and Rescue Services where she spent over twenty-one years. She progressed up the ranks and was Assistant Chief when she left to assume her new position in Prince William County.

DENIS ONIEAL, ED.D., was appointed Superintendent of the National Fire Academy in 1995. A native of Jersey City, New Jersey, he has been a career firefighter since 1971, rising through the ranks to become Deputy Fire Chief in 1991, and Acting chief of a uniformed force of 600 members. He has spent his entire time "in the street" as a line fire officer. He earned a doctorate degree in education from New York University, a master's degree in public administration from Fairleigh Dickinson University, and a bachelor's degree in fire administration form Jersey City State College. He was a professor in the master and doctorate programs in education at New York University prior to his appointment to the National Fire Academy, and has over twenty publications in the field.

STEVE ROBINSON has been a natural resource professional since he began his career with the State of Nevada in 1973. In 1983, he joined the U.S. Department of Interior where he served as National Director of Fire, Aviation and Law Enforcement and Director of the National Interagency Fire Center [NIFC]. For four years, he was the Executive Director of the National Fallen Firefighters Foundation and recently returned to his home state of Nevada as State Forester/Firewarden.

J. GORDON ROUTLEY *(Contributing Editor)* has been involved in the fire service in the United States and Canada for thirty-five years. He served as Fire Chief in Shreveport, Louisiana, as Assistant to the Fire Chief in Phoenix, Arizona, and as Fire Department Safety Officer in Prince George's County, Maryland. Currently, as a fire protection engineer, he provides consulting services to fire departments in the areas of planning, deployment, and incident analysis. He has been very active in the cause of firefighter health and safety, working with the International Association of Fire Chiefs, the National Fire Academy, and the National Fire Protection Association. He is also a member of the Institution of Fire Engineers and the Society of Fire Protection Engineers.

PAUL S. SARBANES is Maryland's Democratic senior Senator serving his fifth term. After graduation from Wicomico High School in Salisbury, Sarbanes received an academic and athletic scholarship to Princeton University (A.B. degree, 1954). He was awarded a Rhodes Scholarship that brought him to Oxford, England, (First Class B.A., 1957). Sarbanes then returned to the United States and attended Harvard Law School. After graduating in 1960, he clerked for Federal Judge Morris A. Soper before going into private practice with two Baltimore City law firms. His political career began the Maryland House of Delegates and then he served as a Congressman from the Third Congressional District for three terms. Since 1977, he has served with integrity and distinction in the United States Senate where he serves as the Ranking Member of the Senate Banking, Housing and Urban Affairs Committee, and is a senior member of the Foreign Relations, Budget and Joint Economic Committees. Senator Sarbanes has served as the Co-Chair and as Chairman of the Congressional Fire Services Caucus, and introduced the legislation that established the National Fallen Firefighters Memorial and the National Fallen Firefighters Foundation.

CHIEF RONALD JON SIARNICKI, a third generation firefighter, began his career with the Prince George's County Fire/EMS Department in 1978. Over twenty-three years, he progressed through the ranks to become Chief of the Department in 1998. Prior to that, he served his hometown as a volunteer firefighter with the Monessen (PA) Volunteer Fire Department Hose House #2. He is currently Executive Director of the National Fallen Firefighters Foundation. As the Executive Director, he is responsible for oversight of all programs, services, and activities of the Foundation, which include the National Fallen Firefighters Memorial Weekend, survivor support programs, fire service training and support programs, and the creation of a national memorial park to honor all of the brave men and woman who have made that supreme sacrifice. Chief Siarnicki is a graduate of the Masters Program, School of Management and Technology, at the University of Maryland University College. He has a Bachelor of Science Degree in Fire Science Management from UMUC. He has also served as a UMUC faculty member for the Fire Science Curriculum since 1997.

CHAPLAIN ED STAUFFER is the Founder and Director of the Federation of Fire Chaplains. He is a retired Chaplain of the Ft. Worth (TX) Fire Department.

DAVID WHITE, publisher of *Industrial Fire World* magazine, has been involved in the fire service for more than forty years. Starting as a teenage volunteer firefighter in McAllen, Texas, White soon took up firefighting as a career. He rose through the ranks to become training officer and assistant to the chief. In 1970, White left McAllen to join the staff of the Texas A&M University Fire School, taking charge of the state's first state-wide recruit training program. In 1982, White left A&M to head his own consulting and training business specializing in industrial fire protection. He has been involved in the emergency response and investigation of many of the nation's largest fire and explosion disasters during his career. These include the Houston chemical plant explosion and Baton Rouge, Louisiana, refinery fire, both in 1989, a burning tanker in Michigan laden with five million gallons of gasoline, the Texas A&M University bonfire collapse rescue, a Houston fire involving 600 railroad cars, the largest storage tank fire ever extinguished (Norco, Louisiana, in 2001), the Las Vegas MGM Grand hotel fire, and the Los Angeles Interstate Bank high-rise fire.

ROBERT A. YATSUK *(Managing Editor)* retired as a Captain with the Prince George's County Maryland Fire Department in 1995, after twenty-two years of service. He worked as a firefighter, paramedic, and Officer. With Greenridge Associates, he worked with the United States Fire Administration and Fire Academy for FEMA. He spent ten days in New York City for the National Fallen Firefighters Foundation following September 11. Currently he is the Supervisor of School Security for Anne Arundel County Maryland Public Schools.

National Fallen Firefighters Memorial

As a tax-exempt, non-profit organization, the National Fallen Firefighters" Foundation supports programs associated with the National Fallen Firefighters Memorial, the official national monument to honor volunteer and career firefighters who die in service to their communities.

The Foundation's distinguished Board of Directors represents the private sector, the fire service, and government. All members have demonstrated interest in fire safety and serve without compensation. They set Foundation priorities and work to enhance the National Fallen Firefighters Memorial and all activities related to it.

Constructed in 1981, the National Fallen Firefighters Memorial features a sculpted bronze Maltese Cross atop a seven foot stone cairn. Throughout the centuries, the Maltese Cross has been used as the traditional symbol by many groups who provide aid in times of distress. The fire service worldwide has used versions of the Maltese Cross as its organizational symbol. Models of fire brigade crosses from several major American departments were used in planning the design of the Fallen Firefighters Memorial Maltese Cross.

At the base of the monument, an eternal flame symbolizes the sprit of all firefighters—past, present and future. A plaza in the shape of a Maltese Cross surrounds the Memorial. Each year, America honors its fallen fire heroes during a National Memorial Service at the monument site. The Ceremony includes the dedication of a plaque honoring those who died in the line of duty during the previous year. Plaques encircling the monument list the names of the men and women who have made the ultimate sacrifice since 1981. Whenever a firefighter dies in the line of duty, a notice is posted at the monument and the plaza flags fly at half-staff.

Work is now underway to expand the monument site to create the first permanent National Memorial Park honoring America's fire service. A brick "Walk of Honor" connects the National Monument and the historic National Fallen Firefighters Memorial Chapel.

In 1990, the U.S. Congress designated the Memorial as the "official national monument" honoring all of America's fire service heroes. The Memorial is open throughout the year to the public and thousands of individuals visit the site annually.

To learn more about the National Fallen Firefighters Memorial and the Foundation, visit its Web site at **www.firehero.org.**

NFFF Board of Directors and Staff

Index